THE IRISH WRITER AND THE WORLD

The Irish Writer and the World is a major new book by one of Ireland's most prominent scholars and cultural commentators. Declan Kiberd, author of the award-winning *Irish Classics* and *Inventing Ireland*, here synthesises the themes that have occupied him throughout his career as a leading critic of Irish literature and culture. Kiberd argues that political conflict between Ireland and England ultimately resulted in cultural confluence and that writing in the Irish language was hugely influenced by the English literary tradition. He continues his exploration of the role of Irish politics and culture in a decolonising world, and covers Anglo-Irish literature, the fate of the Irish language and the Celtic Tiger. This fascinating collection of Kiberd's work over twenty-five years demonstrates the extraordinary range, astuteness and wit that have made him a defining voice in Irish Studies and beyond, and will bring his work to new audiences across the world.

DECLAN KIBERD is Professor of Anglo-Irish Literature at University College, Dublin. He is the author of *Inventing Ireland*, which won the *Irish Times* Literature Prize for 1997, and of *Irish Classics*, which won the Truman Capote Award for the best work of literary criticism published in 2002. He was Parnell Visiting Fellow at Magdalene College, Cambridge, for 2003 and Visiting Professor of Irish Studies at Duke University in 2004.

THE IRISH WRITER AND
THE WORLD

DECLAN KIBERD

CAMBRIDGE
UNIVERSITY PRESS

CAMBRIDGE UNIVERSITY PRESS
Cambridge, New York, Melbourne, Madrid, Cape Town, Singapore, São Paulo

Cambridge University Press
The Edinburgh Building, Cambridge, CB2 2RU, UK

Published in the United States of America by Cambridge University Press, New York

www.cambridge.org
Information on this title: www.cambridge.org/9780521602570

First published 2005

Printed in the United Kingdom at the University Press, Cambridge

A catalogue record for this book is available from the British Library

ISBN-13 978-0-521-84163-4 hardback
ISBN-10 0-521-84163-1 hardback
ISBN-13 978-0-521-60257-0 paperback
ISBN-10 0-521-60257-2 paperback

In memory of Robert Law (1949–2002)

Contents

Acknowledgements

Grateful acknowledgement is made to editors and publishers for permission to reprint material: Ronald Schleifer and Wolfhound Press for 'The Fall of the Stage Irishman' from *The Genres of the Irish Revival*, first printed in *Genre* magazine xll, winter 1979, 451–72; Terence Brown, the late Patrick Rafroidi and Université de Lille for 'Storytelling: the Gaelic Tradition' in *The Irish Short Story*, Lille, 1978, 13–27; Richard Kearney, Mark Hederman and *The Crane Bag* for 'Writers in Quarantine', vol. 2, no. 1, Summer 1979, 9–21; Richard Finneran and *Yeats Studies* for 'Yeats, Synge and Bardic Poetry', 2002, 37–57; Robert Welch and Wolfhound Press for 'George Moore's Gaelic Lawn Party' from *The Way Back*, 1979, 13–27; Wolfhound Press for the introduction to *An Crann faoi Bhláth: The Flowering Tree*, 1989, xi–xliii; the Irish–American foundation, Vera Kreilkamp, Phillip O'Leary and *Éire–Ireland* magazine for 'White Skins, Black Masks: Celticism and *Négritude*', Vol. xxxl, Nos. 1 and 2, Spring–Summer 1996, 163–75; Dele Layaiola and University of Ibadan for 'On National Culture' from *Understanding Post-Colonial Studies: Ireland, Africa and the Pacific*, 2001, pp. 44–50; Susan Shaw Sailer and Regents of the University Press of Florida for 'From Nationalism to Liberation' from *Representing Ireland*, 1997, pp. 17–28; Audrey S. Eyler, Robert F. Garratt and Regents of the University of Delaware Press for 'The War Against the Past' from *The Uses of the Past*, Newark, 1988, pp. 24–53; Damien Kiberd and *The Sunday Business Post* and the Directors of Field Day for 'The Elephant of Revolutionary Forgetfulness' from *Revising the Rising*, Derry, 1991, pp. 1–19; the Raymond Williams Memorial Trust Society for 'Reinventing England' in *Keywords* 2, Nottingham, 1999, 47–57; Cork University Press for 'Multiculturalism: the Strange Death of Liberal Europe', Occasional Pamphlet in Irish and World Development, 1993; Cork University Press and Centre for Border Studies, Armagh, for 'Strangers in their Own Country' in *Multiculturalism: The View from the Two Irelands* (with Edna Longley), pamphlet,

2001, pp. 45–74; the President and Fellows of Magdalene College, Cambridge, for 'The Celtic Tiger: a Cultural History', Parnell Fellowship Lecture, 2003; Stuart Murray, Fiona Becket and the editors for 'Museums and Learning' in *Moving Worlds*, Leeds, vol. 3, no. 1, 2003, 3–17; Franca Ruggeri and Bulzoni editore for 'Joyce's Ellmann' from *Classic Joyce: Joyce Studies in Italy* 6 Rome 1999, 53–68.

The author and publishers also wish to thank the following: Gallery Press and the estate of Beatrice Behan for permission to quote from *Poems and a Play in Irish*, 1978; the Samuel Beckett Estate and Grove Atlantic for permission to quote from *Murphy*; Eiléan ní Chuilleanáin and the Estate of Katherine B. Kavanagh, Caomh and Peter Kavanagh for permission to quote from 'Memory of Brother Michael' and 'Who Killed James Joyce?'; A. P. Watt Limited and Michael Yeats for permission to quote from *Collected Poems* and *Collected Plays*; the trustees of the estate of Lilo Stephens and J. M. Synge and the Board of Trinity College, Dublin, for permission to quote from Synge manuscripts in the College Library; Oxford University Press and the estate of J. M. Synge for permission to quote from *Collected Works*; Colin Smythe and the Society of Authors for permission to quote from *Hail and Farewell*; Wolfhound Press, Gabriel Fitzmaurice for permission to quote lines and translations from *An Crann faoi Bhláth: The Flowering Tree*; Random House and the Estate of James Joyce for permission to quote from *A Portrait of the Artist as a Young Man* and *Ulysses*; Oxford University Press and the estate of Richard Ellmann for permission to quote from *Along the Riverrun*; Seamus Heaney and Faber & Faber for permission to quote from 'Bog Queen'; Salman Rushdie and Jonathan Cape for permission to quote from *Midnight's Children*; the Estate of John Osborne and Faber & Faber for permission to quote from *Look Back in Anger* and *A Better Class of Person*.

I wish to acknowledge a Senior Fellowship from the Irish Research Council of the Humanities and Social Sciences which made the preparation of this volume possible and to thank Dr Noreen Doody, who took my place in the classroom with marvellous success during the period of leave in which this book was prepared.

Finally, I would like to thank Professors John Kerrigan, Maud Ellmann and Eamon Duffy for much kindness during my stint as Parnell Visiting Fellow at Cambridge; Professor John Hobbs of Oberlin College for sound advice on the project; and Dr Ray Ryan, Annie Lovett and Margaret Berrill of Cambridge University Press for their generous encouragement and suggestive commentaries.

A note on the text

I have retained the original referencing system for each of the articles, in keeping with the very varied backgrounds in which they originally appeared. Some are rather heavily annotated, others less fully underpinned, and some had no apparatus at all. In the latter cases, I have added a short bibliography which might help those in search of further reading.

Apart from some deletions in cases of repetition, I have left the work unrevised, even though there are passages in some of the earliest essays which I wish I hadn't written. But since every work is produced at the mercy of its immediate occasion, even the blind-spots may have some exemplary value in tracing the history of cultural debate. Not *every* pub in the 1970s had a resident bard performing nightly, as I seemed to imply in 'Storytelling: the Gaelic Tradition'; nor would I now, as a veteran of too many long nights, refer to the 'fake glamour of the summer schools'. My remarks in the same essay on schoolmasters devoted to extolling folk pieties were wildly in excess of any offences committed: and in subsequent years I came to a different valuation. This was due in great part to friendships with Bryan MacMahon and Gabriel Fitzmaurice, who through the 1980s documented the lore of Kerry villages with the sort of understanding that can only come from love. The high esteem in which both men held W. B. Yeats as an interpreter of Irish culture led me in time to revise the rather harsh assessment offered in 'The War against the Past'. While that essay offers some insights into Yeats's ideas about tradition, it takes no account of the dialectical nature of an imagination which was even more attuned to the future. Denis Donoghue was quite correct in predicting that my generation, soured by the cultural and economic setbacks of the 1980s, would eventually return to Yeats as the inspirational figure of modern Irish culture. I trust that the treatment accorded to Yeats through *Inventing Ireland* and *Irish Classics* does something more like justice to the great writer.

CHAPTER I

Introduction

To write – as to read – is to enter a sort of exile from the world around us. But to go into exile from the world around us may well be a signal to write. Although Ireland has produced many authors, it has on its own land-mass sustained less writing than one might be led to believe. Even a great national poet like Yeats managed to spend more of his life outside the country than in: and the list of artists-in-exile stretches from Congreve to Edna O'Brien. Nor was exile solely a condition of those who wrote in English. Much of the literature produced in Irish during the 'revival' in the early decades of the seventeenth century was composed and published in the cities of continental Europe. It is almost as if Irish writers found that they had to go out into the world in order to discover who exactly they were.

The problem faced by many was the discovery that an 'image' had preceded them to their first overseas encounter. There may be no essence of Irishness, any more than there is of Jewishness, but both peoples have had a common experience – that of being defined, derided and decided by others. If you want to know what an Irishman is, ask an Englishman, for the very notion of a unitary national identity, like that of a united Ireland as an administrative entity, is an English invention. Small wonder, therefore, that some of its staunchest supporters have borne such sturdy English surnames as Pearse and Adams.

The Stage Irishman was a caricature got up in England, based on ignorance and fear of the Other but also on a suspicion that that Other knew better how to enjoy the world. Such a cartoonish creation had its racist overtones but also the merit of making some sort of relationship possible. Out in the world every person is met first as a stranger, with all the simplification which that implies, for we can classify acquaintances in a way that we never would classify close friends. Only much later, after those initial meetings, do we come to know others more subtly, whether as intimate enemies or fast friends. Even as we break through to the true nuances of a relationship, some of the original stereotypes retain a certain authority. That is why Sigmund Freud once said that there are four persons in every relationship – the two actual people, but also the fantasies, entertained by each of the other. As he joked, a bed could sometimes seem a very crowded place. Much the same is true of that bed which has been Anglo-Irish relations, a relation complicated by endless play-acting on both sides or, as Elizabeth Bowen sighed, 'a mixture of showing-off and suspicion, nearly as bad as sex'.

In such a condition of perpetual image-making, it might seem that power lies always with the shapers of discourse, but that has not invariably been so. At the start of the nineteenth century, Hegel suggested that the slave may know more than the master, in the sense of knowing what it is like to lose but also of being able to observe what it must be like to win. Poets and visionaries have repeated the point – in the words of Emily Dickinson, 'success is counted sweetest / by those who ne'er succeed'. The Irish, for two centuries, have read their own newspapers as well as those of England, and savoured the differences with which all parties report on the same event. This has produced in them a sense of the suppleness of language. Hence the strange mixture of insolence and reverence which they bring to the English literary tradition (or, as Liam O'Flaherty's English landlady once put it, 'servile when you must, insolent when you may'). For every character who went *ag sodar i ndiaidh na nuasal* (trotting after the nobility), there was another who mocked the gentry, often by an imitation so exaggeratedly perfect as to constitute a ferocious parody. If Englishness could be so easily performed, then it could not amount to much to begin with. It was even possible that it was more a caricature of an idea than the real thing. That element of performance was rooted in the fact that many colonial agents were out in the tropics precisely because they did not 'fit' back home, either through an excess of creativity or criminality. In the new setting, strangely enough, they were expected to emulate those average home-country types they had so patently failed to be. No sooner did the native notice the element of play-acting, this Stage English aspect of colonialist culture, than the game was up. Perhaps the English were ultimately too self-divided to run a lasting empire.

Underlying that self-division was the strong suspicion that the Irish or Indian personality contained the Englishman's lost spiritual aspect. So it came to pass that the natives could enact what Oscar Wilde called the tyranny of the weak over the strong, 'the only tyranny that lasts'. The Stage Irishman arose from deep and dire needs in the English personality, for a foil which might set off the domestic virtues of efficiency, order and reason: but in that process the feeling for poetry and emotion was projected onto the native. Given that no coherent philosophy bound the English into a unity, this had to come from fighting the Other. The usual paradox ensued: the English depended for their identity on fighting, yet somehow projected a reputation for bellicose behaviour onto the Irish.

Such a view of the Other was a neurosis, for the neurotic is one who behaves as if the identity of his antagonist is all that determines his own (just as male hysterics act as if their masculinity is in all things the reverse of that which is called 'feminine'). Many narrow-gauge Irish nationalists bought into this reactive thinking, patenting an Ireland that was less a truly liberated zone than a sort of not-England, in which every virtue of the colonising country had its equal but opposite Irish counterpart. In that depressing context of endless oppositionism between both parties, the Stage Irishman was of some limited value, offering a recognisable figure through which both sides could at least begin to negotiate. Even though the figure had been created by a succession of English playwrights, there was a very real sense in which Irish people chose to occupy the assigned role, if only to complicate and ultimately to challenge it.

Seamus Heaney's redefinition of the 'bog myth' might be cited as a nuanced contemporary example of the same process, probably modelled (in his case) on the 'black-is-beautiful' movement which he witnessed in Berkeley in the early 1970s. The phrase 'bog Irish' was first applied by English imperial soldiers to those natives who lived on poor land ('bog' is the Irish for 'soft') onto which they lured their armour-clad enemies for battle: but it has been in more recent times internalised by Irish people themselves, so that the word 'bogman' is often used by smart cits to describe an awkward fellow of rural background. For Heaney, this linguistic history would have been further complicated by the knowledge that the 'Bogside' was the Catholic–nationalist enclave of Derry, near which he was educated at St Columb's boarding college.

The tactic was to take a racist stereotype, occupy it until it became one's own, and thereafter invert its meaning, wearing the old badge of defeat with a sort of defiant pride. It should never be forgotten that it was Irish artists themselves who developed many of the simian archetypes in *Punch* magazine of the nineteenth century, and Irish actors who often played Stage Irish roles on the boards of London and Manchester. They may have done so because the stereotype not only precipitated some discussion of the underlying reality but also generated a counter-claim – as when the London Irish objected so strongly to the portrayal of Sir Lucius O'Trigger in the opening production of Richard Brinsley

Sheridan's *The Rivals* that the play had to be taken off and reconfigured. Like much else in English life, from the architecture of the buildings at Westminster to the conventions of social comedy, the figure of the Paddy owed a lot to the ingenuity of Irish minds.

The huge contribution made by Irish immigrants to the shaping of modern Britain has yet to be fully recognised – from soldiers to nurses, architects to politicians, journalists to academics, they have mastered many preserves except the judiciary and police. When loyalists insist that 'Ulster is British', they are – whether they know it or not – conceding that it is Irish by that very virtue. Irish poets like Heaney and Muldoon have been professors of their subject at Oxford in recent times, just as presenters with class-free Irish accents have enjoyed the freedom of Britain's airwaves. A reciprocal process has long been evident in the Irish Republic, where most 'national' rituals seem to be shot through with British thinking, whether it be the annual rivalries of Gaelic football teams playing for counties based on the 'shire' system or the rules of procedure in Dáil Éireann which are so faithfully copied from Westminster.

These types of cultural fusion have long been rehearsed in Irish writing. This collection begins with an essay on the fate of the Stage Irishman as a register of the state of Anglo-Irish relations. Then it moves on to track in a number of essays the confluence of Gaelic and Anglo-Irish literary traditions in the art of storytelling, in the poetry of Yeats and Synge and in the prose of George Moore. Of all literary forms, the short story seems to tap most fully into the energies unleashed by fusing the oral tradition of tale-telling with the writerly virtues of English narrative. If oral tale and bardic poem are forms of the aristocracy and the novel that of the bourgeoisie which succeeds it, then in the period of transition between both orders there may be a phase when the forms of literature go into meltdown. In England, France and Germany that transition occurred rather quickly, but in Ireland it has taken centuries from the fall of the Gaelic princes in 1600 to the establishment of a vibrant middle class in the decades after independence. Throughout this period, the classic novels, so-called, have really been collections of micro-narratives, from *Gulliver's Travels* to *Castle Rackrent*, from *Ulysses* to *At Swim-Two-Birds*, from *Molloy* to *Cré na Cille*. The astonishing persistence of the short story or monologue as the base-narrative in each of these works is to be observed also in many of the foremost contemporary dramas, from Friel's *Faith Healer* through Murphy's *Bailegangaire* to McPherson's *The Weir*. As the old gifts of recital and storytelling pass out of everyday life, they make a compelling reappearance on Stage. For this reason, it seems worthwhile to include some essays which show just how fully these Gaelic traditions survive in English-language laments for their passing.

These essays were written in the later 1970s, during years when I prepared my Oxford dissertation for publication as *Synge and the Irish Language* (1979). The background to my analysis of the interaction of two traditions was not only the 'troubles' of Northern Ireland but also the linked debate about the need for a new national pedagogy, addressed in 'Writers in Quarantine?' The case made there for a plural, multi-disciplinary Irish Studies placed an emphasis on those authors who wrote well in both Irish *and* English: Douglas Hyde, Patrick Pearse, Liam O'Flaherty, Flann O'Brien, Brendan Behan, Eoghan Ó Tuairisc, Michael Hartnett. But the deeper point was that most of the great Irish writers were bicultural in the manner of Swift, who based his Lilliputians and Brobdingnagians on a Gaelic tale, or of Ó Ríordáin, who brought the techniques of Hopkins and Eliot into lyric poetry in Irish.

A central theme in all these essays and studies is that cultural forces which appear to be opposites often turn out to be doubles. My exemplar in all this was Giordano Bruno who wrote in the sixteenth century that 'every power in nature seems to evolve its own opposite – but from that opposition springs reunion'. So the Gaelic and Anglo-Irish worlds, often seen in the past as inimical, are shown to have fused, with new kinds of hybrid art appearing in both languages.

That this scholarly debate located itself along the axis of Anglo-Irish relations was predictable. Most of my generation had grown up reading Enid Blyton and Frank Richards, the *Victor* and the *Wizard*. Though aware that our grandfathers had liberated the country from British rule, we loved the popular culture of the neighbouring island, whose practices we often took for the very definition of a human norm. But the world out of which I came was somewhat different from that British one of which I often read. I was born in Eccles Street, Dublin, in 1951 and given a liberal Catholic education by the standards of the time at local schools in Clontarf. My mother's family had been involved in the Gaelic League and Easter Rising and she herself had been a student at the first Gaelscoil (all-Irish language school) for girls, Scoil Bhríde, under the tutelage of Louise Gavan Duffy. My father's family were, despite their German origins, keen supporters of constitutional nationalism and my grandfather for many years was photographed by the newspapers laying a wreath on behalf of the Parnell Commemoration Committee at the grave of 'the

Chief' in Glasnevin cemetery. Despite these Hibernicising influences, the world of my reading suggested a Britain that was an epitome of all things human and 'normal'. It was only in the 1970s, when I lived and worked in Oxford and Canterbury, that I began to realise how stressed and abnormal Britain really was – still exhausted from running an empire and fighting two world wars. By then I had also travelled in France, where newspapers casually advertised first-communion outfits for children, reassuring me that being Irish was not a completely odd condition. But the appalling intensity of the violence in Northern Ireland through that decade ensured that the Anglo-Irish axis remained paramount to most intellectuals. These were the years when people rather naively suggested that much of the northern problem could be solved by proper education – hence the worthy BBC and RTÉ documentaries that sought to challenge the myths cherished by both sides.

Working from this idealistic analysis, I wrote my essays and studies out of a deep conviction – that if the children of Protestant unionists were to study Irish, they would find that tradition far more open to their ideas than nationalists had often made it seem. Similarly, if the Catholic students in the Republic were exposed more fully to the writings of Swift or Goldsmith, they would find there just the sort of practical humanitarianism which animated young people all over the world in the aftermath of 1968. Culture was the common ground on which the various political traditions of the island might meet, not in some spurious unity but in a zone of free debate which allowed for an intelligent savouring of the differences as well as the similarities between the groups. The studies of Estyn Evans on material lore had long convinced me that Ulster Protestants had more in common with their nationalist neighbours and southern 'enemies' than they had with the distant power elites of London.

Yet there were many people of goodwill in the 1970s who did not feel such hopefulness. The provost of Trinity College, Dublin, F. S. L. Lyons, argued at a time of deep gloom in his Ford Lectures at Oxford that the more you excavated cultural traditions, the more antagonistic and irreconcilable they all began to seem. Far from leading to dialogue, he averred, it was culture itself which had produced the anarchy all around us. Lyons's analysis had, nonetheless, the merit of transcending, to some degree, the idea of just 'two traditions'. Instead, he identified sharp distinctions within unionist politics between working-class loyalism and a more patrician Anglo-Irish upper crust, and equally deep splits between constitutional nationalists and militant republicans. I felt that one could have added further strands to that configuration (traveller culture, Gaeltacht life and the southern proletariat among others).

However, my developing thesis became the reverse of Lyons's: the seeming anarchy of disparate elements, all contending, might lead in time to a genuine cultural fusion. Insofar as there was a split along cultural lines, it existed less between north and south than between east and west, the west being wilder but more conservative, the east more buttoned-down yet at the same time more liberal. This was true whenever you talked to people about issues like divorce, contraception or abortion – the further east you went whether on the upper or lower half of the island, the more likely people were to support these as civil rights; and the further west you went, the less likely.

If politics divided people into warring camps, then a plural vision of culture might help to heal those wounds. This was not a new idea but a return to the fundamental principles of the Gaelic League (founded in 1893), which in its first decade attracted unionists as well as nationalists. In its second decade it began to be co-opted by the forces of militant nationalism with a consequent simplification of the diverse traditions represented by the Irish language, but those traditions needed only to be excavated and then perhaps the possibilities opened by the League's founder, Douglas Hyde (himself a Protestant), could be revisited. My undergraduate studies of Irish and English at Trinity College between 1969 and 1973 had convinced me that both narrow-gauge nationalism and theocratic Catholicism were secondary formations, arbitrarily designated as twin keys to Irish identity only *after* the loss of Irish in many places in the mid-nineteenth century. The equation of 'Gaelic' and 'Catholic' as a basis for 'Irishness' was disastrous in the long term for those who identified with any of these three categories. It led the simple-minded to adopt absurd beliefs – that great republican leaders like Tone and Emmet had somehow enjoyed or endured posthumous conversions to Roman Catholicism, or that there was no word in Irish for 'contraceptive'. These simple beliefs were already helping to generate an equally rudimentary revisionism, which would spend the 1970s and 1980s attacking the cardboard version of Gaelic–Catholic nationalism.

Douglas Hyde had been right in his 1892 lecture on the necessity for de-anglicising Ireland. The great mistake of previous leaders had been to neglect the cultural domain and to be seduced by mere 'politics'. These leaders had bought into a bogus parliamentarianism on the one hand and an even more noxious militarism on the other. Whenever the former failed, the latter was tried, but in the process entire generations had substituted the tradition of the fight for the thing fought for. A common error in revolutionary movements, for whom to strike was always to win, this was dangerously seductive of young, impatient souls. In the later 1970s, that great anatomist of Orientalism, Edward Said, began to point to its folly in the case of his own Palestinian people. He expressed impatience with military comrades in the Palestine Liberation Organisation, whom he accused of fetishising arms and neglecting the more cultural values which alone gave their struggle meaning. Just as Hyde was eventually forced out of the Gaelic League, Said finally had to leave the Palestinian National Congress.

Douglas Hyde was in many aspects of his thought a post-colonial critic *avant la lettre*. A century before Homi Bhabha propounded the 'other question' in terms of a native who was 'not quite/not white', Hyde had in his 1892 lecture described a similar pathology. He also registered the pain of being a flawed mimesis of the real Englander, anglicised but not truly English, and he shrewdly attributed the worst cases of Anglophobia to a bitter resentment of those English-speaking Irish against that country which they did so much to imitate. Hyde was a lower-case unionist, certainly not a nationalist, and his analysis applies as forcefully to contemporary unionists as it did to nationalists a century ago. Today's unionists identify with a Britain that has long been historical (if it ever existed) and they fear that their covenant with it may soon be betrayed. Hence the Anglophobia in loyalist communities and the growing distrust of those very rulers whose principles the loyalists claim to uphold. Just as political nationalists a hundred years ago seized on ancient Irish icons like Cuchulain to project their pride and their fear of disappearance, so also have Ulster's uncertain defenders seen in him a figure who defended their province against attack. That rhetoric of 'the triumph of failure' which once appealed to Pearse and his followers now casts its mesmeric spell over them.

My visits to the Gaeltacht in 1978 and 1979 as a young lecturer in Irish at Trinity simply confirmed these hunches. There political nationalism seemed to have made no headway at all. If nationalism really was just a secondary formation to fill a gap left by a lost ancestral language, then why would Connemara people need such a prop? They were Irish anyway and had no need of abstract demonstrations of that fact, which would also explain the lack of nationalist sentiment in many of the great texts of the native language. This lack was a source of constant frustration to those who wished to enforce the dreary equation of 'Gaelic equals Irish'. What was often just a local or regional pietas in the work of a Gaelic poet was inflated by nationalist commentators into patriotic feeling: but an integrated course in Irish Studies would, I believed, take such texts out of nationalist quarantine and allow for a more open reading.

Again, Edward Said's analysis offered a useful parallel. Towards the close of *Orientalism*, he laments the fact that Arab Studies are practised all over the world, especially in the United States, where they are a crisis-driven discipline which may help students understand and ultimately control the peoples of the Middle East. But Said's regret goes deeper – a multidisciplinary Arab Studies is pursued almost everywhere, he says, except in its natural home among the Arabic peoples. The same was and to a great extent still is true of Irish Studies. Just after I published 'Writers in Quarantine' in 1979, I resigned from a lectureship in Irish at Trinity. I had taken it up in hopes that the college would create an integrated course linking Irish and English. This never happened, so I moved to University College where the portents then seemed more encouraging. There also I was to be frustrated. There were many friendly invitations by individuals to give lectures and seminars in Irish to the Celtic faculty but no joint undergraduate courses were developed over the next two decades. The territorial nervousness of academics at the prospect of turf wars was one factor in this stasis. Another was a genuine fear that Irish Studies could easily become another 'Classical Civilisation' course, leading to a decline in disciplinary rigour and linguistic standards as texts came to be studied mainly in translation. Meanwhile, in places like Boston, Toronto, Liverpool, Kent, Aberdeen and Northern Ireland, Irish Studies took off and flourished. The purist approach taken by Irish departments in the Republic has not arrested the decline in the standard of Irish in schools and colleges.

The dedication of Celtic scholars deserves every respect, yet the policy of compulsory Irish in the nation's schools has proved counter-productive. Although conceived in the 1920s by high-minded idealists, its effect was to turn a gift into a threat. There was a time when, if a child failed Irish, that child thereby failed the entire public examination. The early governments of the Free State were never fully confident of their compulsory policy, so they were afraid to commission a poll on the state of public opinion. After the 1970s, it was no longer required to *pass* Irish in state examinations but its *study* was still compulsory and even less popular than ever. Hence the lowered standard of performance, because less time was devoted to it by teachers aware of their students' need to master other languages and of the impatience of many parents with what they viewed as an anachronism. It is probable that if the subject were made optional in secondary schools, it might be taken up by as few as one in five students but it is certain that it would be taken by their enthusiasm to far higher levels.

All in all, the fate of Irish is a dire example of how policies based on cultural exceptionalism can be self-defeating. At present the Zulu community in South Africa is seeking safeguards for its language from the African National Congress government, including the right to be lectured in Zulu on a Durban campus. Sponsors of that campaign would be well advised to consider the Irish experience. The National University in Galway is officially Irish-speaking, but few third-level textbooks in the native language have ever been seen in its classrooms. The mistaken basis of such policies was well diagnosed by Máirtín Ó Cadhain, who once remarked 'Tá an Ghaeilge ró-cheangailte le scolaíocht' (Irish is too linked to educational processes). If a society really wishes to protect valued traditions or to challenge bad practices, it is futile to think that these changes can be effected simply by tinkering with the syllabus, unless there is a genuine desire for transformation in the society itself. Schoolchildren and teachers – or even university students – cannot be expected to bear all the cultural burdens of a society.

A similar sense of limitation in the United States has led many intellectuals to despair of ever achieving social change and to regroup within the academy, where their highly theoretical form of radicalism tends to lose touch with the community. Hence the daunting jargon in which many intelligent analyses are written. It is noticeable, also, that those Irish or Indian scholars whose work is targeted mainly at an American postgraduate audience often make a virtue of a complex technical language, whereas home-based scholars, such as Ashis Nandy or Terence Brown, still try to write for a more generalist audience. Perhaps the sheer proximity of riots and bombs has left them with no other choice. The troubles in Northern Ireland had many of the elements of a traditional insurrection and although I was never naive enough to believe that narrow-nationalist history-books would be listed as among its causes, I persisted in the conviction that scholars should develop the sort of pedagogy which might contribute to a reconciliation (or at least be useful in its aftermath). Hence my interest in those early artists of the Abbey Theatre – notably Synge and Yeats – who tried to recreate the performance conventions of bardic poetry on the stage of the national theatre, albeit in English. The idea that every text, whether lyric poem or prose passage, calls for the act of interpretation in active performance is one link between the art of Synge and the 'Sirens' episode of Joyce's

Ulysses, for example. Synge's ideas on the duality of literature highlight the difference between words on a page and in live performance. Again, it may be no accident that both he and Joyce would have preferred musical careers, regarding literature as a second-best. Synge's interest in music was, of course, more revivalist than that of Joyce. It would be hard to imagine the latter embarking on an opera based upon 'Eibhlín a Rúin'. Although Synge's Gaelic opera never got written (unless we count *The Playboy* as a sort of verbal opera), the same fusion of native and foreign underlies the project as may be found in George Moore's bizarre orchestration of a Gaelic lawn party in his back garden at Ely Place. The short stories of *An tÚr-Ghort* (*The Untilled Field*) might evoke less derision but they were in their splicing of Gaelic and continental narrative traditions no less hybrid or multiple in conception. There would be many more splicings to follow, from Samuel Beckett's Victorian Gael (a mockery of those nationalists who translated late nineteenth-century British culture into Irish words and called the results a national literature) to the *bialann a la carte*, which greeted more and more tourists on the high road to Connemara.

If England insisted on seeing itself as male and Ireland as female, that was yet another opposition which stood in need of Bruno's reunion. Bruno had himself imagined male and female as two intersecting circles with a dot in the centre of the area of overlap to signify androgyny. The British had projected onto the native Irish or Indians all that poetry and feeling which they suppressed in themselves for the sake of imperial efficiency: but thereafter they often felt more threatened than reassured by the feminised male subject, a Dr Aziz rather than a Michael Collins. The rebel and the military insurgent were types they recognised and could easily deal with, but the exponents of androgyny such as Wilde or Gandhi often found themselves behind British bars – a conjunction first noted and explained by Ashis Nandy. Some nationalists in both Ireland and India opted to fight force with force. In doing so they were trying to validate a virility which the increasingly comfortable conditions of life in the later nineteenth century were throwing into question. This would explain the emergence of polar expeditions, mountain climbs, scouting movements along with the militant nationalisms of the period. Even in the United States there was such a widely articulated fear of feminisation that a preacher named Billy Sunday was despatched to Ivy League campuses to inveigh against the image of 'Gentle Jesus, meek and mild'. 'Jesus was no lick-spittle dough-boy', he gravely told his listeners,

'Why, he even kicked the money-lenders clean out of the Temple.'
These campaigns were all attempts to restore the old stable self of the
heroic male, the imperial protagonist of early romanticism, secure in his
devotion to a singular self-image.

In Ireland that psychology never had much appeal, for it had come
to be known mainly through its rather tiresome exponents, the stiff-
lipped colonels and rigid administrators. By contrast, even before the
projection of femininity onto the native male, the Irish self was always
already multiple – as can be seen in the bards' love of performativity, in
the macaronic and multilingual ballads of the eighteenth century or the
success of dramatists from Congreve and Farquhar down to Wilde. The
use of different narrative voices by writers as varied as Maria Edgeworth,
James Clarence Mangan or W. B. Yeats suggests that the desire to
intensify personality by multiplying it was very deeply established long
before Wilde proclaimed it as a basic principle of art and life.

This explains the androgyny which lasts as a theme from the bardic
poets through Wilde and Shaw down to Yeats and Joyce: the constant
attraction reported in texts between manly women and womanly men. It
also accounts for a linked phenomenon: if the self can multiply, becoming
the opposite of what it seemed by nature and gender, then it may also
become multicultural as well. This is obviously true of some of the central
fictional creations in the literature of the Irish Revival, figures who are
sometimes baptised in more than one religious tradition (as in Wilde or
Joyce's Bloom), but who also reach out to the East as a source of wisdom
too. Shaw's Saint Joan is a truly composite protagonist. Canonised a
Catholic saint in 1920, yet also one of the first Protestants because she
listens to the dictates of her inner voices, she stands as a mystic, French
patriot, a child martyr and a boy–girl. It is but a step from this to a
rereading of the classics of Irish writing as exercises in applied multiculturalism, whether it be Gulliver travelling to foreign parts or the owners
of Castle Rackrent receiving a Jewish or Scottish bride into the family,
Augusta Gregory's adaptation of Moliére or George Russell's use of
theosophy. The biculturalism which I have often celebrated in these
authors may be just an aspect of their wider multiculturalism.

Artists by their very nature are constantly open to outside influences
and ideas, which is what Flaubert meant in saying that Bohemia rather
than France was his native country. This has been especially notable of
modern writers of Irish: being adept linguists, they are often learned in
other languages, which powerfully inform their practices. Pádraic
Ó Conaire, author of the first novel in Irish, was influenced not only by

Gaelic lore but by Dickens, by the Russian novelists and by Guy de Maupassant. Máire Mhac an tSaoi carries traces in her poetry of Provençal and *amour courtois*, as well as of Shakespeare and the romance languages.

As a language with the aura of 'tradition' about it, Irish has often masked the modernity of its users, not just in literature but in the world of practical affairs. Nowhere is this more obvious than in the Gaelscoileanna set up in urban areas over the past few decades. These schools use Irish and become epicentres for all Irish speakers in local communities. Because they are free of the clerical management which was the traditional control-mechanism, they tend to be open and democratic in style, run by parents' committees. The Irish language has also acted as a mask for other forms of cultural radicalism, not least the escape from the Anglo-Irish axis as a measure of all reality. If Beckett moved into French to escape that wit and wordplay which is ritually expected of Irish users of English, then Brendan Behan achieved a similar integrity by his move 'back' into Irish. Small wonder that writing in Irish over the past century has seemed less troubled by what London or New York thinks and far more open to continental Europe, to India and Africa, as explained in my essay-introduction to *An Crann Faoi Bhláth: The Flowering Tree* (1989).

If the Gaelscoileanna and the creation of a national TV service in Irish had by the end of the 1990s turned the whole country into a virtual Gaeltacht, it must also be said that the official Gaeltacht areas themselves had provided many examples of a masked post-modernity in the preceding decades. Often seen as the repository of Gaelic values, these places were chronically underdeveloped under successive governments, which paid only lip service to Irish. A civil rights movement emerged in 1969, a fateful year elsewhere in the world, that made a claim for Irish speakers not on the basis of national piety but of personal rights – to conduct business with the state in the language, to have services in Irish and so on. Within a few years the movement had won reforms in local government and the setting up of a Gaeltacht radio station. This in turn led to the development of publishing houses which specialised in local history and lore. Such a model, challenging the hegemony of the national narrative, was eventually emulated elsewhere in Ireland and the 1980s and 1990s saw the growth of local theatres, radio stations, publishers. If Ireland as a whole served as a sort of laboratory in which the British authorities tested policies in the nineteenth century, it would be no exaggeration to claim that the Gaeltacht was the crucible for Irish post-modernity, the place in which these more general moves were first rehearsed. Like the Irish modernists, Joyce and Pearse, who occluded the futuristic quality of their ideas with back-references to Homer or Cuchulain, Irish post-modernists like Nuala Ní Dhomhnaill or Gabriel Rosenstock could apply the language as a sort of screen behind which they experimented with the ideas of the writer Primo Levi, the musician Ravi Shankar and the like. After the 1960s, these writers correctly identified the Irish language movement as a countercultural force – they, even more than Patrick Kavanagh and his friends, were the authentic indigenous 'beats'.

My essays through the eighties often seemed like a delayed rssponse to the sixties. The seismic shifts of that decade had destroyed many of those instruments which might have measured them, so all one could do was register after-shocks. But then, the 1960s were in many ways a delayed answer to modernism, or as Lionel Trilling joked 'modernism in the streets'. *Men and Feminism in Modern Literature* (1985) was my fullest attempt to explore some persisting themes. By the 1980s that androgyny first exemplified by Leopold Bloom had become a central element in the new art of the music video. My intention was to show how this had been rehearsed not only by the six male modernists treated in the book but also in the working-out of a colonial relationship between a male Britain and a female subject-people.

Implicit in much of this work had been an equation between Ireland and the Third World, at least in terms of a shared colonial past and some persistent similarities in the post-colonial present. One of these similarities was the large number of Irish students who emigrated to the United States on graduation, often as illegal entrants. By 1987 two out of every three of the graduating class at University College, Dublin, seemed to have gone by the following Christmas. During a general election in that year, a witty editorialist for the *Daily Telegraph* of London jeered that 'the only thing keeping Ireland out of the Third World is the weather'. In a series of articles for the *Irish Times* I had already listed those aspects of Irish life which seemed to correspond with the post-colonial pathology so well evoked by Frantz Fanon in *The Wretched of the Earth*: dynastic political families; clientelism; high emigration; low levels of production. Most of my students agreed with the general tenor of those pieces, but some older colleagues voiced anger, as if in writing them I had somehow let the side down and suggested that the entire experiment of Irish independence had ended in failure. On the other hand, anyone who had to listen to Gay Byrne's daily radio show urging young people to quit their 'banjaxed' country could have been forgiven for reaching such a conclusion.

An unshakeable belief in the integrity of the Irish experiment kept me from losing hope. After all, Ireland was a wealthy consumer-democracy compared to most Third World countries; and the corruption of its political elites was far less grievous than that of Italy, much less Africa. It was, as Luke Gibbons would pithily put it, a First World country but one with a Third World memory. The relation between those worlds was enacted somehow in every Irish text or at least in the possible interpretations to which it gave rise – and also in the streets of the country itself. Having played its part in the build-up of the British empire and then in its dismantling, the Irish were in a pivotal position to mediate between First and Third Worlds, between North and South, in the new emerging order. Rather than moan about the racism of the *Daily Telegraph* or the producers who supplied Gay Byrne with his daily prompts, it seemed more useful to seek for some positive meanings in the analogy.

Implicit in the 'double' nature of the Irish condition was a need to dismantle all glib notions of a clear split between First and Third Worlds. This was a dangerous division because, however much it might appeal to left-wing sentimentalists, it overlooked the poverty to be found in many areas of the United States or those regions of vulgar affluence within many of the poorer countries. Missionaries who returned to Ireland from work in Africa, Asia and Latin America brought with them a theology of liberation which might have helped to democratise parish life and reanimate a popular Catholicism whose decline had not been halted by the visit of Pope John Paul II in 1979. Irish missionaries, like development workers, had gone to their tasks without any ulterior political motive and this was why they were in a position to learn from their experiences abroad. In a similar fashion Irish cultural critics were learning from the writings of Léopold Senghor about *Négritude*, from Fanon about the pitfalls of national consciousness or the Subaltern Studies group of India about non-institutional forms of opposition. As director of the Yeats Summer School in the mid-1980s, I invited figures such as Gayatri Spivak, Lyn Innes and Edward Said to address these issues and wrote some essays of my own on such concepts as *Négritude*, Afrocentrism and Orientalism. It was at this time also that I contributed a pamphlet on *Anglo-Irish Attitudes* to the Field Day Company of Derry.

By 1990 post-colonial theory was a fashion on many US campuses, so much so that genuine attempts by friends such as Elizabeth Butler Cullingford to bring Irish Studies under its aegis exposed them to the charge of making nothing more than a career move. At a time when various minorities were clamouring for cultural space within the American scheme,

Irish literature seemed to many Hispanics and Afro-Americans to be part of the problem rather than an element in any possible solution. Back in Ireland, however, post-colonial critics ran the risk of being called the literary wing of the IRA at a time when bombs were still exploding, despite the fact that northern republicans repeatedly insisted that there was nothing 'post' about their colonial problem. A course which I taught at University College, Dublin, with Emer Nolan on 'Emergent Literatures' was removed suddenly from the syllabus in 1994 – and it was for this reason that I wrote *Inventing Ireland* in a style which might appeal, over the heads of my fellow-academics, to the wider community. Luckily, the ceasefires had taken hold by the time of the book's appearance in 1995 and it was well received. The anti-nationalist revisionists were no longer asked to review such a volume in Irish papers, so they had to frame their critiques from the pages of the British press. One such review climaxed in a melodramatic apology for the unconscionable disloyalty of the Easter Rising.

Not all of the revisionist analysis had been wrong, of course. Historians were right to criticise the nationalist morality tale on which the first generations in independent Ireland were raised – but wrong to invert the blame-game along the Anglo-Irish axis and call the result 'demystification'. The indictment of narrow-gauge nationalism became all too easily for some an attempt to deny the colonial aspect of the past, as if this generation might create a new country *ex nihilo*, a wholly understandable desire. Karl Marx had written that a real revolution would draw its poetry from the future rather than the past, which weighed like a nightmare upon the brains of the living. Similarly, Joyce had caused his Stephen Dedalus to call history a nightmare from which he was trying to awaken. Caught up in this mood of impatience which became dominant in the 1980s, I wrote 'The War Against the Past'. One of the vices of colonialism, after all, had been its attempt to erase the historical record and cultural past of the occupied land. To attempt to obliterate one's history in the name of radical self-creation might seem like a strange form of collusion with those policies. Yet there is a certain logic to forgetting, for, as Brian Friel wrote in *Translations*, it can be a form of madness to remember everything. Learning how to forget some things is what allows people to act without excessive scruple in the present – otherwise acts of creation might become impossible. Nevertheless, the past has its untapped potentials too and these may yet – like the vibrant ideas of Douglas Hyde – open a way into a better future.

And not just in Ireland, but also in England. The revivalists, led by Yeats and Gregory, saw themselves as inventing Ireland and in that very act also liberating England. Wilde and Shaw both believed that England should give up its imperial possessions and become the republic dreamed of by Milton, Blake and Shelley. This might necessitate the break-up of the United Kingdom, foretold by Tom Nairn in the 1970s and seemingly begun by Tony Blair two decades later with the installation of devolved parliaments in Cardiff, Edinburgh and Belfast. If these had their home-rule parliaments, how long before London followed? That was the thinking behind my essay 'Reinventing England' (1998) – that the English themselves had become versions of Homi Bhabha's flawed mimesis, anglicised rather than truly English, but that they at least had the chance to recover the full meaning of what being English might be. It was notable that some of the strongest supporters of those Irish prisoners unjustly jailed in England through the 1980s and 1990s were those politicians of the English left, like Tony Benn, Clare Short and Ken Livingstone, who also believed in a truly sovereign English parliament no longer under the yoke of a British monarchy.

Although the Anglo-Irish axis remained important (largely because of the continuing crisis in Northern Ireland), by 1990 it no longer dominated all cultural debate. Ireland's growing role in the European Union and in the emerging democracies of Eastern Europe after 1989 led intellectuals to make comparisons with Berlin, Paris, Tallinn or Prague. The figure of James Joyce was vital to this debate, for here was a writer who had made himself European without ever ceasing to be Irish – such was the emerging orthodoxy as Bloomsday loomed ever larger on the national calendar. But was Joyce a celebrant of European values or their fierce critic? He had chosen to live in some of the great European cities, but his Irish background led him to adopt a global frame of reference which went well beyond the European-style humanism sponsored by his foremost celebrant, Richard Ellmann. His mockery of fashionable European bohemians was one aspect ('My Latin Quarter hat. God, we simply must dress the character'). So was his rather anthropological take on the Judaeo-Christian tradition in *Ulysses*, which he presented in its later chapters as winding down. But at a more directly political level there was also plenty of evidence – not just Joyce's mockery of an education reduced to a means for recruiting colonial servants but also the scene in the Cyclops episode of *Ulysses* in which the drinkers evince a fellow-feeling for Africans under the imperial lash. Ellmann had noted the critique of the drinkers' Anglophobia but it took an Emer Nolan to register their universalist political sympathies (which gave their hostility to Britain a rather nobler meaning).

By the 1990s Joyce's texts had become a major site of contest between those who believed in a European Ireland and those who favoured a post-colonial self-analysis. Perhaps this was yet another false dichotomy in need of dismantling, for Ireland was in fact both a former colony and a consumer-democracy. Its transition from the former to the latter status gave it an exemplary value not only to the re-emergent peoples of Eastern Europe but also to the Scottish and Welsh. The election as President of Mary Robinson in 1990 installed as first citizen a radical lawyer whose career combined agitation for social justice at the European courts in Strasbourg with an active involvement in famine relief in the developing world.

One of her first acts as President was to light a candle in the window of her official residence, Áras an Uachtaráin, in the name of all those who had been forced to emigrate. Throughout the 1970s and 1980s revisionist writers, in the attempt to combat the rhetoric of the IRA, had shrunk the meaning of the word 'Ireland' from thirty-two to twenty-six counties – these were 'the inherited boundaries', according to Sebastian Barry. This represented a deliberate thinning of a concept which, as recently as the 1960s, had had a far wider outreach. On All-Ireland Final days through-out the 1960s broadcasters had regularly sent messages to the Irish in Australia, Africa and the United States at half-time. Now that tradition was back on the agenda and, all of a sudden, *anyone* in the world could be Irish, anyone who felt that he or she belonged.

Meanwhile, the revisionists hadn't gone away but were now playing a different game. Where once they had sought to reduce Ireland to minimal size, now they attempted to expand it so diffusely that the term might come to lack specific meaning. David Pierce's anthology of twentieth-century Irish writing was a flagrant case. It included critiques of those scholars who sought to 'reappropriate' a figure like Joyce for Ireland – hardly a capital offence – but Pierce himself so widened the definition of Irish writing that authors like Scott Fitzgerald and John O'Hara were suddenly admitted to the canon. Now *that* was appropriation.

Nonetheless, there was something decidedly positive about being Irish in the 1990s, though the risk of commodification was very real. Where once emigrants had felt themselves confronted by the image of the Stage Irishman, now they found themselves preceded by a rather different set of cultural symbols – prefabricated drinking bars and high-kicking dancers. Many at home felt equally misrepresented by these rather facile symbols and wished, for example, that the complex history of music and dance as treated in Friel's *Dancing at Lughnasa* might reach as vast an audience as

Riverdance could command in every major world city. Only the more rudimentary forms of Irishness seemed to travel – but travel they surely did. Once upon a time people like Douglas Hyde had felt their home culture besieged by penny dreadfuls and the yellow press, but now aspects of the culture which he favoured were being projected onto a world stage in the forms of big business. Perhaps at a time of worldwide homogenisation, Irish culture offered to many admirers overseas the consoling possibility that some traditional values might yet be preserved. The success of writers like Roddy Doyle and Seamus Heaney suggested that there was still a desire for a good story well told. It was in this rather upbeat mood, much enhanced by the conviction that the northern violence had been ended by the Good Friday Agreement of 1998, that I wrote *Irish Classics* (2000), a celebration of the interaction of Gaelic and Anglo-Irish traditions across a wide range of literary masterpieces.

Some of the cultural events played out in the global setting of the last decade of the millennium seemed a reprise, often in extreme forms, of familiar old themes. Having been the first English-speaking people to decolonise, the Irish experienced some things before other people repeated the process. The censorship of writers was replicated in other newly independent states, often with the added ferocity of jailing and summary execution. The *fatwa* against Salman Rushdie was analagous to other vendettas against free-spirited secularist authors – Synge's alleged blasphemies in *The Playboy of the Western World*, for example. But some of the more facile responses to the *fatwa* were reminders that liberals do not always notice the cultural limits which they set to their own tolerance, a point I explored in two pamphlet essays, 'Multiculturalism' and 'Strangers in Their own Country' (2001). These further developed a theme I treated also in ' Joyce's Ellmann, Ellmann's Joyce' (1998) – that a European humanism, however noble in lineage, might not be enough for a full reading of Joyce, let alone a truly global world.

The problem of how to evolve a genuinely pluralist culture has not yet been solved anywhere, but the raising of the question allows us to reformulate old themes in new ways. If car-bombs in Italian or Spanish cities suggested that the problems of Belfast belonged as much to the twentieth as to the seventeenth century, then there might be a way of redefining the Northern Ireland situation along more contemporary lines. The real problem might be less the existence of the state as such than its failure to provide a public space hospitable to the religious and cultural minority. That might then be seen as a problem analogous to that posed by the wearing of a veil by Islamic girls in French state schools, or to the question of evolving a United States which somehow managed to reconcile its Enlightenment philosophy with a respect for all religious and cultural traditions.

The unfolding developments in other trouble-spots also carried valuable lessons for Ireland – a topic I explored in 'Museums and Learning' (2003). In South Africa the Truth and Reconciliation Commission, with the best will in the world, seemed to reinforce rather than heal some of that country's terrible divisions, mainly because it recreated the binary antithesis of apartheid in its very structure. A similar problem beset the new Northern Ireland executive in its early days, although the emergence of a Women's Coalition held some promise – alas unfulfilled as yet – that old antagonisms could be transcended. It may be too soon for a truth commission in Northern Ireland.

A scholar could in such instances instances use Ireland as a test-case for the world but also see in the culture of globalisation a whole set of issues which needed addressing in his own country. If Joyce was revealed as a major inspiration to novelists of the Latin American boom of the 1960s, and Yeats as a father figure to decolonising poets from Neruda to Darwish, then it might also be possible to argue that the mystical element in the poetry of the 1916 leaders had evoked a powerful set of echoes among the writers of India. But that process was always a two-way street. By the 1990s the challenges posed by growing numbers of immigrants led many teachers to become aware of the need for a new classroom practice which might take account of the diverse biographies of those students now sitting before them. In my essay 'Strangers in Their own Country' (2001) I also explored the likelihood that many of those students might find in the Irish experience telling echoes of their own.

The issues which the incomers posed meant that the canon of Irish writing needed less to be supplanted than to be reinterpreted in ways which revealed more fully its multicultural meanings. My teaching career began with an excited exploration of what might happen in classrooms where students of unionist background confronted the Gaelic world and where children of nationalist families embraced the ideas of the Anglo-Irish. Now it is time to imagine just how the son of a Brazilian worker in a midlands meat factory might read *Gulliver's Travels* or how the daughter of Nigerian immigrants might respond to *Dancing at Lughnasa*.

CHAPTER 2

The fall of the Stage Irishman

(1979)

In Shakespeare's *Henry V* we are given a fleeting glimpse of an Irishman named Macmorris, a captain in the king's army. In this splenetic figure, we find those traits of excitability, eloquence, pugnacity and strong national pride which would later become the stock-in-trade of the Stage Irishman. For Macmorris was, despite his fierce loyalty to the king, a figure of fun on the London stage. For some strange reason, generations of Englishmen, including the open-hearted Shakespeare, have found it amusing that the Irish should be proud of their own nationality. Some of the soldiers in the Globe audience would already have had grim experience of the Elizabethan military campaigns in Ireland, a campaign conducted in treacherous boglands into which the agile Irish repeatedly lured the enemy forces before battle. Hence the endless references to Irish bogs, bogtrotters and bogmen in the subsequent literature of England. Hence, too, the phrase 'wild Irishman' which was used as early as 1608 by the playwright Dekker in *Lanthorn and Candlelight*. By the time the theatres of England were closed under the Puritan ban of the 1640s, the rudimentary image of the Stage Irishman had been formed: he wore trousers, drank endlessly, swore wildly, and spoke a broken but colourful brand of English, salted with Gaelic exclamations. In the eighteenth century, new features were added: now the character invariably carried a shillelagh under his arm, ate potatoes as a staple diet and frequently appeared with a pig in close attendance. More striking than any of these props, however, was his penchant for the 'bull' – the clumsy sentence pregnant with implication.[1]

Although the Stage Irishman proved immensely popular with proletarian audiences in the music halls of Victorian England, the same cannot be said of his real-life counterpart who stole furtively into the major cities and industrial towns. All too often competition for work led to riots between Irish and English labourers and after the fracas the injured were frequently sentenced to deportation. The disparity between the stage character and the real Irishman goes back at least to 1660, but it became extreme in the mid-nineteenth century, when the music-hall creation was loved and the real-life model hated. Previously, the two stock types – the hot-headed soldier and the brainless but loyal servant – had been depicted as amiable fellows, goodhearted and generous despite their bursts of drinking and pugnacity. Now, however, in the satirical cartoons of the gentleman's magazine *Punch* ugly new dimensions were added to the character. The harmless drunken peasant was changed into a dangerous anthropoid or simianised agitator, reflecting a remarkable shift in the attitude of some Victorians about the differences not only between Englishmen and Irishmen, but also between human beings and apes.[2] Of course, it was only when the Irish Question began to bedevil the domestic peace of English politics in the period that the cartoonists decided suddenly that the Irishman should be depicted as a monkey. They portrayed Daniel O'Connell as 'King of the Beggars' and his followers as a bunch of screaming apes. The doctrine of the 'wild Irish', which had arisen through fear of a stubborn enemy, was now compounded with guilt in the years of the Great Famine 1845–8, when the nightmarish metaphors of the cartoonists became literally true. The starving peasantry were reduced in life, as they had been already in the cartoonist's art, to the level of untamed animals. Yet all this time, and for decades afterward, the English audience continued to shower affection on the Irish character of the music hall. It was, perhaps, a classic example of the tendency of all repressive regimes to sentimentalise their victims. After all, those same Victorian ladies and gentlemen who wept over the innocent outraged children in the novels of Charles Dickens were sending six-year-old urchins down into the mines and up into the chimney flues to earn their keep.

The newspapers of Victorian England are studded with reports of the fey, feckless, fighting Irish. Journalists in search of a good story regaled their readers with accounts of Irishmen defending themselves in court. Male defendants were inexorably depicted as 'a broth of a boy', 'as fine a sprig as ever flourished in the Ould Emerald Isle', or introduced as 'Big Blarney' or 'Poor Paddy'. This was the newspaper variant of the music hall phenomenon, an attitude compounded of guilt, fear, affection and racial superiority. The atrocious living conditions of the emigrant Irish gave rise to much violence and crime. In 1861, for example, one quarter of the population of Liverpool was Irish-born, yet that nation accounted for more than one half of the defendants appearing in city courts on charges of assault, drunkenness and breach of the peace.[3]

While the Irishman was being prosecuted in the courts of the realm and mocked to scorn in a thousand music halls, some of his more creative compatriots in London were continuing to win the highest acclaim for their art as playwrights. Englishmen came slowly to realise that their much-vaunted tradition of comedy had been instituted and maintained by a succession of outrageously talented Irishmen. From Congreve and Farquhar in the Restoration drama, through Goldsmith and Sheridan in the eighteenth century, to Wilde and Shaw at the close of the nineteenth, Irishmen had revealed themselves to be past masters of English comedy. While their compatriots were mocked as low buffoons, the intelligence and wit of Wilde and Shaw drew cascades of applause from the most exacting audiences of the London theatre. It was a very Irish paradox and in retrospect its nature is clear. These writers of comedy were all from Protestant or Anglo-Irish stock – a hyphenated race, as one of them complained, treated as English in Ireland but inevitably seen as Irishmen in England. Their predicament called for the sharp ironic intelligence of which comedy is made, since the comic vision delights in revealing those differences and misunderstandings which separate man from man. These playwrights were sufficiently similar to the English in education and background to be acceptable as wry commentators on the British scene – and yet their foreignness gave their views an apparent objectivity and colour which never failed to excite interest. They were different but not too different. In their works they could voice sharp criticisms of John Bull which no Englishman would ever dare to offer himself. If their complaints were acceptable, well and good; but if they went too close to the bone, they could be laughed out of court as Irish folly.

In a sense the role of these playwrights in the London theatre ran parallel to that of the Irish agitators in English politics, for it is now clear to modern historians that the notorious Irish Question was more para-bolic than real in nature. Though often presented as a disruptive force in toppling precariously balanced governments, the Irish members in the House of Commons were used more often as a kind of sounding-board on which the British populace could test the great domestic questions of their politics – land ownership, religion and imperialism. The Irish Question was treated as a parable by which these distressing issues could be raised at one remove, since no English politician would ever have been bold enough to raise them bluntly in the domestic British context himself.[4] Once again, the Irish were accepted as valid commentators, whose judgements could be conceded if they seemed feasible, but if their demands seemed too extreme (as was usually the case), then they could be put down to Irish folly rather than to English malpractice. The Paddies could be patted on the head with an affectionate and condescending sigh, as if they were being whimsical and feckless again.

There was a very real sense in which the image of the Irishman conformed as much to Irish needs as to English prejudice. The English have always presented themselves to the world as a cold, refined and urbane race, so it suited them to see in the Irish the reverse of all these traits – to see them as hot-headed, rude and garrulous. Similarly, British colonists in the Sudan and in India have sought in the natives of those countries the anti-self of the true-born Englishman. They have imputed much the same traits to the 'Fuzzi-Wuzzies', 'Gunga Dins' and 'Pakis' that they had already attributed to the Irish. The fact that the Irish, like the Indians, are on the contrary cold, polite and calculating is beside the point, for their official image before the world has been irrevocably created by a far greater imperial power. In many respects it has suited the Irish in England and even America to conform to the prototype. For all the bogus sentimentality and fawning idiocy of the Stage Irish model, it gave his compatriots a status as folk-heroes at a time when their situation as newly arrived immigrants was bleak indeed. As one commentator has noted:

In spite of the criticisms of later generations of immigrants in less dangerous times, their reasoning was sound: the caricature and ridicule meant that the English considered them harmless creatures. In the East End of the nineteenth century, regularly hovering on the brink of racial conflict, this refusal to take them seriously ensured their safety and marked the thin end of the wedge towards general acceptance.[5]

There were other, more complex, reasons for the donning by immigrants of the Stage Irish mask. Most Irish folk had come straight from the most remote rural communities in the west of Ireland to vast industrial cities which were the living antithesis of all that they had known in childhood. From living in a pious, almost neolithic subsistence community on windswept seashores they were plunged into the secular anonymity of life in the factories and the mines. They had no previous experience of cities and, therefore, no ready-made urban identity. Moreover, their real identity as peasants whose lifestyle had scarcely changed in a thousand years was quite incomprehensible to those English citizens with whom they now had to deal. It was far easier, therefore, to don the mask of the surrogate Irishman than to reshape a complex urban identity of their own. Within their own families and tightly knit communities they continued to subscribe to their traditional culture and ancient pieties, while happily conforming to the folk image of the Irishman in affairs of business and politics. An art of fawning duplicity arose from this predicament. Businessmen acted the feckless brainless Irishman while making shrewd deals which outsmarted their English rivals, who took them at face value. Labourers doffed their caps to gentlemen and ritually intoned in Stage Irish dialect 'Top of the mornin' to you, sor', while secretly gloating over the fact that 'sor' was an ancient Irish word for 'bastard'. The Stage Irish mask could be donned at will and it had two distinct advantages. It permitted some form of rudimentary contact between the immigrant and the native English; but secondly, it called for only a circumscribed relationship which the Irishman could control and regulate at will.

Back in Ireland even those who were not forced to emigrate had learned the value of donning the stage mask in politics, so they chose as their leader the incomparable Daniel O'Connell, a man who was the very incarnation of the Stage Irishman and a godsend to Fleet Street cartoonists. With his torrents of rhetoric, his charm among the ladies and his thick brogue, he charmed his way into the hearts of many English politicians with whom he shrewdly co-operated at all times in his bloodless campaign for the emancipation of his Catholic countrymen. When his later crusade to repeal the Act of Union failed utterly, he suffered an ignominious reversal. Over thirty years later, when the Irish sought a new leader at Westminster, they turned to Charles Stewart Parnell, a man who was the opposite of O'Connell in every respect – aloof, cold and very urbane. The 'great comedian' O'Connell had failed, so they sent to London a man who could speak in the refined cadences of the Englishman's language. With Home Rule a real possibility under Parnell, the Irish finally decided to cast off the stage mask, so they turned to a man who seemed more English than the English themselves. Subsequent events were to show, however, that Parnell's icy exterior was but another mask worn to conceal a passionate and volcanic temperament. Nevertheless, the point was not lost on Irish writers who decided once and for all to have done with the Stage Irishman.

When a young poet named Willie Yeats, newly arrived in London, was introduced in 1888 to his illustrious compatriot Oscar Wilde, he described the meeting as 'an astonishment'. He found in Wilde 'the most finished talker of our time', a man who spoke in perfectly formed sentences, unequalled in elegance even among the Englishmen whom the poet knew. Wilde seemed to have assumed a new, urbane personality;

his utterance had an epigrammatic thrust which could only have been the outcome of rigorous rehearsal; and he seemed to the awkward, gangling young poet to be the very antithesis of the Stage Irishman. In the words of Richard Ellmann, Wilde represented for Yeats an example of the 'allegorical victory of imagination over environment and heredity'.[6] Timidly the poet confessed to Wilde, 'I envy those men who become mythological while still living', and he was told in return 'I think a man should invent his own myth.' To his Irish friends who protested that Wilde was simply a shallow person, Yeats hotly declared that posing was a way of being true to the depth of one's being. He told George Russell that posing 'was merely living artistically, and it was the duty of everybody to have a conception of themselves, and he intended to conceive of himself'. So Yeats saved up at once for a black cape which he wore with enigmatic verve through the years of his young manhood. Having been bullied at the Godolphin School in Hammersmith, London, because of his Irish background, the poet knew from an early age the perils of being type-cast in England. Rejecting the mask of the professional Irishman which London publishers eagerly proffered to him, Yeats created instead his own mask of the anti-self: 'I think', he wrote several years later, 'all happiness depends on the energy to assume the mask of some other life, on a re-birth as something not oneself . . . If we cannot imagine ourselves as different from what we are, and try to assume that second self, we cannot impose a discipline on ourselves.' The discipline Yeats sought was the energy to surmount the inherited image of the Irish as emotional, soft and warm. He wrote: 'I take pleasure alone in those verses where it seems to me I have found something hard and cold, some articulation of the Image, which is the opposite of all that I am in my daily life and all that my country is.' Yeats called this new-found mask the 'anti-self' and he deployed it with lofty austerity for the rest of his days, in confrontation with the prejudices of supercilious Englishmen. This crusade against the Stage Irishman reached its fitting climax after his discussions with Lady Gregory and Edward Martyn to plan the foundation of a national theatre in Dublin. The manifesto which issued from their negotiations was a summons to Ireland's youth to join the fight:

We propose to have performed in Dublin, in the spring of every year, certain Celtic and Irish plays, which whatever be their degree of excellence will be written with a high ambition, and so build up a Celtic and Irish school of dramatic literature . . . We will show that Ireland is not the home of buffoonery and of easy sentiment, as it has been represented, but the home of an ancient idealism.[7]

From this small beginning stemmed one of the major dramatic movements of twentieth-century literature with its home in the Abbey Theatre.

It has been said by Carlos Fuentes that a revolution is 'a battle for faces against masks'. The artistic revolution initiated by Yeats gave to the people their own theatre in which they could depict their own life as it was truly lived, in which they could trace the lineaments of the Irish face rather than the broad caricature of an imposed Stage Irish mask. Some Irishmen might persist in pandering to the prejudices of an English audience in the music halls of London, but at least every young writer was now faced with a challenging choice – either to express Ireland or to exploit her. Fundamentally, the choice lay between the complex but exhilarating task of expressing the emergent nation to itself, or exploiting the experience of the quaint native peasantry for the delectation and amusement of a 'superior' foreign audience. Playscripts came flooding in to the Directors of the new theatre, including a most unexpected offer from George Bernard Shaw. He had jocularly described himself in the past as 'a faithful servant of the British people', indicating that he saw himself as another in the long line of licensed Irish jesters in the history of the English stage. But now in 1904 he submitted to Yeats a new play entitled *John Bull's Other Island,* a witty study of Anglo-Irish relations and a scathing attack on the Stage Irishman. In this work a real Irishman named Doyle is pitted against Haffigan, a type of the feckless stage peasant. Doyle lashes out memorably at the prototype:

The real tragedy of Haffigan is the tragedy of his wasted youth, his stunted mind, his drudgery over his clods and pigs until he has become a clod and a pig himself – until the soul within him has smouldered into nothing but a dull temper that hurts himself and all around him. I say let him die, and let us have no more of his like.

Extending his critique to those Irishmen at home who have conformed abjectly to the image of a race of dreamers and misfits, Doyle goes on:

An Irishman's imagination never lets him alone, never convinces him, never satisfies him; but it makes him that he can't face reality nor deal with it nor handle it nor conquer it: he can only sneer at them that do. He can't be religious. The inspired Churchman that teaches him the sanctity of life and the importance of conduct is sent away empty, while the poor village priest that gives him a miracle and a sentimental story of a saint has cathedrals built for him out of the pennies of the poor. He can't be intelligently political: he dreams of what the Shan Van Vocht said in ninety-eight. If you want to interest him in Ireland you've got to call the unfortunate island Kathleen ni Houlihan and pretend she's a little old woman. It saves thinking. It saves working.

Yeats found *John Bull's Other Island* beyond the technical resources of his infant theatre and politely declined Shaw's offer; but he may also have felt that his ruthless critique of the Irish dreamer might have offended some of the young idealists in the Abbey's audience. Such caution was justified given the passions aroused in the contemporary debate about what constituted the real face of Ireland now that the mask had been tossed aside. Three years later, when Synge portrayed that mixture of poetry and violence at the heart of peasant life in *The Playboy of the Western World*, the audience protested by riot. One newspaper report of the disturbance remarked of the play: 'It is as if we looked into a mirror for the first time, and found ourselves hideous. We fear to face the thing. We shrink at the word for it. We scream.'[8] The protesters were convinced that they had witnessed a revival of the Stage Irishman in the figure of Christy Mahon, the lyrical boy who 'killed' his father with the blow of a loy (spade); but in reality the only Stage Irish scenes had been enacted away from the stage amid the uproar of the pit. The newspaper reporter had shrewdly noted that when a people discard a mask and look for the first time into a mirror, they do not always like what they see. The protesters thought that Synge's dialect was merely another version of the brogue; but the author himself had repeatedly warned other writers against the dangers of what he called 'the rollicking note'. He had carefully chosen his idioms from the speech of rural Ireland, especially from those areas where the Irish language was still flourishing and had conditioned the local brand of English.

Synge's work has often been interpreted as a study in Irish exaggeration, but in fact his plays and essays offer a sharp critique of excess. In an essay written as early as 1904, he rejected the braggadocio and feckless Stage Irishman of the past, but was no less critical of the anti-Stage Irishman of the present. He complained pointedly about the brogue of the Stage-Irish writers in whose idiom he found 'a familiarity that is not amusing'; and he wrote that, as a result 'a great deal of what is most precious in the national life must be omitted from their work, or imperfectly expressed'. When Frank Hugh O'Donnell went from door to door among the denizens of literary Dublin with his pamphlet attacking 'The Stage Irishman of Pseudo-Celtic Drama', he cannot have expected support from a leading playwright of the very theatre which he had denounced most bitterly. But Synge welcomed the pamphlet and wrote:

A young literary movement is never the worse for adverse and candid criticism. It should never be forgotten that half the troubles of England and Ireland have arisen from ignorance of the Irish character, ignorance founded on the biased views of British and Irish historians and on the absurd caricatures which infest the majority of plays and novels dealing with Irish folk and affairs. Lever, Lover, Boucicault and *Punch* have achieved much in the way of making the Irish character a sealed book to Englishmen.[9]

This clear rejection of the Stage Irishman was accompanied in the same essay by an equally trenchant denunciation of the holier-than-thou anti-Stage Irishman of the present. He felt that men such as O'Donnell were so intent on avoiding any taint of Stage Irishness that they had ceased to be real – they had forgotten who they truly were in their endless campaign not to be somebody else. Synge therefore insisted that 'the rollicking note is present in the Irish character – present to an extent some writers of the day do not seem to be aware of – and it demands, if we choose to deal with it, a free rollicking style' (p. 376). For this reason Synge was as anxious to expose the pretensions of the O'Donnells of this world as he was keen to explode the original Stage Irishman, for both prevented the honest depiction of the realities of rural Irish life. He praised the Abbey Theatre which had offered a solution to this problem: 'it has contrived by its care and taste to put an end to the reaction against the careless Irish humour of which everyone has had too much'. That sentence shrewdly implies a criticism not only of the careless humour of the past, but also of the excessive reaction against such caricature in the present. Synge noted with some asperity that 'the effects of this reaction are still perceptible in Dublin, and the Irish National Theatre Society is sometimes accused of degrading Ireland's vision of herself by throwing a shadow of the typical Stage Irishman across her mirror' (p. 398).

Just such an accusation was made against *The Playboy of the Western World* three years later; and it is clear from the 1904 essay that Synge had always anticipated this type of criticism. Far from being another travesty of the national character, however, his play is an attack on the lyric gush, pugnacity and violence popularly associated with the Stage Irishman. It is also, though covertly, an assault on the anti-Stage Irishman of Wilde and Yeats. In *The Decay of Lying* Wilde had constructed an elaborate defence of the mask or anti-self, which took the form of an ingenious justification of lying. Conceding that the mask was founded on a lie, he asserted that lying was no shame: 'After all, what is a good lie? Simply that which is its own evidence.' This is the datum of *The Playboy* where Christy Mahon became great by believing himself so, winning the acclaim of the community, as Pegeen acidly remarks, 'by the power of a lie'. The whole play is simply an investigation of the validity of Wilde's initial observation: 'Many a young man starts in life with a natural gift for exaggeration which, if nurtured in congenial and sympathetic surroundings, or by imitation of the best models, might grow into something really great and wonderful.' Much later, Yeats would describe his own cultivation of the anti-Stage Irish pose as the strategy of a man not so very different from Christy Mahon:

> One that ruffled in a manly pose
> For all his timid heart.

In *The Player Queen* Yeats followed Wilde in his explanation of the underlying idea: 'To be great . . . we must seem so . . . Seeming that goes on for a lifetime is no different from reality.' Synge was not so sure. In *The Playboy* he offered his criticisms of Wilde's theory, of fine words divorced from real action, of gestures struck rather than deeds done – in short, of the fatal Irish gift for blarney. He voiced his own doubts in Pegeen's grief-stricken complaint that 'there's a great gap between a gallous story and a dirty deed'. Synge suspected that, at bottom, the mask of the elegant anti-self purveyed by Wilde and Yeats was merely a subtle latter-day version of ancient Irish blarney.

In portraying an Irish hero who is acclaimed by village girls for a deed of violence, Synge offered what Maxim Gorki was later to describe as 'a subtle irony on the cult of the hero'. His play shows that the so-called fighting Irish can only endure the thought of violence when the deed is committed elsewhere or in the past. But when a killing occurs in their own backyard, then they become suddenly aware of that gap between poetic stories and foul deeds. Far from being another attempt to pander to the British notion of Ireland, Synge's play was an honest attempt to express the nation to itself, to reveal to his own countrymen the ambiguity of their own attitude to violence. He foresaw how Pearse and the heroes of 1916 would evoke only the jeers of an apathetic Dublin populace. He foresaw only too well how generations of Irishmen would sing ballads of glamorised rebellion and offer funds for the freedom-fighters – so long as the fighting took place at a safe distance in past history or at the other side of a patrolled political border. He believed that a writer's first duty may be to insult rather than to humour his countrymen, to shock his compatriots into a deeper self-awareness of their own dilemmas. He exploded forever the stage myth of the fighting Irish and, like Joyce, revealed to his countrymen an even more distressing truth – the fact that their besetting vice was not pugnacity but paralysis.[10]

The arguments about national identity persisted long after the death of Synge and were brought into focus by the rise of the separatist movement known as Sinn Féin. The sense that people were recovering a lost identity is summed up in that name which is the Irish for 'ourselves', and the Abbey Theatre continued to play a crucial role in that voyage of self-discovery and self-conquest. The first man to be shot in the 1916 rebellion was Sean Connolly, a leading actor of the theatre, and the involvement in the rising of many poets and playwrights served to emphasise the deeply symbolic nature of their sacrifice. The plays of Sean O'Casey gave the Irish a true image of themselves as they moved from war, through civil war, to self-government. Inevitably, the same plays caused rioting in the theatre. That pose of lofty austerity which Yeats had once found so useful in breaking down the prejudices of the English audience was now used with equal verve in his magisterial attempts to quell the Dublin mob with the immortal line 'You have disgraced yourselves again.' In retrospect, however, these clashes have something noble about them, and seem exhilarating rather than petty, idealistic rather than bizarre. It was as if the whole nation had entered into a passionate debate about the nature of modern Ireland now that the choice was finally their own. Sinn Féin had won the day on the boards no less than at the ballot box.

If Synge overpowered and disarmed the Stage Irishman, then subsequent writers took him prisoner and went on to use him to their own devices. In *Murphy* (1938) Samuel Beckett warned his readers that he was about to enter for the first time the mind of the Stage Irishman. Endowing his eponymous hero with the most common surname in Ireland, he pointed clearly to his lineage: 'Mr Murphy, the ruins of the ruins of the broth of a boy.' Then he packed him off 'on business' to London, in order to study the phenomenon in his natural habitat and to document the alienation of emigrant life in the English capital. The Cartesian split between Murphy's mind and body has detained even the subtlest of critics, but none has seen the ploy for what it is – a way of depicting the disparity between the Irishman as seen by others (a lazy and crude body) and as he sees himself (a hyperactive, even intricate, mind). It is all too grimly appropriate that this broth of a boy should die at the end of the novel, requesting in his will that the ashes of his body be returned to the lavatory bowl of the Abbey Theatre.

Beckett had merely entered the mind of Murphy, thereby proving, at the very least, that the Irishman had one; but in *An Béal Bocht* (1941), whose English title is *The Poor Mouth*, Flann O'Brien went one better.

He took the most despised of the nineteenth-century music-hall buffoons, named Myles-na-Coppaleen, from that most notorious of Stage Irish melodramas, Boucicault's *The Colleen Bawn*. To this strange persona he turned over the very authorship of his book, thereby making the clown articulate – the articulate author of a work in the Irish language. The fawning, feckless idiot who once blustered in broken English for the amusement of British audiences is now permitted to address the world for the first time in his native tongue, the idiom of his childhood and youth. Those traces of the Stage Irish brogue which linger in his speech are now relegated to the quaintly exotic status of footnotes, where straightforward Gaelic words are used to explain such nineteenth-century monstrosities as 'diversions' and 'advintures' even on the opening page of the novel. It is doubtful that such words were ever spoken on Irish soil, but even if these mispronunciations did occur Myles can now make his meaning clear with the explanation that the first word signifies 'scléip' and the second 'eachtraí'. Similarly, the eclipsing 'g' which had been omitted from his name in Boucicault's play is now restored, so Myles-na-Coppaleen may assume the fuller status of Myles na gCopaleen. In his native language he can be shown for the first time, not as the English have always wished to visualise him, but as he sees himself.

The verbal tricks and sallies which were once a mere object of the nineteenth-century playwright's ridicule have now become the very mode of the new author's vision. That exaggerated language which was once the object of the dramatist's satire has now become the method by which other, more fitting, targets are attacked. Among those targets are Irishmen such as Boucicault, who have abjectly conformed to English notions of the Stage Irishman. Hence the mockery of Boucicault's fabricated brogue, his 'diversions' and 'advintures', which may mean something to the amused English onlookers but have to be pedantically explained to bemused Irishmen, hearing them for the first time.

If Boucicault and the Stage Irishman expired with the nineteenth century, the tendency of certain writers to conform cravenly to prescribed ideas of Irishness did not. The Stage Irishman gave way to an equally spurious stereotype, the Stage Gael, the long-suffering mystical peasantry of the west so beloved of Yeats and de Valera. O'Brien wrote bitterly to Sean O'Casey of the spokesmen for the new mythology, 'the Gaelic morons here with their bicycle clips and handball medals'. In depicting the realities of poverty in the west of Ireland, *An Béal Bocht* is not only a satire on Boucicault's glamorised version of Irish country life in the last century with its scenic landscapes, gothic ruins and romantic music. It is even more urgently an attack on the Dublin revivalists of the twentieth century who could idealise the simplicity of western life only by ignoring the awful poverty on which the whole system was based. Even the acknowledged leader of the literary revival, W. B. Yeats, was forced to concede the truth. As a young boy in Sligo, he had actually approached one of those countrymen whom he was later to idealise in his poems; and the old fellow surprised him by saying that he was tired of Kickham and the other romantic Irish novelists of the nineteenth century. He confided in the startled young Yeats that his real longing was for 'a work in which the people would be shown up in all their naked hideousness'.[11] Many decades were to pass before that wish was granted in the 1940s by O'Brien's *An Béal Bocht* and Ó Cadhain's *Cré na Cille*. Significantly, both of these classic works were written not in English but in the Irish language, which is to say the natural idiom of the west. Both novels are conscious reactions against the sentimental evasions of the Irish Literary Revival, subversive versions of anti-pastoral.

This new generation of writers who came to prominence in the 1940s was following the lead given by James Joyce in *Stephen Hero* and *A Portrait of the Artist as a Young Man*. If *An Béal Bocht* dramatises the lack of identity in a townland where every male rejoices in the sobriquet James O'Donnell, then forty years earlier the sharp-eyed Stephen Hero had come to the selfsame conclusion: 'The glorified peasantry all seem to me as like one another as a peascod is to another peascod. They can spot a false coin but they represent no very admirable type of culture . . . They live a life of dull routine, the calculation of coppers, the weekly debauch and the weekly piety.'[12] Although Yeats had indeed glorified the western peasant with the avowal that 'Connaught for me is Ireland', later poets such as Patrick Kavanagh chose to agree with Joyce. Kavanagh (who was a real countryman as opposed to a Yeatsian peasant) informed the Dublin literati of the 1940s that the impoverished tiller of the fields had scarcely any identity at all. He would have agreed heartily with Marx's dictum about the need to rescue humanity from 'the idiocy of rural life'. Kavanagh wrote with the blunt honesty of a man who knew what he was talking about: 'Although the literal idea of a peasant is of a farm labouring person, in fact a peasant is all that mass of humanity which lives below a certain level of consciousness. They live in the dark cave of the unconscious and they scream when they see the light.'[13] This is closer to Joyce than to Yeats – it is, in fact, a variant of Stephen Daedalus's reverie of the half-naked peasant woman as 'a type of her race and of his own, a bat-like soul waking to the consciousness of itself in darkness and secrecy and loneliness'.[14] The tragedy of waste which lies at the heart of Kavanagh's long poem *The Great Hunger* is the same tragedy depicted by Shaw in *John Bull's Other Island*. Kavanagh's Maguire serves as a latter-day Haffigan, a man without qualities who will never escape from 'his wasted youth, his stunted mind, his drudgery over the clods and pigs until he has become a clod and a pig himself'. The same indignation informs *An Béal Bocht* which takes us beyond the Stage Irish thief who robs the rich for kicks or revenge, to a study of robbers who are so poor that they filch from one another:

Bhíodh gadaíocht ar siúl de ló is d'oíche ag gach éinne sa pharóiste – bochtáin ag rí-bhochtadh a chéile.

Night and day there was constant thieving in progress in the parish – paupers impoverishing each other.[15]

Behind this satiric hilarity lies a real sense of desolation; as Brendan Kennelly has observed 'this black vision sometimes transcends the satirical purpose it so brilliantly serves and achieves at certain moments a real tragic intensity'.[16] The satire and the tragedy are finally one, for in mocking the official clichés of previous Irish writers, O'Brien is emphasising the plight of a peasantry which has had a false romantic identity foisted upon it. If a revolution is truly a fight for faces rather than masks, then O'Brien clearly feels that the new Irish state has failed to disclose to the people its own face – it has merely tricked them into exchanging one mask for another. For him the most distressing aspect of this failure is the alarming number of Irishmen, in the last century and in the present, who were willing to conform to these stereotypes.

It would be wrong, however, to imply that the targets of *An Béal Bocht* are solely local or Irish, for this book has a larger significance. It is a tragedy of mistaken identity, one instance of which is the depiction in the nineteenth century of the Stage Irishman. But such tragedies occur every day in some part of the world, in Aden or India or Pakistan or Vietnam – wherever rival versions of national identity are concocted by coloniser and contested by colonised. It is inevitable that the last people to understand this will be English critics such as John Wain who has glibly announced that O'Brien 'remains a writer whose subject is not Man, but Irishman'. If Myles-na-Coppaleen was the despised buffoon in the sentimental melodramas of the last century, then in this novel as Myles na gCopaleen he has become articulate. His recovery of his true literary identity provides a deeply comic parallel to the serious repossession of a political identity summed up in the words 'Sinn Féin'. Through the use of his once-despised, still-inflated, but now functional language, Myles has succeeded in depicting a world in which all men, and not solely the Gaelic peasant, are seen for the buffoons that they are. The difference between Myles na gCopaleen and Myles-na-Coppaleen is the difference between a vehicle and a target.

If Flann O'Brien deftly chose one Stage Irishman as the fictional author of his greatest novel, then Brendan Behan learned to play the role of Stage Irish author in fact. In his drama of Anglo-Irish relations entitled *The Hostage*, he updated Shaw's critique of the Irish and at the same time wickedly mocked his English audiences for paying good money to be similarly abused. As an author and public character, Behan played up to the Englishman's preconception of the broth-of-a-boy Paddy; but as a playwright he mocked his London audiences for being gulled by that very ploy:

SOLDIER: Brendan Behan, he's too anti-British.

IRA OFFICER: Too anti-Irish you mean. Bejasus, wait till we get him back home. We'll give him what-for for making fun of the Movement.

SOLDIER: (*To audience*) He doesn't mind coming over here and taking your money.

PAT: He'd sell his country for a pint.

The trouble was, of course, that he did – at that very moment and in that very play. He had come to that moment of decision which Yeats had predicted for every Irish writer, the choice between expressing the nation to itself or exploiting the foibles of a quaint island people for the amusement of a 'superior' British audience. To a man such as Behan who had command of both languages, this decision presented itself as a choice between writing in Irish or in English. Nowhere are the consequences of that option more spectacularly dramatised than in the contrast between his play in Irish entitled *An Giall* and its subsequent English version, *The Hostage*.

In 1958 when Behan offered his Dublin audience *An Giall* at the request of the language agency Gael-Linn, he had outwardly little to gain from the decision. Here was an author who in the same year sojourned in Ibiza to start work on a new novel, visited Paris to discuss the French production of *The Quare Fellow* and put the finishing touches to *Borstal Boy* in Sweden. By comparison with such cosmopolitan glamour, Gael-Linn had little in the way of material reward or public acclaim to offer him – in the words of Colbert Kearney, only 'a tiny theatre and the obscurity of a relatively unknown language'.[17] But from a spiritual point of view, this was everything he needed and more. The erstwhile IRA man had always felt himself tugged in opposite directions, between his obligations as a soldier and his desire to succeed as a writer. As a youth in jail for the national cause in the 1940s, he had found a solution in the writing of poetry in Irish – an exercise which allowed him to follow his artistic instinct while still contributing to the struggle against British cultural imperialism. Even after the astounding success of *The Quare Fellow* on the English stage in the mid-fifties, the old boyhood dream of writing a major work in Irish returned to him. As Kearney has so shrewdly observed: 'No amount of foreign applause could satisfy this facet of his personality: he could no more forget his earlier hopes than he could cut himself off completely from the IRA. He had always wanted, among other things, to serve Ireland and now, as something of a world figure, he was in a strong position to do so' (p. 119). *An Giall* was the realisation of this dream and a major success in Dublin. The inevitable call to rewrite the play in English for Joan Littlewood's theatre in London soon followed. What happened next is notorious. The playwright never really rewrote his own play, but ceded it to Littlewood's company who teased it into a new shape calculated to appeal to an English audience. *An Giall*, a spare and simple tragedy, became *The Hostage*, a music-hall variety show with topical references to Profumo, Macmillan, risky homosexuality and Jayne Mansfield. According to Wolf Mankowitz, Behan was 'pissed out of his mind when half the changes were made'. Only on the opening night in London, while the play was winning rapturous applause, did Behan come to an awareness of the damage to his own self-respect. He cursed Joan Littlewood roundly, according to his brother Brian who recalled the occasion: 'I was surprised and I looked at him closely. He looked suddenly as if he knew that he had been 'taken for a ride,' that he had been adopted as a broth of a boy, that they had played a three card trick on him.'

Premonitions of that self-betrayal had dominated Behan's earliest lyrics written in the Irish language. One poem, 'Buíochas le Joyce' (Thanks to Joyce), deals with the way in which the young writer in Paris is bought by foreigners, who ply him with drinks because he is a fellow-countryman of the great modernist:

> Annseo i Rue Saint André des Arts
> i dtábhairne Arabach, ólta,
> míním do Franncach fiosrach thú,
> ex-G. I.'s 's Rúiseach ólta.
> Molaim gach comhartha dár chuiris ar phár
> Is mise san Fhrainc ag ól Pernod dá bharr.[18]

Here in the Rue Saint André des Arts,
pissed in an Arab's tavern,
I dissect you for a curious Frenchman,
ex-G. I.'s and a jarred Russian.
Each sign you wrote on the page I praise,
Rewarded in a Pernod daze.

Such early warnings were whispered in Irish, for that was Behan's truest medium, the language in which he expressed that part of himself which was incorruptible and could not be bought. Even at this early stage of his career, however, he had noted with a mixture of excitement and distaste the ease with which a willing Irishman could entertain a foreign audience. That same cautionary tale is told in 'Do Sheán Ó Súilleabháin' (For Sean O'Sullivan), a poem which chronicles the fate of another great Irishman, Oscar Wilde, a broken genius dying beyond his means in a cheap Parisian hotel:

Aistrith' ón Flore
do fhásach na naomhthacht,
ógphrionnsa na bpeacadh
ina shearbhán aosta,
seod órdha na drúise
ina dhiaidh aige fágtha,
gan Pernod ina chabhair aige
ach uisce na cráifeacht.

Expelled from Flore
to piety's desert;
a Crown Prince of Evil
now aged and bitter;
lust's loveliest jewel
left far behind him;
no Pernod to cure him
save pious church water.

The middle-aged English playwright who won international fame with *The Hostage* could still recall, but never heed, the warnings piped by his Gaelic muse. For he had turned his back on *An Giall* and all that it stood for. In a few short months, he had been converted almost imperceptibly from a major Gaelic dramatist into a music-hall Stage Irishman. The tiny Gaelic stage at Dublin's Damer theatre could never hope to support the broth-of-a-boy who now rollicked through the theatres and television studios of two continents.

That same temptation presented itself to Flann O'Brien, a writer for whom Irish had been the language of conversation in his childhood home. He had distinguished himself as a Gaelic scholar at University College, Dublin, and was awarded a travelling scholarship to the University of Cologne for his achievement in Celtic Studies. In 1939 he began a thrice-weekly column in the *Irish Times* under the pseudonym Myles na gCopaleen, but soon reverted to English on discovering that his brand of humour held a great attraction not only for the paper's largely Ascendancy readership, but also for an English and American audience. O'Brien signified this transition to English in his column by dropping the initial 'c' in the pseudonym, which became Myles na Gopaleen 'in deference to the Anglo-Saxon epiglottis'. It was as if, by this pedantic alteration, he wished to confess to a loss of authenticity, a near-regression to the mistaken spelling and spurious identity of Boucicault's Stage Irishman. Only in *An Béal Bocht* did the author return to his deepest self by entrusting the entire novel to Myles na gCopaleen and the native language. Having ended the ordeal of Myles as perpetual victim of English ridicule in *An Béal Bocht*, O'Brien went on to become the ultimate victim of his newly acquired newspaper persona. So successful was his English column in the *Irish Times* that it ran for over twenty-five years. The cost was massive. Throughout that period, the author produced no works to equal the brilliance of *An Béal Bocht*. The persona to blame was not Myles na gCopaleen, but Myles na Gopaleen. He was the fatal clown, the licensed jester who lurked deep within O'Brien, whom he roundly despised but could never fully suppress. He offered to O'Brien what Littlewood offered to Behan – the quick success and easy laughs which hold a deadly attraction for the young Irish writer who knows he should express, but fears he may exploit, his country.

That temptation is no less real today, over a decade after the deaths of Behan, O'Brien and Kavanagh. It is the fatal call which Kavanagh (the last of that doomed and drink-sodden triumvirate) identified so clearly in his prose. That is the summons to play the fool, to be another 'gas bloody man', to seek in the literary pub and the television talk-show the kind of easy triumph which undid O'Brien and Behan. The Stage Irishman is now a creature of the past, a fabrication of the British bourgeoisie in the nineteenth century; but the home-grown bourgeoisie of twentieth-century Ireland are in real danger of replacing that caricature with an equally spurious fabrication, the Stage Writer. Doubtless, the legendary drinking of Behan, O'Brien and Kavanagh in the forties and fifties gave some credence to this latest stereotype; but the unparalleled affluence of the sixties and early seventies saw the widespread emergence of the phenomenon. The Fianna Fáil government, having banned all good writing in English for almost thirty years, now announced a tax holiday for all creative artists. Exiled novelists and playwrights were encouraged to return to the homeland and claim their share of the new riches. Even in the bad old days Kavanagh had jibed that the standing army of Irish poets had never fallen below five thousand, but that number now grew larger with each passing day. Every self-respecting pub boasted a resident bard who declaimed his verses on six nights a week (Sunday was still reserved for the Lord) in the employ of some publican Paudeen at his greasy till. Writers (as opposed to writing) had become big business and each poet was granted a ritual drunken appearance on television. Summer schools boomed and a thousand college girls welcomed the boozing bards to their seminars with open arms. Some government ministers even appeared in newspaper photographs with writers whose work they had once banned. Everywhere there were rustic geniuses just putting the finishing touches to that great unwritten Irish novel. These men embodied for the bourgeoisie all those qualities which fifty years of moneygrabbing had led the Paudeens to reject in themselves – lyricism, prodigality, spirituality and open-heartedness. They were paid to appear at conferences and seminars, to perform at summer schools, to teach literature (as if anyone could!) – anything was welcome so long as they did not write serious poems or pen criticisms of the prevailing ideology of affluence. The result was a barren decade in Irish literature, which saw many second-rate artists enact in public the role of writer rather than face in private the anguish of real writing. With the eruption of spectacular violence in the north at the close of the decade, the smugness of that unreal world was dispelled for ever. It soon became clear that, apart from some excellent poems by Seamus Heaney, the finest writing in the decade had come from Máirtín Ó Cadhain and Seán Ó Ríordáin, two masters of the Irish language. Untouched by the fake glamour of the summer schools, these men had quietly brought writing in Irish into the twentieth century and had given their countrymen a true image of themselves.

There are some writers in Ireland who can be most true to themselves in the native language. This applies not only to men such as Ó Cadhain and Ó Ríordáin, but also to bilingual writers such as O'Brien and Behan. For the artist who can command Irish there will always be a certain danger in the resort to English, a temptation to play to the gallery and lapse into the role, if not of Stage Irishman then of Stage Writer. Even Joyce, though his knowledge of Irish was negligible, had the honesty to concede the inevitable sense of compromise implicit in his mastery of the language of the invader. In *A Portrait* Stephen Daedalus has a long conversation with the Englishman who is Dean of Studies at the University. During the exchange, he falls into meditation:

– The language in which we are speaking is his before it is mine. How different are the words home, Christ, ale, master, on his lips and on mine! I cannot speak or write these words without unrest of spirit. His language, so familiar and so foreign, will always be for me an acquired speech. I have not made or accepted its words. My voice holds them at bay. My soul frets in the shadow of his language.[19]

Yeats made the same point in a letter to the editor of *The Leader* in September 1900, explaining that he wished to master Irish because 'the mass of the people cease to understand any poetry when they cease to understand the Irish language, which is the language of their imaginations'. That may have been a rather romantic declaration, but in the past seventy years in Ireland many a lesser poet has come to the same conclusion. Yeats's endless war on the Stage Irishman is now being waged most effectively in the native language.

NOTES

1 J. O. Bartley, 'The Development of a Stock Character: the Stage Irishman to 1800', *Modern Language Review*, 27 (1942), 438–47.
2 L. Perry Curtis, Jr, *Apes and Angels: The Irishman in Victorian Caricature* (London, 1971).
3 Kevin O'Connor, *The Irish in Britain* (Dublin, 1974), p. 22.
4 Nicholas Mansergh, *The Irish Question* (London, 1965).
5 O'Connor, *The Irish in Britain*, p. 27.
6 Richard Ellmann, *Eminent Domain* (New York, 1967), p. 12.
7 Lady Gregory, *Our Irish Theatre* (New York, 1913), pp. 8–9.
8 *Irish Times*, 30 January 1907, p. 9.
9 J. M. Synge, *Collected Works: Prose* (Oxford, 1966), p. 397.
10 This was also the diagnosis offered by Pearse in his essays of 1914, where he argued that Ireland had lost the right to nationhood because her people had grown decadent and supine. The rising which he led just two years later proved just how true that diagnosis was, as Dubliners mocked and the rest of the country failed to join in the rebellion. Although today the Irish yet retain the reputation for pugnacity and aggression, there is even less basis than ever to the myth. The fact remains that since 1798 the nation has not fought a war, the much-vaunted risings of 1848, 1867 and 1916 being more in the nature of

skirmishes which only a few had the courage to join. Even today, when the twenty-six counties possess a sizeable army of their own, a handful of crazy idealists with meagre equipment wage a war of liberation in the six counties against the wishes of the majority on both sides of the border. Ireland has been occupied by foreign armies since 1169. It is now almost two hundred years since a disciplined national army resisted the forces of occupation. In the same period the English have fought literally dozens of wars and will in the future doubtless fight many more. And yet there are still Englishmen who believe that the Irish are bellicose. See P. H. Pearse, *Political Writings and Speeches* (Dublin, 1924).

11 W. B. Yeats, *Explorations* (London, 1968), p. 187.

12 James Joyce, *Stephen Hero* (London, 1964), p. 54.

13 Patrick Kavanagh, *Collected Pruse* (London, 1973).

14 James Joyce, *A Portrait of the Artist as a Young Man* (London, 1960), p. 183.

15 Myles na Gopaleen, *The Poor Mouth* (London, 1978), p. 38.

16 Brendan Kennelly, 'An Béal Bocht', in *The Pleasures of Gaelic Literature*, ed. J. Jordan (Dublin, 1977), p. 95.

17 Colbert Kearney, *The Writings of Brendan Behan* (Dublin, 1977), p. 118.

18 Behan's Irish poems were published in *Comhar* (Dublin, April 1964). Translations by the present author.

19 Joyce, *A Portrait*, p. 189.

CHAPTER 3

Storytelling: the Gaelic tradition

(1978)

In 1888, that prince of literary diplomats, Henry James, observed with some tact that 'the little story is but scantily relished in England, where readers take their fiction rather by the volume than by the page'.[1] Pondering this text almost seventy years later, Sean O'Faolain remarked with a kind of baffled triumph that 'the Americans and Irish do seem to write better stories'.[2] The short story as a literary form has flourished in many countries besides Ireland and America. The Russians of the past century are rightly regarded as masters of the genre and Chekhov is justly celebrated as the master of the Russians. France, too, has produced many great storytellers in the tradition of Daudet and Maupassant. In his study of the genre, Mr O'Faolain attempted to explain why the English, who have given the world so many great novels, should have failed so spectacularly to master the short story. He concluded that English readers preferred the social scope of the novel to the more private concerns of the short story. English writers, he believed, found a natural form for expressing their social philosophy in the extended narrative. The short story, on the other hand, was 'an emphatically personal exposition'.[3] Mr O'Faolain offered various explanations for the strength of the shorter genre in other countries. The form had prospered in the United States because 'American society is still unconventionalized', in Ireland because her people were still 'an unconventional and comparatively human people', and in France which was 'the breeding ground of the personal and original way of looking at things'.[4] These are pleasant arguments but there may be deeper reasons for the success of the form in such countries.

It seems, at least to the present author, that the short story has flourished in those countries where a vibrant oral culture is suddenly challenged by the onset of a sophisticated literary tradition. The short story is the natural result of a fusion between the ancient form of the folk tale and the preoccupations of modern literature. We can, with some accuracy, even begin to identify the place and time of such a fusion. For example, the frontier in nineteenth-century America gave us the 'tall tale' of Mark Twain's west, in stories such as 'The Man that Corrupted Hadleyburg' or 'The Celebrated Jumping Frog of Calaveras County'. It was this tradition which provided the basis for the episodic narrative art of *Huckleberry Finn*. In this work, a sequence of anecdotes told in folk idiom became the classic novel of a young nation and, according to Ernest Hemingway, the source of subsequent American literature. The same might be observed of the frontier in Australia and New Zealand, where an indigenous folk culture came into creative conflict with a developing literary tradition. In Russia the vibrant culture of the peasants inspired Nikolai Leskov to write superb short stories at a time of national up-heaval. In more settled countries, such as France, it is no accident that the form was pioneered by writers such as Maupassant, who hailed from Normandy where an oral tradition was still a force in the lives of the people. Indeed, many of Maupassant's finest stories take as their theme that very clash between ancient and modern standards in regional communities which made the development of the genre possible.

For the past eighty years in Ireland, the short story has been the most popular of all literary forms with readers. It has also been the form most widely exploited by writers. Whereas the great Anglo-Irish writers of the Literary Revival, such as Yeats and Synge, excelled in poetry and drama, the short story has been mainly pioneered by the 'risen people' – the O'Kellys, O'Flahertys, O'Faolains and O'Connors. The genre had a particular appeal for the writers of the emerging Catholic bourgeoisie who hailed from regional towns. To take a clear example, Sean O'Faolain and Frank O'Connor both grew up in Cork, strategically poised between the folk and the literary tradition. From lending libraries in the city, they could read the classic works of English literature; but in the countryside all around Cork, the folk storytellers still delighted peasant audiences around cottage firesides and blacksmiths' forges. Even in the heart of the city itself, one or two old people – immigrants from the surrounding country-side – plied the storyteller's art. It was inevitable that such a town would produce, in the twentieth century, some of the nation's greatest exponents of the short story, a genre which was poised, like its authors, between the profane world of contemporary literature and the pious world of the folk. By nature of its origins, the form was admirably suited to the task of reflecting the disturbances in Irish society as it painfully shed its ancient traditions. O'Connor himself has observed that without the concept of a normal society, the novel is impossible;[5] but the short story is particularly appropriate to a society in which revolutionary upheavals have shattered the very idea of normality. In the years in which the modern Irish nation took shape, the short story was the form in which many writers chose to depict their vision of the emerging Ireland. In the earliest phase of the Literary Revival, at the beginning of this century, many of these writers looked to the Gaelic folk tradition for inspiration.

The art of oral storytelling in Ireland goes back over a thousand years and is very similar to that of Brittany. Léon Marillier, in his introduction to Anatole Le Braz's collection, *La Légende de la Mort en Basse-Bretagne*, draws a classic distinction between two types of folk narrative. On the one hand, there is the 'conte', a tale of international provenance with a durable form which scarcely varies from one country to the next. On the other hand, there is the 'légende', which is infinitely variable and deals with more homely matters.[6] The tellers of the 'contes' put little of their own personalities into their remote and marvellous tales, but the 'légendes' arose from the lives of ordinary people and were rooted in a particular place.[7] In Ireland, the same distinction holds good and a discrimination is made between two types of storyteller. The 'sgéalaí' enjoys higher status as narrator of the 'sean-sgéal' or international tale, while the 'seanchaí' narrates local tales and lore concerning familiar places, family genealogies, fairies and ghosts.[8] The 'sgéalaí' was always a man but the 'seanchaí' could be male or female. The tales told by the 'sgéalaí' were long and difficult to remember, filled with amazing adventures and remote wonders narrated neutrally in the third person. The 'seanchaí' told his story as if he himself had witnessed it. These stories were sometimes translated into English, but the versions in the native language were far superior, as J. M. Synge discovered on the Aran Islands.[9]

Perhaps the finest account of the Gaelic storyteller and his art was given by Seán Mac Giollarnáth in his collection published under the title *Peadar Chois Fhairrge*.[10] As a rule, stories were told at night around the winter fire from the end of the harvest until the middle of March. The stories held in highest esteem were tales of heroes such as Oisín and the Fianna, full of astonishing feats and marvellous incidents. Many of the old storytellers believed in these marvels and would suppress the questions of cynical youths in their audience with the exclamation: 'Bhíodh draíocht ann sa tsean-shaol!' (There was magic in the old times!).[11] The tales were often told round the fireside of the 'sgéalaí' himself and folk from the surrounding countryside would crowd into his house to listen. Audiences were critical and not slow to correct a teller who stumbled and made a mistake. They loved to hear a familiar story again and again, having a deep admiration for the skill with which it was told. They became deeply involved in the plot, murmuring with apprehension or sighing with fear as the story progressed. The tellers were often shy, sensitive artists who had to be coaxed into a performance and who did not like to perform before a harsh or unfriendly audience. One famous lady storyteller was so shy of her more critical neighbours that she always locked her kitchen door before starting a story. Very often, a pipe was passed around before the entertainment began and then the 'sgéalaí' would sit back in his chair and prepare himself for delivery. Sometimes the person next to him would hold his hand as he spoke by way of encouragement. A most moving account of a Kerry teller in his eighties was given by Tadhg Ó Murchú in the 1930s:

His piercing eyes are on my face, his lips are trembling, as, immersed in his story, and forgetful of all else, he puts his very soul into the telling. Obviously much affected by his narrative, he uses a great deal of gesticulation, and by the movement of his body, hand, and head, tries to convey hate and anger, fear and humour, like an actor in a play.[12]

The Cork in which Daniel Corkery was born in 1878 was surrounded by a countryside in which traditions of storytelling were still a powerful force. Corkery was a teacher and a writer, a man equally at home by the storyteller's fireside or in the scholar's library. Like his future disciples, O'Faolain and O'Connor, he found in the short story the form most suited to his purposes. He saw his role as that of an artist mediating between two cultures. In 1916, a reviewer in the *Times Literary Supplement* wrote that 'Mr Corkery's stories read as if he had heard them from old Irish peasants and set them down in his own way . . . very deftly, so that the endings of his tales come with a queer, unexpected, epigrammatic turn.'[13] Many of the techniques employed by Corkery in his stories are closely related to those of the folk tale. For example, in 'The Spancelled', a story from *A Munster Twilight*, we read at the start of a paragraph: 'Now, as to the spancelled man who was to meet this spancelled woman. John Keegan his name was . . .'[14] The opening three words, 'now as to . . .', were frequently used by oral storytellers to introduce sequences of action, just as passages in the native language were often introduced by phrases such as 'nós iomarra' (for it was custom) or 'maidir le' (concerning) or 'iomthúsa' (as regards), after a digression on the part of the speaker. The second sentence reproduces the exact order of the words as they would be spoken by a teller, but they would certainly never be written in this way in standard English.

A number of Corkery's stories were unashamedly introduced by their 'author' with the information that they had been gleaned from the folk. There is a sense in which Corkery presented himself not as an artist, but as a collector of folklore, recording the stories of the people and examining the very way in which a story was told. A revealing passage at the close of 'The Lady of the Glassy Palace', from *A Munster Twilight*, runs as follows:

Of course, Watchpole found humour in it, but not for a few days. In this way he now begins the tale; 'Did ye ever hear tell of how Mick Hosford kilt two birds with the wan stone?' As a matter of fact, he killed only one, though at the wake Hawky Sullivan did conduct himself with the reserve that befits one who has had a narrow escape.[15]

In this way, Corkery reasserts his authorial presence and corrects exaggerations in the folk anecdotes with a witty and acid turn of phrase. Each of his oral tales is framed by a literary reference in this fashion. This device is used even with a series of tales, such as those grouped under the collective title, *The Cobbler's Den*.

Corkery was the forerunner of a host of Munster writers who set out to base their stories on folk idiom and belief. In the Irish language, this attempt to preserve the continuity of the Munster folk tradition in the transition to a written literature was even more powerful. The leader of this movement, an tAthair Peadar Ua Laoghaire, explained his policy: 'In order to preserve Irish as a spoken tongue, we must preserve our spoken Irish. That is to say we must write and print exactly what the people speak . . . I am determined to write down most carefully every provincialism I can get hold of. Then I shall be sure to have the people's language.'[16] Even within the language movement, however, there were many writers who dissented from this principle. Aodh de Blácam called instead for a modernist literature which would express 'the individual mind'.[17] The most influential apostle of Gaelic Modernism was Patrick Pearse. In a major statement in the Gaelic League paper, *An Claidheamh Soluis*, as early as May 1906, he explained why a vital modern literature could never be founded on the folk tale:

We hold the folk tale to be a beautiful and gracious thing only in its own time and place . . . and its time and place are the winter fireside, or the spring sowing time, or the country road at any season. Thus, we lay down the proposition that a living literature *cannot* (and if it could, should not) be built up on the folk tale. The folk tale is an echo of old mythologies: literature is a deliberate criticism of actual life . . . This is the twentieth century; and no literature can take root in the twentieth century which is not of the twentieth century. We want no Gothic revival.[18]

One month later, Pearse insisted with uncanny accuracy that the future of Irish literature lay not with the folk tale but with the short story: 'We foresee for this type of composition a mighty future in Irish and indeed in European literature.'[19] Three years later, he defended his own famous story, 'Iosagán', against the traditionalists: '"Iosagán", has been described as a "Standard of Revolt". . . It is the standard of definite art form as opposed to the folk form.'[20]

What can Pearse have meant? In the statement of May 1906, he asserted that 'personality' was the quality which distinguished the individual artist from the folk tradition. This was an elaboration of a point which he had made as far back as 1903: 'Style after all is another name for personality. One cannot always stick to the folk formula and genealogies are out of fashion.'[21] For Pearse the virtue of the short story was that it permitted intense self-expression. Because he lacked the social scope of the novelist, the writer of short stories was bound to select a single aspect of life through which he might reveal his personality. Sean O'Faolain was to make the same observation many years later in his study of the genre:

What one searches for and what one enjoys in a short story is a special distillation of personality, a unique sensibility which has recognized and selected at once a subject that, above all other subjects, is of value to the writer's temperament and to his alone – his counterpart, his perfect opportunity to express himself.[22]

It is this scope for self-expression which distinguishes the short story from the folk tale. The folk tale was impersonal, magical and recited to a credulous audience in a public manner. The short story is personal, credible and written in private for the critical solitary reader. The folk storyteller could win the assent of his listeners to the most impossible of plots. The modern writer is confronted with an audience of lonely sceptics who insist on a literature which reflects their everyday lives. James Delargy has described folklore as the 'literature of escape' through which 'the oppressed and downtrodden could leave the grinding poverty of their surroundings, and in imagination rub shoulders with the great, and sup with kings and queens, and lords and ladies, in the courts of fairyland'.[23] When Lady Gregory went to collect tales in a Galway workhouse, she was 'moved by the strange contrast between the poverty of the tellers and the splendours of the tales'.[24] In the modern short story, however, the teller no longer seeks to flee from his humdrum surroundings, but rather to confront them in all their banality. His motto is that of Katherine Mansfield who promised to tell how the laundry-basket squeaked. Such a literature describes no longer the exploits of kings and princes, but rather the minor triumphs and small sadnesses of the commonplace man. Frank O'Connor has even gone so far as to assert that the short story marks 'the first appearance in fiction of the Little Man'.[25] In the opening chapter of *The Lonely Voice*, O'Connor articulates his belief that the short story is characterised by its treatment of 'submerged population groups',[26] of those lonely people who live on the fringes of society because of spiritual emptiness or material deprivation. America is offered as an example of a society composed almost entirely of 'submerged population groups' in their respective ethnic ghettoes after immigration from Europe. This takes us back to the present writer's contention that the short story flourishes on any cultural frontier, where solitary men daily confront the ambiguities of a changing society which is based on rival folk and cosmopolitan traditions. O'Connor goes on to assert that the short story grew out of folklore and that such stories are 'drastic adaptations of a primitive art to modern conditions – to printing, science, and individual religion'.[27] In the work of writers as diverse as Carleton, O'Kelly, Colum, Stephens, Corkery, O'Connor, Lavin and MacMahon, we find undeniable signs of that adaptation. For example, many of these writers employ in their stories a style which verges on the conversational and this mode of delivery characterised not only the ancient sagas but also the modern Irish folk tale.[28] To a greater or lesser extent, each of these writers has been conditioned by the Gaelic tradition of storytelling.

Having said that much, it is only just to add that the greatest collection of short stories to come out of Ireland, Joyce's *Dubliners*, bears positively no trace of the oral tradition. Where the oral tradition took the spectacular as its subject, Joyce finds poetry in the commonplace. Where the oral tales climaxed in blood-baths and supernatural reversals, Joyce's epiphanies describe nothing more momentous than the passing of a coin. Nor is Joyce alone in this proud immunity to the Gaelic tradition. George Moore and John McGahern might also be cited as writers of real class whose work bears no trace of the folklore of the rural Ireland in which they grew up. One reason for this may lie in the fact that 'tales which had previously been told in the Irish language passed over into English only to a very small extent'.[29]

In such a situation, it might have been expected that the Gaelic tradition of storytelling would have exerted its most profound influence on writers in the Irish language. The work of Mícheál Ó Siochfhradha (An Seabhac) in *An Baile Seo Againne* is an impressive example of this kind of writing. All too often, however, those who relied on folk tales for inspiration did so because they had no art or theme of their own. Anyone who looks back over the literature of the past seventy years will find that the prophecies of Pearse have been vindicated. The finest short stories in Irish have been written by Pádraic Ó Conaire, Liam O'Flaherty and Máirtín Ó Cadhain, not one of whom relied on the art of the folk tradition which was their logical inheritance. Ó Conaire dealt most often in his stories with the middle class rather than the peasants and he rigorously excluded all idiosyncrasies of folk dialect from his prose. Some of his finest collections, like Joyce's *Dubliners* or Sherwood Anderson's *Winesburg Ohio*, are built around a single theme. For instance, the short stories in *Seacht mBua an Éirí Amach* all deal with the ways in which the Easter Rising impinged on the lives of ordinary people. Ó Conaire began to write at the start of the century under the influence of European Realists. With later writers such as O'Flaherty and Ó Cadhain, the short story in Irish became unashamedly modernist. Ó Cadhain even denied that it was a 'story' as such, preferring to see it as a dramatisation of an incident, of a state of mind, or of a person simply passing on the road. For Ó Cadhain, the form is intensely compressed, like that of a lyric poem. More is left unsaid than is said. The story can cover only a short period of time, an hour, a day, a week, and, like the classical drama, it calls for a unity of time, place and action.[30] By these searching criteria, few stories in modern Irish, apart from O'Flaherty's and O' Cadhain's, would survive the test. O'Flaherty's simple lyric descriptions of children, of animals and of evanescent moments in a human relationship, mark off *Dúil* as the finest collection of short stories in the Irish language. These stories have also been published in English, the language in which O'Flaherty composed all his subsequent writing. This leaves Ó Cadhain as the undisputed master of modern prose in Irish. Although his masterpiece is the novel, *Cré na Cille*, his short stories betray similar evidence of his gift for dramatising the human consciousness. Ó Cadhain loved folklore and collected and published many superb tales from storytellers in Galway; but he did not believe that folk tales should be made the basis of a modern literature. In a radio broadcast on the short story, he observed wearily that he would prefer to read a single folk tale in its original form than twenty listless adaptations of that tale in the shape of the short story. In such versions, the distinctive art of the folk tale is not so much adapted as destroyed.

This leads to a final point. Too many bad short stories are written in Ireland today and too few good novels. Foolish people convince themselves that the short story is easily written and that it requires little effort. They know that rewards from newspapers, radio and television are handsome, so they sit down to write. The truth is that the short story, like the lyric poem, is one of the most difficult forms in literature, requiring a concentration and intense economy of effect possible only to a true artist. Nevertheless, a particularly fatuous type of story, which claims to record 'the pieties of the folk', has recently enjoyed a sudden revival. Every town in the west of Ireland has produced some schoolmaster who fancies himself to be a past master of the art. Summer festivals are held in these towns and foreign tourists flock into public houses to applaud the maudlin performances of these rustic geniuses. These men write as if Daniel Corkery were the only model to follow in Irish literature, as if Joyce and Ó Cadhain had never put pen to paper. Such ignoble exercises, carried out on the fringes of the tourist industry, have no artistic value for the contemporary Irish writer or reader. Nevertheless, the phenomenon is worth pondering. It was Corkery himself, in that controversial opening chapter of *Synge and Anglo-Irish Literature*, who declared that every Irish writer is faced with a decision – whether to express Ireland or exploit her.[31] The choice lies between expressing the life of the nation to itself or exploiting that life for the delectation of a 'superior' foreign audience. In Corkery's time, that audience was composed mainly of upper-class English readers who chortled over novels which recorded the foibles of the peasants. In our own day, the nature of that audience has changed, but not the nature of the attendant temptation. The current audience is composed mainly of Irish-American tourists who come to confirm their fondest hope that the fairies are still at the bottom of the garden. Those writers who entertain these tourists by teasing the beautiful old folk tales into shapeless short stories are exploiting their native culture rather than expressing it. They do a signal disservice to the integrity of the folk tales which they travesty.

The folk tale was a valid and beautiful means by which the Gaelic storyteller expressed the Irish people to themselves at a certain phase in their history. That phase lasted for hundreds of years, but it is now past. The vibrant tradition of oral storytelling was one major reason for the triumph of the short story as a characteristic Irish literary form. Seeing this, many writers, with varying degrees of success, applied in the short story the techniques of the folk tale. Some minor writers even tried to adapt folk anecdotes to the form of the short story in the years of national upheaval at the start of this century. This, too, was a valid means of expressing the nation to itself at a time of self-conscious cultural revival. That period, also, is past. It is now clear that the greatest short stories, in both Irish and English, owe more to the narrative genius of their authors than to the Gaelic tradition of storytelling. Pearse's prophecy is fulfilled and it is the modernist artists who have written, in Joyce's lucid phrase, a chapter of the moral history of their country.

NOTES

1 Henry James, *Partial Portraits*, London, 1888, p. 264.
2 Seán O'Faolain, *The Short Story*, 2nd edn, Cork, 1972, p. 43.
3 Ibid., p. 44.
4 Ibid., pp. 44–5.
5 Frank O'Connor, *The Lonely Voice, A Study of the Short Story*, London, 1963, p. 17.
6 Léon Marillier, Introduction to *La Légende de la Mort en Basse-Bretagne* by Anatole Le Braz, Paris, 1892, p. xviii.
7 Ibid., p. x.
8 Ibid., pp. v, xiii, and xiv.
9 J. M. Synge, *The Aran Islands* in *Collected Works, Prose*, ed. Alan Price, Oxford, 1966, p. 61.
10 Seán Mac Giollarnáth, ed., *Peadar Chois Fhairrge*, Dublin, 1934.
11 James Delargy, 'The Gaelic Storyteller' in *Proceedings of the British Academy*, vol. xxxi, London, 1945, 8.
12 Quoted by Delargy, 'The Gaelic Storyteller', 16.
13 Quoted in frontispiece to Daniel Corkery, *The Threshold of Quiet*, Dublin, 1917.
14 Daniel Corkery, *A Munster Twilight*, Cork, 1967, p. 57.
15 Ibid., p. 51.
16 Quoted by T. F. O'Rahilly, *Papers on Irish Idiom*, Dublin, 1920, p. 138.
17 Aodh de Blácam, 'Gaelic and Anglo-Irish Literature Compared', in *Studies*, March 1924, 71.
18 Patrick Pearse, 'About Literature' in *An Claidheamh Soluis*, 26 May 1906, 6.
19 Patrick Pearse, 'Literature, Life, and the Oireachtas Competition' in *An Claidheamh Soluis*, 2 June 1906, p. 6.
20 Quoted by Máirtín Ó Cadhain, 'Conradh na Gaeilge agus an Litríocht' in *The Gaelic League Idea*, ed. Seán Ó Tuama, Cork, 1972, p. 59.
21 Patrick Pearse, 'Reviews' in *An Claidheamh Soluis*, 14 March 1903, 3.
22 O'Faolain, *The Short Story*, p. 44.
23 Delargy, 'The Gaelic Storyteller', 24.
24 Lady Gregory, *Poets and Dreamers, Studies and Translations from the Irish*, Dublin, 1903, p. 129.
25 O'Connor, *The Lonely Voice*, p. 15.
26 Ibid., p. 18.
27 Ibid., p. 45.
28 Delargy, 'The Gaelic Storyteller', 33.
29 Sean O'Sullivan, *The Folklore of Ireland*, London, 1974, p. 15.
30 Máirtín Ó Cadhain, 'An Gearrscéal sa nGaeilge', Radio Éireann, 1967.
31 Daniel Corkery, *Synge and Anglo-Irish Literature*, Cork, 1931, pp. 10–11.

CHAPTER 4

Writers in quarantine? The case for Irish Studies

(1979)

> If we once admit the Irish-literature-is-English idea, then the language movement is a mistake. Mr Yeats' precious 'Irish' Literary Theatre may, if it develops, give the Gaelic League more trouble than the Atkinson–Mahaffy combination. Let us strangle it at its birth. Against Mr Yeats personally we have nothing to object. He is a mere English poet of the third or fourth rank and as such he is harmless. But when he attempts to run an 'Irish' Literary Theatre it is time for him to be crushed.
>
> Patrick Pearse, Letter to the Editor, *An Claidheamh Soluis*, 20 May 1899

When Patrick Pearse wrote in 1899 that the concept of an Irish national literature in the English language was untenable, he cannot have reckoned with the emergence of a writer such as Synge. Pearse's doctrinaire statement became a major policy of the Gaelic League and this led to an artificial division between writing in Irish and English on the island. Such a division persists in Irish schoolrooms to this very day, where Anglo-Irish literature is studied in one class and literature in the Irish language is considered in another. The short stories of Liam O'Flaherty are examined in courses on the Anglo-Irish tradition, with no reference to the fact that many of them were originally written in the native language. Similarly, the Irish-language versions of such stories are studied in a separate class, with no attempt to appraise the author's own recreation of these works in English. It was Synge's particular achievement to ignore this foolish division and to take both literatures out of quarantine. In an article introducing Irish literature to a French audience in March 1902, he criticised his fellow-writers for their neglect of Irish and pointed out how much more inspiration was to be found in Old Irish literature than in the less vibrant Anglo-Irish tradition of the nineteenth century. This did not imply a repudiation of his heritage as an Anglo-Irishman, but rather an attempt to synthesise the two traditions. During the Parnell split, the 'chief' had called upon all Irishmen to resign themselves to the cursed versatility of the Celt. Synge also believed in a fusion of the two Irelands, Gaelic and Anglo-Irish, so that neither should shed its pride – a challenge which confronts Irishmen more urgently than ever today. While Pearse argued against the logic of history that the Irish language alone could save the soul of the nation, writers like Yeats and Synge had set their course with greater realism. There were now two traditions to be confronted and the more exciting challenge was to forge a literature which would bring into alignment the world of Berkeley, Swift and Burke with that of O'Hussey, Keating and Raftery. At home Synge was always keen to emphasise his Anglo-Irish heritage, but he invariably presented himself in foreign countries as a Gael. In his strictures to the narrow nationalists of the Gaelic League, he celebrated the Anglo-Irish tradition as a vital component of 'the nation that has begotten Grattan and Parnell'; but, in a programme note for a German audience, he was also at pains to insist that the Synges 'have been in Ireland for nearly three centuries, so that there is a good deal of Celtic, or more exactly, Gaelic blood in the family'. In his art, he succeeded in his search for a bilingual style through which he could translate the elements of Gaelic culture into English, a language ostensibly alien to that culture. Of course, he ignored the division between those rival traditions at his peril and, in the Ireland of his time, he paid the inevitable price. Those who might have admired him for his commitment to the native culture denounced him for his belief in the higher claims of art. Those who admired his art could never fully appreciate the extent of his commitment to the native culture.

It is one of the most cruel ironies of literary history that the attempt to restore the Irish language coincided with the emergence of some of the greatest writers of English whom Ireland has ever produced. It is certainly true that many of these writers drew their initial inspiration from the revival of interest in the native culture; and it is even possible that one or two of them might never have emerged without that inspiration. Nevertheless, as Yeats, Joyce, Synge, Moore and, later, O'Casey proceeded to win the admiration of readers of English throughout the world, the quality of writing in Irish continued on its drastic decline, as art was renounced in favour of nationalist propaganda. In time, however, the leaders of the Gaelic movement succeeded in convincing their readers and writers that a vibrant literature could not be founded on the propagandist play and the patriotic lyric. They prayed for the emergence of a writer of European stature who might deliver the language from its bondage; but the self-imposed quarantine in which writers of Irish had placed themselves, from the time of Pearse, retarded such development. As Synge had predicted, these writers failed to become European lest the huckster across the road might call them English. When a genius of international stature finally did emerge in the Irish language, it was too late. By the time Máirtín Ó Cadhain's *Cré na Cille* was published in 1949, there were few readers left who could understand the rich idiom of that book, much less the magnitude of its intellectual achievement.

The artificial division between writing in English and Irish still holds sway. Synge was its first and most spectacular victim. He bravely broke the quarantine decreed by Pearse only to find it sedulously observed by the nation's theatregoers and readers. His work, so deeply rooted in the Gaelic tradition, was rejected by the strident professional Gaels of his own time because it was written in the English language. If Joyce and Beckett had to endure the hardships of exile in order to write their masterpieces, then the kind of inner exile endured by Synge in his own country can have been scarcely less severe. He was, of course, a victim of such intolerance only in Ireland; in the eyes of the world he was seen, even in his own lifetime, as a master. The ultimate victim of the introversion of the Gaelic movement was its greatest modern writer, Máirtín Ó Cadhain. He had steeped himself in the literature of modern Europe and expressed his sophisticated mind in his native and mother tongue, only to find that his readers had no sense of the significance of his achievement. Unlike Synge, he wrote in Irish and could not appeal over the heads of his detractors to the more enlightened tribunals of Europe.

Seventy years after the death of Synge, a literary partition between writing in Irish and English divides the classroom of Ireland as surely as a political partition divides the land. This division begins on the child's first day in primary school and is maintained even at post-graduate level in the universities. This is the major reason why no scholar has ever been able to write a systematic study of Synge's creative confrontation with the Irish language. Such work is not encouraged by a system which ignores the fact that writers of Irish and English live on the same small island and share the same experiences. The absurdity of this division becomes acutely apparent in any attempt to study the work of such writers as Patrick Pearse, Brendan Behan, Flann O'Brien or Liam O'Flaherty, all of whom wrote with facility and fame in both languages. It is ironic that Pearse, whose critical pronouncements were the major cause of this partition, should, as a creative writer, have become one of its foremost victims. In the case of O'Flaherty, so enmeshed are both traditions in his work that there is a protracted critical dispute as to whether certain of his stories were originally written in English or Irish, following his own wicked admission that he cannot remember himself. It is greatly to the credit of most modern Irish writers that they have not succumbed to the partition-ist mentality in their art. Synge was one of the first writers of twentieth-century Ireland to incorporate his experience of Gaelic literature into his art, but he has had many followers since – Thomas MacDonagh, Austin Clarke, F. R. Higgins, Frank O'Connor, Brendan Behan, Flann O'Brien. That list reads like a roll-call of modern Irish writers, for the problem which Synge confronted is as acute as ever today. A contemporary poet and translator, Thomas Kinsella, has expressed the dilemma well:

A modern English poet can reasonably feel at home in the long tradition of English poetry . . . An Irish poet has access to the English poetic heritage through his use of the English language, but he is unlikely to feel at home in it. Or so I find in my own case. If he looks back over his own heritage the line must begin, again, with Yeats. But then, for more than a hundred years, there is almost total poetic silence. I believe that silence, on the whole, is the real condition of Irish literature in the nineteenth century – certainly of poetry; there is nothing that approaches the ordinary literary achievement of an age. Beyond the nineteenth century there is a great cultural blur: I must exchange one language for another, my native English for eighteenth-century Irish. Yet to come on eighteenth-century Irish poetry after the dullness of the nineteenth century is to find a world suddenly full of life and voices, the voices of poets who expect to be heard and understood and memorised. Beyond them is . . . the course of Irish poetry stretching back for more than a thousand years, full of riches and variety. In all of this I recognise a great inheritance and, simultaneously, a great loss. The inheritance is certainly mine but only at two enormous removes – across a century's silence and through an exchange of worlds. The greatness of the loss is measured not only by the substance of Irish literature itself, but also by the intensity with which we know it was shared; it has an air of continuity and shared history which is precisely what is missing from Irish literature, in English or Irish; in the nineteenth century and today. I recognise that I stand on one side of a great rift, and can feel the discontinuity in myself. It is a matter of people and places as well as writing – of coming from a broken and uprooted family, of being drawn to those who share my origins and finding that we cannot share our lives.

The problem is succinctly summarised by the title of Kinsella's essay, 'The Divided Mind'. The division is symbolised by the virtual absence of good writers in both languages through the whole nineteenth century, when the people were painfully shedding one language and slowly acquir-ing another. Synge, who began to write in the closing years of that century, stood on the very edge of that great rift. He saw that he could never hope to return to the other side – that an attempt to reimpose Irish would lead only to another barren century for literature – but he resolved to fill the rift by uniting the divided traditions. Those writers who knew no Irish, such as Yeats and George Russell, relied on translations and popularisations of the ancient Irish literature for the same purpose. To Standish James O'Grady's *History of Ireland: Heroic Period* Russell said he owed the reawakening of his racial memory. It was doubtless for the same reason that Yeats remarked that to O'Grady every Irish writer owed a portion of his soul. Like Kinsella, each writer since the Irish Revival has recognised that he stands on one side of a great rift and has tried, as best he can, to heal the sense of discontinuity in himself. That sense of severance from one's own heritage has been poignantly expressed by John Montague in his poem, 'A Lost Tradition', which deals with his homeland in County Tyrone. The map of his native county is studded with place names derived from the Irish language, which has been dead in that area for generations. In an ancient Gaelic manuscript, which no contemporary reader can understand, he finds an image of his own geography of disinheritance:

> All around, shards of a lost tradition . . .
> The whole countryside a manuscript
> We had lost the skill to read,
> A part of our past disinherited,
> But fumbled, like a blind man,
> Along the fingertips of instinct.

Once again, in 'A Lost Tradition', a contemporary poet has described that very rift which his poem seeks to fill, by drawing on both traditions of the island.

Many other writers in English have sought to bridge the rift by producing occasional translations from Irish poetry and prose. This exercise had real validity in the early decades of the century, when writers such as Yeats and Russell yearned for a glimpse of the poetry hidden in a language which they could never hope to learn. Nowadays, however, when most Irish writers have a reading knowledge of Irish, these translations are less immediately useful. They appear, more and more, as conscience-stricken gestures by men who feel a sense of guilt for producing their major creative work in an Anglo-Irish or even an English literary tradition. Synge was one of the earliest of these twentieth-century translators, but he did not see such work as an end in itself, nor even as a public expiation for the sin of writing in English. Rather, his translations were a deeply private exercise, written not for public approval but as a practice which helped him to forge his own literary dialect and to recreate the Gaelic modes in English. To this day, there are in Ireland a number of writers who produce translations from Irish for public consumption on the one hand, while continuing to compose straightforward modern English poems on the other. They place their works in the same kind of quarantine as that in which the study of Irish and English is placed in their schools. Synge did not believe that an artist could so divide his own creations, neatly slotting each work into one or other tradition. Each of his plays and poems represents a fusion, *in a single work*, of both traditions and an attempt by the power of his imagination to make them one. He saw that those who neatly produce translations from Irish on the one hand and modern English poems on the other are doomed only to perpetuate the very rift which they profess to deplore. It was for this reason, perhaps, that he never published in full any of his own translations from Irish poetry and prose. This reticence was costly, for it gave further credence to the allegation that he knew little Irish. Nevertheless, it was necessary if he was to achieve his aim of filling rather than deepening the rift in his own mind.

To teach Irish and English in separate classes of our schools and universities is surely to deepen the chasm. When Pearse decreed that Irish and English were separate literatures, he still had visions of a perilous but rewarding crossing to the other side of that chasm, back to an Irish-speaking Ireland. Nowadays, it would seem more sensible to fill the gap and unite the two traditions. Pearse's latter-day followers who persist in his belief that Yeats and Synge are not Irish writers should learn from the mistakes of their forerunners in the nationalist movement. All through the nineteenth century, Irishmen had fought and argued for the freedom of their country while, at the same time, they permitted the virtual extinction of the native language and culture – a major basis of their claim to recognition as a separate nation. In 1892 in his classic address on 'The Necessity for De-Anglicising Ireland', Douglas Hyde pointed to the anomaly of 'men who drop their own language to speak English . . . nevertheless protesting as a matter of sentiment that they hate the country which at every hand's turn they rush to imitate'. By 1901, D. P. Moran had extended Hyde's analysis and had set out to challenge 'the accepted view that politics was the begin-all and end-all of Irish nationality'. His diagnosis was simple and devastating. Irishmen had exalted the unending fight against England into a self-sustaining tradition and had forgotten the very things which they fought for – the native language, dances, music, games, a whole civilisation. According to Moran, a nation was the natural outcome of a distinct civilisation and any power that killed the one was guilty of the death of the other. He observed wryly that his fellow-Irishmen 'threw over Irish civilisation whilst they professed – and professed in perfect good faith – to fight for Irish nationality'. This may still be the case today, when some Irishmen persist in rejecting the matchless achievement of Yeats, Synge and Joyce, because they wrote in the English language. For a narrow nationalist principle, they have thrown over a major part of their inheritance.

There is, of course, misunderstanding on the other side too. Some of those who wrote in English displayed an alarming ignorance of the Gaelic tradition which they professed to mock. Patrick Kavanagh, in his role as recalcitrant peasant, even wrote a brilliant poem on the subject, entitled 'Memory of Brother Michael':

> It would never be morning, always evening,
> Golden sunset, golden age –
> When Shakespeare, Marlowe and Jonson were writing
> The future of England page by page,
> A nettle-wild grave was Ireland's stage.
>
> It would never be spring, always autumn
> After a harvest always lost,
> When Drake was winning seas for England
> We sailed in puddles of the past
> Chasing the ghost of Brendan's mast.
>
> Culture is always something that was,
> Something pedants can measure,
> Skull of bard, thigh of chief,
> Depth of dried-up river.
> Shall we be thus for ever?
> Shall we be thus for ever?

The Brother Michael of whom Kavanagh wrote was one of the Four Masters who compiled the Annals of Ireland in the 1630s; and the literary period in Irish which Kavanagh contrasted unfavourably with its counterpart in England was the late sixteenth and early seventeenth century. In fact, this was the last age of high achievement in the native language, a period when poetry and prose enjoyed a superb revival as the ancient Gaelic order disintegrated. As a literary period, it might more aptly be compared with the Anglo-Irish revival at the start of the twentieth century, when a whole group of writers burst into a kind of swansong as their own class suffered its final decline and disintegration. When all this was pointed out to him, Kavanagh cheerfully shrugged and announced that his lines were 'good poetry but bad history'; yet the attitude which underlies his poem is still prevalent in Ireland. When Sean O'Faolain concluded a long essay on 'Fifty Years of Irish Writing' in 1962, he devoted only a couple of

sentences to those who wrote in Irish in the twentieth century. Although
the work of men like Synge, Clarke and MacDonagh testifies to the
inspirational value for an artist of both languages, a lasting rapprochement
between writers of Irish and English on the island has yet to be achieved.

It may be objected that such a rapprochement is of little significance
when our two greatest writers in this century – Yeats and Joyce – knew
little or nothing of their native language. Such an objection, however,
takes little account of the deeper implications of this situation. It was a
matter of constant regret to Yeats, throughout his life, that his poor skills
as a linguist caused his repeated attempts to master Irish to come to
nothing. The poet who finally confessed that he owed his soul to
Shakespeare, to Spenser, to Blake and perhaps to William Morris was
the same man who had also insisted that the Irish language held the
key not only to the west but to the lost imagination of the whole nation.
Yeats wrote with a mixture of rue and pride: 'I might have found more
of Ireland if I had written in Irish, but I have found a little, and I have
found all myself.' That little had been found mainly in translations such
as those made by his friend, Lady Gregory. It is not surprising, therefore,
that Yeats should have come to regard such translations as the 'true
tradition' for the movement which he led. In the Preface to *A Book of
Irish Verse* he wrote: 'It was not until Callanan wrote his naive and
haunting translations from the Gaelic that anything of an honest style
came into verse.' Sensing that Samuel Ferguson's knowledge of Irish gave
him an intimate appreciation of Ireland's legends, such as no previous
Anglo-Irishman had possessed, Yeats argued that he was 'the greatest poet
Ireland has produced because the most central and the most Celtic'.
Translations such as Callanan's conveyed to Yeats a sense of the style
and themes of Gaelic poetry, which he yearned to incorporate into his
work. But, at best, Callanan's poems were only translation. Ferguson was
the greatest poet because he had gone beyond mere translation. His
treatment of the Deirdre legend was a powerfully original poem in
English, informed, nevertheless, by the Gaelic poetry in which he had
so immersed himself. His poem was recognisably a work in the Anglo-
Irish tradition, but it was also an unmistakable recreation within the spirit
of the Gaelic original, possible only to an artist with a feeling for Irish.

Towards the end of his life, Yeats found in a young writer named Frank
O'Connor the translator of whom he had always dreamed – a man with a
profound insight into the texture of Gaelic poetry and an equal mastery of
the English language. In a late poem, *The Curse of Cromwell*, Yeats did not
scruple to borrow the final line of a stanza from the last line penned by

Aogán Ó Rathaille. Yeats shared with this poet an aristocratic contempt for the rising philistine classes; and in 'The Curse of Cromwell' he made an explicit equation between the uncultured bailiffs and middlemen planters who dogged the great Gaelic poet in the eighteenth century and the bourgeois arrivistes and gombeen-men who harassed the Anglo-Irish poet in the newly founded Free State. His poem, which is in effect another Gaelic lament for fallen noblemen, loots many of its finest lines from the Irish language:

> The lovers and the dancers are beaten into the clay
> And the tall men and the swordsmen and the
>   horsemen, where are they?
> And there is an old beggar wandering in his pride,
> His fathers served their fathers before Christ was crucified.

That closing line comes straight from O'Connor's version of 'Cabhair Ní Ghairfead', that final statement of wounded nobility and stubborn pride by Ó Rathaille:

> Rachad a haithle searc na laoch don chill,
> Na flatha faoi raibh mo shean roimh éag do Chríost.

> I shall go after the heroes, ay, into the clay,
> My fathers followed theirs before Christ was crucified.

The lovers and dancers 'beaten into the clay' are clearly another borrowing from Ó Rathaille; but other phrases of Yeats's stanza have evidently been looted from a quite different source – that classic lament for fallen woods and fallen nobles entitled 'Cill Cais':

> Níl trácht ar Cill Cais ná a teaghlach
> Is ní cluinfear a cling go bráth.
> An áit úd na gcónaíodh an deighbhean
> Fuair gradam is meidhir tar mhnáibh,
> Bhíodh Iarlaí ag tarraingt thar tuinn ann
> Is an taifreann doimhin dá rá.

If Yeats and Lady Gregory achieved some sort of rapprochement with Irish literature in translation, then other writers such as John Eglinton and St John Ervine fought shy of the native language and even denounced it. Not all who abandoned it did so without scruple and James Joyce is an interesting case in point. He opted, of course, for Europe and modernism, as he playfully explained in *Finnegans Wake*: 'He even ran away with hunself and became a farsoonerite, saying he would far sooner muddle through a hash of lentils in Europe than meddle with Irrland's split little pea.' Never has a writer commented more wryly on Ireland's divided mind and body. Understandably, Joyce's encounter with Gaelic Ireland in the shape of Michael Cusack, 'Emma Clery' and the pale young men of the Gaelic League had given him a restricted view of the Irish tradition. Had he followed the example of Synge in reading the work of Keating or the love songs of the folk, he might have come to share the playwright's belief in the possibility of creating a European modernist art which would nevertheless draw on the Gaelic tradition – a national art which would, for all that, be international in appeal. He might have seen that the shortest way to Tara was indeed through Holyhead. On rare occasions Joyce did turn to the native literature for an idea or an idiom, such as 'silk of the kine' (síoda na mbó) in *Ulysses* – an image of Ireland culled from the famous lyric, 'Droimeann Donn Dílis'. He had halting imitations of the bardic *deibhidhe* in mind when he wrote mockingly in the same book:

> Bound thee forth my booklet quick
> To greet the callous public,
> Writ, I ween, 'twas not my wish,
> In lean unlovely English.

Apart from his admiration for the free translations of James Clarence Mangan, Joyce turned to the native poetry on only one other occasion – and then to use the Gaelic tradition in mockery against itself. In *A Portrait of the Artist as a Young Man* Stephen's friend, Davin, has enjoined on him 'Ireland first, Stevie. You can be a poet or mystic after.' But Stephen is too clever for Davin. He knows the lines of Keating, the great Gaelic poet who did put Ireland first and who found expression for his frustration only in the most bitter images: '"Do you know what Ireland is?" asked Stephen with cold violence. "Ireland is the old sow that eats her farrow."' In Keating's poem, 'Óm Sceol ar Árdmhagh Fáil', the sow is destroyed by her greedy farrow; but in Joyce's work the image is inverted and the sow consumes her own children. It is an ingenious use of the Gaelic tradition against itself, of a kind which we shall find often in the plays of Synge. Another such device may be found in the burlesque of an elementary Gaelic lesson in the Citizen passages of *Ulysses*: '"Ah, well, says Joe, handing round the boose. Thanks be to God they had the start of us. Drink that, citizen." "I will", says he, "honourable person."' Pádraic Colum has pointed out that the pseudo-Gaelic phrase, 'honourable person' (based on the Irish, 'a dhuine uasail'), has a humour that only those who knew Dublin at the time could fully appreciate.

The Irish Ireland which he rejected with such coldness haunted Joyce all his life in the shape of Nora Barnacle and his liberation from it was more apparent than real. In the final story of *Dubliners*, 'The Dead', Gabriel (the central character) is forced to come to terms with the spiritual gulf between himself, a sophisticated Dublin intellectual, and his homely wife from the west. He is chided by a young woman named Miss Ivors for holidaying on the continent rather than on Aran. As the story closes, his thoughts are moving west, across the Central Plain over a snow-bound Ireland, to the peasant boy whom his wife had once loved. The ambiguity of Gabriel's position in 'The Dead' is the predicament of his author. Joyce's uneasy feelings towards the west are elaborated with an almost painful clarity in the closing pages of *A Portrait of the Artist as a Young Man*. The reader is given extracts from Stephen's diary which cover the days immediately prior to his departure for Paris. Stephen is flippant about the Gael and seeks to belittle him in a European context:

April 14. John Alphonsus Mulrennan has just returned from the west of Ireland. (European and Asiatic papers please copy.) He told us he met a man there in a mountain cabin. Old man had red eyes and short pipe. Old man spoke Irish. Mulrennan spoke Irish. Then old man and Mulrennan spoke English. Mulrennan spoke to him about universe and stars. Old man sat, listened, smoked, spat. Then said: – Ah, there must be terrible queer creatures at the latter end of the world.

What one notices here is not just the parody of the dialect of Synge's plays in the final sentence, nor even the travesty of his conversation with a countryman about the constellations in *The Aran Islands*. Remarkable above all else is the corrosive realism in the portrayal of Mulrennan's encounter with the peasant – an encounter which was hopefully initiated in Irish, but soon lapsed (as the contents of Mulrennan's phrase-book were exhausted) into the English language. It was the first of many such encounters. Joyce has made his brilliant little joke against Synge (to be repeated and amplified in *Ulysses*) and against Mulrennan; but his treatment of the peasant, when finally he comes to him, is downright frightening, even defensive. The split-mindedness of Gabriel in *Dubliners* has now grown to near-hysteria: 'I fear him. I fear his red-rimmed horny eyes. It is with him I must struggle all through this night till day come, till he or I lie dead, gripping him by the sinewy throat till . . . Till what? Till he yield to me? No. I mean him no harm.' Clearly, the author of this passage turned his back on Gaelic Ireland with mixed feelings and no absolute certainty that silence, exile and cunning were answers to the challenge of the native tradition. Joyce was a middle-class Dublin Catholic, born into that very society which, through organisations like the Gaelic League, was staking its claim as the logical heir to the Gaelic tradition. To deny that gospel was indeed to kick against the pricks. Joyce's rejection of this tradition did not arise out of ignorance – rather it was planned and dynamic, at once a cunning strategy of self-defence and wilful opposition. But even if in one sense he formally rejected this Irish tradition, there is a deeper sense in which he could not avoid being its beneficiary. As Flann O'Brien observed in a letter to Sean O'Casey, every Irish writer who uses the English language with resource and imagination owes an indirect debt to his native language, whether he has learned to speak it or not: 'I agree absolutely with you when you say that the Irish language is essential, particularly for any sort of literary worker. It supplies that unknown quantity in us that enables us to transform the English language – and this seems to hold good for people who know little or no Irish, like Joyce. It seems to be an inbred thing.' On another occasion, O'Brien observed that 'if Irish were to die completely, the standard of English here, both in the spoken and written word, would sink to a level probably as low as that obtaining in England and it would stop there only because it could go no lower'. These are, of course, some of the deeper implications of a situation which urgently demands further study. Such an investigation can be carried out with full rigour only in the context of a major course in Irish Studies, which would take 'Gaelic' and 'Anglo-Irish' literature out of quarantine.

The initial steps towards such a study were taken by Thomas MacDonagh in his epoch-making *Literature in Ireland*, which was published some months after his execution in 1916. The sub-title of this book was 'Studies Irish and Anglo-Irish' and in it the author asserted the essential continuity of the two traditions. He argued that by the time of the Penal Laws Gaelic literature had become decadent, but for more than a century afterwards English 'was not yet able to carry on the tradition or to syllable anew for itself here'. It was only in the most recent decades that a writer such as Synge had emerged who was 'at once sufficiently Gaelic to express the feeling of the central Irish tradition, and sufficiently master of English style to use it as one uses the air one breathes'. Rejecting Pearse's doctrine that a national literature could be created only in the Irish language, he went on to declare that modern Irish suffered from the very same defects which afflicted modern English – journalese, cliché and fatigued imprecision. The ideal solution of this dilemma had been found in the dialect of Synge which 'at its best is more vigorous, fresh and simple than either of the two languages between which it stands'. MacDonagh conceded that 'all of us find in Irish rather than in English a satisfying understanding of certain ways of ours and the best expression of certain of our emotions – so we are expressing ourselves in translating from Irish'. However, he was quick to point out that such translations were purely a temporary expedient during the transition to English: 'At present a large amount of translation is natural. Later, when we have expressed again in English all the emotions and experiences expressed already in Irish, this literature will go forward, free from translation.'

These enlightened precepts had been taught by MacDonagh in his university lectures in Dublin. Had he lived longer, he would certainly have worked for a rapprochement between both literary traditions, a rapprochement which Pearse himself began to favour in the closing years of his life, doubtless under the influence of his friend and colleague at St Enda's. Unfortunately, it was the earlier and more strident doctrine of Pearse which Daniel Corkery chose to reassert for the next generation of writers. In his notorious pamphlet *What's This About the Gaelic League?* (1941) the eloquent Corkman thundered in open defiance of MacDonagh: 'The English language, great as it is, can no more throw up an Irish literature than it can an Indian literature. Neither can Irish nationality have its say in both English and Irish.' The fact that his own grasp of Irish was weak and that his fame as a master of English extended to Britain and America did not seem to blunt Corkery's ardour in expounding this extreme theory. In his most important critical work *Synge and Anglo-Irish Literature* (1931), he had gone even further, arguing that no writer could truly claim to be Irish unless his work contained three specific notes – (i) Nationality, (ii) Religion (Catholic, of course) and (iii) the Land. By these rigid criteria, Yeats and his colleagues were written off as mere interlopers. It will not have escaped the alert reader of Joyce's *Portrait* that Corkery's three notes were the very forces which had driven Stephen Daedalus into exile. The Joycean hero exclaims 'I will not serve that in which I no longer believe, whether it call itself my home, my fatherland, or my church'; and again, 'You talk to me of nationality, language, religion. I shall try to fly by those nets.' The rigid prescriptions of men like Corkery were to drive many other disillusioned idealists out of the inaptly titled Free State.

It must be added that the influence of Corkery was more often healthy than harmful for, like many strident dogmatists before him, he tended to flout his worst theories by his best practices. Though he was foolish enough in theory to deny the very existence of Anglo-Irish writing as a body of literature, he was sensible enough in practice to ignore the classroom division between English and Irish. So he produced brilliant essays in which he contrasted the Nativity Odes of Aodh Mac Aingil and John Milton and compared the homely intensity of Robbie Burns and Eoghan Rua Ó Súilleabháin. In *The Hidden Ireland* (1924) this man, who was soon to be honoured with the Chair of English at University College, Cork, provided the first sustained book of literary criticism on the Gaelic poetry of the eighteenth century. Furthermore, in the preface to that scintillating if wrong-headed book, he bravely outlined his reasons for invading the preserves of Gaelic scholarship – the fact that the revival of Irish had fallen out of the hands of imaginative writers and into the hands of grammarians. It was a complaint to be amplified seventeen years later by the poet Austin Clarke, during his memorable clash with Osborn Bergin on the controversial love poem 'Féuch Féin, an obairse, a Aodh'. Bergin was the ultimate scholar–pedant, a man whose favourite hobby was to walk down the streets of his Dublin suburb, scouring the novels of Agatha Christie for errors of grammar and spelling. On at least one famous occasion, a surprised neighbour spotted Bergin diligently pencilling in corrections to a particularly tattered novel, impervious to the fact that rain was pouring hard all around him. In a reply to Bergin's testy remarks, Clarke remarked with some bitterness in the *Irish Times* in January 1941 that

Dr Bergin's letter shows why there is scarcely any literary criticism of Gaelic poetry. When a timid literary man (like myself) dares to approach this preserve, grumbling grammarians and thin textualists try to scare him away with ogreish frowns and fee-faw-fummery. But this is pantomime month, so let us climb the beanstalk and see whether there is a giant up there or only a scholar on stilts.

The language movement was afflicted with pedants and puritans of every kind, tight-lipped young idealists who dreamed of creating a republic with bicycle clips and handball medals. Irish had become fatally associated with the purgatorial fires of the classroom, the terrors of the irregular verb and the distortions of ingrown virginity. Those madmen or idealists who were brave enough to write in the language found themselves all too often under strict instructions to create a literature which would be marketable in the classroom, a literature which would parade the noble simplicity of de Valera's pastoral vision of athletic youths, comely maidens and wise old prophets. If Stalin and Zdhanov crippled a generation of Soviet writers with injunctions to map out a scenario for 'Girl Meets Tractor', then de Valera and Corkery had their own subtler but no less rigid prescriptions for Irish writers. The result of this literary bureaucracy was An Gúm – creative geniuses like Máirtín Ó Cadhain and Seosamh Mac Grianna were relocated in government offices and paid to translate the famous novels of Victorian England into Irish. Some of these works were unreadable in English anyway, and it is doubtful if the Irish versions were ever read by any but the most intrepid of country parsons. Even more dispiriting were the 'creative' policies of An Gúm, which rejected such masterpieces as *An Druma Mór* by Mac Grianna and *An Stráinséara* by Ó Cadhain, but blithely published sentimental bilge by tenth-rate writers. As Ó Cadhain wearily observed in retrospect, to read the mass of modern writing in Irish is to be confronted with a body of literature composed explicitly for an audience of credulous schoolchildren and preconciliar nuns. In the early decades of the century, most writers of Irish were so busy trying to teach it in classrooms or mounting public campaigns in its defence, that their creative endeavours were relegated to third place. Considering that there were only five books in Irish in print when Hyde founded the Gaelic League in 1893, many enthusiasts came to feel that the fact that books were written at all in the language was miracle enough. This gave rise to the uncritical attitude satirised by Joyce in *Stephen Hero*, when the young artist remarks with indignation to his nationalist classmate Madden: 'It seems to me you do not care what banality a man expresses so long as he expresses it in Irish.' Complacency such as Madden's was widespread, because there was no critical tradition in Irish over and above the internecine pedantries of rival grammarians. Even in more recent decades, those few critics who have emerged in Irish seem to suffer from the same complacency, a compound of understandable defensiveness and grotesque self-satisfaction. Many believe that simply by virtue of being in Irish, a book deserves a wide readership. This calls to mind the recent suggestion that all those books which are banned in Ireland should now be made available in Irish, as this would provide the greatest possible incentive for people to learn their native language.

In such a depressing situation it may seem an act of madness for a talented poet to forsake a career in English for the more frugal rewards of Irish. Yet that is exactly what Michael Hartnett, the young Limerick poet, has recently done, announcing his decision in that fine volume *A Farewell to English* and following in 1978 with a no less admirable collection in Irish. Of course, the decision is not as absolute as Hartnett might seem to suggest, for the contemporary poets of the native language have mapped out a territory of their own, full of fascinating intersections between many cosmopolitan traditions. The echo of Yeats is never far from the lines of Máirtín Ó Direáin, who also owes a major debt to the religious poetry and social criticism of T. S. Eliot. Even Synge, the man who was vilified by the Gaelic League seventy years ago, has been the subject of an ode by Ó Direáin, an Aranman who returned the compliment paid to his people in *The Aran Islands* with 'Omós do John Millington Synge'. In prose the achievement of Máirtín Ó Cadhain, a self-confessed 'Joycean smutmonger', is unthinkable without the example of *Ulysses* and *Finnegans Wake*, but this major author has also acknowledged exemplars as disparate as Norman Mailer and Teilhard de Chardin, Raymond Williams and Hugh MacDiarmid. All over Europe the borders between national literatures are rapidly disappearing and this is especially true of the fake border between Irish and English – a division which was never recognised by our finest writers but which is still observed and reinforced in every classroom on the island. Our schoolmasters and professors seem blithely unaware of the fact that it is impossible to study the work of Ó Cadhain or Ó Direáin in the sealed vacuum that constitutes a course in Irish. For the same reason, those who lecture on Synge and Lady Gregory, with no understanding of the native culture which so inspired them, can only be regarded as pious frauds.

In some respects the most interesting contemporary writers in Ireland are those who have rejected the stark choice made by Hartnett as a constricting and unnecessary decision – and have chosen instead to work simultaneously in both languages. Names such as Pearse Hutchinson, Eoghan Ó Tuairisc and Críostóir Ó Floinn spring instantly to mind, but these are simply the current disciples of a bilingual tradition which reaches back through Mícheál MacLiammóir to men like Pearse and Hyde. The most exemplary exponents of this tradition are Brendan Behan and Flann O'Brien, for the careers of both men read like parables on a familiar theme. That theme had been enunciated by Yeats, who asserted at the start of the Literary Revival that, sooner or later, every Irish writer would be faced with a choice – either to express Ireland or to exploit her. As Yeats saw it, the choice lay between the boring traditional ploy of exploiting the foibles of a quaint island people for the amusement of a 'superior' foreign audience or the exciting and complex new challenge of expressing the nation to itself. For that band of writers who had command of both languages, this often presented itself as a choice between writing in Irish or in English. Nowhere are the consequences of that option more spectacularly dramatised than in the literary careers of Brendan Behan and Flann O'Brien.

The questions raised in this tentative essay can only be debated fully in a comprehensive course in Irish Studies. Such a course would take both Anglo-Irish and Gaelic literature out of quarantine and reassess each writer in the context of the culture of our whole island, its politics and history, its folklore and geography. Professors in our universities continue to pay lip-service to this aspiration, while they make no serious attempt to create such a course themselves. As far back as 1970, during a symposium at Trinity College, Dublin, Sean Lucy remarked with some gusto that he 'would take no student of Anglo-Irish literature seriously unless that student were bilingual' – but the professors who applauded this comment most loudly have continued to appoint to lectureships those who are not. Those students who tried in their graduate work to vindicate the logic of Sean Lucy's argument have found the doors of Irish academe slammed in their faces. This, surely, is one of the main reasons for the failure of modern Irish scholarship – the fact that our critics have been riven by divisions which have never afflicted the creative writers whose work they profess to interpret. The denizens of our English departments patrol their corridors daily to ensure that no Gaelic expert penetrates the building, least of all a Gaelic scholar with the highest qualifications in English. The members of our Irish departments (with one or two honourable exceptions) continue to frown on literary criticism of any kind.

Across this small island, a partitionist mentality has divided north from south, unionist from nationalist, Anglo-Irish from Gael; in even the smallest parishes we have built separate Protestant and Catholic schools; and in the schools themselves we have parcelled up the literature of the island into two separate packages. It is not surprising that our division has assumed notorious and warlike form. Most Irish teachers and critics today are still caught in the pretence that they are the heirs to one narrow tradition; while their creative writers have shown them over and over again that their inheritance is richer and wider than that. Every Irish person who has passed through the classrooms of the country has emerged from this educational mauling with a chronically divided mind; and at the root of many a man's inability to live in peace with his neighbour is the inability to live in peace with himself.

Such problems are not solved in a single generation, but a start must be made and scholars have a small but significant contribution to offer in this enterprise. There have been persuasive calls for multidenominational schools in Ireland and these calls will hopefully be answered. However, such schools will be self-defeating if they persist in sanctioning the current divisions in the educational curriculum. It is imperative that wide-ranging courses in Irish Studies be instituted in all schools and universities now. Such courses are already pursued with success in foreign universities and they offer the interdisciplinary study of Anglo-Irish and Gaelic literature, Irish history, folklore, politics and language. The schools and colleges of Ireland are already filled with experts trained in these various fields, so that the organisation of a course in Irish Studies, on both sides of the border, would require not so much an expenditure of money as of imagination and will. The battle will finally be won or lost in thousands of parish schools across the land, but the universities have the chance to play a leading role. Over ten years ago, Frank O'Connor called for a chair of Irish Studies which would integrate courses on the Gaelic and Anglo-Irish traditions. His call yielded only a number of posts in Anglo-Irish literature, most of them held by men who care little for Irish. Yet in his book *The Backward Look* O'Connor had offered a brilliant model of what such a course of studies might achieve. After a decade which has been filled with political violence and literary stagnation, his call seems more pressing than ever.

FURTHER READING

Anne Clissmann, *Flann O'Brien: A Critical Introduction to His Writings*, Dublin, 1975.

Gearóid Denvir, *Litríocht agus Pobal*, Indreabhán, Conammara, 1997.

Douglas Hyde, *Language, Lore and Lyrics*, ed. Breandán Ó Conaire, Baile Átha Cliath, 1986, pp. 153–70 ('The Necessity for De-Anglicising Ireland').

Augusta Gregory, *Ideals in Ireland*, London, 1901.

Colbert Kearney, *The Writings of Brendan Behan*, Dublin, 1978.

Declan Kiberd, *Synge and the Irish Language*, London, 1979 (1993).

Thomas Kinsella, 'The Divided Mind', in *Irish Poets in English*, ed. Sean Lucy, Cork, 1972.

Thomas Mac Donagh, *Literature in Ireland*, Dublin, 1916 (reprinted Nnenagh, 1996).

Vivian Mercier, *The Irish Comic Tradition*, Oxford, 1962.

Robert Welch, ed., *The Oxford Companion to Irish Literature*, Oxford, 1996.

CHAPTER 5

Synge, Yeats and bardic poetry

(2002)

DYING ACTS

The old order of the *fili* or Gaelic poets began to disintegrate after 1600, as the English extended their conquests over Ireland. In response, many poets began to proclaim the death of their tradition: but they did so in lines of such vibrancy and power as to throw the thesis into question. They were rather like those soldiers who play dead on a battlefield, the better to rise and fight again. Ever since the early 1600s, the Irish language has contained statements of its imminent doom in every generation, yet four hundred years later it faces into the new millennium still truculently alive.

The best poems of the *fili* were in fact written after the crisis of 1600 and in direct response to it. 'Ceist, Cia Cheannóidh Dán?' (Question, who'll buy a poem?) captures the crisis of men deprived of ancient patronage and forced instead to contemplate the indignities of the open market. Like Baudelaire's *flâneur* they traverse their society, ostensibly to take a look at it but in reality to find a buyer. As such, these ruined bards provide a spectacularly early case of modernism *avant la lettre*. Their attempt to fit the old mandarin forms to the needs of a new social order put them in the classic predicament of the dandy – courtiers dispossessed of a court. Yet there was always something slightly suspect about the elegant phrases in which they confessed to being tired of life: if they were truly exhausted, they could hardly have expressed their fatigue so beautifully. The new tradition which they founded – that of dandiacal stoicism – lasts for centuries, down to Wilde's *Dorian Gray* and Beckett's protagonists who can't go on but go on anyway. The account of the death of one order becomes, in effect, a major narrative of its successor. And the attempt to express and defend a sensibility nurtured in one century against the depredations of the next is what links the author of 'Ceist, Cia Cheannóidh Dán?' forward to Yeats. Irish modernism had in effect two governing methods – some of its protagonists sought to protect old ideas by affording them the protective coverage of experimental, contorted new forms (a line going from Swift to Yeats), while others who believed more deeply in the newer ideas sought to give them the defensive armour of the older literary forms (a current which runs from Sheridan through O'Casey).

It is part of Synge's complexity that, at various phases in his work, he employed both of these tactics of representation in a transitional society. His poetry was based on his recognition of the need for brutality and violence of form in order to survive in the harsh climate of modernity. Yet he also proved capable of expressing many modern ideas in rather traditional modes. In both of these manoeuvres, the legacy of the *fílí* proved invaluable. Synge was not a revivalist in the sense of someone who wished to restore some previous form of poetry or society: rather, he believed that the potentials latent in past moments of the Gaelic tradition had been cut off before they could fully realise themselves, and that it was the task of the radical traditionalist to unleash and liberate those spurned but still potent possibilities. For him the Gaelic tradition was not a set of canonical texts so much as a *medium* by which past moments might be retransmitted, their energies made once again current. He had no wish to revive the past, but every wish to repossess its still-available energies. In some ways, his use of bardic tradition seems surprisingly unprogrammatic, as if it can be reactivated as an incidental outcome of trying to write an occasional poem of praise or blame – and in those moments it can take on a quality rather akin to Proust's involuntary memory. At other moments, however, it can seem far more deliberated: and it is with these exercises that I shall now deal.

CAVALIER OR BARD?

The conscious imitation of the function of the ancient bard is a feature of Synge's writing. It is a characteristic element in the work of most post-Classical Irish poets, whether they wrote in Irish, like Aogán Ó Rathaille or Eoghan Rua Ó Súilleabháin, or in English, like Samuel Ferguson or George Russell. In the work of Synge, it took many forms, the most important of which was the emulation of bardic techniques.

W. B. Yeats had written, in 1890, with unconcealed envy of the power of the Gaelic bards:

Their rule was one of fear as much as love. A poem and an incantation were almost the same. A satire could fill a whole countryside with famine. Something of the same feeling still survives, perhaps, in the extreme dread of being 'rhymed up' by some local maker of unkindly verses.[1]

Synge drew on the satiric traditions of such poetry in Christy's biting curse on Old Mahon:

May I meet him with one tooth and it aching, and one eye to be seeing seven and seventy divils in the twists of the road, and one old timber leg on him to limp into the scalding grave. *[Looking out.]* There he is now crossing the strands, and that the Lord God would send a high wave to wash him from the world.[2]

This power is revealed even more memorably in 'The Curse':

> To a sister of an enemy of the author's who
> disapproved of 'The Playboy'
> Lord, confound this surly sister,
> Blight her brow with blotch and blister,
> Cramp her larynx, lung and liver,
> In her guts a galling give her.
> Let her live to earn her dinners
> In Mountjoy with seedy sinners:
> Lord, this judgement quickly bring,
> And I'm your servant, J. M. Synge.[3]

This curse falls wholly within the bardic tradition, even to the detail of raising blisters on the brow of the cursed one. Eleanor Knott, in *Irish Classical Poetry*, explained that there are ten varieties of the brand of satire known as *aircetal aíre*, the last of which, known as *glám dicend*, could raise blisters.[4] James Carney pointed out, in *The Irish Bardic Poet*, that a satire was an injury to a king's honour 'which may show physically as blisters on his face'.[5]

The bardic poets were renowned for two types of poetry – eulogies of their chieftain and satires on his enemies. Sometimes, they wrote satires on personal enemies of their own, who refused to support their art. This is precisely what Synge did in 'The Curse' with Molly Allgood's sister, Mrs Callender, who had expressed disapproval of his play. The professional bards also wrote occasional poetry, compliments, inscriptions, and, of course, personal love lyrics. It is within this tradition that Synge's own poetic achievement falls.

Few of the scholars who have written on the poetry of Synge have shown any realisation of this. The editor of Synge's poems, Robin Skelton, is undoubtedly their subtlest explicator and critic, but he has seen fit to locate Synge's poetry within the English 'Cavalier' tradition. This approach illustrates the problems confronting critics with little or no knowledge of the Gaelic tradition in poetry who try to interpret Synge's work. Skelton finds that Synge shares with the Cavalier poets a vital self-mocking humour, a 'careless ease'. With this technique, the poet is able to 'make it seem as if each poem were an impromptu, or, at the most, the work of an hour or two of pleasurable industry'.[6] The poem is offered more as a virtuoso performance for an admiring audience than as a serious statement about life. It never commits the error of taking itself seriously, except, of course, when it praises the poet's patron, or lampoons his enemy. Skelton's description of the distinguishing features of Synge's poems is an eloquent attempt to locate them within this Cavalier tradition. It would be wholly persuasive if Synge had not already inherited from the Gaelic bards a courtly tradition, as vibrant as that of the Cavaliers.

Skelton's account of Synge's poetry might serve as a fair description of the modes of Irish bardic poetry:

There are curses – poems which are constructed as if poetry could alter reality. There are inscriptions – poems made for the flyleaves of books and for tombstones, as if the poet really had a social function as a maker of sentences for special places and occasions. There are poems which are stray thoughts versified, spasms of the heart or intelligence. And there are several poems which tell an anecdote in the kind of language which presumes the existence of a listening audience. (Skelton, 155)

There is nothing here with which we might wish to quarrel. All court poetry possesses common features, whether it is composed for the court of Elizabeth in London or for the court of Maguire in Fermanagh. Compliments, encomia, curses, satires, love-outbursts, inscriptions and anecdotes, wrought in a style of brilliant nonchalance, are the stuff of which courtly literature is made. We might justly ask, however, what Cavalier tradition ever believed in the power of satire to cause permanent injury to the body of its victim. We might further ask if there is one shred of evidence that Synge actually studied or read the Cavalier poets. There is no such evidence in the reading lists kept at Trinity College in his days as a student, nor in the later diaries where he scrupulously recorded all his later reading. There is, on the other hand, plenty of evidence that Synge sought to imitate the exponents of the bardic mode in Irish poetry, an interest which he shared with Yeats. Here is Robin Skelton's verdict:

Synge, as a poet, succeeded in making for himself a persona which few poets have been able to imitate in the twentieth century. Perhaps only Yeats could make full use of it after Synge had died. It is this persona which is, to my mind, Synge's greatest contribution to the poetry of our time; it was also quite certainly an immensely formative influence upon the poetry made by Yeats after 1908. (Skelton, 155)

This is too ingenious by far. The persona employed by Synge to such telling effect is an impressive part of his poetic equipment, but it was not created by him. He didn't need to create a persona, for he found one ready-made in the bardic tradition. His notebooks, as we shall soon see, testify to the strength of that influence.

Skelton is clearly unhappy with his own 'Cavalier' theory. As he struggles to isolate the features of Synge's poetic persona, he cannot wholly reconcile that theory with his scholarly scruples:

It is not easy to define this persona accurately. It is partly that of the Cavalier, as I have described it. It is also, however, partly that of the poet who saw his vocation as a social function, and who had a strong sense of his role as orator. (Skelton, 155)

It is a tribute to the honesty of Skelton's perceptions that he can identify so clearly that element of Synge's writing which does not conform to the conventions of Cavalier poetry. The strong sense of social vocation and the public tone of the poet's voice – so conspicuously lacking in Cavalier poetry and so blatantly present in Synge's work – are directly attributable to the influence of the Gaelic bards.

Skelton rightly sees this persona as one increasingly adopted by Yeats. The part played by Synge in this process was doubtless 'formative'. But that persona is not Synge's greatest contribution to the poetry of our time; it is the logical inheritance of every Irish poet who writes in the wake of the bards. Synge did not invent the persona and public tone of voice which, through his poetry, he passed on to Yeats; he simply rediscovered these features in the bardic mode. Yeats would have embraced them with particular enthusiasm, knowing that they came to him from the work of an esteemed friend and that they were sanctioned by ancient Gaelic practice.

Synge was not the first Irish poet of his age to revitalise the bardic modes. Lionel Johnson had written of how the bardic poet 'passed through a long discipline of the strictest severity, before he reached the high dignities of his profession'.[7] Like Yeats and Synge, he had been appalled at the disregard for technical rigour and craftsmanship of the Young Ireland poets. He strongly disapproved of the belief that patriotic

Irish verse must be the utterly free outpouring of spontaneous emotion. He cited the example of the bardic poets to demonstrate that concern for technical rigour was a thoroughly Irish literary tradition. This was, of course, a point often made by Yeats himself, who had remarked in his important essay on 'Nationality and Literature' that 'we have shrunk from the labour that art demands, and have made thereby our best moments of no account' (*Uncollected Prose, Vol. 1*, 274).

For Yeats, the labour that art demanded was the stern bardic code of painstaking attention to detail, 'the fascination of what's difficult'.[8] The rules of bardic poetry had been complex, involving assonance, consonance, alliteration and syllabic rhyme. For ceremonial public poems, the rules for the use of ornament were even stricter: 'the number of internal rhymes in each stanza and the number and position of alliterating words in each line [were] precisely determined' (Knott, 56). The more difficult the technical discipline which the bardic poet imposed upon himself, the greater his sense of achievement and the larger his reward. The work was read aloud to a courtly audience, who were asked to admire its apparent effortless complexity. This was akin to the method described by Yeats in 'Adam's Curse':

> A line will take us hours maybe:
> Yet if it does not seem a moment's thought,
> Our stitching and unstitching has been naught.
> (*Collected Poems*, 80)

Both Yeats and Synge worked for this achieved simplicity. We find it in the contrived artlessness of 'The Curse'. This poem seems like a burst of invective unleashed in the heat of the moment, but is, in fact, a work of ornately patterned alliteration.

This ideal of complex thought in apparently effortless expression was shared by Yeats and Lady Gregory, both of whom liked to quote the aphorism that the poet should think like a wise man, but express himself like the common people. This is exactly the procedure followed by Synge in his versions of Petrarch. The success of these translations is, in the words of Robin Skelton, 'due to his setting a much simplified diction against a highly elaborate construction of thought' (Skelton, 156). Synge projects complex sequences of thought in the clear idioms of the Irish peasant.

SYNGE, YEATS AND THE BARDIC REVIVAL

Robin Skelton does recognise that one of Synge's shortest lyrics, 'Abroad', is indeed a reworking of Gaelic tradition:

> Some go to game, or pray in Rome
> I travel for my turning home
>
> For when I've been six months abroad
> Faith your kiss would brighten God!
>
> *(Poems,* 62)

This is a variation on an old Irish stanza preserved in the margin of a ninth-century manuscript:

> Techt do Róim
>   Mór saítho, becc torbai;
> In Rí con-daigi i foss
>   Manim bera latt ní fhogbai.[9]

This has since been translated by Frank O'Connor in language remarkably close to that of Synge:

> To go to Rome
>   Is little profit, endless pain;
> The Master that you seek in Rome,
>   You find at home or seek in vain.[10]

Skelton goes so far as to suggest that Synge's poem is so close to the original text that 'one might even call it an "imitation"'. However, he contents himself with the observation that 'the balance of passion and mortality' is 'almost Jacobean' (Skelton, 157). It may be almost Jacobean, but it is altogether Gaelic. 'Abroad' is not just a variation upon its original, nor even an 'imitation', but a direct and creative confrontation with the Gaelic text.

Synge rejects far more of his original than he retains. The Gaelic text is wholly religious; Synge's is at once a religious and a love poem. As a love lyric, it draws on another tradition – that of *amour courtois* – where the love of Christ for the soul is often compared to the love between man and woman.[11] 'Abroad' is immensely more complicated than its source. Its nouns and verbs enact its ironies, which flicker between the sacred and the secular. The poem presents 'Rome' and 'home' as clashing concepts. The Gaelic poet had expected to find God in Rome but had discovered that He was all the time to be found at home. For the Gaelic poet, Rome is abroad, home with God. Synge's work plays with the same opposition, but in a different way. He remarks that some seek God in religious ecstasy in Rome; but that the ecstasy of lovers kissing after a homecoming is brighter than that offered by God. 'God' is a religious concept employed by Synge to a brashly profane purpose. After the kiss, 'God' is no longer an object of ecstasy, but merely an instrument by which the happiness of the lovers may be measured. 'God' is repudiated for a lover's kiss, yet he continues to provide a measure of its delight. This image of God, placed in a disadvantaged relationship with humans who love, will appear again and again in Synge's plays.

One is scarcely surprised to find that Yeats himself, in a late poem of 1938, employed the same poem for a stanza of 'Those Images'. He decided, like Synge, to emphasise the antithesis between 'Rome' and 'home':

> I never bade you go
> To Moscow or to Rome,
> Renounce that drudgery,
> Call the Muses home.
> (*Collected Poems*, 319)

Yeats had edited the first edition of Synge's collected poems and would, therefore, have had occasion to study 'Abroad' quite closely.

We could multiply such examples, where Yeats and Synge, in common, adopt features of Gaelic poetry. The bardic mode was studied and emulated by other contemporary writers, such as George Russell, who wrote, in 1902, that he was seeking for 'the old, forgotten music once heard in the dunes of kings, which made the revellers grow silent, and great warriors to bow low their faces in their hands'.[12]

One of the major functions of bards at royal feasts was the listing, in encomiastic poetry, of the names of dead kings and heroes, queens and heroines. The celebratory list was a device which Synge, Yeats and Russell each incorporated into his poetry. In 'Queens', Synge built a whole poem around the process:

> Seven dog-days we let pass
> Naming queens in Glenmacnass,
> All the rare and royal names
> Wormy sheepskin yet retains,
> Etain, Helen, Maeve, and Fand,
> Golden Deirdre's tender hand . . .
> Queens who wasted the East by proxy,
> Or drove the ass-cart, a tinker's doxy,
> Yet these are rotten – I ask their pardon –
> And we've the sun on rock and garden,
> These are rotten, so you're the Queen
> Of all are living, or have been.
> (*Poems*, 34)

Again, we are confronted with the ironic renewal by Synge of an ancient poetic tradition; and, as ever, the irony subverts the original convention. Synge recalls not only the great queens of old. In his reference to the vellum ('wormy sheepskin') which yet enshrines their names, he also recalls the age when it was common to celebrate those names in a poetry of genuine gravity. Synge's poem, on the other hand, must be shot through with mocking ironies, for it must register the subsequent decline from Etain and Helen to the latter-day 'tinker's doxy'. We are reminded that the beautiful women of the past are all rotten in earth. Even the vellum of the bards, who thought that they had at least salvaged the royal names from oblivion, is now but a 'wormy sheepskin'. As heir to these bards, Synge sets out to write an encomium of ancient queens, but instead produces a love-lyric to his lady. He does indeed write in praise of the queens; but this praise is framed by other statements, more important to him as a man writing in the twentieth century. He is no court poet of the sixteenth century, a powerful man with an influential audience and a recognised social function. He is a modern poet, that is to say, a man devoid of influence or social authority, who can register only the heartfelt intensities of private emotions. He can engage in the ritual name-dropping of the bardic encomium; he can even register the decline of the queens, after the fall of the Gaelic aristocrats, into tinker's doxies; but, finally, he is left with the reality of his own lover and must excuse himself of his bardic duty – 'I ask their pardon.' If this poem seems to mock the pretensions of the bards, it is only in the sense that all writers mock the conventions which they most avidly embrace. The ancient feeling of deference is mocked, but also maintained, through the very stridency of the lines which disclaim it. Only the poet who has deep feelings on a subject experiences the need to deny them so furiously.

The same naming-device was used by Yeats in 'Easter 1916', and with qualifications remarkably similar to those voiced by Synge in 'Queens'. In the final lines of the poem, Yeats recites the names of the leaders who have fallen in the rebellion:

> I write it out in a verse –
> MacDonagh and MacBride
> And Connolly and Pearse
> Now and in time to be,
> Wherever green is worn,
> Are changed, changed utterly:
> A terrible beauty is born.
> (*Collected Poems,* 182)

In this way, Yeats discharges one of the primary functions of bardic elegy – the listing of the warrior dead. The ancient bard would have left it at that, or might simply have added that the dead heroes were rewarded with a place in heaven and the knowledge that their land had been redeemed by their sacrifice. That would have been the public voice, which intoned the phrase 'Wherever green is worn'. However, Yeats, like Synge before him, cannot resist his duty, as a modern poet, to speak in an individual capacity about the questions which personally agitate him. In fact, the tragic power of the last stanza arises directly from the heartfelt tension in the mind of Yeats between his bardic duties, as poet of Irish Ireland, and his more complicated personal reactions to the event. It opens with a deeply personal statement of a belief about political commitment, which had long dominated his poetry and which had been confirmed by his hopeless love for the revolutionary, Maud Gonne:

> Too long a sacrifice
> Can make a stone of the heart.
> O when may it suffice?
> (*Collected Poems*, 181)

At once, however, he suppresses the question. In keeping with his function as an Irish bard, the social voice reasserts itself and reminds him of his traditional bardic duty:

> That is Heaven's part, our part
> To murmur name upon name,
> As a mother names her child
> When sleep at last has come
> On limbs that had run wild.
> (*Collected Poems*, 181)

The poignant, personal question insistently repeats itself, however. The bardic refrain, with which Yeats concludes his poem, has the customary dignity, but is shot through with irony and doubt. It is intoned as much to suppress the awkward questions raised by the event, as to celebrate its protagonists. The closing refrain, which has been sounded throughout the poem – 'A terrible beauty is born' – seems suddenly very complex. It is dignified, beautiful, appropriate, sanctioned by triple repetition, but, somehow, more richly ambiguous than ever.

THE DUALITY OF LITERATURE: PROBLEMS OF RECITAL

The poetry of the classical bards was recited for an aristocratic company on festive occasions, to the accompaniment of a harp, according to the *Memoirs of the Marquis of Clanrickarde*:

The Poet himself said nothing, but directed and took care that everybody else did his part right. The Bards having first had the Composition from him, got it well by Heart, and now pronounced it orderly, keeping even Pace with a Harp, touch'd upon that Occasion . . .[13]

This, of course, does not mean that the poems were songs. They were written in syllabic metres, with scant regularity of rhythm. There could, therefore, be no basis for a truly regular melody (Bergin, 20–1). In the opinion of Anne O'Sullivan, however, the musical accompaniment to these syllabic metres must have been rhythmical.[14] This is borne out by Clanrickarde's remark about the accompanist 'keeping even Pace with a Harp'. This music would have had to be toned down, so that the qualities of the voiceless consonants in bardic poetry might be clear. After the break-up of the bardic schools about 1600, later Irish poetry seemed to call for some kind of musical accompaniment within the verse. Hence, the increased use of assonance, alliteration and balanced cadences. It is as if the accompanist's harp, which once provided a background music, had been subsumed into the poem – just as in a famous English poem, 'My Lute Awake', Thomas Wyatt annihilates his lute and incorporates it into the music of his courtly lyric.

Synge was aware of the importance of all this for the modern writer of poetry – and, indeed, for the composer of modern music. In the first chapter of an unfinished novel entitled *Flowers and Footsteps* (1899), he described two young artists in conversation at a window overlooking the Luxembourg Gardens. One of these men recalls the way in which traditional folk poetry seems to contain its own self-interpreting musical accompaniment:

'These folk melodies', said his friend, 'contain their own signature in a way complex art cannot do. They require no notes of expression or crescendo to lead the performer. But a page's Schumann or Chopin without aesthetic indication is not always legible . . .'[15]

The discussion is soon extended by Synge to a consideration of the practice of the bardic poets and to the implications of this for modern music:

'Folk songs', said the other, 'have the same relation to modern poetry.' 'Not altogether. The folk melody is complete in itself. The folk poem needs a music which must be drawn from the words by the reader or reciter. In primitive times every poet recited his own poem with the music that he conceived with the words in his moment of excitement. Any of his hearers who admired his work repeated it with the exact music of the poet. This is still done among the Aran Islanders. An old man who could not read has drawn tears to my eyes by reciting verse in

Gaelic I did not fully understand. The modern poet composes his poems with often extremely subtle and individual intonations which few of his readers ever interpret adequately . . .'

'Is there any means of noting this?'

'Sometimes in my MS I have marked all the intonation ff. rall. etc. but it has a certain unpleasantness and what is more would become mechanical with the reader. Take this verse:

> I love you least for your long lips
>   And the sweeter voice of your smiling dreams
> I love not the woman of mortal lips
>   Nor the soul where your glory gleams.

With slow movement pausing slightly after "least" "lips" "voice" "dreams" and dwelling on the first syllable of "woman" and "glory". If the line were read without this pause on the "glory" the alliteration becomes frightful.

> The wail of the winds
> Is wound in the pines
> An ancient eighty
> My soul entwines.

Here without prolonged intonations the continued assonance and alliteration are lost and the poem is absurd. Observe that even now as I recite them for you I cannot give them their full value . . . with the poet there are often moments when he cannot read nor musically understand his own poetry.'[16]

The desire to recapture 'continued assonance and alliteration' in the sensitive recitation of modern poetry is part of Synge's deliberate attempt to revive bardic modes. He emphasises the fact that every bard 'recited his own poem with the music that he conceived with the words in his moment of excitement'. Other theorists, such as William Larminie and George Sigerson, saw the task of incorporating assonance and alliteration as a problem of poetic creation. Synge alone showed himself aware that a crucial element of bardic tradition was the recital of the poem in public performance.

The use of assonance and alliteration made strict demands, not only on the poet, but also on the reciter who was expected to bring out the subtle potential in every vowel and consonant. Assonance and alliteration occur so regularly in Synge's poetry and plays that they call for a sensitive interpretation in performance. The reciter must not rush through the lines, or they will seem drearily mechanical and formulaic. The solution to these problems in the passage quoted is similar to that later recommended by Synge to the actors of the Abbey Theatre – the use of

'prolonged intonation' and the skilful deployment of pause. The intonation was prolonged in order to bring out the rich texture of assonance;
the pauses were to occur after rhymed or alliterated words, in order to
prevent those devices from declining into mere jingle. In this way, the
movement of the lines is both slowed and varied, bringing them closer to
a lilt, or even, at times, a slow chant. Hence, no doubt, the significance of
Willie Fay's comment on the speeches of the plays: 'They had what I call
a balance of their own and went with a kind of lilt.'[17]

Máire Nic Shiubhlaigh's account of her difficulties, as an actress, in
reciting Synge's lines is illuminating:

The speeches had a musical lilt, absolutely different to anything I had heard
before. Every passage brought some new difficulty and we would all stumble
through the speeches until the tempo in which they were written was finally
discovered.[18]

She recalled that Synge did not offer much help in this process. His
characteristic reticence was doubtless due to the belief, expressed in
Flowers and Footsteps, that to mark the intonations 'ff'., 'rall'. etc. was to
impose a mechanical interpretation on the lines. Like the folk melodies
admired because they 'contain their own signature', Synge's own lines
revealed their hidden tempo to the actor or actress who studied them
closely. The tempo had been insinuated into the lines by Synge, to be
rediscovered by the actor; just as, in the classical period, the bard
conceived the music of his words in a moment of excitement and 'any
of his hearers who admired his work repeated it with the exact music of
the poet'.

Under the watchful, if reticent, direction of Fay and Synge, Máire
Nic Shiubhlaigh worked on her part as Nora in *The Shadow of the Glen*.
She made for herself all the discoveries about the use of pause and the
value of a retarded intonation, which Synge had already outlined in his
unfinished novel: 'I found I had to break the sentences – which were
uncommonly long – into sections, chanting them, slowly at first, then
quickly as I became more familiar with the words' (Nic Shiubhlaigh and
Kenny, 43). These breaks occur not according to the logic of grammar but
to the cadences of the speech. The pauses recommended in *Flowers and
Footsteps* seldom fall where the printer would insert a period-mark, but
rather where the poet has employed alliteration or rhyme. This is also true
of the speeches in Synge's plays. These are published with the punctuation
of normal grammar, but clearly have a poetic punctuation of their own, as
Máire Nic Shiubhlaigh soon discovered.

Synge supervised the production of his own plays and the recitation of his lines, just as the highest grades of professional poets in classical Irish directed the presentation of their own compositions. In this capacity, Synge was sometimes forced to do what he scrupulously refused to do when setting down his work – to write, in effect, 'ff.' or 'rall.' beside a line of his speech, interpreting its cadence for the puzzled actor. It is no surprise, therefore, to find among the Synge papers a special Abbey Theatre edition of *The Well of the Saints*, with annotations in Synge's own handwriting.

These annotations are of two kinds. Firstly, we find the insertion of certain short phrases to emphasise rhythms or to separate cadences with a kind of verbal pause; for example:

> I'm saying
> You'd do right / not to . . . .[19]

Secondly, all through this copy, we find the insertion of pause-strokes to guide the actor.

Thus, the methods adopted by Synge in the production of his plays were refined many years earlier in the unfinished novel, *Flowers and Footsteps*, of 1899.

A further discussion of these problems can be found in Synge's unpublished essay on 'The Duality of Literature', written less than a year earlier, in 1898. Again, we encounter the belief that it is the duty of the reciter to reproduce the passionate cadences of the artist as faithfully as he can:

In drama, music and literature, the work of art has a twofold existence, first as it is created by the artist, then as it is rendered by the actor, reader, or performer. Mallarmé seems to have considered the reader of a book as the equivalent of a spectator in a theatre but it seems juster to consider him as a real actor or performer.[20]

Here Synge expressed the bardic doctrine that a purely mental or visual reading of literature is worthless and that good writing relies for its effect on the spoken word. The true lover of poetry reads aloud, sharing with the author the nuances of his moments of inspiration. He is closer by far to the creating poet than to the passive audience, which merely listens to words which have been wholly decoded, first by the author and secondly by the performer. Like Yeats, Synge restored to literature the primacy of the spoken word. He was quite intransigent in this belief and mocked all who read books in silence, arguing that 'dumb reading is only a pantomime.'[21]

Next Synge turned to the question of 'complex art' which he also discussed in his novel – that complex art which requires accompanying notes of interpretation. In music, the composer may write 'rall.' or 'ff.' over the bars, but the poet or playwright cannot do so without reducing his lines to a dreary scheme:

In a page of Chopin or Franz Schubert every nuance of expression is indicated with extraordinary care but at the present time the writer sends out his work – a tissue of the subtlest intonation – with no warning for the reader and in numerous cases a great part of his conception is not understood.[22]

Synge believed that reticence concerning his intentions was a necessary part of a writer's art. However, he was uncompromising enough to point out that the price of this reticence is often incomprehension, or, worse still, misinterpretation.

In Ireland, according to Synge, the art of public recitation had flourished and passed unaltered through the centuries:

. . . there exist yet in lonely places the unlettered literature which was the real source of all the art of words. In the Gaelic-speaking districts of Ireland for instance recitation is of an extraordinary merit.[23]

The art of public recitation stands at the point of intersection between literature and music. Synge believed it was an art towards which many modern writers were preparing to return.

In the next section of the essay, Synge asked if the poet is necessarily the best reciter of his own verses. Great poets have read their own work badly, but have lived to hear the beauty intrinsic to their lines captured by the recitations of less gifted men. Synge readily conceded it

. . . possible that the poet himself does not inevitably reach the perfect utterance of the words with which he evokes our excitement, but if his own melody is transmitted by two or three persons of taste a beautiful rendering is provided.[24]

Nevertheless, Synge inclined to the opposite view and cited the example of Paganini, who 'was not ill advised to let his compositions reach the world during his life from his own violin only.'[25]

The value of the bardic tradition for Synge was that it reconciled this conflict – the awful disparity between the poem as imagined by the poet and the poem as recited by the performer. On rare occasions, the performer drew from a work a melody impossible to the composer; but all too often the real music of a poem died with the poet who wrote it. The gap between maker and interpreter threatened to make a mockery of the whole idea of poetry as communication, as an artefact which would outlive its maker. The art of recitation in the Gaeltacht, on the other hand, had been so highly developed that this problem had never arisen. In a predominantly oral culture, the ears of a good reciter are so sensitive that he need listen only once to a song in order to repeat its words and music. In *The Aran Islands*, Synge remarked on how the islanders could reproduce 'with admirable precision' the sounds of a foreign language after hearing them only briefly.[26] In his unpublished notes, as we have seen, he decided that this was a legacy of the bardic tradition:

In primitive times every poet recited his own poems with the music that he conceived with the words in his moment of excitement. Any of his hearers who had admired the work repeated it with the exact music of the poet. This is still done among the Aran Islanders. . .

The precision with which a reciter recaptured the original cadences and intonation of the poet meant that a work could be transmitted unmodified from generation to generation. The voice of the poet did not die with him.

Synge's essay underwent constant revision and many of its paragraphs went through four drafts. In every draft, the solution to the 'duality of literature' is a return to the discipline of the spoken word. Synge endorsed the bardic belief that a printed poem is an incomplete creation until it has been reconstructed in the sounds of the poet's own voice. He was realistic enough to concede that this ideal might never be fully achieved:

But when all has been attempted a certain duality will continue; the personality of the reader will refuse to acquire the whole intonation of the author and the same poem read by five different men of culture will show much greater differences than the same fugue played by five musicians.[27]

Synge ended with a call to contemporary writers to advance beyond the written word. His belief in the possibilities of a post-literate society anticipates that of Marshall McLuhan by over sixty years. It is even more remarkable that in an unpublished essay of 1898, Synge should have voiced his belief in the need for modern literature to engage the living voice, at the very time when Yeats himself was evolving similar ideas.

Synge's awareness of the close relation of words to music in bardic tradition was not unique. His interest was shared by W. B. Yeats. In an article in *Samhain* (1906), entitled 'Literature and the Living Voice', Yeats called for a return to the art of the reciter.[28] In the same magazine, he devoted much space to the importance of musical recitation and to the value of a learned recitative tradition. He endorsed Synge's belief in the dual existence of poetry, in the imagination of its creator and in the voice of its speaker:

If they are to read poetry at all, if they are to enjoy beautiful rhythm, if they are to get from poetry anything but what it has in common with prose, they must hear it spoken by men who have music in their voices and a learned understanding of its sound. There is no poem so great that a fine speaker cannot make it greater or that a bad ear cannot make it nothing.

(Explorations, 212)

So, Yeats shared Synge's belief that a good reciter can enhance a work and become a kind of co-creator with the author.

In bardic recitals, the *reacaire* (reciter) was given strict direction by the author whose work he performed. The poet, or *file*, was in absolute control, and the *reacaire* must defer to his judgment. The position of an actor in the Abbey Theatre was almost identical to that of the *reacaire*. The Abbey was first and foremost a literary theatre, where the major authors of plays were also directors and producers. Democratic revolts by actors or other personnel were crushed with matchless severity. Lady Gregory wrote that the Directors of the Abbey must not be guilty of 'giving in to stupidity in a Democracy', [29] and Yeats reminded the readers of *Samhain* that 'theatres cannot be democracies' (*Uncollected Prose, Vol. 2,* 377).[30] The actors were merely the exponents of the theories of Yeats and Synge. No doubt, they excelled the authors in their powers of acting and recitation, just as the *reacaire* was a professional reciter precisely because he had a finer speaking voice than the bard. But that was all the power that they had. It was not enough for Yeats and Synge that the company should act only those plays favoured by the Directors. They also insisted that the players should understand their art only in those terms laid down in the pages of *Beltaine* and *Samhain*. However, a technique of acting which drew on the discipline of the *reacaire* would not have been unwelcome to a team of actors which had been recruited from the Gaelic movement. They might bridle, as Gaels, at the imposition of 'unpatriotic' plays by the Directors; but they would have been delighted to know that, in their techniques of recital, they followed the ancient traditions of the bards. A leading article in *An Claidheamh Soluis*, written by Patrick Pearse in 1906, endorsed the Abbey's mode of acting, with its ruthless suppression of all unnecessary physical movement and its overwhelming emphasis on the spoken word. In particular, Pearse recommended that all actors in Irish should 'study the art of the traditional Irish reciter'[31] – eight years after Synge had made an identical observation in his unpublished essay of 1898. Pearse, however, qualified this insight with the warning that the Gaelic reciter was not a model to be religiously followed, 'for – other considerations apart – acting is essentially different from recitation'. Nevertheless, he gave the technique his blessing because, in restoring to the spoken word its lost primacy, it 'puts the student in touch with Ireland'.

Yeats had been interested in the relationship between words and music in the bardic tradition for some time before he met Synge. The 'chanting' or 'lilt' achieved under Synge's direction by Máire Nic Shiubhlaigh is related to the experiments with musical recitation performed by Florence Farr in the 1890s under the guidance of Yeats. Yeats saw this work as an extension into modern drama of the bardic tradition. Like Synge, he could not capture with his own voice the intonation which he desired, but could teach actors and actresses to do so.

In the first issue of *Beltaine* (1899), Yeats had written of his endeavour to have *The Countess Cathleen* spoken 'with some sense of rhythm' (*Uncollected Prose, Vol. 2, 160*). In the same article, entitled 'Plans and Methods', Yeats outlined the reasons why a return to bardic modes of recitation was necessary on the modern stage:

The two lyrics, which we print on a later page, are not sung, but spoken, or rather chanted, to music, as the old poems were probably chanted by bards and rhapsodists. Even when the words of a song, sung in the ordinary way, are heard at all, their own proper rhythm and emphasis are lost, or partly lost, in the rhythm and emphasis of the music. A lyric which is spoken or chanted to music should, upon the other hand, reveal its meaning, and its rhythm so become indissoluble in the memory. The speaking of words, whether to music or not, is, however, so perfectly among the lost arts that it will take a long time before our actors, no matter how willing, will be able to forget the ordinary methods of the stage and to perfect a new method. (*Uncollected Prose, Vol. 2, 160*)

This was to be a method of reciting poetry which brought out its musical cadences and emphasised its metrical structure; but the words rather than the music were to be primary. On no account was the music to distort the subtle rhythms of the words or to overwhelm them in mere melody. A musical instrument known as the 'psaltery' was invented by Arnold Dolmetsch, a renowned maker of instruments with a special interest in the music of the sixteenth century.[32] This instrument had thirteen strings and was attuned to the vocal range of Florence Farr, an actress who intoned the lines of poetry to the accompaniment of the psaltery.

The word 'intoned' is used, since the object of Farr's performance, according to William Archer, was neither to speak nor to sing, but rather to perform a kind of lilt or chant:

with such insistence on the rhythm, and such clear transitions from note to note, as can be recorded in musical symbols, and reproduced by anyone who knows what these symbols signify. The psaltery, meanwhile, is to be used as a sort of tuning-fork, striking the new note at each transition.[33]

The instrument was only to be sounded at points of transition and these would not occur very frequently, as Yeats insisted that phrases of remarkable length be spoken on one note. This Yeatsian theory was applied, according to William Archer, 'to the delivery not only of lyric, but more especially of dramatic, verse' (Archer, 2). In fact, the theory relates closely to Synge's dramatic practice. His speeches contain phrases of considerable length, punctuated by pauses, which marked the change from cadence to cadence and from note to note.

Synge had written that the art of the *reacaire* persisted in the recitation of poetry on Aran. In a letter to the editor of *The Academy* in June 1902, Yeats, too, affirmed that the declamation which he sought could still be heard in the singing of Irish countrywomen who 'speak their little songs precisely as Miss Farr does some of hers, only with rather less drama'. He went on to say: 'I imagine men spoke their verses first to a regulated pitch without a tune, and then, eager for variety, spoke to tunes which gradually became themselves the chief preoccupation until speech died out in music.' [34]

Arnold Dolmetsch summarised the problem of attuning the phrases of Yeats's verse to the notes of the psaltery: 'The point was to find the "time" to which the poet recited his own verse.'[35] This was the same problem which faced anyone who wished to recite Synge's lines, as Máire Nic Shiubhlaigh recalled: 'At first I found Synge's lines almost impossible to learn and deliver. Like the wandering ballad-singer I had to 'humour' them into a strange tune, changing the metre several times each minute' (Nic Shiubhlaigh and Kenny, 42).

Her problem was also to find the 'tune' to which the author had imagined the cadences of his speech. It was compounded by the fact that Synge deliberately refused to help and that he could not give his own lines their full musical value, 'perhaps partly because his years abroad had removed every trace of brogue from his speech' (Fay and Carswell, 137-8). His later experience at the Abbey, therefore, vindicated his statement in 'The Duality of Literature' that the author is not necessarily the best reciter of his own lines. When Dolmetsch asked Yeats to perform his own poetry to the psaltery, he encountered a similar problem, for the great poet, he found, 'did not recognise the inflexions of his own voice' (Hone, 191).

So, in both his private critical speculations and in his published plays and poems, Synge turned to the practice of the bardic poets for instruction and inspiration. He did this at a time when their work was still a sealed book to most of the Irish men and women who came to watch his plays. He shared the bard's belief in the necessity to close the gap between the poem which the poet wrote and the poem as recited in performance. His was an age when poetry was becoming an increasingly private affair, when the attention of post-Romantic poets and critics alike was on the creative moment and on the transaction between the poet's imagination and the paper to which he committed its creations. Synge's stern emphasis on other aspects of poetry – on poetry as a spoken art involving a listening audience – was wholly revolutionary. It went beyond a mere consideration of the workings of the poet at the moment of creation and asked how best could the nuances of such moments be recaptured by an independent reciter. In a literary tradition in English which gives all too little attention to such questions, Synge's analysis of these problems was salutary. In the native Irish literary tradition, these questions and insights are the logical, conservative inheritance of every practising poet.

NOTES

1 'Bardic Ireland', a review of Sophie Bryant's *Celtic Ireland* (1889), was published in *Scots Observer*, 4 January 1890; reprinted in W. B. Yeats, *Uncollected Prose*, ed. J. P. Frayne (London: Macmillan, 1970), vol. 1, p. 164. Hereafter cited as *Uncollected Prose*.

2 J. M. Synge, *Plays, Book II*, ed. Ann Saddlemyer, vol. 4 of the *Collected Works* (London: Oxford University Press, 1968), p. 125.

3 J. M. Synge, *Poems*, ed. Robin Skelton, vol. 1 of the *Collected Works* (London: Oxford University Press, 1962), p. 49. Hereafter cited as *Poems*.

4 Eleanor Knott, *Irish Classical Poetry* (Dublin: Colm O Lochlainn, 1960), p. 75–6. Hereafter cited as Knott.

5 James Carney, *The Irish Bardic Poet* (Dublin: Dolmen Press, 1967) 11.

6 Robin Skelton, *The Writings of J. M. Synge* (Indianapolis: Bobbs-Merrill, 1971), p. 154. Hereafter cited as Skelton.

7 Lionel Johnson, 'Poetry and Patriotism', *Poetry and Ireland: Essays by W. B. Yeats and Lionel Johnson* (Dublin: Cuala Press, 1908), p 22. Johnson's lecture was delivered in Dublin in 1894.

8 W. B. Yeats, *Collected Poems* (Macmillan, 1951), p. 93. Hereafter cited as *Collected Poems*.

9 W. Stokes and J. Strachan, eds., *Thesaurus Palæo-hibernicus* (Cambridge University Press, 1901), vol. 2, p. 296.

10 Frank O'Connor, *The Backward Look* (London: Macmillan, 1967), p. 51.

11 A. J. Denomy, *The Heresy of Courtly Love* (Gloucester: P. Smith, 1965), p. 29–33.

12 George Russell, 'The Dramatic Treatment of Heroic Literature', *Samhain* (October 1902): 15.

13 Quoted by Osborn Bergin, *Irish Bardic Poetry* (Dublin: Institute for Advanced Studies, 1970), p. 8. Hereafter cited as Bergin.

14 Anne O'Sullivan, 'Giolla Brighde Mac Con Midhe', *Early Irish Poetry*, ed. James Carney (Cork: Mercier Press, 1969), p. 92.

15 Synge Manuscripts, TCD, MS 4382, f.41.v.

16 Ibid. f.41.v.– f.42.r.

17 W. G. Fay and Catherine Carswell, *The Fays of the Abbey Theatre* (London, 1935), p. 138. Hereafter cited as Fay and Carswell.

18 Máire Nic Shiubhlaigh and Edward Kenny, *The Splendid Years* (Dublin, 1955), p. 43. Hereafter cited as Nic Shiubhlaigh and Kenny.

19 Synge Manuscripts, TCD, MS 6408, f.53. For pause-strokes, see in particular ff. 90–1.

20 Synge Manuscripts, TCD, MS 4349, f.3–f.4.

21 Ibid. f.4.

22 Ibid. f.4–f.5.

23 Ibid. f.8.

24 Ibid. f.11–f.12.

25 Ibid. f.12.

26 J. M. Synge, *Prose*, ed. Alan Frederick Price, vol. 2 of the *Collected Works* (London: Oxford University Press, 1966), p. 60.

27 Synge Manuscripts, TCD, MS 4349, f.15 and f.17.

28 W. B. Yeats, *Explorations* (London:Macmillan, 1962), pp. 202– 21. Heareafter cited as *Explorations*.

29 Lady Gregory, *Our Irish Theatre* (New York: Putnam, 1913), p. 104.

30 'Events', *Samhain* (November 1908): 5.

31 Patrick Pearse, editorial, *An Claidheamh Soluis* (7 July 1906): 6.

32 Robert Donington, *The Work and Ideas of Arnold Dolmetsch* (Haslemere: Dolmetsch Foundation, 1932).

33 Quoted by Florence Farr, *The Music of Speech* (London: E. Mathews, 1909), p. 2. Archer's article, which Farr reproduces, was originally published in May 1902. Hereafter cited as Archer.

34 *Letters of W. B. Yeats,* ed. A. Wade (London: Rupert Hart-Davis, 1954), p. 374.

35 Quoted by Joseph Hone, *W. B. Yeats* (New York: Macmillan, 1943), p. 191. Hereafter cited as Hone.

CHAPTER 6

George Moore's Gaelic lawn party

(1979)

'Strike a blow for Irish by speaking it', urged Eoin Mac Néill in an address to the first recruits of the Gaelic League, adding the afterthought that 'if we cannot learn Irish we can at least stand up for it'. The history of Ireland in the decades after the foundation of the League in 1893 was to prove how much easier Mac Néill's second option was than his first. The brief career of George Moore as a leader of the Gaelic revival provides an apt and amusing illustration of that point.

It was a campaign which began, as all campaigns should, in a garret in London just one year after Mac Néill's rallying cry. One evening Moore's friend Edward Martyn expressed regret that he did not know enough Irish to write his plays in the language. Moore was astounded and remarked derisively to his friend: 'I thought nobody did anything in Irish except bring turf from the bog and say prayers.'[1] Martyn was the first Anglo-Irish writer to give serious consideration to the possibility of employing Irish as a literary medium, but the nearest he ever came to his ideal was in his drama *The Enchanted Sea*, whose hero speaks fluent Irish, but only off stage. Despite his initial misgivings, Moore was soon excited by the possibility of Ireland 'awakening at last out of the great sleep of Catholicism'. As he strode restlessly along the King's Bench Walk in the following days, he fantasised about 'writing a book in a new language or in the old language revived and sharpened to literary usage for the first time' (*Hail and Farewell*, p. 56). The reasons for his sudden enthusiasm were more personal than patriotic, for he had despaired of ever writing another creative work in English, a declining language which was 'losing its verbs' and in which 'everything had been already written' (p. 84). The noble idioms of Shakespeare could never be equalled, having been passed 'through the patty-pans of Stevenson into the pint-pot of Mr Kipling'.[2] Moore was convinced that primitive peoples invented languages and that journalists destroyed them. He laid his curse on the journalists of England and decided to campaign for Irish, a language which had not been debased by abstract thought.

In that sense, the return to Irish might also be seen as an advance towards the modernism of Ezra Pound, who would soon revile journalists with his credo 'No ideas but in things'. From Yeats, Moore soon learned that there were no ideas in early Irish literature, only things: 'through dialect one escapes from abstract words, back to the sensation inspired directly by the thing itself' (p. 246). Knowing no Irish, Yeats was happy to study the concrete images and homely idioms of the Hiberno-English dialect, but such half measures could not satisfy Moore. Taking his cue from Edward Martyn, he denounced the dialect as a shoddy compromise: 'I like the English language and I like the Irish, but I hate the mixture' (p. 333). He was scathing in his rejection of Lady Gregory's 'Kiltartan whistle'; 'a dozen turns of speech' which could be easily emulated by any journalistic parrot (p. 550). Synge was scarcely any better, though Moore did pay him the compliment of parodying his idiom and his celebrated Parisian encounter with Yeats, who is caused to advise: 'Give up your schoolmaster words that have no guts left in them, and leave off thinking of Loti and his barley-sugar, and go down into Country Wicklow and listen to what the people do be saying to each other when they're at ease without any notion of an ear cocked to carry off what they say.'[3] All of which simply proves that Moore could never have mastered the dialect, so he preferred to denounce it in accordance with the approved policies of the Gaelic League.

'I came to give Ireland back her language', he remarked shortly after his return to the capital, and the cynics of literary Dublin wondered just how long it would take Ireland to give the native language back to George Moore. In the event their disbelief was justified, as he settled for Mac Néill's second option. Though he struggled through some early lessons, he soon abandoned the enterprise. Yeats uncharitably put it down to weakness of character: 'He did not go to Mass because his flesh was unwilling, as it was a year later when the teacher, engaged to teach him Gaelic, was told that he was out.'[4] His attempts to reform Irish cooking were no more successful and after a vicious argument as to the correct preparation of omelettes, his cook promptly resigned and called a policeman. Increasingly, the door at Ely Place went unanswered.

But Moore did speak up for Irish, with an intensity that bordered on absurdity, with a sincerity that seemed to many to come very close to parody. Having failed to master the language, he invested his hopes in the younger generation. 'That one child should learn Irish interests me far more than the production of a masterpiece',[5] he wrote in a letter to Yeats. At a meeting in February 1900 he explained his position:

I have no children and am too old to learn the language, but I shall arrange at once that my brother's children shall learn Irish. I have written to my sister-in-law telling her that I will at once undertake this essential part of her children's education. They shall have a nurse straight from Aran; for it profits a man nothing if he knows all the languages of the world but knows not his own.[6]

He expected that his audience would giggle at this and it did.

Douglas Hyde took his distinguished recruit aside and informed him that there was no need to kidnap an unsuspecting nurse on Aran, as there were many excellent speakers of Irish in the neighbourhood surrounding his nephews' home at Moore Hall. Apparently, this public announcement came as a great surprise to the nephews, who had heard nothing of their uncle's plans. Five months elapsed before their mother was to receive a letter from Ely Place asking her to 'enquire about the woman who speaks the best Irish and engage her to speak Irish all day to the children'.[7] The hapless nephews were not amused to find their days consumed by an Irish-speaking nurse who rattled off sentences, not a word of which they could understand. Not surprisingly, they revolted and the nurse was despatched. Moore was not beaten, however, and at his next public appearance he threatened to disinherit the children unless they attained fluency in the language within a single year. Having failed in his appeal to the idealism of the younger generation, he now tried outrage and threat. In a final outburst to their recalcitrant mother he wrote: 'It must be clear to you now that the first thing that concerns your children is to learn Irish, that whether the nurses are dirty or ill-mannered is of no moment whatever.'[8] When the appeal went unanswered, he duly carried out his threat.

Mrs Maurice Moore was just one of a number of women who were subjected to Moore's inveterate crusading. He outraged Lady Gregory at this time with his threat to have Yeats's *The Shadowy Waters* played in Irish during the third and final session of the Irish Literary Theatre in 1901. She insisted on its being acted in English and recorded this shrewd analysis of Moore in her diary:

I believe that what gives him his force is his power of seeing one thing at a time; at the moment he only sees the language, whereas I see the Theatre is the work in hand and our immediate duty. *Shadowy Waters* in Irish! It would appear to the audience as *Three Men in a Boat* talking gibberish![9]

This diagnosis of the brevity and fury of Moore's devotions bears a suspicious resemblance to that offered by Max Beerbohm earlier that year in the *Saturday Review*:

It is one of Mr Moore's peculiarities that whatever is uppermost in his mind seems to him to be the one thing in the world, and he cannot conceive that there will ever be room for anything else . . . But if the Keltic Renascence prove to be the most important movement ever made in Art, it will not long enchain him.[10]

For the time being, however, Moore's enthusiasm only gathered fire. Despite the strictures of Lady Gregory, he knew that both the theatre and the Gaelic League had much to gain from a diplomatic alliance. The theatre could recruit actors and stage-hands from the ranks of the League, while the language movement would find in the stage the ideal platform for its gospel. In the *New Ireland Review* Moore wrote in April 1900:

The performance of plays in our language is part and parcel of the Irish Literary Theatre, which was founded to create a new centre for Irish enthusiasm, a new outlet for national spirit and energy. This is the first object of the Irish Literary Theatre; I may say it is its only object, for if we achieve this we achieve every object.[11]

He then announced that they planned to produce *The Land of Heart's Desire* by Yeats in an Irish translation prepared by Douglas Hyde. Clearly, Lady Gregory had won her point. Defending his choice of a translation for the first production of a Gaelic play, Moore pointed to the difficulties of acquiring the craft of writing for the stage and to the limited number of writers in Irish. He emphasised the potentially drastic long-term effects on Gaelic drama of producing a bad play in the language, while cheerfully conceding that at this early stage in the progress of the Gaelic League, 'there will be few in the theatre who will understand an Irish play'.

This article came to a climax with a warning that the native language, 'in which resides the soul of the Irish people', was 'slipping into the grave'. He called for 'a great national effort to save it'.[12] Answering the stock objections that Irish literature was merely a formless folklore and an improper medium for art, Moore argued that the words of Ibsen, written in a language used by only a few million people, were known all over Europe. Furthermore, the glories of ancient Irish literature were celebrated by scholars from all parts of the world. It was the English rather than the Irish language which was unsuitable for artistic production. 'From universal use and journalism, the English language in fifty years will be as corrupt as the Latin of the eighth century, as unfit for literary usage, and will become, in my opinion, a sort of Volapuk, strictly limited to commercial letters and journalism.'[13] He recalled how he had been struck by the refined beauty of some passages translated from the Irish writings of an islander, but that the English written by the same person was coarse and ugly. 'In either case the writer wrote artlessly, without selection, but in one case he was using a language in which all expressions are true and appropriate, and in the other case he was writing in a language defiled by too long usage.'[14] His belief was that the future of poetry lay with the languages of national minorities, Irish, Flemish, Hungarian, Welsh and Basque. When this article was published with minor alterations one year later in *Ideals in Ireland* (1901), he outlined his policies even more clearly, offering a partial retraction of his earlier statement that there would be few to understand an Irish play. An addendum to page 45 now read: 'Mr George Moore wishes to add that at the time he wrote this passage he did not know of the extraordinary revival of the Irish language in Dublin.' Lady Gregory, who was the editor of *Ideals in Ireland*, considered this sentence sufficiently important to have it printed in red ink on a specially inserted page in the collection. However, the most important addition to the earlier article was Moore's blunt declaration of his position: 'Our desire is to make Ireland a bilingual country – to use English as a universal tongue, and to save our own as a medium for some future literature.'[15]

Moore's belief in the theatre as an important, but secondary, weapon of the language movement was calculated to recommend him to the Gaelic League. Its leader, Douglas Hyde, had declared himself 'convinced of the importance of using the stage to promote the revival of the native Irish language as a medium of literature'.[16] In an interview with the *Freeman's Journal* in 1901 Moore agreed that 'the central idea of the Theatre would be the restoration of the Irish language'.[17] In the same year Frank Fay expressed his hope for actors who would be native speakers, but he was realistic enough to admit his fear that 'we shall not be so lucky as to get people of this sort'.[18] Within twelve months Fay had settled for a national theatre in English, to the great dismay of Moore who would have preferred to see him touring the provinces with a group of Gaelic players. The closing months of 1901 were filled with preparations by Yeats and Moore for the production of the play *Diarmuid and Grania*, to be performed in conjunction with Hyde's one-act drama, *Casadh an tSúgáin*. Despite his genuine enthusiasm for the English work, Moore could not help treating that part of the project with some flippancy, as when he suggested a master plan to purify the idiom of the noble characters – he would compose the play in French, Lady Gregory would translate it into

English, Tadhg Ó Donnchadha ('Tórna') would then render it in Irish, and finally Lady Gregory would remould that version in English. The result of these perverse manoeuvres was greeted with some disdain by the nationalist press. The drama critic of *The Leader* unleashed a diatribe against the authors: 'Mr Yeats and Mr Moore have twisted the Gaelic story beyond recognition and have changed Diarmuid from a Fenian chief into a modern degenerate.'[19] But Moore couldn't have cared less, for he was in full agreement with the editor of *The Leader* that 'the chief use of Irish drama at present is to popularize the use of the Irish language'.[20] All through the rehearsals, he had stressed that point in conversations with Yeats which are recalled in *Salve*: 'But our play doesn't matter, Yeats; what matters is *The Twisting of the Rope*. We either want to make Irish the language of Ireland, or we don't; and if we do, nothing else matters' (*Hail and Farewell*, p. 315). Though Yeats could never assent for long to such patriotic rather than artistic priorities, there were occasions when he demonstrated a willingness to condone Moore's way of thinking. For example, at the famous luncheon party at which Moore threatened to disinherit his nephews, Yeats had pleased Hyde with the statement that 'the vital question of the moment was the Irish language question', and that it was their own misfortune that the literary society had had to work in the English language.[21]

Moore's commitment to the Gaelic League reached a climax in the first issue of *Samhain*, the journal of the Irish Literary Theatre, where he introduced *Casadh an tSúgáin* in October 1901:

In a way, it would have pleased our vanity to have been the first in Dublin with an Irish play, but this would have been a base vanity and unworthy of a Gaelic Leaguer. There has been no more disinterested movement than the Gaelic League. It has worked for the sake of the language without hope of reward or praise; if I were asked why I put my faith in the movement I would answer that to believe that a movement distinguished by so much sacrifice could fail would be like believing in the failure of goodness itself.[22]

In the same year, he continued to bombard the press with interviews and articles in defence of the language, remarking in 'A Plea for the Soul of the Irish People' that 'in five years it has become an honour to know the language which in my youth was considered a disgrace'.[23] Addressing himself to his many readers in England, he declared that the death of a language was 'an act of iconoclasm more terrible than the bombardment of the Parthenon'.[24] In return for the lost Gaelic legends and the open fields of Connemara, the English could offer only 'the gutter press of London' and 'the universal suburb, in which a lean man with glasses on his nose and a black bag in his hand is always running after the bus'.[25] Londoners were suitably insulted, but the Gaelic League was not particularly impressed. The very stridency of Moore's language caused suspicion and amusement – and there were even some ignoble souls who suggested that this stridency arose not from Moore's desire to convince others but from his incapacity to convince himself. When Moore called on the little office of the Gaelic League in Dublin, he was dismayed to find that his name was unknown to the secretary and compensated for his lost dignity by muttering 'seamstresses, seamstresses' under his breath.

However, he had devised a master plan to bring himself to the notice of the Leaguers: the preparation of a collection of short stories for translation into Irish. By its very title *The Untilled Field* proclaimed itself an example to future Gaelic authors of the kind of work to be done. Accordingly, it was first published in an Irish version in 1902 as *An tÚr-Ghort*. Moore later described it as 'a book written in the beginning out of no desire for self-expression but in the hope of furnishing the young Irish of the future with models'.[26] It became a great deal more than a literary model, however, developing into a study of clerical oppression and written in a corrosively realistic style. Moore was overjoyed to see the Irish version of his name 'Seorsa Ó Mórdha' on the book's cover, which also featured the name of Pádraig Ó Súilleabhain of Trinity College, who translated all but one of the stories. The remaining story, 'An Gúna-Phósta' (The Wedding Gown) had been translated by Tadhg Ó Donnchadha in a version that particularly pleased Moore. When he got T. W. Rolleston to translate 'An Gúna-Phosta' back into English, Moore was entranced with his own lines, finding them 'much improved after their bath in Irish'. He gave as an example 'She had a face such as one sees in a fox', which he deemed far superior to his own flaccid 'She had a fox-like face.' He compared this revitalised phrase to 'a jaded townsman refreshed by a dip in the primal sea'.[27] However, scarcely a hundred copies of *An tÚr-Ghort* were sold and the author never achieved his ambition of seeing the volume displayed in the Gaelic League window. The only real benefit he derived from the experience was the assistance of Rolleston's versions of the Gaelic as he made final preparations for the publication of *The Untilled Field* in the following year. He continued, though, to assert the importance of providing Gaelic writers with the best models and constantly nagged Hyde with suggestions for translating various English and continental classics into Irish.[28]

His finest hour was yet to come. At the start of 1902 he went into conclave with Hyde, in order to lay plans for that contradiction in terms, a Gaelic lawn party. He wrote in a state of high excitement to his brother, Colonel Maurice Moore:

I want to give a party. The garden in front of my house belongs to me and it will hold five or six hundred people easily; and there are apple trees; and nothing will be easier than to build a stage . . . On this stage I want to have performed a play in Irish. I want to have a Gaelic-speaking audience. I think this would be a very good thing, and I think it would annoy Dublin society very much, which will add considerably to my pleasure.[29]

Soon Hyde's play *An Tincéar agus an tSídheog* (*The Tinker and the Fairy*) went into rehearsal with the actors all drawn from the Gaelic League, including the author himself and Sinéad Ní Fhlannagáin (later to become Mrs Éamon de Valera). Moore treated the actors who trooped through his house during rehearsals with the most exquisite tact, but when the great day dawned he seemed at a complete loss, for he had never before given a party. 'What am I do to?' he asked the Leaguers, and in the event decided simply to do nothing other than beam beatifically at all of the guests. They must have been a motley collection of people, those shopgirls and office clerks mingling in Ely Place with professors and portrait painters, under the disapproving gaze of Moore's neighbours who looked down in derision from their high windows. Or so John Butler Yeats thought, as he recalled the strange event in a letter to his daughter Lily:

There was a great crowd there. Tyrrell, F.T.C.D. was the only F.T.C.D. there . . . The weather held up alright at the play. There had been a bitter, black storm of rain in the morning, but it cleared up . . . The play ought to have started at 3 o'clock when the sun was shining and it was quite warm, and that was the time appointed. But the delegates (I don't know what delegates) did not arrive. Meanwhile, the sky began to blacken and we all felt anxious while Moore, in his peculiar manner, kept softly gesticulating his despair. At last, the wretches arrived and the play began, and though expecting every moment to be drenched through, we got safely to the end; though for a time all umbrellas were up, which might have been pleasant for the people trying to see. Fortunately, this happened towards the end, when the musicians and singers (out of sight behind a screen of leaves) had the performance to themselves.[30]

As Moore waved farewell to Hyde later that afternoon, he must already have been studying the shape of the gentle scholar's head in search of an appropriate satirical phrase. By the time Moore had embarked on his autobiography, Hyde had been transformed from a genial scholar in a suburban garden to the abject butt of his most lethal lines. 'Nothing libels a man so much as his own profile', wrote Moore. 'Hyde looked like an imitation Irish speaker; in other words, like a Stage Irishman' (*Hail and Farewell*, p. 139). He recalled 'the droop of the moustache through which his Irish frothed like porter, and when he returned to English it was easy to understand why he desired to change the language of Ireland' (p. 238). Why this sudden contempt? An answer may be found in Moore's growing anti-clericalism. He was greatly irritated by the way in which Hyde curried favour with all sections of the rising Catholic bourgeoisie, 'members of Parliament, priests, farmers, shop-keepers'. 'By standing well with these people, especially with the priests,' complained Moore, 'he had become the archetype of the Catholic–Protestant, cunning, subtle, cajoling, superficial and affable.' By such devices Hyde had managed 'to paddle the old dug-out of the Gaelic League up from the marshes'. For Moore, just then engaged in an announcement of his defection to Protestantism in the *Irish Times*, such abject deference by a distinguished Protestant to the Catholic clergy was lamentable. So he poured scorn on the man whose work he had once compared with that of Homer.

Already the Catholic clergy were taking control of entire branches of the League, to the dismay not only of Moore but of the young James Joyce. In his early novel *Stephen Hero*, Joyce acidly noted that 'the meetings of Friday nights were public and were largely patronised by priests'.[31] Joyce's own view of the League emerges in a conversation between Stephen and the enthusiast Madden. Stephen considers the Roman, not the Sassenach, to be the real tyrant of the island. He suggests that the belated support for the dying language was given by a clergy which considered it a safeguard for their flock against the wolves of disbelief, 'an opportunity to withdraw their people into a past of literal, implicit faith'. Moore would have heartily agreed. He had made the cynical observation that 'the Roman Catholic church relies upon its converts, for after two or three generations of Catholicism the intelligence dies' (*Hail and Farewell*, p. 434). His study of translations of early Gaelic literature had vindicated Yeats's belief that it was healthily bereft of abstract ideas; but the pathetic inadequacy of later Gaelic art demonstrated, he felt, just how corrosive was the effect of Catholic teaching on the artistic intelligence. 'The only time Ireland had a litera-ture was when she had no ideas – in the eighth and ninth centuries' commented Moore (p. 344). 'As soon as the Irish Church became united to Rome, art declined in Ireland . . . Irish Catholics have written very little . . . After a hundred years of education it [Maynooth] has not succeeded in producing a book of any value' (pp. 352–3). Now that the products of

Maynooth were beginning to appear on Hyde's platforms, Moore began to look upon them with a very jaundiced eye. In *Ave* he offered the same analysis as Joyce:

. . . a young cleric said that he was in favour of a revival of the Irish language because no heresy had ever been written in it. A fine reason it was to give why we should be at pains to revive the language, and it had awakened a suspicion in me that he was just a lad – in favour of the Irish language because there was no thought in its literature. What interest is there in any language but for the literature it has produced or is going to produce? (p. 241)

Moore had returned to Ireland in the belief that the Gaelic League would waken the land from the great sleep of Catholicism; but now, under the indulgent eye of Hyde and his clerical cohorts, Ireland was slumbering more peacefully than ever.

Of course, Moore had suspected as much all along. Hence the covert irony and self-mocking extravagance of his more extreme pro-Gaelic statements. Even the description of the *Daily Express* dinner for the Irish Literary Theatre is shot through with the misgivings which had haunted the new recruit as he mounted the platform of dignitaries and listened in consternation to the sounds of his native tongue:

It seems to be a language suitable for the celebration of an antique Celtic rite, but too remote for modern use. It had never been spoken by ladies in silken gowns with fans in their hands or by gentlemen going out to kill each other with engraved rapiers or pistols. Men had merely cudgelled each other, yelling strange oaths the while in Irish, and I remembered it in the mouths of the old fellows dressed in breeches and worsted stockings, swallowtail coats and tall hats full of dirty bank-notes, which they used to give my father. Since those days I had not heard Irish, and when Hyde began to speak it an instinctive repulsion rose up in me, quelled with difficulty, for I was already a Gaelic Leaguer. (p. 139)

The repulsion is *instinctive*. Subsequent experience was simply to increase Moore's misgivings; and even the model for a future Gaelic literature, *An tÚr-Ghort*, is filled with that same repulsion, as if the author's unconfessed mission was to have that repulsion expressed for the first time in his native language. Distaste for the language all too easily became distaste for the entire country. So Ned Carmady in 'The Wild Goose' opts for emigration in the belief that it is better to die than to live in Ireland, a maxim curiously prophetic of Beckett's avowal that he preferred to live in France at war than in Ireland at peace. The hero of 'In the Clay' makes a similar observation: '[Ireland] is no country for an educated man.'[32]

It was, perhaps, the failure of the Gaelic League to respond to the challenge posed by *An tÚr-Ghort* which – more than anything else – convinced Moore that its writers would never create a major literature. He could have endured praise or enjoyed abuse, but he had no use for apathy. Even if (as Patrick Pearse repeatedly stressed) the language could be a realistic medium for a modern writer, Moore estimated that it would take him ten years to acquire an adequate knowledge of it, a more charitable span than that which he had allotted to his disinherited nephews. 'But ten years among the fisher-folk might blot out all desire of literature in me.' The only remaining hope was that a native Aran Islander, endowed with literary genius, might put pen to paper, 'but the possibility of genius, completely equipped, arising in the Arran Islands seemed a little remote' (*Hail and Farewell*, p. 75). It was more than twenty years later that Liam O'Flaherty began to make his name, but apart from some skilful short stories by Pádraic Ó Conaire and Patrick Pearse, there was no revival of Gaelic literature while Moore sojourned at Ely Place. By 1908 he could write to Edouard Dujardin that 'the Celtic Renascence does not exist – it is a myth, like a good many other things'.[33] Nevertheless, he was modest enough to aver before his English audience that if he had managed to learn Irish and write in it, the language would now be 'a flourishing concern' (*Hail and Farewell*, p. 74).

In his autobiography Moore chose to treat his brief career as a Gaelic revivalist with a dismissive and insolent flippancy. This led most critics to assume that the entire affair was from the very outset an elaborate joke at the expense of literary Dublin. Moore connived in this interpretation by suggesting that his public speeches and articles were pure fabrications, 'merely intellectual, invented so that the Gaelic League should be able to justify its existence with reasonable, literary argument' (p. 235). But it would be wrong to assume that the corrosive tone of *Hail and Farewell* had also characterised his relations with the Gaelic League and the Literary Theatre. The insolent satire which permeates that brilliant but wilful book tells us a great deal about Moore's state of mind between 1910 and 1914, but reveals nothing of the passionate intensity with which he threw himself into the work of the Gaelic League in 1901 and 1902. Those who knew him well in his Dublin years – men like John Eglinton and George Russell – were in no doubt as to the depth of his commitment, which they found at times ridiculous, but which he himself learned to mock only when it had abated. At the time of his passion he was perfectly capable of expressing grave doubts about the authenticity of George Russell's visions, on the grounds that the mystic poet did not know the Irish language and could not therefore expect to converse with the Celtic gods. If there is a note of scornful irony in the pages of *Hail and Farewell*, then that scorn is directed not so much at the idealists of the Gaelic League as at the intensity of the author's earlier devotion.

For all his subsequent disclaimers, Moore's flirtation with the Gaelic movement proved surprisingly influential. His dream of translating the classics of England and the continent into Irish was finally realised with the foundation of An Gúm in 1926, the government-sponsored press which employed such fine writers as Máirtín Ó Cadhain and Seosamh Mac Grianna to do just that. Furthermore, Moore's disenchantment with the corrupting effects of journalism was shared by many contemporaries, including Yeats, who later went on to blame 'a violent contemporary paper' and 'a patriotic journalism' for the attacks on Abbey art.[34] The theory that English had become worn from over-use became a subject of impassioned debate in the ensuing decade. Yeats endorsed the ideas of Moore, while Russell insisted that words can never be utterly debased by anyone, that even the threadbare idioms of the journalist can be revitalised by an artist of vision and emotion. It was left to Synge to reconcile these conflicting theories. He conceded Moore's point that words have a cycle of life, but insisted that the time came when they were too exhausted, even for the journalist. At such a time, they might be restored to their original power, in line with Emerson's belief that 'every word was once a poem'.

It was, however, the policy of selective bilingualism which proved the most durable of Moore's legacies, for it is that ideal which still dominates the debate on the future of the Irish language. Moore saw English as the language of business, journalism and commerce with the outside world, Irish as the idiom of culture, education and the domestic life. In many respects his ideas remarkably anticipate the more sophisticated concept of *diglossia* expounded by Máirtín Ó Murchú in his study *Language and Community* (1970). *Diglossia* is defined as the societal patterning of two codes in sets of situations, usually exclusive, where the use of each code is clearly defined by social convention. As a concrete example of this, Ó Murchú cites the normal division of Arabic into a set of domains where a high sub-code is used (church sermons, university lectures, news broadcasts), and an informal set of domains where a low sub-code is used (instruction to servants, domestic conversation, captions in political cartoons). Moore would have been in profound agreement with the immediate goal of 'an Irish–English *diglossia* along such lines, in which

Irish would have a significant part to play consistent with its function as the national language'.[35]

For good or for ill, the ideas of George Moore still prove a fertile source of discussion among writers and scholars, over sixty years after he himself abandoned them. The ripples of appreciation and amusement which emanated from his quaint garden party at Ely Place have never quite died.

NOTES

1 *Hail and Farewell* (Colin Smythe edition, Gerrards Cross, 1976), p. 55. All further references to this edition are indicated in the text.
2 'Literature and the Irish Language', *Ideals in Ireland*, edited by Lady Gregory (London, 1901), p. 49.
3 *The Untilled Field* (Colin Smythe edition, Gerrards Cross, 1976), p. xix.
4 W. B. Yeats, 'Dramatis Personae', *Autobiographies* (London, 1955), p. 428.
5 Unpublished letter, 31 July 1901, National Library of Ireland Collection.
6 *Ideals in Ireland*, p. 51.
7 Quoted by Joseph Hone, *The Life of George Moore* (London, 1936), p. 226.
8 Ibid., p. 230.
9 Lady Gregory, *Seventy Years* (Gerrards Cross, 1974), p. 357.
10 Max Beerbohm, 'Au Revoir', *Saturday Review* (3 February 1900); reprinted in *Around Theatres* (London, 1953), pp. 59–61.
11 'The Irish Literary Renaissance and the Irish Language', *New Ireland Review* (April 1900), 66.
12 Ibid., p. 67.
13 Ibid., p. 69.
14 Ibid., p. 70.
15 'Literature and the Irish Language', 47.
16 Quoted by Alice Milligan, Letter to the Editor, *Dublin Daily Express* (21 January 1899), p. 3.
17 'The Irish Literary Theatre – an Interview with Mr George Moore', *Freeman's Journal* (13 November 1901), 5.
18 Frank Fay, *United Irishman* (11 May 1901).
19 *The Leader* (2 November 1901), 3.
20 *The Leader* (19 October 1907), 5.
21 *Freeman's Journal* (23 February 1900), 6.
22 *Samhain* (October 1901), 13.
23 'A Plea for the Soul of the Irish People', *Nineteenth Century* (February 1901), 287.
24 Ibid., p. 294.
25 'Literature and the Irish Language', p. 48.
26 See also John Cronin, 'George Moore: the Untilled Field', *The Irish Short Story*, edited by Patrick Rafroidi and Terence Brown (Gerrards Cross, and Atlantic Highland, 1979), p. 114.

27 Quoted by Joseph Hone, *The Life of George Moore*, p. 244.
28 John Eglinton, *Irish Literary Portraits* (London, 1935), pp. 87–8.
29 Quoted by Joseph Hone, *The Life of George Moore*, p. 240.
30 *J. B. Yeats: Letters to his Son W. B. Yeats and Others 1869–1922*, edited by Joseph Hone (London, 1944), p. 71.
31 *Stephen Hero*, edited by Theodore Spencer (London, 1966), p. 61.
32 *The Untilled Field*, p. 330.
33 *Letters from George Moore to Edouard Dujardin 1886–1922*, edited by John Eglinton (New York, 1929), p. 64.
34 W. B. Yeats, Letter to the Editor, *United Irishman* (24 October 1903). See also 'J. M. Synge and the Ireland of His Time', W. B. Yeats, *Essays and Introductions* (London, 1961).
35 Máirtín Ó Murchú, *Language and Community* (Dublin, 1970), p. 12.

CHAPTER 7

The flowering tree: modern poetry in Irish
(1989)

It has been said more than once that a writer's duty is to insult, rather than flatter. Yeats inclined to the view that whenever a country produced a man of genius, he was never like that country's idea of itself. Without a doubt, the literary movement now known as modernism consisted primarily in a revolt against all prevalent styles and a rebellion against official order; and yet, by its very innovative nature, it was precluded from establishing a fixed style of its own. 'Modernism must struggle but never triumph,' observed Irving Howe, 'and in the end must struggle in order *not* to triumph.'

By the 1960s, this movement had come to an end, as society tamed and domesticated its wild bohemians, converting them from radical dissidents into slick entertainments. 'The avant-garde writer', bemoaned Howe, 'must confront the one challenge for which he has not been prepared: the challenge of success . . . Meanwhile, the decor of yesterday is appropriated and slicked up; the noise of revolt magnified in a frolic of emptiness; and what little remains of modernism denied so much as the dignity of an opposition.'

Irish modernism had been largely an emigrant's affair – and those Gaelic writers who remained at home produced not a literature which peered into the abyss or fought the new establishment, but one which (in the view of Máirtín Ó Cadhain) was more suited to an audience of credulous schoolchildren and preconciliar nuns. In his novel *Cré na Cille* (1949) Ó Cadhain produced the one undisputed masterpiece of Gaelic modernism. If Beckett had to cope with a language of exhaustion, then in that book Ó Cadhain offered a response to the exhaustion of a language. There were many who believed that Ó Cadhain's graveyard, with its talking corpses, was the epitome of the state to which the Irish language had fallen in the mid-century. Among politicians, the argument seemed no longer about ways of saving the language, but rather about who had responsibility for the corpse. But, in the words of Nóra Sheáinín, the fey philosopher of that narrative, *ars longa, vita brevis*, Ó Cadhain was already shoring against his ruins, looking forward to a time when his book would survive even the death of the language in which it was written. The book's central location in a graveyard is not a metaphor of the fate of Irish, but of the fate of itself. Ó Cadhain shared with Beckett the secret knowledge that even when language dies, the voices continue:

> All the dead voices.
> They make a noise like wings . . .
> To have lived is not enough for them.
> They have to talk about it.

Unlike Beckett, however, Ó Cadhain did not have to seek out debility, self-impoverishment, and estrangement. The culture in which he functioned was estranged from the start.

It was this apparent weakness of the Irish language which became the saving of its literature. If modernism is a literature of extreme situations, then few groups have professed this sense of extremity more obviously than the Irish – Synge's Aran peasants live on the outermost edges of Europe; Tomás Ó Criomhthainn reminds us that the next parish is America; and Muiris Ó Súilleabháin goes so far as to say that he is not an Irishman but a Blasketman (rather like Flaubert who claimed Bohemia, and not France, as his native country). By the 1960s, however, Irish modernism was at a virtual end. Having lived for decades on the edge of things, at limits where other lungs would have found the air unbreathable, writers of English were encouraged to return to the homeland and claim their share in the new riches. The government, which had banned most good writing in English over the previous decades, announced a tax-holiday for creative artists.

The results were predictable. As Howe foretold, bracing enmity gave way to wet embraces. Many second-rate figures appeared to enact in public the role of writer, rather than confront in private the anguish of real writing. By the end of the 1970s, the Fianna Fáil government instituted the *Aosdána*, a group of about 150 artists who would be paid an annual stipend and accorded state homage. Cynics remarked that this honeymoon between politician and artist might end when the *aos* became truly *dána* and emulated the cantankerous behaviour of ancient bards dissatisfied with the behaviour of a chief. But the *Aosdána* proved as tame as they were grateful.

The position of writers in Irish during the 1960s was somewhat different. For decades, they had been engaged in a protracted honeymoon with the government and state agencies; but the marriage had proved less than fruitful. The massive attempts to revive and spread the Irish language, at the beginning of the century, had been attended by no great revival of Gaelic writing. Indeed, writers of English had seemed to draw the last drops of blood from the expiring body, and to inject those toxins into their own offspring to invigorating effect. Anglo-Irish literature fed like a parasite off its dying parent; and yet the more extensive the efforts at reviving Irish, the poorer the quality of the literature actually produced.

By the 1970s, when the official pretence of revival was less and less convincing, and when a pass-mark in the language was no longer compulsory in state examinations, the literature of Irish enjoyed a minor renaissance. Much of this energy was due to the inspiration of Máirtín Ó Cadhain, by 1970 at the end of a great career as Professor of Irish at Trinity College, Dublin; and much of the zest came from the skill with which men like Desmond Fennell presented the language movement as part of the counterculture – a return to healthy rural values, to peripheries rather then centres, to civil rights for small communities rather than national emblems for large, impersonal bureaucracies. While the youth of America marched with black leaders on the Pentagon and while Bernadette Devlin (herself a student of Irish at university) marched for democracy on Stormont Castle in Belfast, men like Ó Cadhain and Fennell marched through Connemara in a movement that would lead to a devolved government, local radio stations and, by no coincidence, a revival of Gaelic poetry.

And this, too, was grounded in a paradox, for the youthful poets who supported Cearta Sibhialta na Gaeltachta in 1969 would make their subsequent careers not in the Gaeltacht, but in large cities from which most of them anyway came. And they would renew not the prose tradition so beloved of Ó Cadhain, but the poetic forms for most of which he had such ill-disguised scorn. In his last major lecture, delivered just a year before his death, *Páipéir Bhána agus Páipéir Bhreaca*, Ó Cadhain mocked the very movement which he, more than any other, had helped to create:

Staid bhagarach, drochthuar é, an iomarca tóir a bheith ar fhilíocht a chuma le hais an phróis. Seo mar tá sé i mionteangachaí eile ar nós Gáidhlig na hAlban, a bhfuil triúr nó ceathrar filí den scoth inti freisin . . . Na cúpla file maith atá againn, níl siad ag cuma a ndóthain. Is fusa go fada liric dheas neamhurchóideach ocht líne a chuma anois agus aríst ná aiste a scríobh, urscéal, ná fiú gearrscéal féin a scríobh. Seo í an éascaíocht agus an leisce ar ais aríst. Chó fada is is léar dhomsa is mó go mór a bhfuil d'fhilíocht dhá scríobh sa nGaeilge ná sa mBéarla in Éirinn . . . Sé an prós tathán coincréad, clocha saoirsinne an tsaoil, agus é chó garbh, míthaitneamhach leis an saol féin. Sileadh gur gaile-maisíocht a bhí ar Phatrick Kavanagh nuair adeireadh sé gurbh fhileata go mór iad na prós-scribhneoirí, daoine mar O'Flaherty nó O'Connor, ná na filí Gall-Ghaelacha. Le galra seo na filíocht a bhí sé ag plé . . . Is beag atá fághta ag an bhfilíocht inniu. Níl tada fághta aici sa nGaeilge ach liricí gearra . . .

It is a threatening and ominous portent when there is an excessive zeal to compose poetry rather than prose. This is also the situation in other minority languages, including Scots Gaelic, which has three or four first-rate poets working in the language as well . . . The few good poets of our own are not composing a sufficient amount. It is easier by far to write an essay, a novel, or even a short story. This heralds a return to glib facility and laziness. As far as I can make out, far more poetry is being written in Irish than in English here in Ireland. Prose is the concrete base, the mason's cornerstone of life; and it is as rough and unpleasant as life itself. It was thought that Patrick Kavanagh engaged in special pleading when he said that prose writers such as O'Flaherty and O'Connor were much more poetic than the Anglo-Irish poets. He was referring to the disease of poetry . . . These days there is little left for poetry to do. Nothing is left to poetry in Irish but brief lyrics . . .

Ó Cadhain asserted that nothing should be written in the lyric form which could not be equally well said in prose (hardly a revolutionary demand); but he seemed to imply the superior range and versatility of prose when he skilfully deployed the criticism of Edmund Wilson to make his point for him: 'The technique of prose today seems thus to be absorbing the technique of verse; but it is showing itself equal to the work.'

At the time of its delivery, this lecture was construed as a frontal assault on poetry (and Seán Ó Ríordáin responded accordingly); but also as a covert critique of the woolly-mindedness of the young. The University College, Cork, poets associated with *Innti* magazine through the 1970s – Davitt, Rosenstock, Ó Muirthile and Ní Dhomhnaill – had to bear the burden of this formidable disapproval; but bear it they did, remaining steadfast in their defence of the Gaelic lyric, which they infused with the cultural deposits of the 1960s, from Zen Buddhism to Dylanesque symbology.

The death of Ó Cadhain in 1970 saw the proseman raised to canonical status and made the task of the younger poets, if anything, more difficult. They were helped from the beginning by enthusiastic and large audiences among their own generation. For the first time ever, writing in Irish was addressed not to the Gaelic race (whatever that might be), but to specific groups, illustrating Scott Fitzgerald's dictum that an artist writes for the youth of today, the critics of tomorrow and the schoolmasters of ever afterward. The rate of social change in Ireland was such that the old seemed to occupy a time-warp of their own; and though an occasional young poet might write a lyric of homage to an established master, such as Davitt's to Ó Direáin, astute readers often found that the laconic recreation of the senior lyricist's modes skirted the edge of insolent parody. Of course, nobody would know better than Máirtín Ó Direáin, the leading survivor of the older generation, just how essential such insolence is to a living tradition. Ó Direáin might not catch all the countercultural resonances of 'Positively Sráid Fhearchair', but he had read and well understood 'Tradition and the Individual Talent'. The war on the past took many forms, but, in a case such as this, an insulting imitation was the sincerest form of flattery.

Poets like Davitt, Rosenstock and Ní Dhomhnaill spoke for, as well as to, a wide audience, most of whose members were urban, middle-class and radical, unlike the previous generation of authors who tended to hail from the Gaeltacht or semi-Gaeltacht, and to be rural, impoverished, and conservative in ideology. Instead of pandering to the placid, already converted audience of senior Irish-speaking citizens, the *Innti* poets went out and created a largely new audience for poetry. Not only that, but the interviews and essays published in their journal helped to create the taste by which they would eventually be judged. At the height of this revival, it was widely believed that there were more readers in Ireland for a poem written in Irish than for one in English, though whether all these enthusiasts applied aesthetic (rather than nationalistic) criteria is debatable. It is, of course, the peculiar destiny of innovators to seem less and less remarkable in proportion to their success in changing public taste; and if, by the 1980s, both *Innti* and its poets were attracting smaller audiences they could at least console themselves with the knowledge that the senior critical figures in universities had finally admitted their work as a valid and valuable extension of the Gaelic canon. In December 1984, writing in *Comhar*, Eoghan Ó hAnluain gave *Innti* a clean bill of academic health. It is, perhaps, a measure of the growing conservatism of the *Innti* poets that some pronounced themselves grateful and pleased.

Had Máirtín Ó Cadhain lived for another decade, he might have wished to rephrase, if not reverse, his judgements. The war which he proclaimed was phoney from the outset, for if Ó Cadhain could write poetry in prose, then it was also possible for Áine Ní Ghlinn to flirt with the possibility of a kind of prose in verse. The very Kavanagh whom Ó Cadhain had invoked in his attack on the young poets had himself proclaimed that it was his lifelong ambition 'to play a true note on a dead slack string', to deflate the modernist intensity of a Yeats with the ad-lib techniques of 'Not-caring':

> No one will speak in prose
> Who finds his way to those Parnassian
>   Islands . . .
> – but he will do the next best thing!

The notion that the distinction between poetry and prose is a typographical conceit is part of a much wider post-modern attempt to annul all polarities. The poets after 1970, or at least the younger among them, ask us to unlearn the illusory differences between men and women, reason and emotion, Irish and English.

The premier literary journal of the period *Scríobh* recognised no division between creative and critical writing, opening its pages to the academic specialist and the working artist alike; while, at the same time, poets incorporated elements of auto-criticism into their creative texts. This may have been motivated by the desire to render these texts invulnerable to academic exegesis, by beating the scholar to the critical punch, for, from its beginnings, Gaelic poetry, though practised by persons of wit and erudition, has shown a healthy disrespect for pedantry. As Seán Ó Ríordáin wrote of his poems;

> Má chastar libh fear léinn sa tslí
> Bhur rún ná ligidh leis, bhur mian, –
> ní dá leithéid a cumadh sibh . . .

> If you meet a learned man on the way
> Do not let slip to him your secret, your desire –
> It wasn't for his sport that you were made . . .

But it was also, and more probably, part of the international attempt by poets to create a wholly self-sufficient work of art, containing within itself its own critical apparatus.

What all this proved was simple enough – that the best literature is an act of consummate criticism, and the best criticism is literature in the profoundest sense. In the great works of this century, the two became indistinguishable, as the French novelist Alain Robbe-Grillet observed:

It seems as though we are making our way more and more towards an epoch in fiction in which the problems of writing will be seen clearly by the novelist, and in which critical concerns, far from sterilising creation, will be able on the contrary to serve it as a motive force.

The inevitable consequence is that, as criticism grows more academic and solemn, literature is increasingly learning to laugh at itself. Though many of the poems in this volume are, predictably, about the process of making poetry, all but a few are written with a degree of irony and self-effacement. Like Kavanagh – a significant source for poets in Irish as well as English – these artists are happy to treat literature as a mere aspect of life, rather than a high road to salvation. By reducing the extravagant claims made by Yeats for poetry, they manage to lodge the reasserted, but more modest, claim with a fair degree of conviction. The poems, as a result, are not irritatingly self-conscious, but healthily self-aware; and the learning, quite impressive in some cases, is lightly carried. At a time when Irish poetry in English grows more heavily allusive each year – as if the text were created in, and not just written for, the university seminar – this poetry is blessedly free of Dante-esque echoes or mythical claptrap. Indeed, so resolutely anti-academic had it been in its earlier phases, that the educational establishment responded in kind by keeping many of the younger poets off school courses.

If the Gaelic tradition offered a life-support mechanism for Yeats, Synge and the many Anglo-Irish contemporaries during the period of national revival, then the reverse has been the case in recent decades, as Gaelic poets turn for inspiration to the work of these figures. There has, indeed, been a real rapprochement between the two traditions; and this is clear also in the number of translations from Gaelic to English performed by a range of leading poets from Heaney to Kinsella. Even more crucial to this closening of ties has been the sheer number of artists producing high-quality work in both languages – Brendan Behan, Pearse Hutchinson, Críostóir Ó Floinn, Michael Hartnett and Mícheál Ó Siadhail are simply the latest exponents of a great tradition of bilingualism that reaches back, *via* Flann O'Brien and Liam O'Flaherty, to Patrick Pearse.

The phrase *ag obair as lámha a chéile* (working out of one another's hands) might well characterise the current relationship between writers of English and Irish. Paul Muldoon's translation of Davitt's *An Scáthán* is probably as well known as its brilliant original; while Mícheál Ó Siadhail's English versions of his own lyrics have achieved a reputation in their own right. The deference shown to Yeats, especially by the young, is remarkable. Mícheál Ó Siadhail's compliment to the women in his life

> Two or three drew the thread together
> And wove for me a shirt . . .

though nicely ironical in its image of shirt as shroud, is clearly indebted to Yeats's

> Three women who have wrought
> What joy is in my days . . .

as, indeed, to Kavanagh's 'God in Woman'. The cultivation of an itali-cised balladic refrain is another Yeatsian ploy favoured by many, while Ó Direáin's characteristic imagery of tree, stone and wave-whitened bone has its acknowledged source in Yeats.

In a somewhat similar fashion, the use of sacred imagery to brashly profane purpose, which was a feature of Synge's art, may be found in poets as varied as Ó Searcaigh

> On the altar of the bed,
> I celebrate your body tonight, my love . . .

and Mac Fhearghusa

> Give us a hint, God,
> What kind of place is Heaven?
> According to what I hear
> The place isn't greatly to my liking . . .

This is in keeping with the Gaelic proverb which says that God possesses the heavens but covets the earth; and also with Christy Mahon's pity, as he squeezes kisses on his lover's lips, for the Lord God sitting lonesome in his golden chair.

The homages to Yeats and his Anglo-Irish contemporaries may spring from a deep-felt desire to fuse the two island traditions in a single work of literature as an emblem of Irish possibility; but such homage is all the more remarkable in view of the fact that contemporary Irish poetry in English is increasingly identifying its true parent as Joyce. Dillon Johnston's *Irish Poetry After Joyce* (1985) was just the first of what will doubtless be a succession of books written to substantiate that claim. Hence, our paradox – that while Ó Direáin was penning heartfelt tributes to Yeats in *Comhar*, Kavanagh was pouring scorn on the man whom he saw as the last of the Eminent Victorians:

> Yes, Yeats, it was damn easy for you, protected
> By the middle classes and the Big Houses,
> To talk about the sixty-year-old public protected
> Man, sheltered by the dim Victorian muses.

What attracted Kavanagh to Joyce was his rediscovery of the mythical in the matter-of-fact, his evocation of the wanderings of Odysseus in the voyage through Dublin of a nondescript canvasser of ads. Kavanagh's 'Epic', in sonnet form, casts a small-town quarrel over the ownership of fields against a similar backdrop:

> That was the year of the Munich bother. Which
> Was more important? I inclined
> To lose my faith in Ballyrush and Gortin
> Till Homer's ghost came whispering to my mind.
> He said: I made the Illiad from such
> A local row. Gods make their own importance.

While, at first glance, it might seem as if the ancient epic is invoked to belittle the struggles of latter-day pygmies, in the end it is clear that the banal concerns of everyday men are used to question the notion of ancient heroism.

This was not exactly the understanding on which Yeats's poetry was based, which is, of course, why Joyce steered clear of the warlike Cuchulain and chose instead as his model the homely and draft-dodging Odysseus. Seamus Heaney's poem 'The Tollund Man' bases itself on a comparable strategy. Here, the sacrifical victim of an ancient fertility rite is dug out of the Danish bog, his body preserved down even to his half-digested seedcake, to recall for us the banality of ancient as well as contemporary evil. Heaney says he could consecrate the bog as holy ground, install the Tollund Man as a pagan god

> and pray
> Him to make germinate
>
> The scattered, ambushed
> Flesh of labourers,
> Stockinged corpses
> Laid out in the farmyards.

Pádraig Mac Fhearghusa uses the figure of Neanderthalus in identical fashion, addressing him in his grave beneath the Zagros mountains:

> Moistly may the pollen grains
> of your body
> fecundate us,
> That we may lay aside
> at the mouth of your grave
> the scorched briars
> of shiftless power,
> That from our eye
> may fall

a black fertile tear
on the grey ashes
of our tribes consumed . . .

The elevation of Joyce to a position of primacy in the story of modern
Irish poetry is another illustration of Ó Cadhain's contention that
prose could now take on most of the tasks traditionally assigned to verse.
The consequent diminution of Yeats is not without its cruel ironies, for
the 'Joycean' commingling of the mythical and the material had its actual
roots in the Yeatsian theatre. 'What we wanted', said Lady Gregory of the
Abbey Theatre, 'was to create for Ireland a theatre with a base of realism
and an apex of beauty' – or, as Lennox Robinson later phrased it, a
reconciliation of 'poetry of speech' with 'humdrum facts'. Yeats himself
endorses the method in his play *On Baile's Strand* where the irrelevance of
Cuchulain's poetic posturing to the needs of the proletarians in the
prosaic sub-plot is the drama's underlying theme.

Wherever we look in the contemporary zones of Gaelic poetry, we may
come upon this interrogation of the mythical by the matter-of-fact. This
works, most often, in terms of the humiliation of tradition by the
individual talent, the denial of national myths in the face of authentic
personal feeling. The self is the new touchstone; and so the source of
ethical judgements changes. The impact on the self, and not the moral
consequences for society, becomes the most popular yardstick for meas-
uring an action. So, in 'Spring Thaw', Declan Collinge's lovers rekindle
their flame against an ice-age backdrop; and even though the legendary
giant of Kippure mountain starts to stir in his sleep, he seems strangely
ancillary to the scene. Perhaps Mícheál Ó Siadhail pursues this strategy
best. His 'Stony Patch' is a complex reworking of the same theme, because
he is as anxious to humanise the past as the present. If Joyce's ancient
hero turns out on closer inspection to have been a draft-dodger, then
Ó Siadhail is also aware that the remnants of a life are a mimicry rather
than a full representation. What is left is the search for some sign of the
persistence of the person, some hint of the complexities lost to the ravages
of time. Our respect, hints Ó Siadhail, should be given to the matter-of-
factness of the Egyptian hermits and Skellig monks, rather than to the
post-factum myths of simplification – for, like Yeats's meditators on
Mount Meru, and like the modern artist, they too were self-invented
men, each one 'scratching his song in the wax of his soul', or working 'in
the tradition of himself'.

Ó Siadhail's 'Nugent', though superficially a very different type of
poem, is an even more astute reworking of the same materials, for here

the matter-of-fact is elevated to the status of the mythical. The first republican prisoner is released, after two years and three quarters on the blanket-protest, to become an instant newspaper celebrity, only to be diminished almost at once by his proximity to banal news of 'the last race from Naas'. The single photograph, a moment frozen in time, is all we moderns know of Nugent, and all he will finally be allowed to know of himself. It cruelly deprives the nationalist rebel of his own history, of the tradition of himself for 'what space has news or history?' The remainder of the poem becomes Ó Siadhail's attempt to reinsert this figure into his own narrative, with irony as well as love, since Nugent is a name not of Gaelic but of foreign origin. This republican may even be descended from those very Dutch mercenaries who invaded Ireland to found the Orange ascendancy which Nugent himself now fights. Cast in this European perspective, Nugent becomes a kind of universal soldier:

> But in the fear of Nugent's eye
> Walks the last private soldier,
> Famished, bedraggled after Napoleon;
> All camp followers who ever tramped,
> Smarting for our comfort,
> Across the cold land of history.
> Were those his own crazed eyes
> Who terrified us so?

Already, this still-born myth has been almost erased by the matter-of-fact, for 'tomorrow the back-room must be put in order', and even now Nugent's photograph has been 'covered over / by a spatter of paint'.

The poem, though it lovingly celebrates this domestic ritual, seems nevertheless profoundly troubled by its elevation of the private over the public world. Though the poet repeats Daniel O'Connell's aphorism that the cause may not be worth a drop of blood, he has the artistic courage to leave the last word to Nugent and to that question which forms in the prisoner's eyes. As is the case in 'Patient', the pain in those eyes is but an aspect of the suffering of the poet, who looks into them with an acute awareness of other lives which the prisoner might have had. There is, however, nothing patronising about the sympathy offered in either poem. On the contrary, there is humility in the poet's admission that he cannot gaze on the unfathomable, but can merely 'by indirections find directions out' and look quizzically into the eyes of those who have the courage to peer into the unknown. Only he experiences a need to name and, therefore, to control – he itemises the nature of a patient's disease or the history of a surname – and that is his foremost duty as poet. He offers a private judgement of Nugent's wasted years, as they appear to him, but concedes the awesome integrity of the man's option, and tenderly restores to him that full history which the news photograph had threatened to abort.

Integrity, here, lies in the scrupulous balance kept between sympathy and condemnation. Where most poets would lapse into facile condemnations of violence, or (less likely) glib endorsements of Nugent's heroism, or (very common and worst of all) automatic attempts to steer some middle course of suspended judgements, Ó Siadhail has the courage to make his own views clear, while conceding that Nugent remains finally mysterious, ineffable, beyond the neat formulations of the local newspaper or, indeed, the home handyman's poem.

Something of a similar complexity is achieved by Michael Davitt in 'For Bobby Sands on the Day before he Died'. This is a poem which perfectly captures the luxurious marginality of the south in the face of all northern suffering, and the fake intensity of its debate. Davitt is the gentlest of poets and there is a streak of sentimentality in the final prayer, which is an attempt to rewind the reel of history rather than play it through. Nevertheless, both this and 'Nugent' are among the very few political poems written in Irish under the strain of the northern crisis which manage to be political and yet remain poems. Others have generally opted for the easier, and fashionable, strategy of calling down a plague on all public worlds and celebrating instead the intensities of the personal life. One is left with the impression that nationalism, perhaps because there was so much of it in the bad poetry of previous generations, is deemed radioactive – so much so that it cannot be condemned, or praised, or even mentioned at all. No poet of the *Innti* generation would echo the hopeful simplicities of Ó Direáin:

> I dtír inar chuir filí tráth
> Tine Cásca ar lasadh,
> Ní lastar tinte cnámh
> Ar árda do do shamhail . . .
> Is abair nuair is caothúil
> Gur dhí na céille an galar
> A bhí ar na móir atá marbh
> Anois nuair nach mairid
> Ní heagal duit a nagairt.

> In a land where poets once
> Put Easter fires ablaze,
> Bonfires are not lighted

On hilltops for your like . . .
And say when it is convenient
That stupidity was the illness
Which beset the great ones who are dead.
Now that they are no longer living,
You need not fear their challenge.

The irony is that these words were addressed to those younger poets, who, for the most part, have politely refused to be drawn into such debates.

For some younger writers, 'politics' is a debate not about hunger strikes and dirty protests, but atom bombs, US foreign policy and the cost of living. In 'The Harlot's Secret' the most common poetic strategy of our time is followed by Declan Collinge, as the private resolution of a prostitute to live respectably on the money earned by her memoirs rocks the composure of bishop and politician. For this generation, all isms are wasms; and frequently it is only the labyrinth of sexual relations which can evoke a truly complex poem. National ideals, where they survive, can only be treated tangentially; and so Collinge's poem on the bald eagle in Philadelphia Zoo seems to discern in the decay of one republic the fate of another. Caitlín Maude's 'Vietnam Love Song' is even more resolute in its avoidance of all public worlds:

the hawk hovering in the air
awaiting the stench of death

and in its, by now suspect, assurance that private havens may be found in an otherwise heartless world:

we could stay on the field of slaughter,
but the sad faces of the soldiers
made us laugh
and we chose a soft place by the river.

Rarely enough is there any recognition of the fact that the personal refuge may itself recapitulate all the distortions and wickedness of the outside world. Far more typical is Maude's option for the soft place by the river, in whose depths the unconscious may be plumbed, and by whose shores the self may be dramatised. Perhaps all this is predictable enough, for even an intensely political poet like Yeats, after his writings on the civil war, never again conceived of happiness in social rather than domestic terms.

It is only in the work of Seán Ó Ríordáin and Máirtín Ó Díreáin – both, significantly of an older generation which started out in the 1940s – that there is any extensive attempt to chart the links between the private and public world. By another curious paradox, this is achieved by these most lonely and most private of men. Their poems are based on the notion that only the outsider-figure truly knows the values held by a community, whose members are always too busy living life to appraise, and therefore to possess, it. There is, says Ó Ríordáin, 'a local music / that its speakers do not hear'. As an isolate, Ó Ríordáin is filled with contempt for mass-culture, where freedom turns out to be the freedom to be like everybody else and true freedom is a bleakness which very few can endure. On the other hand, however, he envies the Gaeltacht community which he visits its apparently effortless achievement of communal value:

> The love of my heart I'll give to people
> to whom nothing has appeared
> but other's thoughts.

But there is no final relief to be found in the Gaeltacht, either. Like Synge, the poet feels himself a mere 'interloper'; and, anyway, the community is revealed as a degenerate fiction, a myth which has been exploded. The 'Gaelic community' is a zone for tourists, but not a recognisable place where anyone lives.

A remarkable number of poems in the volume do, indeed, take the form of spiritual tourism of one kind or another – Ó Ríordáin in Mount Mellery (anticipating Heaney's *Station Island* in tone and theme by decades), Ó Muirthile in Maoinis, Collinge in Philadelphia Zoo. The impression is given of the world – and especially Ireland – as a gigantic open-air museum, in which remnants of the past can be examined by a process of instant archaeology. The past, like art, exists as just another item to be consumed; and, since nothing is more remote than the recently abandoned past, nothing is treated with more ferocity.

The official pretence – that there was still a sizeable Irish-speaking community in the Gaeltacht – was exploded by Desmond Fennell at the end of the 1970s; and he himself returned to a Dublin where most of the poets were already trying to gear Irish to a post-Gaeltacht, post-industrial, post-Christian, post-everything society. Davitt's jibe at the 'céad míle fáilte' (hundred thousand welcomes), offered to the incoming visitor by the Irish Tourist Board, took the form of a hundred and one farewells offered to the few post-inflationary visitors and departing emigrants; but such nose-thumbing could not conceal the fact that the Irish were virtual tourists in their own country now. The same material greed which priced Irish holidays out of the international market had served also to erase centuries-old traditions. Thatched cottages were abandoned to ruin, as hacienda bungalows rose up in their stead, with names like 'South Fork' and 'High Chapparal'. So rapid were the changes that the native Irish themselves began to take the place of absent foreign visitors, in an attempt to exhume on a fortnight's holiday their all-but-buried past. Tourist slogans which, a generation earlier, might have been beamed at a British or American audience, were now directed at the Irish themselves: 'Discover Ireland; it's part of what you are.' Significantly, the latter phrase had already been used in government promotional campaigns for the Irish language. Some city boys, like Ó Muirthile in Maoinis, or even Behan, in an earlier generation, on the Blaskets, were beguiled for a time by such pastoralism; but a majority endorsed the war against the past.

So, in *Entreaty*, Caitlín Maude implores her man not to impose any past pattern of Celtic lovers (Diarmaid and Gráinne) upon the present fact:

> do not speak
> o 'Diarmaid'
> and we will be
> at peace.

The rejection of 'literature' and of literary stances is a recurrent theme, along with the suspicion that there is corruption at the very heart of beauty. The latter, of course, is an ancient Gaelic notion, to be found in the legend of Deirdre, who threatened to destroy her beauty in order to thwart the besotted king who tried to kill her lover. Even more notable is an awareness of the past as a burden rather than an enrichment. Áine Ní Ghlinn's 'Racial Pride' concedes that the cry of ancestors, though it may tear us apart, must be kept alive, and not because that cry is a sign of self-confidence but because the only alternative is a grey, dreary meaninglessness. Culture thus becomes a self-confessed tautology by which, in Eliot's terms, we rejoice in being able to construct something upon which to rejoice.

We fear to pay the full costs of our debt to the past – as we fear the steady gaze of Nugent – and yet we also desire to clear the bill once and for all, lest our refusal to do so constitute an allegation against ourselves as well as our ancestors. Not all, of course, are so tender towards the tradition. The continental poet Apollinaire once said that you can't lug the corpse of your father around on your back for the rest of your life; and so Davitt can call for a clean slate, creation *ex nihilo*:

> We will singe our barren bards
> in a bonfire
> and scatter their ashes
> on the mildew of tradition . . .

though it must be added that he is equally dismissive of Marxist notions of political determinism:

> We will bid farewell
> to the historic train
> that goes astray.

Creation out of nothing is, in the end, impossible and a Gaelic poet may burn his bards only to find himself reaching for the writings of Joyce, Keats, Wordsworth or whomever. Gaelic poetry has always enjoyed a living connection with European art, from the age of *amour courtois* to the versions of Catalan by Pearse Hutchinson; and that, in turn, has been complicated, as well as enhanced, by the growing American connection. If Seferis and the Greeks lie on the shelves of Seán Ó Tuama, or the love-poets of France on the mantelpiece of Máire Mhac an tSaoi, then John Berryman lies alongside the collections of local folklore which animate the muse of Nuala Ní Dhomhnaill. Pop-art and Bob Dylan may inform a lyric by Davitt or Collinge; Kavanagh and Bronislaw Malinowski may inspire Mícheál Ó Siadhail; Eliot's human voices may awaken Caitlín Maude to a whole series of American accents, the most detectable of which is Emily Dickinson's:

> the loss of
> Heaven
> is the worst Hell.

seems to echo

> Parting is all we know of Heaven
> And all we need of Hell.

There is a Keatsian ring to her 'sweeter still / is the word / that was never uttered'.

There can be no doubt, however, that the major influence is Joyce, most palpable in the work of Ó Ríordáin, far and away the leading poet of the period. Like Joyce's, his mind was saturated with the symbols of the Roman Catholicism which he had learned to reject; and, like Joyce, he put the repudiated terminology of theology to use in evolving a personal aesthetic theory. If Joyce spoke of 'epiphanies' as moments of sudden spiritual manifestation, Ó Ríordáin wrote of the 'beo-gheit' which leaves us sacramentally 'fé ghné eile' (under a different aspect). If Joyce annexed the Eucharist for his *epicleti*, Ó Ríordáin stole the notion of 'Faoistin' (confession) and 'Peaca' (sin), reworking these words until they became artistic terms. Joyce's surrender to 'the whatness of a thing' is recapitulated in Ó Ríordáin's desire to achieve 'instress' with his objects. Thus, for Ó Ríordáin in his poems, *I* becomes *Thou*, and every seeming opposite is revealed to be a secret double. Turnbull becomes his horse, and the horse Turnbull; a woman's eyes are reborn in her son's; male blends with female, the poet with his *anima*; and, of course, if Yeats's English poems are also a part of the Gaelic tradition in 'translation', then Ó Ríordáin's may, with equal validity, be seen as an experiment with the English tradition. There are times when creation *ex nihilo* seems to this particular poet but a polite phrase for the process of pillaging English:

> A Ghaeilge im pheannsa
> Do shinsear ar chaillís?
> An teanga bhocht thabhartha
> Gan sloinne tú, a theanga?
>
> An leatsa na briathra
> Nuair a dheinimse peaca?
> Nuair is rúnmhar mo chroíse
> An tusa a thostann?
>
> O Gaelic in my pen
> Have you lost your ancestry?
> Are you a poor illegitimate,
> Without surname, o language.
>
> Are the verbs yours
> When I commit a sin?
> When my heart is secret,
> Is it you who are quiet?

The poet who began by writing sprung rhythms in imitation of Hopkins finally concedes that his ideas are often stolen from the very language which he seeks only to escape:

> Ag súrac atáirse
> Ón striapach allúrach
> Is sínim chugat smaointe
> a ghoideas-sa uaithi.
>
> You are escaping from
> The foreign harlot
> And I proffer to you the ideas
> Which I stole from her.

The chauvinism underlying the word 'harlot' may offend some; but in general terms, these lines are a graphic illustration of the cultural trap described by Daniel Corkery as facing every Irish schoolchild in the 1920s and 1930s: 'No sooner does the child begin to use his intellect than what he learns begins to undermine, to weaken and to harass his emotional nature. For practically all that he reads is English . . . Instead of sharpening his own gaze on his neighbourhood, his reading distracts it.' Ó Ríordáin's poems bear palpable traces of his readings of Hopkins, Eliot and Wordsworth. In this context, Corkery's bitter attack on 'the want of native moulds' in Anglo-Irish writing seems extremely ironic, especially in view of his rather naive recommendation of the Irish language as the natural remedy for such a lack. The diagnosis offered by Corkery had been astute when he said of the aspiring poet that 'his education provides him with an alien medium through which he is henceforth to look at his native land'. But Corkery's mistake was to believe that Irish was, by some mysterious privilege, immune to the incursions of international culture and modern thought. Ó Ríordáin suffered from no such delusion, but steeped himself in post-Christian philosophy, thereby disproving not only the chauvinist theories of Corkery, but also the defeatist assertion of Thomas Kinsella that to write in Irish means 'the loss of contact with my own present . . . forfeiting a certain possible scope of language'.

Faced with the fact that most of his background reading was in English, Ó Ríordáin said that the best he could hope for was to de-anglicise the material in his imagination, under the imprint of the Gaelic mind. This may be feasible for those to whom the Irish language comes more naturally than does English, but, in the case of other practitioners, Ó Direáin has said that what they produce by this means is all too often neither good Irish nor good poetry. This is the double bind experienced most notoriously by Yeats who wished to be counted one with Davis, Mangan and Ferguson; but who conceded at the end of his life that he owed his soul to Shakespeare, Spenser and William Morris, because all that he loved – including a wife – had come to him through English. And this is the plight of a writer like Michael Hartnett who bade farewell to English, only to find, in due course, that language is inescapable. In a poem to his English wife, he writes:

> I abandoned English
> but never you:
> I have to hone my craft
> in a wood that's new;
> for my English grave
> is naked, barren:
> but I hope your day

of happiness is coming.
You'll have the silk of your heart one day,
We'll find us both our America.

That the option for Irish should culminate in a line which echoes John Donne is a perfect illustration of the constraints on the Gaelic poet.

So, although Anglo-Ireland and Gaelic Ireland may indeed have evolved quite separate cultures and traditions, they do, indeed, share what Conor Cruise O'Brien once called 'a common predicament'. It is thus quite proper to speak of Ó Ríordáin or Hartnett as Anglo-Irish authors, in the most literal sense of that term, for, just as much as Yeats or Synge, they also belong to a hyphenated literary tradition, with Gaelic and Anglo-Irish components. Apart from this common predicament, these writers share the sense of speaking for a dead tradition. The Gaelic poets, once dubbed 'voices from a hidden people', seem to speak, like the corpses in *Cré na Cille* or the voices in Beckett's trilogy, from the edge of the grave. Reading Ó Ríordáin, we have the sense of every lyric as a little death, when something of himself is expressed and lost, in a kind of grim rehearsal for death. In 'Mise' he seems to suggest that his splintered selves will only be fully reintegrated 'on our deathbed'. In the meantime, the poem is as near as he can get, but it remains a marginal gloss on an unlivable, unknowable life. Ó Ríordáin's is a sensibility whose plight is to have lived through the consequences of its own extinction, even before it had a chance to know the self that died.

Many Gaelic poets seek in silence an escape from the stain of sounds, while conceding that sound is all they have. Like Beckett, they know that the search for the means to put an end to speech is what enables discourse to continue. Caitlín Maude repeatedly asks her interlocutor not to speak, while her own lines grow shorter and shorter. Ó Direáin's 'Dínit an Bhróin' has the energy of its powerful reticence. Áine Ní Ghlinn, though verging on slack conversational prose, is actually a minimalist who equates caring with silence, loss with speech, and who follows Joyce in her predilection for the unfinished sentence. This is a technique especially appropriate to her world of echoes, filled by puzzling people who never quite constitute personalities, and personalities who never quite become characters. The trailing sentence is a fitting vehicle for people who can never quite become themselves.

This liminal state, of one who is neither dead nor living, neither poet nor proseperson, neither Irish nor English, neither male nor female, neither rational nor emotional, is the central zone of contemporary Gaelic poetry. Such destitution has its compensations, the most obvious being the opportunity it affords the poet to search for an absolute idiolect. The danger, of course, is of idiocy in the root-meaning of that word, of becoming a hopelessly private person who acknowledges no social debts.

Such boundary states, wherein both mind and body are annulled, are grist to the Buddhist's mill, for Buddhism, unlike the West, delights in contradictions. Gabriel Rosenstock has an Eastern relish for silence. He floods words with space, divesting them of all context and freeing them from their traditional moorings, in hopes of rediscovering their pristine value. On the principle that 'every word was once a poem', he produces vertical lyrics deliberately designed to slow down the reading or recitation. He deploys the techniques of meditation in a Beckettesque manner with an unfinishable sentence. If Ní Ghlinn's personae are half-constructed persons, Rosenstock's, in the main, do not even aspire to the bogus glamour of being dispossessed of personality. A sense of self is something they can gladly do without, for they are mystically large enough to contain multitudes. Genius here becomes not an identity, but a capacity to take on the identity of every person or thing that lives. The poem is less an artefact than a radiant absence, which implies but never achieves its true correlative in the real world, an authentic lyric. Like the Whitman who sent those who would understand him to the nearest drop of water, Rosenstock can advise us, in 'The Search', to find his poems in rivers, clouds, stars.

The boundary between me and not-me in such poems disappears, as the distance between text and world is drastically reduced. If the person is a part of speech, then speech is also a part of the person. The dream of the 1960s – the eclipse of all distance and distinction – is complete.

The dangers of such poetry are manifest in the notorious illnesses and early deaths of many American exponents, as well as in the vagueness and diffuseness of much of their literary remains. Davitt and Rosenstock share with Ginsberg and Corso a love of the list, an inventory of the endless opulence of created things. There is something very American about this exhibition of affluence. It can all too easily seem another case of conspicuous Western consumption rather than serene Eastern impassiveness in the face of the world's variousness; but, of course, there is adequate sanction for it in the lyrical lists and inventories of synonyms which characterise the Gaelic poetic tradition. At times, such lists may lead only to the banality parodied by Flann O'Brien ('I am a flower in the wind. I am a hole in the wall') or lambasted in Whitman:

> Over-Whitmanated song
> That will not scan:
> With adjectives laid end to end,
> Extol the doughnut and commend
> The common man.

The deeper danger of a poetry where subject becomes object, and all distinctions are obliterated, is the tendency to a deadly narcissism. This is less a problem for Davitt and Rosenstock than for some of their contemporaries. If Gaeilgeoirí have betrayed a fatal propensity to navel-gazing and to writing incessantly about the state of Gaeldom, then their poets seem, at times, incapable of writing about anything except the act of writing poetry. Where once the bards, or even the senior contemporary figures like Ó Direáin, Ó Tuairisc and Mhac an tSaoi could aim satiric barbs at a deserving enemy, now we are confronted by a gentler generation whose deepest wounds are self-inflicted. They find in art the source of their disease, as well as its diagnosis. Rosenstock's obsession with Billie Holiday is a tell-tale, as well as a brilliant, instance:

> You squeezed pain
> From the height of sweetness
> Sweetness
> From the height of pain.
> When you were raped
> At ten years old
> That was the first nail
> In the crucifixion of your race, your womanhood
> And your art,
> Till in the end
> Your own voice frightened you
> Lady in satin.

It could be as near as Rosenstock will ever get to writing 'An Ghaelig Mhilis Bhinn', for, in the fate of the jazz-singer he seems to read his own. If your own voice is so frightening, then perhaps it is better to be a phoney-man, a skull filled with echoes.

Yet the poem *is* powerful, precisely because it senses that self-hatred, rather than self-love, is the actual basis of such narcissism. It is less an example than an indictment of the illness which it diagnoses. If the signs of that illness were apparent even in some of the most powerful Gaelic poems of the previous generation, then the cure may be found in the uncompromising self-criticism to which such self-scrutiny finally leads. James Joyce once complained that Gaelic enthusiasts did not care what banalities a writer uttered, just as long as he uttered them in their precious language; but today's Gaelic poets are strong and brave enough to insist on the most candid of criticism. They stake their claim as artists rather than as Gaelic-speakers. That they should be the first generation in the twentieth century to do this gives them, and us, infinite grounds for hope.

FURTHER READING

Gabriel Fitzmaurice and Declan Kiberd, eds., *An Crann faoi Bhláth: The Flowering Tree – Contemporary Irish Poetry with Verse Translations*, Dublin, 1991 (1994).
Máirtín Ó Cadhain, *Páipéir Bhána agus Páipéir Bhreaca*, Baile Átha Cliath, 1970.

CHAPTER 8

On national culture

(2001)

Frantz Fanon's account of *libération* in the third phase of decolonisation was anything but detailed in outline, perhaps because it was more a utopian inference than a recollection of lived experience. The dream of creating *ex nihilo* a new species of man or woman, capable in inventing themselves rather than being the effects of others, was too easily assumed to be about to become a reality.

A major reason for this may be found in Fanon's *déraciné* status: he grew up in Martinique, thinking himself French and white, only to discover that he was a West Indian to those whom he met after his arrival as a student in Paris. Thereafter, he lost all sense of local particularisms (a phrase he used with contempt in *The Wretched of the Earth* to describe the nationalist phase). According to the Tunisian writer Albert Memmi: 'Fanon's private dream is that, though henceforth hating France and the French, he will never return to *Négritude* and the West Indies . . . never again set foot in Martinique.' In that, he had much in common with early writers of the Irish Renaissance such as Oscar Wilde: for Wilde was another instance of the colonial intellectual who came to the metropolitan centre only to discover that he was Irish, not English, and who evolved there a vision which, lacking local specificity and addressing itself more to an English than an Irish audience, found in the end 'an equal welcome in all countries'.

In both writers' texts, there is a dramatic sense of struggle with inherited form, a sense of the artist submitting to received forms with an over-determination that verges on parody or downright disavowal. Wilde's hilarious mimicry of the well-made play is a little like Fanon's use of Hegel and Sartre. In either case, the writer adopts the protective coloration of a prestigious 'European' mode, and then proceeds to improvise within it a little space for his own expressive freedom. The same techniques were adopted by Yeats, as he subjected the Shakespearean form to the disruptions of the Cuchulain cycle. Equally, the tension so often set up by Yeats between the title of a poem and its following text provides a blatant example of this battle with available modes, a mockery of the expectations accompanying the poem which he announces but then refuses to write in works like 'The Second Coming' or 'Easter 1916'.

The rationale for all this was announced by Wilde when he said that one's first duty in life was to adopt a pose, and what the second was nobody had yet found out. By this formula, a writer slipped into an available persona or mode in hopes of learning something new about himself. Such a strategy was similar to the adoption of the apparatus of the coloniser in Fanon's second phase. Central to Fanon's analysis, however, was the assurance that this was nothing but a transitional playing out of adolescent roles: a moment would come, however delayed, when the masks were set aside to reveal the face beneath.

For many intellectuals, the act of writing, of imagining oneself in somebody else's shoes, became a prelude to revolution. So, by a rather obvious paradox, it became necessary for people to wear a mask as a precondition of finally disclosing a face.

The first mask was that of the *assimilé*: and Wilde's example existed to prove that it need not be abject at all, for the mask could be worn with a mockery that shaded into insolence. If the representatives out in the occupied territories were often the rejects of the imperial culture back home, sent to impersonate those types they had manifestly failed to be, then they were already found in a state of high anxiety upon arrival. This was one reason why the English, wherever they went, gave the impression of a people forever at play, eternally acting an over-the-top drama called *Mad Dogs and Englishmen*.

A further reason was detected by Fanon as the fundamental contradiction of the colonial mission: any successful attempt to erase the 'difference' of the natives, either by extermination or assimilation, could only result in the erasure of the category coloniser. The master created the slave, observed Fanon in a sly parody of Hegel, and the slave in turn defined the master: for the master to abolish the native was to do away with the very grounds of his own being. The ambivalence of feeling which ensued led to the familiar wavering in government policy. The 'natives' couldn't be ruled by out-and-out coercion (for in that case the raw underlying reality of the imperial mission would be clear to all), nor could they be completely assimilated (for then the very grounds of difference would be ceded). The native was expected to ratify the ruler's self by emulating it, but whenever he refused to pander to this narcissistic fantasy, he could be brutalised to such a degree that he would seem far more different in the end.

The historian Richard Ned Lebow has contended that the invention of the stereotyped 'Paddy' or 'Sambo' allowed for a negotiation of these anxieties, insofar as these figures provided targets for the approved release of aggression. The notion of an idle, lawless, superstitious Paddy, for example, protected an administrator from a knowledge likely to cause stress, that knowledge of the discrepancy between Christian avowal and colonial practice, or, repeatedly in the Irish context, between the official goal of reconciliation and the frequent outbursts of martial law. This stereotype had the merit of allowing a relationship: but, according to Lebow, it left its authors in a perceptual prison which blinded them to the turn which events were taking. Hesitations revealed in the official personality could be exploited by natives astute enough to mimic *either* the ideal Englishman each was supposed to become *or* the hopeless Paddy/Sambo each was held actually to be. Wilde turned in the former performance, as has been shown, and the experience of the younger Senghor, teaching perfect French to the most able French children, provided another instance: generations of natives did the latter, pretending to be the kind of person their masters believed them to be. In Fanon's famous description of the consciously play-acting 'nigger' may be noted a tell-tale excess of energy, a parody of over-determination which raises similar suspicions. The 'extravaganza' mounted by J. M. Synge in celebration of a patricide in *The Playboy of the Western World*, and framed by his reservations about factitious eloquence, seems a rather *literary* instance of the technique: but it may be found also in the very different world of political detainees under interrogation, as Edward Said reported of a famous exchange between an Israeli policeman and a Palestinian suspect: 'the ideological mufflers of the interrogator's mind are so powerful as to shut out any alertness to the Palestinian parody of terrorism: each line he speaks repeats and, by rhetorical overkill, overdoes what his interrogator wants from him'.

This type of 'answering back', taking on the protective coloration of approved, official forms, could not easily be detected as such, much less punished. Once adopted in a strategic encounter with the occupier, it could take on a momentum of its own among the people, who often developed a tendency to return to one another, with minor alterations, a version of what the interlocutor had already said: for the guardedness of conversation in a colony was legendary. It was a device often deployed in India, as the acute ear of E. M. Forster received it. At the garden party in

A Passage to India, even those English ladies who wish to know the land and people better are frustrated by the refusal of the local women to reveal themselves. Instead, the Englishwomen come up against 'the echoing walls of their own civility', and this in a book where snakes are seen to adopt the same sort of protective mimicry to secure themselves from human attack. That book's central epiphany is the famous echo from the Marabar Caves, the symbolic point being, as one Englishman recognises, that though the original sound of English people at home is always good, the echoing falseness which they induce in themselves and their subjects in a colony is bad. That echo could come in two ways: as the abject deference of the *assimilé*, or in the polar defiance of the nationalist.

The stereotype of the native, 'as anxious as it is assertive', has been compared by Homi Bhabha to the sexual fetish. The fetishist's mastery of the Other, he recalls, is no sooner asserted than it is lost, in a perpetual act of displacement.

The fetishism and the mimicry led to the creation of a native who was almost English but never quite so, what Bhabha jokingly calls 'not quite/not white'. As well as feeling ratified by this apprentice straining so visibly to be like themselves, the colonisers felt more often threatened and mocked: for if the impersonation could be so easily and so nonchalantly done, then the fear was that it was only that, an act which concealed no real essence in the coloniser himself. Interestingly, T. E. Lawrence reported that the English tended to regard imitation as parody, where the French preferred to take it as a compliment.

The more like the master the native became, the less willing was the master to accept the presentation: and that unease, disabling enough for an administrator out in Africa or India, took on an extra terror in the neighbouring island of Ireland. In 1860, the novelist Charles Kingsley went through just such a process of identification and disavowal in post-Famine Connaught, a pathology complicated by the fears so recently unleashed by Darwinian evolutionists, and he wrote a letter home to his wife:

But I am haunted by the human chimpanzees I saw along that hundred miles of horrible country. I don't believe they are our fault. I believe there are not only more of them than of old, but that they are happier, better, more comfortably fed and lodged under our rule than they ever were. But to see white chimpanzees is dreadful; if they were black, one would not feel it so much, but their skins, except where tanned by exposure, are as white as ours.

Even more remarkable was the returned Indian civil servant who met Horace Plunkett in the west of Ireland in 1891 and confided in him that he could not bear to treat the Irish 'like white men'.

What unnerved such visitors was the moment when 'the look of surveillance returns as the displacing gaze of the disciplined, where the observer becomes the observed'. In that instant, the movements of disavowal which attended the master's performance were repeated and even magnified in those of the subject, for mimicry 'emerges as the representation of a difference that is itself a process of disavowal' (disavowal by the master of the ideal type he is supposed to represent, by the colonised of that which is represented). It was 'a sign of the inappropriate'. The onlooker had to guess at the native's hidden intention, much as English administrators tried to figure out the meaning of the ever-changing Irish Question, or as English audiences struggled to decipher the latent meanings in experimental Irish texts. It was but a short step from the recognition that the observed could turn observer to an awareness that the natives might have an alternative set of criteria, by which their masters could be judged vain, foolish, even weak.

In short, there was locked into the colonial culture 'an insurgent counter-appeal', which every so often had caused members of the garrison to go over to the other side, or at least to remember that they also had a country. Each of these defectors – and they began as far back as Jonathan Swift – discovered at some point that they were the effects of a flawed colonial mimesis, 'in which to be Anglicised was *emphatically* not to be English'. Hence, Douglas Hyde's famous appeal to the Irish that, since they would not or could not be English, they should not be anglicised, but instead throw in their lot with the native culture. Otherwise, they would be mere mimic-men, pitiful illustrations of that famous minute of Lord Macaulay which recommended that a class of interpreters be placed between the English and the millions whom they governed, native in blood but 'English in tastes, in opinions, in morals and in intellect'.

Homi Bhabha's investigation of such mimicry is subtle and deft, but he carried it even farther to argue that the truly unnerving element of this encounter was its revelation to the occupier that he had no self, no identity at all, and that the mimicry engaged in by coloniser and colonised alike was structured over a painful absence. In other words, there was *only ever* a mask, which existed to conceal the absence of a face. To the native, the suggestion that the centre of meaning was always elsewhere seemed normal, but to the master this was frightening stuff: the knowledge, reported by Joseph Conrad in *Heart of Darkness*, that there might be no authority whatever behind his performance. Such a model has its attractions and indeed a certain beauty at the level of theory, but what it describes at this point is not the way that history happens. There is in the world an English personality-type and a countervailing native identity which, even though it cannot always define itself for interviewers, can nonetheless feel its own oppression. Its tragedy is to suffer, while not retaining any assured sense of the self that is suffering. Nor could Bhabha's model account for such phenomena as Ashis Nandy's revolutionary feedback (already discussed), or for the refusal of the rebels described by Fanon and Said to be broken under interrogation. Some part of the self in all these models remains untouched by oppression: and this may even be true of Bhabha's own protagonist – for what self opts to perform the mimicry which he so devastatingly describes? To suggest the workings of an agency without a subject, as he does, is to impute to the colonial encounter a randomness which anyone still caught up in it will find hard to credit.

In Ireland, mimicry eventuated in two traditions: a political resemblance called nationalism (which tended to repeat old models) and a literary movement dubbed Irish modernism (which tended to subvert them). In either case, such mimicry returned the initiative to the colonial subject: and this allowed writers to disrupt the master-narratives of the neighbouring island with their own secret knowledge. It was at this juncture that many began to contemplate what Fanon, decades later, would describe as the liberationist phase.

FURTHER READING

Bhabha, Homi. 1994. *The Location of Culture*. (London: Routledge.)
Fanon, Frantz. 1973. *The Wretched of the Earth* (New York: Ballantine Books.)
Foster, E. M. 1962. *A Passage to India* (Harmondsworth: Penguin.)
Kingsley, Charles. (1890) 1901. *His Letters and Memories of His Life*. Edited by his wife (London: Macmillan.)
Lawrence, T. E. 1993. *Lawrence of Arabia, Strange Man of Letters: The Literary Criticism of T. E. Lawrence*. Edited by Harold Orlans. (London: Cranbury, N. J.: Associated University Presses.)
Lebow, Richard N. 1976. *White Britain and Black Ireland: the Influence of Stereotype on Colonial Policy*. (Philadelphia: Institute for the Study of Human Issues.)
Said, Edward. 1986. *After the Last Sky*. (London: Faber and Faber.)
Synge, J. M. 1968. *The Playboy of the Western World in Collected Works*. (Oxford University Press.)

CHAPTER 9

White skins, black masks: Celticism and Négritude

(1996)

The late nineteenth- and early twentieth-century programme of cultural decolonisation in Ireland is an important precursor of a related struggle in Africa more than forty years later. Undoubtedly England's only European colony differed from imperial territories in Africa, most obviously as a result of Ireland's centuries of enforced intimacy with England – an intimacy based on proximity and affinities of climate, temperament and culture. And while Europe's race for empire in Africa occurred in the latter half of the nineteenth century, England had occupied Ireland for more than 700 years. Thus at the time of Irish decolonisation, the imperial culture had penetrated far more deeply than in Africa or Asia. Despite such differences, however, the shapers of modern Africa (as well as India) looked on occasion to Ireland for guidance. But if Ireland once inspired many leaders of the 'developing world', today the country has much to learn from them.

In spite of episodic involvement with India's decolonisation, Irish nationalists and writers were slow to identify with other resistance movements, preferring to see their own experiences as unique. Moreover, a strain of white triumphalism, running from John Mitchel to Arthur Griffith, would never countenance Irish solidarity with the anti-imperial struggles of other racial groups. And although many nineteenth-century Irishmen, serving in the British army, had assisted in the conquest of India and Africa, the English colonisers imputed many of the same qualities to natives in these remote territories that they were attributing to the Irish.

A comparative cross-cultural study identifies significant similarities between the Irish experience and that of other emerging nations. In addition, post-colonial theory from Africa, India or the West Indies provides useful interpretation of Irish resistance, a movement less richly theorised than later decolonisations. In both Ireland and Africa, for example, the central role of the artist was to question the assumption that culture arises only when imperialists arrive. The comparable roles of an alienated urban elite in African and Irish nationalisms, similar debates about the role of native languages, and parallels between cultural movements like Celticism or *Négritude* (arising in French Africa) reveal how native cultures the world over contain, in the words of West African polemicist Amilcar Cabral, the seeds of resistance.

In Ireland, anti-imperialism emerged in different stages, often creating an identity merely reactive to that imposed by the ruling colonial class. Thus if England characterised its subject people as imaginative, childlike or feminine, political nationalists, in reaction, created a hyper-masculine identity. The limitations of Celticism (and *Négritude* in Africa) emerge from its sources in such a binary opposition to imperial definitions, a reaction with origins in a sense of inferiority rather than in a vision of liberation. However, Irish cultural nationalists – such as Douglas Hyde, through his founding of the Gaelic League in 1893, or William Butler Yeats in his early poetry – sought to create alternative modes of expression for a nation struggling to invent an autonomous identity. Hyde's project of de-anglicisation, as well as Yeats's use of fairy lore and Gaelic saga material in his early poetry, drew on an explicitly Irish cultural memory. Both writers, although never moving from cultural nationalism to political resistance, emphasised returning to the sources of a national identity. Like John Millington Synge, Hyde and Yeats avoided a narrowly anti-British focus of a politicised Irish-Irelandism, even as they provided the cultural basis for liberation.

This process pioneered by Hyde and Yeats had followers also in Africa. The subtle programme of cultural freedom mapped by Amilcar Cabral, the scourge of Portuguese colonialism, was one that 'without underestimating the importance of positive accretions from the oppressor' (Cabral, 43) found in native culture the seeds of resistance. Because the conquest of Africa had been confined to major cities and their immediate hinterlands, the urban middle class there seemed to have assimilated the new codes, which led its members foolishly to consider themselves superior to their own people (very much in the manner of Ireland's 'Castle Catholics' and 'West Britons'). Outside of these centres, the influence of colonial codes was much weaker: for the peasants in the African countryside, the question of a return to the source did not arise (Cabral, 61), since the fount was intact. It was among the 'marginal' petit-bourgeoisie, caught painfully between the vast masses and the tiny group of foreign rulers, that the pressure was felt in the form of estrangement and disorientation.

A frustration complex was soon established in those who felt the need to question their marginal status and to dream of a return to native traditions. This return was very like the programmes mapped out by Hyde, though in Africa there may have been economic factors at work too. In Ireland, as in many African states, an educated elite had emerged, not all of whose members could be employed in the imperial administration: these individuals – 'anglicised' in Ireland, 'Europeanised' in Africa – came to conclude that as long as the colonial occupation continued, they would remain marginal. A moment came when members of this elite rejected further assimilation and turned back to their own culture, hoping to create a new society and to attain the wealth and status previously denied them by the imperial and native codes. To Amilcar Cabral, therefore, it came as no surprise that movements like Pan-Africanism (based on the assumption that all black Africans have a common culture) should have been propounded first by educated black thinkers outside of Africa (62–3). The first Pan-African Congress had been convened in London in 1900 and it was addressed by W. E. B. Du Bois, a leader of the black movement in the United States.

By no great coincidence, in the same period a Pan-Celtic movement (based on a unitary theory of the 'Celtic personality') held similar meetings in London and other cities. As early as 1856, the French critic and ethnographer Ernest Renan had written of the Breton Celts in his *The Poetry of the Celtic Races*, contrasting the barbarous warmongering of the Teuton with the imagination, justice, loyalty and humour of the Celt. A decade later, Matthew Arnold made these ideas current in England with a lecture on the study of Celtic literature; and in 1891 the London writer and publisher Grant Allen could seriously contend that the Celt was responsible for most of the intellectual movement of England (267–71). After 1900, the Pan-Celtic Congress evoked a mixture of amusement (Synge lampooned it in a playlet), thoughtful support and nervous opposition.

The Gaelic League at first found it difficult to decide what policy to follow. Hyde and his younger, more radical colleague in the League, Patrick Pearse, adopted the line that would be taken on Pan-Africanism by Kwame Nkrumah and Léopold Senghor, future leaders of Ghana and Senegal, respectively, who believed that strength could be found in numbers. But hard-line Irish-Irelanders, led by the prose fictionist and language activist Father Peter O'Leary, declared for a specific Irish essence and against 'the Pan-Celtic humbug'. O'Leary alleged that *An Claidheamh Soluis* was 'possessed of a dumb devil' (McCartney, 47) on the subject. It was even rumoured that Pearse, the magazine's editor, while visiting Wales as a representative of the League at the Eisteddfod, had partaken of a toast to the Queen during a Pan-Celtic lunch. Synge mocked the Pan-Celts for holding their congresses in great cities rather than in the countryside, among the peoples who actually spoke Celtic languages; and a somewhat similar complaint was made against the Pan-Africanists by Cabral for their removal from the masses in whose name they propounded their theories.

Cabral insisted that the 'return to the source' could never in itself be an act of struggle, being simply a rejection of the pretended superiority of foreign culture. Unless it actively contested foreign domination, a movement was 'of no historical importance' (63), the point made by Pearse in his final breach with Hyde. The reassertion of traditional identity by a minority of the native middle class would cause another minority in that group to make noisy assertions of the identity of the foreigners, warned Cabral. But it was the paradoxical nature of the resistance that struck him most strongly: the intellectual who returned to the source remained, on the one hand, subject to daily humiliations and insulting jibes by the ruling elite and, on the other, painfully aware of the injustices endured, often half-consciously, by the masses. Even though this liminal group was a product of colonialism, it also produced from within its ranks the forces to dismantle it. In this manner, V. I. Lenin's Marxist analysis of the revolutionary nature of the lower-middle class in *What Is To Be Done?* found itself applied, with only minor inflections, during the process of decolonisation.

Cabral was quick to point out how much more slowly a national (as opposed to a class) revolution would proceed: liberation movements seeking to form new nations were trying to achieve in a few years something that in Europe had taken centuries. Cabral told an American audience that the people of the United States were still trying to decolonise their minds even two centuries after independence; and he warned of the dangers when such peoples take over without modifying the forms inherited from the occupier: 'For example, we must not use the houses occupied by the colonial power in the way in which they used them' (84). This was also true of literary forms and of political structures such as the apparatus of the state, that last and most seductively ambiguous gift of the occupiers. Failure to solve these problems was 'the secret of the failure of African independence' (84).

The Martinican poet and anti-colonial propagandist Aimé Césaire concurred on that point, if on few others: the problems of Latin America, one hundred and fifty years after independence, proved that 'the fight against colonialism is not over as fast as one thinks, nor *because*

imperialism has suffered military defeat' (157). His analysis was less econ-
omistic than Cabral's – and somewhat more Yeatsian. He agreed that
'national sentiment generally survives in the most immediate and also
most obvious fashion . . . among the common people', but he felt that it
required the 'man of culture' (154) to fashion and discipline it into
appropriate artistic form. Césaire did not suggest that the artist literally
invented the nation or created the sentiment: rather it was a case of the
artist finding a satisfying expression. 'And by the very fact of its being
expressed, and therefore brought to light, this expression itself creates
or dialectically recreates in its own image the sentiment of which it is
by and large the emanation' (154). People invented – or rather were – their
own nation; it was simply the task of the artist to solve the problem of
form, and this would never be easy. Where Yeats had to complain
of 'three sorts of ignorance' and Synge of the 'cruder forces' latent in
Irish-Irelandism, Césaire observed, 'there is never a paucity of national
sentiment: there is only an insufficient number of men of culture' (154).

The value of the writer lies in the challenge art implicitly poses to a
colonial hierarchy, for the artist ceases to be a *consumer* and becomes a
creator instead. This was a disruption as radical as any challenge to the
master–servant relation, and so 'the colonizer can only look with suspicion at all indigenous artistic creation' (Césaire, 155). Césaire's insights
may explain why Irish artists, like their African and Indian counterparts,
often found their early audiences among liberal well-wishers in the
imperial cities of the 'home countries', for out in the remoter provinces
officialdom had set its face against them. To the artist fell the task of
restoring the disrupted continuum and of questioning the conceit that
culture and history began only when the invader arrived. In so doing, he
or she should assert that the people's is a 'sacred literature', their art 'a
sacred art' (Césaire, 160). This was a resolutely Yeatsian prescription,
based on the notion that races identified themselves by a mythology that
married them to rock and hill.

By far the most vivid debates among African writers would be
prompted by the later theory of *Négritude* (see Arnold, 21–103). *Négritude*
arose among those peoples who had been colonised by the French and
whose writers usually worked in the French language. The analogy with
conditions in Ireland at the start of the twentieth century is actually
closer than any between English-occupied Africa and Ireland would
be – simply because the French in Africa (like the English in Ireland)
sought to assimilate the natives to their own culture, whereas the English
in Africa tended to leave the native cultures intact. Léopold Senghor,

the Senegalese leader, taking his cue from the Pan-Africanists, defined *Négritude* as 'nothing more or less than what some English-speaking Africans have called the African personality' (179). He did not find anything suspect or degrading in this definition from without rather than from within: it appeared to him, and to others, as the inevitable product of a liminal group, but it was nonetheless 'the sum of the cultural values of the black world' (179). His own intellectual exemplars were Europeans like the philosopher Henri Bergson, who taught that scientific matter was nothing unless animated by intuition, and the palaeontologist–priest Teilhard de Chardin, who denied the old Cartesian split between matter and spirit.

This anti-materialist philosophy recalled that of Yeats, not least in its insistence that matter was but 'a system of signs which translates the single reality of the universe: . . . an infinitely large network of life forces which emanate from God' (Senghor, 185). The distrust of analytic philosophy, a philosophy which had led to the crass polarities of urban versus rural, male versus female, spirit versus matter, led Senghor to the rejection of art as an activity separate from society. He despised a self-enclosed art with a capital A, preferring the Yeatsian ideal of arts that combined together again into a popular craft, 'a social activity, a technique of living, a handicraft in fact' (189). The connecting tissue was to be *rhythm*, the source of Negro beauty (191) – just as 'an indefinable Irish quality of rhythm and style', in keeping with Gaelic poetic tradition, was sought by Yeats (255). This was to issue in an anti-representational, even supernatural art, which moved on its trajectory to a moment not of analysis but of participation, away from photographic realism or empirical impressionism. Senghor, who was a student in Paris in the 1930s, conceded that *Négritude* might seem at moments like surrealism, but he distinguished between the abstract, European variety and the more physical, intuitive African kind. He was supported in this by the Martinican poet Césaire and by Léon Damas, a Guyanan writer.

The limits of such an analysis had already emerged with some clarity in the case of Celticism: its fatal willingness to take the coloniser at his word and convert every insult into a boast, leaving his basic categories of thought unchallenged and unmodified. Yeats's happy acceptance of a Civil List pension from the British government, like Senghor's pride on being nominated to membership of the Académie Française, might be taken as a sign of such capitulation, though the very offer of recognition was even more likely an attempt by the authorities to challenge their potency as separatist influences. By its slot-rolling psychology, *Négritude* could reinterpret every shameful attribute of the black in a more positive light. It carried entire peoples from abject self-hatred to overweening chauvinism, and this acted as a discouragement to critical self-analysis. There were some traces of such thinking in the earlier work of Yeats, as I have shown in the early section devoted to the poet in *Inventing Ireland*. A sedulously cultivated Irishness, invoked either for blame or for praise, but deemed quite distinct from the rest of humanity, was a dubious blessing, even if it was a necessary and inevitable phase through which a people had to pass en route to freedom. The problem was that, in its failure to disrupt the inherited categories of thought, *Négritude* submitted to the very binarism which Senghor wished only to challenge. Thus the French existentialist Jean-Paul Sartre would eventually (in *Orphée Noir*) dub it 'an antiracist racism' (qtd Bishop, 144), and the Ghanaian government would, rather comically, commission a poem entitled 'I Hate *Négritude'*.

To invert, rather than abolish, colonial hierarchies would never be enough: it was the intellectual equivalent of Cabral's nightmare that the former houses of the colonialists would be reserved for new, elitist African occupants. To plant a free people's flag on the old apparatus would achieve nothing but the ongoing disempowerment of local communities by a monolithic administration in the capital. The corresponding identity, whether calling itself *Négritude* or *Irishness*, would simply remain a label *to have* rather than a way *to be*. Such a national sentiment could easily contain the seeds of some future imperialism, for that was how the models of the European nation–state tended to see their eventual evolution. In the words of the philosopher of history Wolfgang Mommsson, 'they all preached the doctrine that true nationalists . . . had to become committed imperialists, since the possession of an empire was an essential precondition for the free development of one's own national culture in time to come' (34). Though Yeats could never have countenanced such thinking, other Irish leaders, like Arthur Griffith, the founder of Sinn Féin, did, and many modern African rulers suffered similar delusions of grandeur. The nation–state that many took over was seen as an apparatus that encouraged a psychology of domination and dependence, and it often replicated those relations in its own dealings with greater powers.

In consequence, a nationalism which remained caught in this chauvinist phase could not only lapse into racism but become itself a tool in the subjugation of a people, and so bring about the very negation of its own original impulses. Mood-swings between self-abnegation and self-assertion would be a feature of much post-colonial public opinion, as if people were trapped in a posture of perpetual adolescence, whose features were sketched early by the satirist George Moore: 'the Irish do not know themselves, but go on vainly sacrificing all personal achievement, humiliating themselves before Ireland as if the country were a god . . .' (qtd Mansergh, 259). The self-doubt, which lay not far beneath the surface of national chauvinism, was detected by Mary Colum, a leading Irish literary critic domiciled for some years in the United States, who noticed on return visits that Dublin newspapers continued to refer to 'The Irish poet, Mr So-and-so' . . . 'as if', she sardonically noted, 'there was something rather peculiar about being an Irish writer in Dublin' (69). Moore's answer to this was almost penitential in its rigour: 'It is the plain duty of every Irishman to dissociate himself from all memories of Ireland – Ireland being a fatal disease, fatal to Englishmen and doubly fatal to Irishmen' (qtd Mansergh, 259).

To Senghor, such thinking was too abstract, too dialectical for comfort. Peoples had fought for independence to recover, defend, and illustrate their personalities, as he put it, and no sooner had the right to such selfhood been won than the militants were being asked to give it away. For his part, however, Senghor might have been accused of forgetting the original purpose of independence: the expressive freedom of the individual. There were moments when he seemed to forget that a culture exists so that a people can express themselves rather than a people existing to provide illustrations (a tell-tale word, that) of a culture. When black radicals contended that an inferiority complex lay at the root of *Négritude*, Senghor grew impatient with his critics:

the same word cannot mean both 'racialism' and 'inferiority complex' without contradiction. The most recent attack comes from Ghana, where the government has commissioned a poem entitled 'I Hate *Négritude*' – as if one could hate oneself, hate one's being, without ceasing to be. (179)

In his high idealism, Senghor could not understand that racism was indeed an attempt to cope with an inferiority complex, the fear of one's mediocrity, yet this process should have been clear to any student of colonialism. Briefly, the process works as follows: the racist invents the enemy to relieve himself of the laborious task of self-authentication. Instead, he defines himself by others, by a strategy of consolatory mechanisms, which tell him that if others are taking the idea of 'Ireland' or 'Africa' from him, then those ideas must belong to him. Only by virtue of such an inferiority complex does the racist function as such. In that respect, he resembles the colonisers, for if the objects of their contempt were destroyed, they too would be destroyed. Their vital need, often erotically charged, is for the very enemy they dream of exterminating. It was from such an analysis in his *Anti-Semite and Jew* that Sartre derived his idea of an anti-racist racism, of a nationalism that annuls itself (13–46).

The young men and women who followed Senghor could never have suspected that in his proud message might lurk the makings of a new colonialism; a generation that had been raised to despise its own skin and to censor its own utterances found in the countries of the white man *émigrés* from their own lands expressing themselves with verve in the language of the masters. Senghor, in the Paris of the 1930s, enacted for African intellectuals a role similar to that played by Yeats for Irish artists in the London of the 1890s – and with similar results. The notion of Ireland as the sole saviour of spirituality in the modern world would be replaced, in due time, by the contention that only *Négritude* could save the soul of mankind from crass commercialism. Such hopeful simplicities had a corrective and polemical value, but they were degradingly dependent on the very stereotypes they inverted – and could not satisfy subtle minds for long.

The debate concerning nationality and cosmopolitanism in literature, which had so exercised the Irish at the start of the century, would be taken up with full rigour in Africa. The Nigerian playwright Wole Soyinka, addressing his fellow artists at a Lagos conference, was utterly dismissive of *Négritude*: 'a Tiger does not shout about its Tigritude' (qtd Bishop, 151). By way of reply, Senghor's friends contended that the tiger, being among the most powerful of animals, had never been denied its natural expression, and some understandably asked if the analogy was not even more degrading than the one its author set out to expose. 'A tiger does not have to proclaim its tigritude', they said, 'but Africans have proved their ability to think in abstractions. And that is why they can, and the tiger cannot, proclaim their *Négritude*' (qtd Bishop, 152). Even in this statement, however, the desire to establish that Africans could think may have seemed to some caustic observers a rather humble, possibly abject, goal. Nonetheless, in his essay on 'The Failure of the Writer in Africa', Soyinka performed a useful service in exposing the mediocrity of many exponents of Africanness, whose simple-minded conformity to 'cultural definitions' encouraged sentimental well-wishers in European capitals vastly to overrate their achievements and value (135–8).

The professional Celt, who had once made lucrative rounds of the London publishing houses, now had a counterpart in the professional

Negro who strode the boulevards of Paris and New York. The problem
with *Négritude*, as Soyinka saw it, was that it tried to return to Africans
something that they had never lost: an identity. The fascination with the
past of Africa was bogus: it was, deep down, a fascination of the writers
with their own power over it, but the only past worth encountering was a
past still dynamic, still pressing, still coexistent in present awareness. 'The
myth of irrational nobility, of a racial essence that must come to the
rescue of white depravity, has run its full course', Soyinka believed; and
he concluded with a bitter rebuke to the *Négritude* school: 'It never in fact
existed, for this was not the problem but the camouflage' (141). A concern
for national mythology or social mores must give way to a response by
every writer to this 'essence of himself'. To such a point had Yeats come
when he, too, renounced nationalist imperatives for the task of 'expressing
the individual' – indeed, those who portray him as moving at this point
from a 'Celtic' to a more 'Irish' note might see in this an anticipation of
Nkrumah's move from the Pan-African to the Ghanaian.

Early twentieth-century calls by sceptical liberal critic John Eglinton for
writers to make not an Irish but a human literature now found many
echoes in African demands for a humanist universalism. Yet the old
nationalist conceit of saving civilisation persisted, as Soyinka sourly noted,
in 'a call to the bridge, to bring about the salvation of the world by a
marriage of abstractions' (141). The sad fact was, he insisted, that not a
single French writer had yet sent out a call for rescue to the black artist.
(Strictly speaking, this wasn't true: many French surrealists from André
Breton onward had turned to African art for inspiration, just as many
English writers had felt jolted into modernity by the works of Yeats and
Joyce. But it was a salutary warning against the delusions of messianism.)
These strictures led the theorists of *Négritude* to become more humble
and more precise in their claims: no longer did they dream of a recover-
able past, admitting now that the past is always at the mercy of the
demands of the present moment. They also began to concede that there
were no essentially negro themes, that the element of *Négritude* was a
matter of style rather than substance. More subtly still, they confirmed
what Yeats had long asserted: that style was recruited in the search for,
rather than in the definition of, a personality, and that such a search was
'the very thing that makes the artist' (Kiberd, 115–16). The problem with
Négritude was its assumption that the search was over. The modern
African was a product of history, landscape, climate, a being as adaptable
as any other, and a *Négritude* that museumised a people's past as over and
done with was no better than a tourist's cliché.

The Senegalese poet David Diop shrewdly remarked on the link between *Négritude* and the commodification of native traditions for the benefit of the visiting international bourgeoisie. It seemed to him bleakly apt that an idea spawned in the *salons* of Europe should find its way back to its luxuried sponsors in the form of African *kitsch*: 'Believing he is "reviving the great African myths" to the excessive beating of the tom-tom and tropical mysteries, [the artist] in effect gives back to the colonial bourgeoisie the reassuring image it wants to see' (qtd Bishop, 162). Such a museumisation committed the native intellectual to endless apologetics, to endless demonstrations that there really *was* a native African culture, rather than to its actual modernisation and development. Soyinka, on the contrary, could see culture as a perpetual becoming and the past as necessarily flawed rather than uniformly admirable: something neither to be fetishised nor erased, but sifted for those vital elements that might be adapted in the future. In a sense, what Soyinka wanted was a restoration to history of the openness that it once had before the onset of colonialism; for him history begins not when the occupier comes but when he leaves.

The critique of *Négritude* by radical thinkers has been overemphasised, to the point where figures like Senghor and Sartre have been presented as utterly opposed. Senghor's vision has been taken to be an account of a timeless African personality and Sartre's of a historical agent who set out on the long march to freedom in a non-racist world order. Senghor, however, was fully aware that most of the theories of race which Europeans had evolved were the basis for hatred and consequent injustice, but this did not finally discredit them in his eyes: difference need not lead to subjugation. Moreover, Senghor never really intended to turn the clock back to a past, pre-invasion Africa: rather he wished to tap the genius that informed his people's traditions and to make it current again in modern African society. Like some of the Irish leaders, he believed that the native genius could evolve its own characteristic forms of everything from socialism to lyric poetry (Irele, 73). His socialism, for instance, relied on the communal nature of African society, emphasising the group rather than the individual, but distinguishing itself from European socialism in its high regard for spiritual values, including the conviction that man is more than the effects of his material conditions. His notion of culture was often misrepresented by simplifying critics, but its basis was a civilisation, a structure of feeling and thought that allowed to a people a certain manner of expressing itself, an idea of a sacred art produced by a people alert to the numinous all around them. Moreover, though Sartre came to see *Négritude* as a process to be transcended, he never questioned its value as a phase in which to rehabilitate the victims of oppression. Nor would he have been unduly worried by its critique of the limits of the analytic philosophy of the European Enlightenment. That critique had been mounted, even as the Enlightenment was still forming, by Edmund Burke and the thinkers of the Celtic periphery; and many 'Third World' philosophers have simply taken up where Burke and Hume and Berkeley left off.

What did dismay many was Senghor's totalising project, his assumption that black people in all continents and societies would share in a unitary African personality. But what might be true for his Senegalese citizens would not necessarily pass muster for a Ghanaian, much less a black New Yorker. And if geography offered one kind of challenge, history suggested another: that the African personality was not timeless, but the outcome of conditions likely to be found in any society where rural traditions were challenged by the onset of modernity. The sheer number of echoes and overlaps between Celticism and *Négritude* should be proof enough of that. Senghor and his friends were not exactly reinventing the wheel: but they were inventing a wheel, their own wheel, which might easily enough have been attached to an Irish or an Indian carriage as it carried its occupants to freedom.

FURTHER READING

Allen, Grant. 'The Celt in English Art'. *The Fortnightly Review* (Feb. 1891), 267–77.

Arnold, A. James. *Modernism and Négritude: The Poetry and Poetics of Aimé Césaire.* Cambridge, Mass.: Harvard University Press, 1981.

Bishop, Rand. *African Literature, African Critics: The Forming of Critical Standards, 1946–1966.* New York: Greenwood Press, 1988.

Cabral, Amilcar. *Return to the Sources: Selected Speeches by Amilcar Cabral.* Ed. African Information Service. New York: Monthly Review Press, 1972.

Césaire, Aimé. 'The Responsibility of the Artist'. *The Africa Reader: Independent Africa.* Ed. Wilfred Cartey and Martin Kilson. New York: Random House, 1970, pp. 153–161.

Colum, Mary. *Life and the Dream.* Dublin: Dolmen Press, 1966.

Eglinton, John. *Anglo-Irish Essays.* Dublin: Unwin, 1917.

Irele, Abiola. *The African Experience in Literature and Ideology.* London: Heinemann, 1981.

Kiberd, Declan. *Inventing Ireland: The Literature of the Modern Nation.* Cambridge, Mass.: Harvard University Press, 1996.

McCartney, Donal. 'Hyde, D. P. Moran and Irish Ireland'. *Leaders and Men of the Easter Rising: Dublin 1916*. Ed. F. X. Martin. London: Methuen, 1967, pp. 43–54.

Mansergh, Nicholas. *The Irish Question*. London: Allen and Unwin, 1965.

Mommsson, Wolfgang. 'Power, Politics, Imperialism and National Emancipation'. *Nationality and the Pursuit of National Independence*. Ed. T. W. Moody. Belfast: Appletree Press, 1978.

Sartre, Jean-Paul. *Anti-Semite and Jew*. Trans. George Becker. New York: Grove Press, 1962.

Senghor, Léopold Sédar. '*Négritude*: a Humanism of the Twentieth Century'. *The Africa Reader: Independent Africa*. Ed. Wilfred Cartey and Martin Kilson. New York: Random House, 1970, pp. 179–92.

Soyinka, Wole. 'The Failure of the Writer in Africa'. *The Africa Reader: Independent Africa*. Ed. Wilfred Cartey and Martin Kilson. New York: Random House, 1970, pp. 135–42.

Yeats, William Butler. Letter to the Editor. *United Ireland* 17 Dec. 1892, in *Uncollected Prose*. Vol. 1. Ed. J. P. Frayne. London: Macmillan, 1970, p. 255.

CHAPTER 10

From nationalism to liberation

(1997)

For most of the nineteenth century, and for some time before that, England and the English had been presented to Irish minds as the very epitome of the human norm. Only with the onset of the Irish Renaissance did it begin to become clear that, far from being normal, England's was an exceptionally stressed society, whose vast imperial responsibilities were discharged only at an immense psychological and social cost. In some ways, the invention of modern Ireland had far more in common with the state-formation of other European countries such as Italy or France. In other respects, the analogies – especially in the domain of culture – would be with the emerging peoples of the decolonising world. The debates about language revival, like the arguments about nationality and cosmopolitanism in literature, anticipated those which would later be conducted in Africa and Asia, just as Pan-Celticism seemed to resonate with Pan-Africanism. One abiding difference, however, which left the Irish experience unique, was the sheer proximity of the imperial power, as a not-always-appreciated model, as a source of ideas, and as a market for surplus theories and labour. Also important was the significant number of Irish persons recruited into the imperial service overseas, as Joyce acidly noted in his passage about examination results in *A Portrait of the Artist as a Young Man*.

The revivalist myth of the Irish as 'a people like no other race on earth' militated against the comparative method. Being the first English-speaking people this century to decolonise, the Irish were doomed to walk in relative darkness down a now-familiar road. Even when some comparisons were finally made by such intrepid analysts as Joseph Lee, they were cast mostly in terms of smaller and middle-sized countries of Europe. It may be useful, therefore, to widen the angle of vision somewhat and analyse movements in Ireland that prefigured those in the 'developing' world.

The value of nationalism was strategic rather than inherent; it helped to break up the self-hatred within an occupied people, which led them to dream of a total, seamless assimilation to the colonial culture. Aimé Césaire called this assimilation *bovarisme*, because it reminded him of a Martinican chemist who wrote lyric exercises that won prizes at the Toulouse Games from judges who did not even realise that their author was a man of colour (Césaire, 73). Such undetectability was abject, yet, in a different, deeper sense, it would become a hallmark of the post-*Négritude* phase of Martinican writing, when a new sort of universalism might replace the imperial model.

In the opening assimilationist phase, however, it became a point of honour with the colonial author that the white audience could read his book without guessing his skin colour. The obsessive quality of such a desire was manifest also in the exaggerated correctness with which many natives spoke the occupier's tongue and wore his clothing, and in the anxiety of parents to raise children who could do these things even more convincingly. In Hocquet, Léon-Gontran Damas portrayed a Guyanese mother berating her son for not speaking 'le français de France / le français au français / le français français' (qtd by Innes, 15). From his Kenyan perspective, Ngugi Wa Thiong'o recalled how this policy was implemented in schools, where children caught speaking Gikuyu faced an experience similar to that of the tally-stick in nineteenth-century Ireland:

A button was initially given to one pupil who was supposed to hand it over to whoever was caught speaking his mother tongue. Whoever had the button at the end of the day would sing who had given it to him and the ensuing process would bring out all the culprits of the day. Thus children were turned into witchhunters and in the process were being taught the lucrative value of being a traitor to one's immediate community. (Ngugi, 11)

In Ireland, of course, children studied even more assiduously how to become traitors to themselves. For centuries, the English had not tried especially hard to teach the natives their language, because language (in the absence of a different skin colour) served to distinguish ruler from ruled. The occupiers were content to make the natives ashamed of their own language, with the result that the Irish learned English mainly from one another and from books. Nonetheless, the effect was self-estrangement, the sense, reported by Ngugi, that 'the language of my education was no longer the language of my culture' (11).

The breaking of that harmony meant nothing to the colonisers, who had already experienced the split between nature and nurture themselves; indeed, they may have accepted it as one of the sophisticated pleasures of a post-Renaissance world that they hoped in time to share with the natives.

The Irish cultural critic Daniel Corkery seized gratefully on Eliot's notion of a 'dissociation of sensibility' to recount the split between reading and the lived experiences of the child in nineteenth-century Ireland. His famous diagnosis bears a striking similarity to Ngugi's account of how 'the language of the African child's education was foreign' (17), with the result that thought itself took the visible form of a foreign language; the written language of school became completely divorced from the language of the home. Such disorientations, far from making people confident, actually bred in them a sense of inadequacy, reinforcing their conviction of 'their inability to do anything about the forces governing their lives' (Ngugi, 56). For those, however, who assimilated so fully that they grew into the adopted mask, a measure of poise was possible, albeit at a terrible psychic price. Writers of such a kind were fearful of experiment or innovation, of attempting any form that was not already deeply respected and sanctioned by the occupier culture. This gave to their productions an archaic tone, a resolutely antiquarian tinge, yet the strain of maintaining this pretence was immense – out of all proportion to the benefits that accrued – and thus it could not indefinitely last.

Négritude was the predictable, polar response. As Césaire later explained: 'Since there was shame about the word *nègre*, we chose the word *nègre*', in order to wear the taunt as a badge of pride. Such a surging-out of repressed feeling was uncontrollable when once released: 'All the dreams, all the accumulated rancour, all the formless and repressed hopes of a century of colonialist domination, all that needed to come out and when it comes out and expresses itself and squirts bloodily, carrying along without distinction in the conscious and the unconscious, lived experience and prophecy, that is called poetry' (Ngugi, qtd in Arnold, 126). The danger there is the assumption that one had only to express a native culture to become a poet – a conceit common to Irish revivalists, who used to say that if Gaelic were translated word for word into English, then the inevitable result would be poetry. Only a foreign ear could have found such deviations from the standard 'poetic', or, at any rate, an ear long attuned to the accents of the colonialist. From the outset, there was something short-term, something not fully convincing, about this manoeuvre. Bernard Shaw's warning in *John Bull's Other Island* about dreams anticipated many African warnings about the way in which fantasies of a 'return to the source' may take such a hold on a people that the reality is often submerged beneath their dreams.

The psychiatrist Frantz Fanon thought that all this had a 'hysterical element', of a kind to be found in patients who respond reactively to categories imposed by another, and who try in consequence to be as opposed to that other as it is humanly possible to be. Hysteria of that sort might take many forms, from stories of raising the dead to the deification of criminals and murderers. Most notable in this phase, said Fanon, was 'the will to be a nigger, not a nigger like all other niggers, but a real nigger, a Negro cur, just the sort of nigger that the white man wants you to be' (*Wretched*, 178). The English, by easy analogy, were perfectly happy to find the Irish just the sort of 'bucklepping', gallivanting rebels they had always proclaimed them to be, the rebel being one reassuringly familiar kind of Irishman whom the liberal, book-buying English had taken fatally to their hearts.

Such a phase had, nonetheless, a cathartic value; as the novelist Chinua Achebe observed, *Négritude* was a prop that could eventually be thrown away, but for its duration the artist needed 'to announce that we are not just as good as the next man but that we are much better' (*Hopes*, 30). It promised adherents something of the clarification afforded by the intermediate stages of psychoanalysis: those moments of dawning lucidity, between illness and health, when the repressed contents of a psyche are dragged back into consciousness. This was one way of challenging those *bovaristes* who had refused to recognise the extent of their own alienation; Césaire took the Freudian method and applied it with imaginative daring to the community rather than to individuals. He rejected the reductionist Marxist analysis of colonialism as a consequence of the capitalist search for materials and markets, and linked all this back to the much more complex question of racism.

In literary terms, Césaire's celebration of a writing that would disrupt European narratives was quite at variance with the realist modes then favoured by even the more developed Marxian artists. 'I became a poet by renouncing poetry', he explained in an interview: 'Poetry was for me the only way to break the stranglehold the accepted French form held for me' (66). This was done by surreal effects, which shook up every norm, dredging up a repressed Third World of the mind. All this struck Césaire as a return to pagan energies that had been denied by a Christianity arrogant enough to equate itself with civilisation, 'from which there could not but ensue abominable colonialist and racist consequences' (11). Such an account may also explain the paganism espoused by Irish writers such as Yeats and Synge, and the repeated debates between Oisín and St Patrick in revivalist writings, which assume all the intensity of a battle between orality and print culture, pristine codes and colonial discourse.

Writing generated in this way was not an entirely free activity, but a rather desperate attempt to do two things at once: to renovate a national consciousness while opening a space in a sub-category of the master's literary history. Césaire's relation to surrealism re-enacts, in many ways, that of Yeats to late English romanticism; the Frenchman's use of African techniques may be compared to Yeatsian pastoral, the espousal of which was immensely consoling to those English readers who found, surviving in Ireland, a peasantry all but erased in their own country. The loneliness of such a position was felt by the decolonising artist and by the political leader too: 'To an unprecedented extent', writes Benedict Anderson, 'the key early spokesmen for colonial nationalism were lonely, bilingual intelligentsias unattached to the sturdy local bourgeoisies' (30).

The resistance movement always had to adapt itself to the behaviour and character of the colonial power, and the danger was that, in submitting itself to an already loaded language, the revolution would be taken away from people even as they performed it, and taken sometimes by the very weapons they chose for the fight. Those zealous Irish-Irelanders who shouted about 'Gaeilge Ghaelach' (Irish Irish) in *An Béal Bocht* (*The Poor Mouth*, 1941) were simply the mirror image of those *assimilés* who talked in Guyana of 'le français français'. The insistence of the imperialists on a standardised language would lead new nationalist regimes to compel children to learn an artificial, homogenised version of Irish, unrelated to any living dialect, but a fitting riposte to the complaints of Professor Atkinson about the lack of a standard language (see Tomás Ó Fiaich, 'The Great Controversy', in *The Gaelic League Idea* (Cork, Ireland: Mercier Press, 1972, 67 ff.)); and it led many teachers to beat children at the end of the day for speaking English, as their ancestors had once been beaten for speaking a native language.

An overweening nationalism, which based itself on the lie that its people were better than any other, could learn from its enemies only what Achebe called 'the art of conquering without being in the right' (*Hopes*, 35). The Irish disappointment has been tracked already in the imperial images that insinuated themselves into Yeats's Easter Rising poem (Kiberd, 113–14). As long as a significant part of the implied audience for such writing was in the occupiers' home country, nationalism would remain a damage-limitation exercise rather than a real platform for freedom, an exercise in apologetics rather than in self-authentication. It failed fully to embrace the resilient, unseen inheritance in native cultures, yet at the same time it confirmed many ancient stereotypes of native 'soul' and 'rhythm'. Soyinka devastatingly parodied it as a sort of down-market Cartesianism: 'I feel, therefore I am' (speech at Lagos, Nigeria, 1964). His joke about tigritude implied his hope for a writing that would be branded neither by racist clichés nor by their programmatic refutation.

The fabled puritanism of Irish nationalists had a counterpart in African movements in ways that suggest it may have been far less rooted in Jansenist Catholicism than its critics seem to have thought. The dread of obscenity among Synge's audiences or Joyce's printers makes sense, if it is understood as rooted in an anxiety not to appear coarse to those in the colonial power who are adjudicating the national claim. Some Irish people even felt squeamish about seeing their own place names and slang words committed to print – as Joyce observed in 'Gas From a Burner' – but this feeling did not prevent them from continuing to use such terms. It was the apologetic character of the revivalist phase that led to such extreme responses, responses that (like the theatre riot at the *Playboy*) had the effect of convincing administrators that the natives were not yet ready for self-government. The title of Yeats's collection *Responsibilities*, published in 1914, becomes all the more poignant in that context.

Most of these reservations about national revivalism must have been in Frantz Fanon's mind when he began his critique of *Négritude* with the corrosive slogan: 'after the great white error, the great black mirage' (qtd in Arnold, 96). He wrote them out at length in *The Wretched of the Earth* (1967) and to devastating effect. Fanon describes the history of such movements as falling into three phases: the colonial, during which artists mimic the occupier culture; the national, in which movements like *Négritude* assert that 'black (or green) is beautiful'; and the liberationist, in which the binaries are exploded in a sort of Hegelian synthesis. (The fact that Hegel had written insultingly of Africa did not prevent the eclectic Fanon from using his categories.) Fanon's description of the secondary period, during which 'old legends will be reinterpreted in the light of a borrowed aestheticism and a concept of the world which was discovered under other skies' (*Wretched*, 179), might seem to account for many texts of the Irish revival. It would explain the strange blending in *The Shadow of the Glen* of Aran folk tale and Latin Quarter decadence (which so troubled Arthur Griffith), or Yeats's re-creation of Cuchulain as a sort of Celtic Hamlet (which so distressed Patrick Pearse). Fanon claimed that the second-phase writer stamps such texts with a hallmark that he wishes to be national but that is, in fact, strangely reminiscent of exoticism.

This indictment is sadly similar to Yeats's strictures on the failure of the Young Ireland poets to do anything more than clothe their thoughts in ungainly foreign garb; his famous injunction to Synge to learn Irish (after Yeats had returned from a fruitless 1896 trip to Aran, where he was stymied for lack of the language) makes sense as his attempt to cope with this very crisis, a crisis that he and Synge would solve. Yeats's solution was a disciplined attempt to purge his idiom of all exoticism, while Synge in *The Playboy of the Western World* became at once Irish exoticism's greatest exponent and foremost critic, moving from the 'poetry talk' of Act 2 to the terse, cutting eloquence of the conclusion. Indeed, what remains most striking about Fanon's categories is not their mechanical rigidity so much as the sense in which they trace, in their very transitions from one phase to another, the inner development of so many major artists through their careers and, indeed, the inner movement of certain classical texts of decolonisation.

Fanon's analysis was much more subtle than his verbal energy made it seem; here was no prescription for a return to the source, but a celebration of hybridity that brought his dialectic to a triumphant synthesis. He chose to broadcast his programmes on Radio Fighting Algeria in French rather than in any native language; every French sentence until that moment had been an order, a threat or an insult, and so he wished to challenge those associations (*Dying*, 73). This move recalled the surrealism of Césaire, which became a weapon to explode received French and place in its stead 'a black French, an Antillean French that while still being French, had a black character' (Césaire, 67). Using points of departure in French, it would become 'a new language, one capable of communicating the African heritage', much as Synge had resolved on creating a bilingual weave out of an English as Irish as it was possible for that language to be.

This need was even more pressing in those African countries that lacked a single native language; Achebe spoke for them all in saying, 'I feel that the English language will be able to carry the weight of my African experience. But it will have to be a new English still in full communion with its ancestral home but altered to suit new African surroundings' (qtd in Ngugi, 11). The struggle to disrupt and remodel the received language was often a painful one, shadowed by feelings of colonial guilt and national apostasy. At the *Playboy* trials, for instance, Yeats apologised to the court for his scant knowledge of Irish, but much later in his life he was apologising to sponsors of an English tradition that he feared he had too often attacked. In making such attacks, he had denied a vital part of himself and so he confessed, quite late in the day, that he owed his soul to Shakespeare, Spenser, Blake and William Morris. His love tortured him with hatred, he explained, and his hatred with love. Achebe reported identical symptoms when he remarked in 1964 that 'those of us who have inherited the English language may not be in a position to appreciate the value of the inheritance' ('African Writer', 59).

It might uncharitably be said of such manoeuvres that they represent the twistings and turnings of a rudderless mind in search of an identity, a freedom that could have easily enough been found by a return to a native language. Nigerian radicals denounced the staging of a Soyinka play in English at their country's independence celebrations, on the grounds that only 1 per cent of the population could have understood it; when there are so many native languages, however (as Fanon found in Algeria), it may often seem wisest to use that of the occupier. Senghor, nonetheless, opted for French with what Ngugi called 'lyrical subservience', preferring its universal profile to African ties of blood. After such early optimism a certain jadedness set in, an uncertainty about whether, in choosing the European language, this group had chosen well. Faced with the disappointments of independence, many grew less sure of the merits of European languages, and the obsession with definitions of identity in their work indicated minds no longer clear about whose interests they represented. Like Shakespeare's Caliban, they had learned a new language, only to find themselves obliged to translate their own thoughts and feelings into an idiom that named them savage. Finding their identities consistently negated, they had to pinch themselves and ask, 'Who am I?' and in that questioning, they became objects even to themselves, viewing their very bodies through the implied eyes of the occupier. This splitting of the self afforded a certain bleak consolation, because it allowed the fiction that the real self was not undergoing humiliation (which, in turn, of course, led to a rather humiliating identification of the real self with the humiliator).

Nevertheless, it *was* possible to argue that it was no quality intrinsic to English or French that attracted writers like Yeats or Senghor, nor any essence of the native languages that eluded them, but rather that in the space opened between both codes, they might find the 'absent texts' that could harmonise both languages, the dream of a lost pre-Babelian harmony. That yearning would, of course, seem the more inevitable to those who had felt in themselves the split between the language of cradling and of schooling.

The bilingual weave evolved by Synge was a curious anticipation of Fanon's dialectic of decolonisation. The linguistic version of this dialectic has Irish ritually pulverising English, so that the Hiberno-English that eventuated is a code that has shaken free of all standardised subjugations. Another example might be found in jazz music, the creation of those black slaves shipped over to America who, deprived of their native instruments, took trumpet and trombone in hand and began tinkering. 'Is anyone going to say', wrote Achebe, 'that this was a loss to the world or that the first Negro slaves who began to play around with the discarded instruments of their masters should have played waltzes and foxtrots?' (*Hopes*, 60). It was no surprise, then, that James Weldon Johnson called for a Harlem Renaissance among black American artists based on the technique of Synge, 'in a form that is freer and larger than dialect, but which will still hold the racial flavour' (4).

Such Hegelian struggles, though they sound ferocious enough, illustrated what everyone caught up in them always knew: that two cultures, native and foreign, though they experienced moments of interpenetration, were always finally separated by the exploitation practised by one on the other. The nations that emerged from this battle of the shadows were fictions, imagined communities inserting themselves into the precarious zones between even more glaring make-believes.

The attractions of the Fanonite analysis are obvious, for it makes possible that golden moment when the negro or the native can appear in his or her human capacity, can in fact live to see the day when the very words 'negro' or 'native' fall into disuse. The peril lies in the assumption that this can be no sooner said than done. A movement that fails to work through its revivalist or nationalist phase may too hastily proclaim itself freed of all embarrassing local pieties in the name of some glorious universalism. The temptation to call a global humanism what is in fact a shallow cosmopolitanism assailed Achebe as it did John Eglinton, but the former, at least, was proof against it:

Africa has had such a fate in the world that the very adjective *African* can call up hideous fears of rejection. Better then to cut all the links with this homeland, this liability, and become in one giant leap the universal man. Indeed I understand this anxiety. But running away from yourself seems to me a very inadequate way of dealing with an anxiety. And if writers should opt for such escapism, who is to meet the challenge? ('Africa and Her Writers', 127)

The lesson is that if anyone tries to push history forward faster than it wants to go, history will give such a person a back kick. Africa in the early 1960s was filled with writers who longed soon to see the day when all monotonous talk of colonial wounds and cultural identity could give way to the sort of sophisticated irony that they thought possible to free persons. Yet for even daring to dream this dream and for organising an anti-government theatre, men like Ngugi woke up in jail. They began at that moment to learn that before it disappears, every class must first disgrace itself completely.

If the nationalist phase cannot be transcended until it has been fully worked through, it can, nonetheless, be subjected to rigorous critique by writers and artists. These often complain against its wish to make time stand still, to freeze everything in the state it was just at the moment of independence, so that the native elites inherit not a dynamic society so much as a post-colonial museum, in which the new rulers merely stand as custodians. In Salman Rushdie's *Midnight's Children*, a departing Englishman sells his estate for a bargain price to an Indian merchant named Ahmed Sinai on two conditions: that the sale be legally concluded on Independence Day and that, until then, every item of ornament or furniture be left exactly where it is:

'Tell me, Mr. Methwold,' Ahmed Sinai's voice has changed; in the presence of an Englishman, it has become a hideous parody of an Oxford drawl, 'why insist on the delay? Quick sale is the best business, after all?' (96)

The new Indian elites were bending over backwards to prove to the English that they could be trusted to do the same job in the approved English way; thus with every year of independence, Ahmed Sinai is observed to lose the darker pigmentation of his skin. The sheer effort of removing the occupier has proven so great that, in India as in Ireland, there was little left over for reimagining the national condition, and every new disappointment drained a little more colour from once-hopeful faces. Purchasing a period house, Rushdie's Indians effectively embalmed themselves alive.

This was the fear that gripped Aimé Césaire too, the dread of being petrified in the second, nationalist, phase: 'It is not a dead society we want to revive. We leave that to those who go in for exoticism' (31). To take over, without modifying, the old colonial forms was to submit to the one-directional ethnography that had Europeans perpetually studying natives, who were assumed to make no reciprocal observations. The ethnographer never for a moment considered that it might have been better to allow the natives to develop along their own lines, 'that it would have been better to let them fulfill themselves than to present for our admiration, duly labelled, their dead and scattered parts; that anyway, the museum by itself is nothing' (Césaire, 54). Such museumisation was not even a romanticisation of the culture by artistic souls from the ruling country. It was rather a last-ditch attempt to freeze it.

To Césaire the tragedy of Africa was not its belated contact with the rest of the world; it was, instead, the manner of that contact. The proof of this lay in the frequency with which the natives asked for roads, machines, heavy industries: 'it is the colonised who wants to move forward and the coloniser who holds things back' (Césaire, 25). Natives, so often accused of fatalism, now were suddenly being told that they were asking too much.

The fullest elaboration of this analysis was provided by Fanon. In his account, the revivalist comes onto the scene only very late in the day, to collect the despised husks of a culture that even most of the natives have largely cast off. The visiting Englishman Haines at the start of Joyce's *Ulysses* would be a telling instance, a man come over to Ireland to collect in his notebook the scraps of Gaelic and melancholy shafts of wit that still remain as potential cultural plunder for the metropolitan power; when material resources have all been extracted, a colourful culture of poverty may yield its own riches to be catalogued and exploited by the right taxonomist. Such admirers exalt native custom but only as the mummification of a culture; thus Joyce in *Ulysses* has the Orange headmaster Mr Deasy, a defender of the British connection, preside over a school that, with its glass displays of shells and ancient spoons, seems more like a museum. The young Stephen Dedalus, on the other hand, intent on renovating the consciousness of his race, happily treads the same shells and husks underfoot on Sandymount Strand as he searches for protean signatures; the revivalist, however, seeks only what Fanon sarcastically calls 'a knowledge which has been stabilized once and for all' (*Wretched*, 181). For the revivalist, culture is invariably something that was; for the liberationist, it is something that yet may be. Thus *Négritude* or nationalism runs the risk, at a certain danger point in its development, of sentimentalising backwardness and, in this way, of becoming a force opposed to its own original intentions.

Even well-meaning nationalist artists can find themselves drawn into endless, demeaning demonstrations of the fact that there *is* a native culture – an activity that is little better than taxonomy. In the midst of this distraction, artists often turn in good faith away from actual events of the contemporary struggle and toward the cast-offs of tradition. However, for Fanon as for Pearse, a national culture cannot be reduced to a folklore: 'to believe that it is possible to create a black culture is to forget that niggers are disappearing' (Fanon, *Wretched*, 188). The sudden, intense interest among intellectuals of the colonising power in conserving literary forms of the native tradition is not always as intelligent, or as altruistic, as it may seem; the more credulous are simply failing to recognize the new forms assumed in the experiments of writers like Joyce, while the more cynical are actively touting the 'native style' as a bulwark against just such innovation. The production in the early phase of national revival of large numbers of exotic, archaizing texts, filled with florid effects of eloquence, proves profoundly reassuring to the by-now-nervous rulers. The radical intellectual, therefore, wishes to move beyond these effects.

This was why, even in his early writing, Fanon predicted that *Négritude* would never be sufficient in itself, unless 'it serves to prepare the way for the synthesis or the realization of the raceless society. Thus *Négritude* is dedicated to its own destruction' (*Black Skin* 159).

FURTHER READING

Achebe, Chinua. 'Africa and Her Writers'. *Morning Yet on Creation Day*. London: Heinemann, 1975.

'The African Writer and the English Language'. *Morning Yet on Creation Day*. London: Heinemann, 1975.

Hopes and Impediments. London: Heinemann, 1988.

Anderson, Benedict. *Imagined Communities*. London: Verso, 1983.

Arnold, A. James. *Modernism and Négritude*. Cambridge, Mass.: Harvard University Press, 1981.

Césaire, Aimé. *Discourse on Colonialism*. New York: Monthly Review Press, 1972.

Fanon, Frantz. *Black Skin, White Masks*. New York: Grove Press, 1967.

A Dying Colonialism. London: Penguin, 1970.

The Wretched of the Earth. London: Penguin, 1967.

Innes, C. L. *The Devil's Own Mirror: The Irishman and the African in Modern Literature*. Washington, D.C.: Three Continents Press, 1990.

Johnson, James Weldon. *The Book of American Negro Poetry*. New York: Scribners, 1931.

Kiberd, Declan. *Inventing Ireland: The Literature of the Modern Nation*. Cambridge, Mass.: Harvard University Press, 1996.

Ngugi Wa Thiong'o. *Decolonising the Mind*. London: Heinemann, 1986.

Rushdie, Salman. *Midnight's Children*. London: Jonathan Cape, 1981.

CHAPTER 11

The war against the past

(1988)

The best women, like the best nations, have no history.

(George Eliot)

The greatest sin a man can commit against his race is to bring the work of the dead to nothing . . . We all hope that Ireland's battle is drawing to an end, but we must live as though it were to go on endlessly. We must pass into the future the great moral qualities that give men the strength to fight . . . It may be that it depends upon writers and poets such as us to call into life the phantom armies of the future.

(W. B. Yeats)

Just after the triumphant production of the play *Cathleen ni Houlihan* in 1902, W. B. Yeats wrote the above words. Like so many nationalists before and since, Yeats there seemed to extol the notion of the fight as a self-sustaining tradition, rather than the more humane idea of the culture fought for. It is the mark of many conservative thinkers to see in sacrifice not the highest price a man may pay to assert his self, but an end in its own right. Even more sinister is Yeats's implied view of the Irish Revival not as a restoration of personal freedoms but as bleak revenger's tragedy, in the course of which this generation will get even with England on behalf of Ireland's patriot dead.

This fatalistic view of history leaves little room for the autonomy of the person. In his dramatisation of the Deirdre legend, Yeats showed how slender are the resources of individual protagonists when pitted against the destiny embodied by the chorus. The play *Deirdre* opens with the first musician declaring:

> I have a story right, my wanderers,
> That has so mixed with fable in our songs,
> That all seemed fabulous.[1]

At first it seems as though the tale already has its final form, needing only to be narrated. The second musician yearns for that sense of an ending that will ensure her significance as a professional teller:

> The tale were well enough
> Had it a finish . . .
>
> (113)

But Fergus, the king's man, insists that history is still open. Deirdre and her lover Naisi *have* been forgiven, despite the terrible prophecy. Each time the first musician reopens her story on the appointed line – 'There is a room in Conchubar's house, and there' (115) – and just as often Fergus brutally cuts off the fated tale, asserting the rights of the individual to curve, or even break, the line of history. Yet even he too stumbles, almost against his better judgement, into piecing together the missing elements of the plot that he is so keen to abort. He recalls an ancient tale of how Lugaidh Redstripe and his wife played at chess on the night of their death. He conjures up a ghost from the very past that he seeks to escape:

> I can remember now, a tale of treachery,
> A broken promise and a journey's end –
> But it were best forgot.
>
> (117)

Yet he remains oblivious of the fact that Deirdre and Naisi seem about to re-enact that half-remembered story. Half-remembered, and for that very reason wholly to be repeated.

At this point in Yeats's play, the men are all agreed that ancient tales are the appropriate concern of terrified and superstitious women, while men alone have the courage to 'meet all things with an equal mind' (118). They have not reckoned with Deirdre, however – a woman who has already decided that she is both musician and tragic protagonist, both rebel and poet recording and extolling her rebellious act. It has often been remarked that whereas the men in the play are still intent on sorting out their relations to one another, Deirdre alone realises that the only crucial task remaining is to establish a fitting relationship with the chorus:[2]

> But I have one (she boasts)
> To make the stories of the world but nothing.
>
> (121)

There will still be moments when Deirdre is tempted to tamper with the fatal tale, as when she threatens to destroy the beauty that so dazzles and inflames the king; but, on that occasion, Naisi dutifully takes up the chorus line:

> Leave the gods' handiwork unblotched, and wait
> For their decision; our decision is past . . .
>
> (123)

Inevitably Fergus, the congenital interrupter, is himself interrupted by the king's message, which heralds death for Naisi and the betrayal of Fergus's precious trust. There is nothing left for the lovers but to put a brave face on things, so that the long-remembering harpers will have matter for their song. As they plunge to inevitable death, the phantom armies of the future will derive comfort from the inspiring story of how Deirdre and Naisi composed themselves in the face of the grave. Naisi nerves himself for his plunge into history by casting himself in a role from the ancient costume-drama of Lugaidh Redstripe:

> What do they say?
> That Lugaidh Redstripe and that wife of his
> Sat at their chess-board, waiting for their end.
>
> (124–5)

Deirdre is torn by conflicting impulses, between the desire for 'a good end to the long cloudy day' (125), which further affiliates her to the musicians who voice this need, and, on the other hand, a growing awareness of the dangers of playing like that 'cold woman' (125) of the old story. Whenever one of the lovers loses relish for the assigned role, the other coaches the offending partner in the stratagems of performance. Naisi advises; 'It is your move, take up your man again . . .' (126), just as Deirdre had coached the chorus to 'make no sad music' (125). Curiously, it is at the moments when the characters seem most resigned to the plot that the musicians grow restless with their assigned parts. The more Deirdre appropriates herself to the chorus, the more the musicians empathise with the characters caught in the web of events. The first musician effectively makes available the knife with which Deirdre will kill herself. She doesn't exactly give it, for Deirdre snatches it, but the impression is nevertheless created that, for all their human sympathy, the musicians need a shaped story and have a vested interest in giving history a shove. The first musician says:

> You have taken it,
> I did not give it you; but there are times
> When such a thing is all the friend one has.
>
> (127)

By this stage, both Deirdre and Naisi have resigned themselves to their roles in history, which are likened to a net that entraps the tragic hero; the more he struggles to free himself, the more enmeshed he becomes. In her own mind Deirdre has already passed beyond life, and she loiters only to ask the singing women what words they will find to praise her and Naisi. Like Hamlet breathing his last words to Horatio, she gives the first musician a bracelet and prophesies that many welcoming doors will be opened to her

> . . . because you are wearing this
> To show that you have Deirdre's story right.
> (127)

It is almost as if she decides to die, less a martyr to the king than to the literary tradition, which will derive sustenance from the tale of her death and inspire future lovers, as the tale of Lugaidh Redstripe inspired this pair, to repeat the deed, never as farce, but always as tragedy.

Many of the classic elements of the authoritarian personality are latent in Yeats's tragic protagonist – particularly the courage to suffer the decrees of destiny without complaint, but not the courage of trying to stop pain or, at least, to reduce it. 'Not to change fate, but to submit to it, is the heroism of the authoritarian character', says Erich Fromm in *The Fear of Freedom*. Fromm extends his analysis by showing that such a character worships the past, believing that what has been will eternally be. 'To wish or work for something that has not yet been before is crime or madness. The miracle of creation – and creation is always a miracle – is outside his range of emotional experience.'[3] It is, of course, hard for any man to love that which does not exist, and yet it is the very nature of true love to effect such a miraculous creation. A passing Samaritan, when faced with the broken flesh and bones of another's past, offers tenderness not really to the ravaged body so much as to the full person whom this very act of kindness will bring into being. It was for this reason that Simone Weil wrote that 'creative attention means really giving our attention to that which does not exist'.[4] What is true of individuals may also be true of the love one gives to a nation, so that a real patriotism would base itself not on the broken bones and accumulated grudges of the national past, but on an utterly open future. A true hero would thus be one who imagines future virtues, which would be admirable precisely because others could not conceive of them. In a land where the word *past* is interchangeable with the word *guilt*, the idea of an uncertain future has a liberating force, as much because it is uncertain as because it is the future. The theologians of liberation have, indeed, seen such heroism as the duty of every Christian person. Rudolf

Bultmann has gone so far as to redefine the sinner as the one who fears the future and desperately tries to forestall its coming.[5] Such a person – and Yeats was one – sees history not as the story of a people creating itself, but as a series of meetings with remarkable people, who turn out to be remarkable not for any individual qualities but simply and solely for their ability to submit, ostentatiously, to the approved patterns of the past.

Colonialism had denied the Irish personality the right to know itself. It was not surprising that those who suffered in consequence from a tenuous sense of selfhood should have prostrated themselves before apparently charismatic leaders. Unable to be self-sufficient, the colonised race nursed feelings of hatred for the authority that had so humiliated it. The way out of this crisis was to idealise some ordinary man as a superepitome of the history that was overtaking them all. Fromm's description of this process in Germany can be translated, with only a little straining, into Irish terms. The idealisation of the new leader harmlessly drained off the accumulated feelings of hatred, while the glamour surrounding the 'uncrowned king' converted the humiliation into intelligent obedience.[6] Hence, Yeats viewed nineteenth-century Irish history as the story of O'Connell and Parnell.

Unfortunately, the Yeatsian view of history inserted itself into the school textbooks. As an analysis it is, of course, not really historical at all, based as it is on a rupture of chronology by the endless repetition of familiar crises, with no hope of a resolution. It is in just such a context that the fight becomes more important than the thing fought for, and 'history' is deemed history only if it exactly repeats itself. New leaders may climb to power, but only if they have a gift for verbal repetition. In *Life Against Death*, Norman O. Brown points out that 'under the condition of repression, the repetition-compulsion establishes a fixation to the past, which alienates the neurotic from the present and commits him to the unconscious quest for the past in the future. Thus neurosis exhibits the quest for novelty, but underlying it, at the level of the instincts, is the compulsion to repeat.'[7] There could hardly be a more fitting description than this of the psychology of literary revivalism, or of its effect in reducing history to a narrative stutter tending towards infinity, in the manner of Christy Mahon telling his story six times since the dawning of the day, before leaving the stage to repeat his short, sharp, meaningless encounter in every other Mayo parish.

INTERNAL COLONIALISM

The situation is tragic rather than ludicrous because, even after the coloniser has gone, the obsessive pathology of repetitiousness remains, visible in the career of Eamon de Valera, the new Yeatsian leader. The paralysis that Frantz Fanon detected in certain newly independent African states also gripped 'independent' Ireland:

> The leader pacifies the people . . . unable really to open the future. . . . We see him endlessly reassessing the history of the struggle for liberation. The leader, because he refuses to break up the national bourgeoisie, asks the people to fall back into the past – and to become drunk on remembrance.[8]

This is doubtless the kind of thing that Conor Cruise O'Brien had in mind when he accused his countrymen of seeming intent on commemorating themselves to death. It is instructive, in this context, to contrast the behaviour of the Irish electorate in the 1930s and 1940s – which consistently re-elected ex-gunmen who talked repeatedly about past gun-play – with that of their counterparts in Britain, who unsentimentally disposed of Winston Churchill after World War Two lest his once-valued martial rhetoric come between them and a welfare state.

The Irish leader, on the other hand, was as lacking in a sense of self as the public that supported him. Revivalist leaders – and there are many in the world today – have no comprehensive programme. They desire not to lead but to occupy the position of leader. It is this very emptiness that gives them their charm, allowing them to reflect back to their followers whatever it is that the followers want to see. Karl Marx spotted such a figure on the world stage in the middle of the nineteenth century and wrote an essay about him entitled 'The Eighteenth Brumaire of Louis Bonaparte'. Marx regarded him as a comic buffoon who 'can no longer take world history for a comedy and so must take his comedy for world history'.[9] So, in the Irish parallel, the boy from Bruree must be the subject of endless radio broadcasts that remind listeners of his rise from humble country cottage dweller to shaper of a nation. That the nation is *not* being shaped is what this self-mythologising is designed to occlude – just as the Yeatsian hero dies for nothing beyond his own gesture of heroism, fights for nothing beyond the notion of the fight, and lives for nothing beyond his own place in literature. Confronted with each crisis of statecraft or economics, the new leader, like Deirdre and Naisi in the play, can do little but repeat the tale of his own apotheosis. The classic political career in 'independent' Ireland thus becomes a farcical repetition of Yeats's own progress, which began with a youth intent on reshaping an entire nation and ended with a besieged and weary old man merely defending an archaic sensibility. In such a culture, persons are judged on what they are – or more precisely on what they say they are – rather than on what they do. No wonder, therefore, that de Valera is best remembered for his sole witticism – that in most countries it doesn't matter what you say, so long as you do the right thing, but in Ireland it doesn't matter what you do, so long as you find the right formula of words.

It need not necessarily have been so. To restore to history the openness it once had, one has only to reread James Connolly's warning that the worship of the past was really an idealisation of the mediocrity of the present:

In Ireland . . . we have ever seized upon mediocrities and made them our leaders; invested them in our minds with all the qualities we idealized, and then when we discovered that our leaders were not heroes but only common mortals, mediocrities, we abused them, or killed them, for failing to be any better than God made them. Their failure dragged us down along with them . . . Our real geniuses and inspired apostles we never recognized, nor did we honour them. We killed them by neglect, or stoned them whilst they lived, and then went in reverent procession to their graves when they were dead . . .[10]

That passage remarkably parallels Patrick Pearse's famous retraction of his attacks on J. M. Synge. In *An Claidheamh Soluis*, 21 November 1908, Pearse wrote: 'In our sentiments and tastes, we are often too extreme. We worship our poets and politicians for a time, as if they were gods, and when we discover them to be human we stone them. Some writers of the Abbey may have sinned against our deepest sentiments, but the good they have done outweighs all their shortcomings.'[11] By 1913 Pearse had come to identify very strongly with Synge in his martyr's role and to regret that he was no longer around to dramatise the events of the Dublin Lock-Out. Stirring indeed were those events: in that year the average circulation of Larkin's socialist paper the *Irish Worker* peaked at ninety thousand copies, while the nationalist paper *Sinn Féin* was selling two thousand.

THE SEARCH FOR AN ABUSABLE PAST

It is significant that Pearse should have endorsed not only Synge plays but, by implication, their anti-heroic vision as well just when he regarded the people as its own messiah. For no better critique of the authoritarian heroism of Yeats's *Deirdre* has ever been offered than Synge's last play on the same theme, *Deirdre of the Sorrows*. His Fergus, betrayed by the king at the end, throws his sword into the lovers' grave in symbolic repudiation of the bankrupt aristocratic code. Here the place of the chorus is taken by the old woman Lavarcham, but she interprets her assigned role with far greater flexibility than did Yeats's musicians. Although she does, on occasion, invoke the coercive power of the plot to influence the other protagonists, this is done not to propel the ancient prophecy but rather to save the lovers from themselves, as when she warns Naisi against violating the king's prerogative: 'That'll be a story to tell . . . that Naisi is a tippler and stealer . . .'[12] Throughout the play, what distinguishes Lavarcham is her submission to her part as recounting chorus, *along with* her insistence that the malign destiny need not be fulfilled. Most observers note how Synge humanised his characters, treating them as fallible mortals rather than as stiff Yeatsian royalty, but few remark on how he also humanised his chorus. Here the lovers return from Scotland, not under *geasa* (ritual obligation), but because of the more human fear of old age in Alban. Lavarcham is as unimpressed by this more homely reasoning as she was by the claims of the fated prophecy. 'There's little hurt getting old', she warns Deirdre, 'saving when you're looking back, the way I'm looking this day, and seeing the young you have a love for breaking up their hearts with folly' (235). Deirdre, however, incorrigibly Yeatsian, is anxious to hear Lavarcham tell stories of past queens Maeve and Nessa and is already a connoisseur of her own literary performance in the same tradition, posing fatally for posterity: 'and a story will be told forever' (229). Lavarcham's more pragmatic impulse is to ask – like a certain Anglo-Irish joker – what has posterity ever done for us; but the self-dramatising Deirdre suffers the last infirmity of the romantic mind, the belief that all nature is in reckless collusion with her mood. The little moon, she thinks, will be lonely when she is gone, as lonely as the woods of Cuan. It is part of Synge's realism that he can let the Celtic nature poets have their eloquent say, only to mock such self-delusion in the final lines of the play, in which Lavarcham questions those very notions of pathetic fallacy that helped to nerve Deirdre on the way to her death: 'Deirdre is dead, and Naisi is dead; and if the oaks and stars could die for sorrow, it's a dark sky and a hard and naked earth we'd have this night in Emain' (268). But the oaks and stars disobligingly survive our deaths and that is the loneliest discovery of all, as Synge once remarked.

Those lines are a wonderfully ambiguous conclusion, for in them Lavarcham discharges the traditional role of telling the tale to its finish while sustaining her reservations about its romantic predestination. In many respects Lavarcham is Synge's most complex creation for, like all his heroes and heroines, she can provide the imaginative appeal of a good story, while also retaining a healthy respect for those elements of human experience that resist imaginative transformation. As he got older and wiser, Synge's interest in the recalcitrant elements grew, until he seemed to find in their imperviousness to literature the basis for a strange kind of hope. It is that part of the person that refuses the surrender to the prescribed patterns of the past that truly excited Synge, just as it was soon to animate the similarly anti-heroic James Joyce.

In one respect, the burdens borne by Joyce's Mr Bloom are immeasurably lightened by the fact that he is not even aware that his wanderings around Dublin re-enact the voyages of Odysseus. Yet re-enact them he does and, in a deeper sense, his very unawareness may seem to indicate an even ruder curtailment of his freedom. If, as Engels said, freedom is the *conscious* recognition of necessity, then most definitely Leopold Bloom is unfree – his whole existence is an inauthentic rehash of someone else's. His very being is a literary revival, for his life is lived in inverted commas or, as the structuralists would say, perverted commas. There are crucial moments in *Ulysses* when the Homeric plot seems a great deal more real than the tenuous and uncertain self on which it is imposed. Bloom thus partakes of the same inauthenticity as an Irish Renaissance staged in manifest quotation marks, as a revival of various revivals. Yet to say this is to say little enough, for what delights us in Bloom are not his mindless concurrences with the past but rather, as Hugh Kenner first argued, those moments when history repeats itself with telling human variations, as in the immortal Dublin witticism, 'the same, only different'.[13] In such a context the repetitions no longer seem purely constricting, but give to the differences savour and meaning. The very unpretentiousness of Bloom, his utter innocence of the parallels between himself and the ancient Greek hero, adds not only to the poignancy of Joyce's character, but also to the final likeness. It repeats Homer's most telling point – that heroism is never conscious of itself as such. It is in this light that we are forced to reread Yeats's plays and to concede that, far from being a heroine, his Deirdre is merely a Celtic Hedda Gabler who was caught in a plot that prevented her from becoming herself. Like Ibsen's fatal woman, she kills herself when she discovers that her role leaves her with no self to kill. Ireland was to do much the same in 1922, as we shall presently see.

By far the most brilliant retelling of the Deirdre legend in recent times is Brian Friel's *Faith Healer*, a play whose protagonists, like its critics, are as unaware as Bloom that they are re-enacting an ancient legend.[14] Yet Friel's plot tells of a well-brought-up girl who is destined for a noble calling in the north of Ireland but spirited away to Scotland by an attractive but weak young man, to the great dismay of her elderly guardian. In Scotland, and also in Wales, the lovers live well enough for many years, supported by their manager Teddy, who performs the same role as Naoise's brothers in Synge's play. Ultimately, however, this nomadic life is felt to be stressful and, not without foreboding, they return to Ireland only to find no sense of homecoming. In both Synge's and Friel's versions the characters delight in listing the names of places loved and lost, but Friel's heroine lives on for a year of misery before her suicide, in keeping with the Old Irish version of the legend.

Constrained by a time-honoured plot, the characters, like the author Friel, improvise what little freedoms they can. They each face the audience in soliloquy and tell discrepant versions of the old tale, altering the story with a twist that gratifies their vanities. Like the artist–healer, they remould their shattered lives to some private standard of excellence, just as Friel has remoulded the story to his current artistic needs. In *The Anxiety of Influence* Harold Bloom suggested that every major artist is a kind of Francis Hardy, creatively distorting and misreading a work from the past to clear some imaginative space for himself in the present and avoid being smothered by past masters.[15] In similar fashion, James Connolly creatively misinterpreted the landholding systems of Gaelic Ireland to pave the way for the communist systems of his ideal future. If the artist – and in his reading of history Connolly was nothing if not an artist – fully understands his ancient model, then he will be overwhelmed by it, as Yeats was by the official version of Deirdre. On the other hand, what Harold Bloom calls the 'strong artist' will imperfectly assimilate the past model and be thereby saved by the mistake. So, for Friel and Synge as for Joyce, the same can also be the new. By a somewhat similar process, Pearse summoned Cuchulain to his side in the General Post Office (GPO) of 1916, but only to validate his dream of a welfare state; while Joyce smuggled the most subversive narrative of the century into polite society, having first gift-wrapped it in the likeness of one of Europe's oldest tales.[16]

To explain this manoeuvre, the Spanish philosopher Ortega y Gasset used the beautiful metaphor of the step backward taken by the bull-fighter before delivering the mortal thrust. Ortega believed that the man of antiquity 'searched the past for a pattern into which he might slip as into a diving-bell, and being thus at once disguised and protected might rush upon his present problem'. Thomas Mann saluted this attitude as, quite literally, festal, a constant making present of the past as in an anniversary.[17] There is, however, another view. All too often the fighter of Irish bulls takes one step back only to be impaled on the horns of the past and never recovers to deliver the mortal blow. Such a manoeuvre leads not to personal liberation but to tragedies of mistaken identity, such as one finds in a modern Ireland whose people have never had the opportunity to become themselves. After the Easter Rebellion, they abandoned the Irish Renaissance as a search for personal freedom and turned it into a Yeatsian tragedy; they made it an attempt to vindicate 'the work of the past' (in Yeats's terms) rather than one to forge the 'uncreated conscience of the race' (in Joyce's definition). All of a sudden the national stage was filled with the ghosts of dead men insisting that the living simplify and abandon their daily lives, to the point of becoming agents of the dead. History, as Marx explained in 'The Eighteenth Brumaire', became a nightmare in the minds of the living, a phrase that would re-echo in the opening pages of Joyce's masterpiece. The revolutionaries had sought to create themselves out of nothing; those who remained were reduced to revivalists, seeking mere revenge.

The national dilemma was dramatised by the career of Shakespeare's Hamlet, as writers as diverse as Yeats, Joyce, and, more recently, Heaney have testified.[18] Yeats's Hamlet was a deployer of masks, Joyce's became his own father, and Heaney's stands by graves dithering and blathering. But the full implications of the parallels have never been traced. At the age of thirty, after a protracted education as courtier, soldier and scholar, Hamlet was about to come into his own when he met a ghost and, henceforth, could never become himself. Although the role of revenger was one to which he was ill-suited and ill-disposed, once the ghost had seized the centre stage Hamlet was destined to fill it. Hamlet becomes in consequence, as Yeats noted, a character obsessed with role-playing.[19] He coaches Polonius and the players in the art of acting, tells the queen to assume those virtues she doesn't have, and punctures the thin disguises of Osric, Rosencrantz, Guildenstern and the usurping king. His gift for mimicry is unbounded but, in the end, it is his tragedy to be able to discover and play virtually every part except his own. Like Yeats's Deirdre – also something of an expert in stratagems of performance – to know his deed he has to postpone and finally cancel the moment when he might know himself. By Act 5 he reappears among the graves, not really as the mature man sought by Joyce, but more as a kind of ghost come back from the dead – much as Pearse, Connolly and the other dead men eternally return, their words simplified and insisting that those who follow simplify themselves too. In a radical reinterpretation of the theme, Harold

Rosenberg has shown how Hamlet wiped away all trivial fond records of his own half-constructed past and abandoned himself to a merely historical role.[20] Having hovered precariously in the first four acts between an assigned role and a putative self, he finally surrenders to the *ur-Hamlet*, the preordained revenger's plot. The living man capitulates to the dead. To murder the false king, he must first abort his scarcely born self. Yet that is not all; as Rosenberg argues, the dilemma of the man–actor remains:

On the stage which is the world the plot is written by nobody and no one can denote himself truly . . . The drama in which the living man attempted in vain to seize his life as particular to himself concludes by proclaiming the utter irony of human existence, as Fortinbras orders a soldier's burial for Hamlet, not for what he did but for what he might have done.[21]

In similar procession, Pearse and Connolly pass into Irish iconography attired for ever in that most inappropriate garb, the military uniform. Even the ghosts of our fathers are thus simplified before they are allowed to terrify and haunt us, clanking around in their unwieldly and incongruous armour.

ESCAPE FROM FREEDOM

The rebellion of 1916, and the Irish Revival that surrounded it, may have led people into a similar tragedy of mistaken identity. The question to be asked is not how the socialist Connolly could have thrown in his lot with the nationalist Pearse, but rather how two such complex and radical thinkers, intent on instituting 'the people' as its own messiah, could have so dreadfully mistaken their historic moment. In 'The Eighteenth Brumaire' Marx had already warned about the lamentable tendency of ghosts to appear on the eve of revolutions. So the men of 1789 nerved themselves for the unthinkable by casting themselves as resurrected Romans. As Caesar had worn the mask of Alexander, and Alexander of Miltiades, so the rebels of 1916, without the irony of a Pearse or a Connolly, donned the mask of Cuchulain. The whole of history had been a story of mistaken identity, said Marx, staged as a bizarre costume drama in which the protagonists could never be themselves. Even the radicals of recent times, just when they seemed on the point of creating themselves out of nothing but their own desires, had relapsed into the farce of revivalism:

An entire people, which had imagined that by means of a revolution it had imparted to itself an accelerated power of motion, suddenly finds itself set back into a defunct epoch and, in order that no doubt as to the relapse may be possible, the old dates rise again, the old chronology, the old names, the old edicts, which had long become a subject of antiquarian erudition, and the old minions of the law, who had seemed long decayed.[22]

History becomes a farce without events, where 'nothing happens' not just twice but indefinitely, 'wearying with constant repetition of the same tensions, the same relaxations'.[23] The ancient plot takes over, much as the individuals are suppressed by the emphatic chorus in Yeat's play. However, Marx had no doubt that when a real revolution finally came, the people would not mistake themselves for historical actors but would wear their own clothes.

This was exactly the point made by Sean O'Casey when he opposed Captain Jack White's introduction of military uniforms into the Irish Citizen Army. He argued that formal costumes would simply set up Connolly's men as highly visible targets for the opposing army. In the opening acts of *The Plough and the Stars*, the rebels and their supporters strut in the most outlandish historical uniforms, complete with ostrich plumes, evoking a mixture of awe and contempt among the tenement-dwellers, but when the fighting nears its end the rebels are pathetically anxious to shrug off their incriminating clothing and seek shelter in the anonymity of proletarian dress and tenement life. One of the escaping rebels threatens to shoot the 'slum lice' if they continue to loot shops. In using that phrase to characterise the people in whose name he has helped to lead the rebellion, the officer confirms the suspicion that here is yet another tragedy of irrelevance.

It is well known that colonialism always makes its subjects seem theatrical so that even their gestures of revolt seem 'literary' rather than 'real'. Hence the theatricality of the 1916 rebellion, led by poets and playwrights who brandished ceremonial swords, sported kilts and played the bagpipes during a guerilla confrontation at a potently symbolic time of the year, invoking sacrifice, renewal and resurrection. But the more poignant the gesture is in literary terms, the more tragic is its irrelevance to human needs. For example, the rebels of 1916, as elsewhere in Europe that year, seem to have affected every form of dress except their own. In his essay 'The Suit and the Photograph', John Berger marvelled at the crumpled and ill-fitting suits worn by most labourers, peasants and craftsmen at the time. Such workers did not lack the skill to choose good cloth or the knowledge of how to wear it, but the suits were designed for the sedentary administrators of a ruling class. The vigorous actions of the labourers merely spoiled the suits, which were clearly inappropriate for the lives they led. A clear example of class hegemony, the suits worn by Dubliners on the barricades at Talbot Street in 1916 showed their acceptance of cultural norms that had nothing to do with their daily experience, and condemned them 'to being always, and recognizably to the classes above them, second-rate, clumsy, uncouth, defensive'.[24]

Even less appropriate, more archaic forms of costume were worn by some rebel leaders inside the GPO, most notoriously the kilt. They mistakenly believed that kilts had been worn by Irish chieftains and their pipers as they marched into battle; the aristocratic connotations pleased the more snobbish elements among the revivalists. In fact, the ancient Irish wore hip-hugging trousers long before the English (and were reviled for it), but they never wore kilts, which offer few defences against the insinuating moisture of the Irish climate. Indeed, it has recently been shown that the kilt, far from being an ancient Highland dress in Scotland, was invented by an English Quaker industrialist in the early 1700s and 'was bestowed by him on the Highlanders not in order to preserve their traditional way of life but to ease its transformation: to bring them out of their heather and into the factory'.[25]

Many other 'ancient traditions' of the Irish Revival turn out, on inspection, to be cases of instant archaeology. History becomes a form of science fiction by which people can pretend to find in the endlessly malleable past whatever they secretly desire in the golden future. So 'Gaelic' football was invented in the 1880s as a consciously wrought antidote to soccer. Such ploys were at once a rejection of Englishness and a craven surrender to the imperialist English notion of an antithesis between all things English and Irish. So, if the English had hockey, the Irish must have hurling; if the English wore trousers, the Irish wore kilts; if John Bull spoke English, Paddy spoke Irish, and so forth. This slot-rolling mechanism was derided in recent decades by Seán de Fréine as 'the ingenious device of national parallelism', whereby for every English action there must be an equal and opposite Irish reaction. De Fréine acidly noted the failure of the Irish mind to clear itself of imposed English categories: 'It was felt that the Irish could not claim as theirs anything that was characteristic of England; on the other hand, not to have it could betoken inferiority.'[26] Irish people were so busy being not-English that they had scarcely time to think of what it might mean to be Irish. They forgot who they were or might be in their hysterical desire not to be taken for something else. J. M. Synge laughed at the knee-jerk nationalism of a Gaelic League that could define itself only according to English categories. 'With their eyes glued on John Bull's navel', he mocked, 'they are afraid to be Europeans for fear the huckster across the street might call them English.'[27]

If any hucksters had had the temerity to hurl such an insult, they would probably have been right. The IRA created its military structure with the help of manuals stolen from the British army, while the nationalist courts deliberately aped the legal rituals of the power they fought. Even today something of that trend persists as IRA funerals, shown on British (but not fully on Irish) television, exactly parallel the obsequies for English soldiers killed in the north of Ireland. Indeed, at the height of the revival, the very worst excesses of imperialism seemed to have built a replica of themselves in Irish brains. So Arthur Griffith, a founder of Sinn Féin, could call for a stronger Irish industry, lest Ireland never 'be placed in a position to influence the cultivation and progress of less-advanced nations and to form colonies of its own'.[28] It was small wonder that the political and legal institutions in the far-from-Free State were slavish imitations of English models. One cannot avoid suspecting that the new leaders, having no clear sense of selfhood, were bending over backwards to win the approval of those English authorities whom they had just ejected. Nowhere is this more obvious than in Yeats's hopeless rehabilitation of the modes of Irish deference. The English had deemed the Irish backward, superstitious and uncivilised, but Yeats urged the Irish for 'backward' to read 'healthily rooted in tradition', for 'superstitious' to read 'religious', and for 'uncivilised' to read 'instinctive'. Thus the racist slur was sanitised and worn with pride.[29] The deepest insults could now be happily internalised in the post-colonial mind. Irish people could postpone indefinitely the moment of self-identification. Instead they could spend their lives acting out assigned roles that might not be their own, but had the advantage of being well known.

For many years, up to 1922, the Irish had hovered, Hamlet-like, in the no man's land between a role and a self. True independence would have meant further years in hard search of that self, but instead partial freedom saw them resign themselves to a time-honoured role. In *The Fear of Freedom* Erich Fromm describes this familiar capitulation: 'To put it briefly, the individual adopts entirely the kind of personality offered to him by cultural patterns; . . . the discrepancy between the "I" and the world disappears . . . This mechanism can be compared with the protective colouring some animals assume . . . But the price paid is high; it is the loss of the self.' That lost self is replaced by a pseudo-self (what Beckett would later call a 'vice-exister'), as a result of which 'thoughts can be induced from the outside and yet be subjectively experienced as one's own'.[30] The costume-drama continues and a whole population goes on playing a part not its own. Independence means only that the old imperialist style of administration will be deployed by boys from Clongowes and Belvedere rather than from Eton and Ampleforth; when, in 1933, the less-colonised Tweedledum replaced the more-colonised Tweedledee, nothing changed. And in the 1940s and 1950s while England reformed her own society and created a welfare state, the Irish persisted in administering themselves through the old structures of imperialist England. The lookalikes replace the lookalikers. They are all in on the 'act'.

REVIVAL OR REVOLUTION?

Yet, now and then, a person will speak out on behalf of that tenuous (but never quite extinguished) Irish self, which feels demeaned and violated by all this play-acting. Like characters in a Beckett play, such people feel that others they do not know have been living their lives. Some years ago, a correspondent to the *Sunday Press* wrote:

It is as if the Irish people are still living as an underground movement in their own country. The 'shape' of Irish society and institutions fits Irish people like a badly tailored suit. We do not acknowledge the suit as our own; we do not feel at home in it, but we tolerate it as we have always tolerated everything. I never hear Irishmen talking about *our* courts, *our* gardaí, *our* representatives, etc.[31]

This condition gives rise to the suspicion that every Irish deed is an impersonation rather than an avowal, an 'act' rather than a truly complete 'action'. 'To say "I" in a poem is hard for me', reports contemporary poet Eiléan Ní Chuilleanáin. This problem also agitated Yeats from start to finish, for despite repeated resolutions to 'walk naked' he found it impossible to commit the ultimate revolutionary deed of speaking with his own face instead of performing through a rhetorical mask. Even the beautiful image with which he sought to dignify the executed rebels in 'Easter 1916'

> . . . our part
> To murmur name upon name
> As a mother names her child,
> When sleep at last has come
> On limbs that had run wild[32]

manages also to trivialise the insurgents' theatrical gesture in a recognised colonialist way. In the words of that great purveyor of imperialist fictions, Captain Marryat, 'what a parallel there is between a colony and her mother country and a child and its parent'.[33] Yeats has infantilised the fallen rebels in much the same way as they obligingly, if unconsciously, infantilised themselves in the opening sentence of their proclamation. His poem ends by hinting that the rebels were really children, not full moral agents, and therefore forgivable – as far beyond or below the law as a black in the American South in the mid-nineteenth century.

More self-aware writers, such as Samuel Beckett, constantly monitor themselves for traces of just such an impersonation. In *The Unnamable*, the third volume of his trilogy, Beckett's narrator complains of the 'vice-existers': 'All these Murphys, Molloys, and Malones do not fool me. They have made me waste my time, suffer for nothing, speak of them when, in order to stop speaking, I should have spoken of me and of me alone.'[34] Though this is primarily a search for the authentic language of the self, the political implications of such a programme should never be underestimated. Like the Irish, Beckett's characters must constantly shake off the masks proffered by others and invent themselves *ex nihilo*, on a stage with no props to offer reassuring clues from the past as to how such a programme might begin. In *Murphy* the Stage Irish mask imposed by English onlookers on 'the ruins of the ruins of the broth of a boy' is manifest enough, as is his refusal to live in any zone of physical buffoonery when he can come alive in the pure world of the mind. By *Endgame* Clov overtly dissociates himself from centuries of play-acting, from tradition and the prison-house of other people's language, in contrast to the theatricalised Hamm who 'was never really there'. In many respects, the war against the past is waged most insistently in the political unconscious of Ireland's least politicised writer. Beckett, a dramatist without any obvious tradition, writes instead about the attempt by characters without context to create one: 'Yesterday. In my opinion, I was here, yesterday.'[35]

The politics of impersonation are a burning issue in the work of Joyce from first to last. Stephen Daedalus complains of the foreignness of certain English words like 'home', 'Christ', 'ale' and 'master' that he cannot use 'without unrest of spirit,' for his soul frets in the shadow of an 'acquired speech'.[36] And Joyce's own fate, as Richard Poirier observed, was to have been able to parody all available English styles, yet achieve no finally recognisable style of his own.[37] It is now fashionable to see this escape into stylelessness as Joyce's deliberate mimicry of the spiral of modernism that 'must always struggle, but never quite triumph, and in the end must struggle not to triumph'.[38] Such a reading would find in the endless succession of styles a version of the consumer spiral, whereby each fashion must be usurped by the next at breakneck speed.[39] But it is surely a different kind of usurpation that Joyce points to here; as Stephen complains, his ancestors threw off their own language and allowed themselves to be subjugated by a pack of foreigners, leaving him to carry the debt. And carry it he does, like Flann O'Brien after him, whose restless changes of pseudonym betoken a corresponding admission that he too could play many parts except his own. Both men's vaunted experiments with the English novel arise from their sense that the form does not truly fit the Irish experience that they seek to record. The English novel describes a land of stable gradations of made lives, whereas Irish writers must depict a land of instability, of lives in the making. It was their ambiguous fortune to impersonate the novelist by writing books that themselves aped the form of novels, in an age that found in their self-evident sham an echo of its own. Nonetheless, that should never blind one to the underlying postcolonial strains, for it never blinded Joyce. His Stephen, usurped in the tower by the neo-colonial Mulligan, who toadies to the English Gaelic revivalist, knows the exact implications of the story of Hamlet – a tale of usurpation, of player kings, and of ghosts whose injunctions press like nightmares upon the brains of the living.

What Stephen resents most is the Englishman's desire to convert him into another obliging Irish actor, a flashy Wildean phrasemaker: 'A jester at the court of his master, indulged and disesteemed . . . Why had they all chosen that part?' he asks himself.[40] Yet Haines too is forever acting – acting the part of a reasonable Englishman who can always find in history, but never his own history, the handy scapegoat. His Gaelic revivalism is not just a grotesque impersonation, but a hint from Joyce that all revivalism is just such impersonation, demanded by colonisers and their Yeatsian agents at a certain stage in the development of the colonised. As Frantz Fanon wrote in *The Wretched of the Earth*, revivalists only come onto the scene very late in the day, to collect the despised husks of a culture that even the natives have largely cast off. They exalt custom – as Yeats does in 'A Prayer for My Daughter' – but only because it is always the mummification of culture. They pick, says Fanon, among shells and corpses not the protean signatures read by Stephen on Sandymount Strand but 'a knowledge which has been stabilized once and for all'. The revolutionary intellectual, on the other hand, 'who wishes to create an authentic work of art . . . must go on until he has found the seething pot out of which the learning of the future will emerge'.[41] The revivalist embraces the native culture and mummifies it, as a bulwark against the revolution announced by Joyce. Culture for the revivalist 'is always something that was',[42] but for the revolutionary it is something that will be. The revival thus becomes a valued weapon of the counter-revolution, for it sentimentalises that backwardness that the insurgents are hoping to end. And it reveals itself as an insincere act, performed by mumming companies, rather than a purposeful action, for it is buried in the inauthenticity of quotation marks.

That inauthenticity of life among the colonised was epitomised by E. M. Forster in the famous echo from the Marabar Caves in *A Passage to India*, a noise that convinced the English liberal Fielding that 'the original sound was always good – the echo always bad'. In other words, English people are all right in England, but in India or any other colony they become false to themselves and induce an echoing falseness in others. Similarly, among his fellow-Indians Dr Aziz is a reputable doctor, but when faced with an Englishman he loses his impeccable sense of evidence. Worse still, he begins to act, becoming 'greasily confidential' to those English ladies whom he promises to take to 'some frightfully super places'.[43] At much the same time, this most civil of men becomes stagily aggressive to the English official Ronnie Heaslop. The echo set off by imperialism is always bad, especially when it has an Englishman antici-pating the idioms of an Enid Blyton, but the worst echo of all comes from the native intellectual who confirms English hegemony by his willingness to accept and dignify the coloniser's valuation of the colonised. Forster knows, however, that there is also a resounding echo from the imperial Englishman who is impersonating himself. In *Howards End* Forster captured this staginess in a mundane scene in Simpson's Restaurant: 'The guests whom it was nurturing for imperial purposes bore the outer semblance of Parson Adams and Tom Jones. Scraps of talk jarred oddly on the ear: "Right you are. I'll cable out to Uganda this evening . . ."'[44] This is a delightful exposure of the contradiction inherent in the myth of a primitive people overtaken by industrial and imperial power. V. S. Naipaul has offered a brilliant gloss on the scene:

Between the possession of Uganda and the conscious possession of Tom Jones there is as little connection as there is between the stories of Kipling and the novels of his contemporary Hardy. So, at the height of their power, the British gave the impression of a people at play, a people playing at being English, playing at being English of a certain class. The reality conceals the play; the play conceals the reality.[45]

The hypocrisy of such a performance is strictly functional, but it is nothing compared to the bad faith it induces in the colonised. The English ploy is usually designed only to fool others, for at heart they know who they are, but the Indians, or Irish, end by deceiving themselves. Before the colonisers leave, they place replicas of themselves in the rebels' heads.

This process occurred in Ireland with astonishing swiftness. The middle-class civil servants and office workers who tittered in 1926 at the urban leprechauns on Sean O'Casey's stage were the same people who, fifteen years earlier, would have accused the same author of mounting Irish shenanigans on stage for the delectation of a Castle audience. Yeats had hoped that by gathering a national audience in Dublin he could express Ireland to the Irish rather than exploit it for the foreigner; but he had not reckoned with the capacity of the occupier to insinuate an entire symbology into his own and his audience's minds.

The story of how a revolution was reduced to a revival has been told many times, most often as a cautionary political tale. Maurice Goldring has shown how the myth of a rural nation played a spuriously unifying role by giving a common vocabulary to Irish people who were, in fact, deeply divided on many issues.[46] For one thing, the myth could never include the peasants themselves, whose activities in the Land League often led to attacks on the property of Anglo-Irish writers. Gaelic revivalism was, of course, a largely urban phenomenon offering a brand of self-respect to a somewhat snobbish lower-middle class. Yet even within the cities class tensions could surface, as when the nationalist rebel Cathal Brugha sacked an employee for trying to form a union. As late as April 1920, however, it seemed as if the revolution might be carried through. On the fifth of the month, workers organised a general strike for one hundred republican prisoners who were fasting for political status. The neo-colonial union leadership sedulously avoided committing itself, and leaving rank and file members to wage a campaign commandeering buildings, vehicles and so on. Within twenty-four hours they had produced an organisation so awesome that the government preferred to concede than to see such self-confidence develop. The *Irish Times* saw the shrewdness of this concession: 'A continuation of the fight which ended yesterday might have witnessed the establishment of soviets of workmen in all parts of Ireland.'[47] Certainly the previous few years had witnessed an astounding decline in deference to all forms of authority. No doubt the Great War had helped to discredit figures of authority from fathers to property owners. As David Fitzpatrick has pointed out: 'The post-Rising labour movement was radical because, far from begging government or men of property to raise the labourer's status in traditional fashion, by granting him land, it arrogantly asserted that the landless worker, as chief producer of the nation's wealth, was a superior person in his own right.'[48] This is an image quite at variance with the stoic and enduring Yeatsian peasant.

Though the politics of the Labour Party's subsequent strangulation by conservative nationalism are well known, the psychological aspects have been less often analysed by Irish intellectuals, perhaps because they are so painful to contemplate. Yet, in the words of Ortega y Gasset, 'every life is a ruin among whose debris we have to discover what the person ought to have been'.[49] It would be plausible to argue that the revivalists, having won the day, rewrote the history books and edited the radicals out of their narrative, which to the historians had the inevitability of a Greek tragedy. Such a conservative view of history mistakes what happened for the inevitable 'given', the very terms of reality itself. It has always been a ruse of colonialism to confirm in its victims a fatalistic conviction that the world as given to them could never be changed, merely accepted.

Yet there are, it must be admitted, severe liabilities to futurology. Those who catch a whiff of the future may be so intoxicated by the smell that they cannot afterwards recall it at all. They have not the consolations of some well-plotted appointment with the past, but instead the nerve-wracking tensions of going on stage, like a Beckett character, without benefit of a script, which can itself only take form in the future. It was René Char who said that our heritage is not preceded by any testament. Pondering this notion, Hannah Arendt decided that

the first who failed to remember what the treasure was like were precisely those who had possessed it and found it so strange that they did not even know how to name it . . . The point of the matter is that the 'completion', which indeed every enacted event must have in the minds of those who then are to tell the story and to convey its meaning, eluded them; and without this thinking completion after the act, without this articulation accomplished by remembrance, there simply was no story left to be told.[50]

If one tried to complete the tale not as a political fable but as a psychodrama between fathers and sons, one might at least end the story one began, and not some other. The official ending emphasises the Irish Revival as a tale of recovered national identity; but the story, at its outset, was to concern itself with increasing the freedom of the Irish individual.

FATHERS AND SONS — IRISH STYLE

In all societies in the throes of revolution, the relation between fathers and sons is reversed. The Irish *risorgimento* was, among other things, a revolt by angry sons against discredited fathers. The fathers had lost face, either because they had compromised with the coloniser in return for safe positions as policemen or petty clerks, or because they had retreated into a demeaning cycle of alcoholism and unemployment. The Irish father was a defeated and emasculated man, whose wife sometimes won the bread and often usurped his domestic power while the priest usurped his spiritual authority. Most fathers accepted colonialism as part of the 'given' and warned their sons against revolt. This did not prevent the fathers from being enthusiastic revivalists; on the contrary, their very caution made revivalism all the more necessary as a form of cultural compensation. In *A Portrait of the Artist as a Young Man*, Simon Daedalus recalls the athletic feats of his youth and asks if his son can vault a five-barred gate. Wherever one looks in the literature of the Irish Renaissance, one finds fathers lamenting the red-blooded heroes now gone and evoking the conquests of their own pasts. Joxer and Boyler, Michael James and Philly Cullen are all debased versions of Yeats's searched-for hero, who can only be a hero if his deed is done in the past, as the Mayomen discover in Synge's greatest play and as Yeats was finally to admit, with honest split-mindedness, in 'Easter 1916'.

In a colony the revolt by a son against a father is a meaningless gesture because it can have no social effect. Since the natives do not have their hands on the levers of power, such a revolt can neither refurbish nor renew social institutions. To be effective it must be extended to outright revolution, or else sink back into the curtailed squabbles of family life. The pressure and intensity of family life in a colony cannot be overestimated, for (as Albert Memmi has reported in the case of Tunisia) the family is the only social institution with which the colonised can fully identify. The law, the state apparatus, the civil service and even the colonised church are in some senses alien. Because these social forms are repudiated by the young in a colony, they petrify, in much the same way as the language of Elizabethan and Cromwellian England petrified in Ireland. Memmi noticed disconsolately how few of his countrymen had any awareness of, much less aptitude for, government.[51] In Rousseau's terminology, such persons were subjects, not citizens. This lack of civic commitment is often adduced as the major reason why colonised peoples are among the last to awaken to national consciousness. When the sons of each generation rebelled, they soon saw the meaninglessness of their gesture and lapsed back into family life, as into 'a haven in a heartless world'. Yet it was a haven that, in every respect, reflected the disorder of the outside colonial world. The compromised or broken father could provide no true image of authority. In Memmi's words: 'It is the impossibility of enjoying a complete social life which maintains vigour in the family and pulls the individual back to that more restricted cell which saves and smothers him.'[52] All that remains is for the son, thus emasculated, to take the place of his weak and ineffectual father.

The classic texts of the Irish Renaissance read like oblique meditations on this theme. Many secondary artists, such as Pearse and Kavanagh, write about the overintense, clutching relationship between mother and son without displaying any awareness of the underlying implication that the very intensity of the mother–son relationship suggests something sinister about the Irish man, both as husband and as father. Women sought from their sons an emotional fulfilment denied them by their men, which suggests that the husbands had failed as lovers. But the women could not have achieved such parental dominance if the husbands had not also abdicated the role of father. The space vacated by the ineffectual father was occupied by the all-powerful mother, who became not just 'wife and mother in one',[53] but surrogate father as well. The primary writers of modern Ireland, the Joyces, Synges and O'Caseys, therefore sidestepped the cliché and resolved to examine the deeper problem of the inadequate Irish male.

O'Casey is famous for his juxtapositions of industrious mothers and layabout fathers, of wronged girls and unscrupulous, sweet-talking men. In *Juno and the Paycock* Mary Boyle is left pregnant by a rascally schoolmaster and then disowned by her boyfriend of long standing. All this she can take. It is only when her father disowns her and her child that she breaks down completely: 'My poor little child that'll have no father'. Mrs Boyle's rejoinder is O'Casey's epitaph on the Irish male: 'It'll have what's far better. It'll have two mothers.'[54]

That same indictment of Irish fatherhood echoes through the work of Joyce, who chronicles a whole series of unreliable, inadequate or absent fathers, priests and authority figures. The Stephen who at the start of *A Portrait* proclaimed his father 'a gentleman' ends by scoffing at him as a 'praiser of his own past' (241); by the start of *Ulysses* he has fled the father in search of an alternative image of authority and self-respect. 'Why did you leave your father's house?' asks his saviour, only to be told: 'To seek misfortune' (608). At the root of Joyce's art is the belief that 'paternity may be a legal fiction' (252), that fathers and sons are brought together more by genetic accident than by mutual understanding, and that most sons are compelled to rebel. 'Who is the father of any son that any son should love him or he any son?' (191) asks Stephen; wryly he concludes that a father is a necessary evil, but not before he has repented of his refusal to fulfil his dying mother's wish that he pray at her bedside. As he teaches school in Dalkey, Stephen ponders his dead mother's love: 'Was that then real? The only true thing in life?' (33). So the basic groundwork of *Ulysses* is identical with that of *Juno* – the truth of maternity interrogates the myth of paternity.

Similarly, Synge's plays depict a rural Ireland where enterprising males are either in jail, the grave or America, leaving such 'puny weeds' as Shawn Keogh to inherit the land. In such a place, father-slaying may be a moral necessity as well as a dire compulsion. In *The Playboy of the Western World* the frustrated young women of the area lament the banality of their confessions to Father Reilly, 'going up summer and winter with nothing worthwhile to confess at all' (33), just as Pegeen condemns a father who believes so little in protecting his daughter that he abandons her for the flows of drink at Kate Cassidy's wake – an all-male affair that ends with 'six men stretched out retching speechless on the holy stones' (67). What brings Pegeen and Christy together is their shared conviction that fathers are intolerable, for Christy was driven to 'kill' his father, who tried to earn some extra drinking money by marrying off his hapless son to the horrendous Widow Casey. It is no surprise to learn that, although Mahon's other children have abandoned him, they are still haunted by his ghost: 'and not a one of them, to this day, but would say their seven curses on him, and they rousing up to let a cough or sneeze, maybe, in the deadness of the night' (25). It is remarkable that both Synge and Joyce depicted motherless sons in their masterpieces, the better to dramatise the real roots of the problem of the Irish male as inadequate father. This tradition is taken up as well by Brian Friel in *Philadelphia, Here I Come*.

Although Joyce, Synge and O'Casey all vividly describe the widespread disenchantment with the Irish male as father, none of them offers a convincing analysis of the causes of parental failure. And this despite the fact that a remarkable number of the foremost writers of the period either lost their fathers at an early age (Synge, O'Casey), had ineffectual fathers (Joyce, Shaw, O'Connor), or had fathers who saw themselves as gifted failures (Yeats, Wilde). The tortuous attempts by foreign critics to explain the recurring theme of weak paternity may make us glad that the artists did not similarly seek to explain away the phenomenon. One reason for the obsession is hinted at in the opening story of *Dubliners*, where Joyce depicts an orphaned boy fighting free of the oppressive aura that surrounds a dead and discredited priest. In Synge's *Playboy*, as in Joyce's story, the priest never appears on stage, as if to suggest that he is no longer an authoritative force in the people's lives. The orphaned youth and discredited priest seem paradigms of a late-Victorian culture deprived both of God and of the consolations of a received code. 'If there is no God', cries out a baffled soldier in a novel of Dostoevsky, 'then how can I be a captain?' Many a Victorian father may have asked the same question about his own fatherhood, just as many a Victorian son may have decided, like another of Dostoevsky's characters, that after the death of God anything – even father-murder – was possible. It is no accident that the self-invented Christy Mahon promises Pegeen Mike the illicit delights of poaching fish in Erris 'when Good Friday's by' (64). Henceforth the day on which God dies will be the day on which man learns to live.

This revolt of the artistic son against an unsatisfactory father is a leitmotif that spans the literature of Europe from D. H. Lawrence to Thomas Mann in the early years of the twentieth century. The breakneck speed of change in society gave added force to the concept of 'generation', and the gap that had always separated fathers and sons grew so wide as to suggest that the young and old inhabited totally different countries. For the first time in history, perhaps, writers found themselves forced to write solely for their own immediate generation – as F. Scott Fitzgerald joked, an artist speaks to today's youth, tomorrow's critics and posterity's schoolmasters. To a modernist generation intent on 'making it new', the fact of fatherhood was an encumbrance and an embarrassment. The emerging hero was self-created like Jay Gatsby, who sprang from some Platonic conception of himself, or an orphan of indeterminate background, or a slayer of fathers.

There were, however, particular colonialist pressures in Ireland that gave that revolt an added urgency. The fathers, as has been shown, were already defeated and broken men, and emigration had robbed the community of many potential innovators. In such a context Yeats's search for heroic models takes on a sinister overtone for, in a world peopled by Michael Jameses and Simon Dedaluses, the cult of the hero is more a confession of male impotence than a spur to battle. To those revivalists who might sigh 'Unhappy the land that has no hero', the radicals could reply 'No! Unhappy the land that *needs* a hero!'

Whenever a colony starts to crumble, these dramas are enacted as a reversal of the relations between fathers and sons. In the Algeria of *A Dying Colonialism* in the 1950s, Frantz Fanon found that as families broke into their separate elements under the new stress, the true meaning of a national revival emerged: 'Each member of this family has gained in individuality what it had lost in belonging to a world of more or less confused values.'[55] Women asserted their independence of fathers and husbands, often appearing more manly than their partners. This masculinisation of woman may also be found in the major Irish works written in the period of national resurgence.[56] Even more telling, however, is Fanon's account of the men. At first, he says, the colonised father gives the impression of indecision and evasiveness, while even those sons who have adopted nationalist positions remain deferential in the home. With the start of the revolution in 1954 'the person is born, assumes his autonomy and becomes the creator of his own values'. The father still counsels prudence but the son, in rejecting the counsel, does not reject the father. 'What he would try to do on the contrary', says Fanon, 'would be to convert the family. The militant would replace the son and undertake to indoctrinate the father.'[57] Thus, Christy Mahon walks off the stage in control of his delighted parent, 'like a gallant captain with his heathen slave' (80), in a situation that Fanon has described: 'At no time do we find a really painful clash. The father stood back before the new world and followed in his son's footsteps.'[58] The old-fashioned respect for the young, which Wilde feared was dying out at the start of the 1890s, would be evident again for three decades, even in the poetry of Yeats, whose denunciations of old age are a pervasive theme.

It was in this very period that Freud in Vienna developed the notion that all politics are reducible to the primal conflict between father and son. As a boy he had been reprimanded by his father for urinating in his trousers: 'The boy will come to nothing!' This was, according to Freud, the source of all his subsequent ambition, as though he had decided at that moment to show his father that he *could* amount to something. Years later as a successful adult he had what he called, significantly, his 'revolutionary dream', in which a strong son reprimanded a guilty father for the same offence. It was, says Carl E. Schorske, a kind of revenge.[59]

In Ireland, however, matters did not unfold as they had in Synge's play, Fanon's country or Freud's dream. Instead the fathers had their revenge on the sons for daring to dream at all. After 1922 the shutters went up and the emigrant ships were filled not just with intellectuals but with thousands of young men and women. People started to emigrate not from poverty or the hated English law, but because the life offered to them was boring and mediocre. Those who stayed created a new myth to appease and explain their disappointment. According to this myth, the most creative and promising intellects had been lost after the executions of 1916 and subsequent hostilities to a small country that could ill afford such a reckless expenditure of its most gifted youth. Yeats, again, was the prime creator of this myth; in 'Easter 1916' he explicitly mourned not just Pearse, but also MacDonagh, the 'helper and friend' who 'might have won fame in the end'.[60] This – as with everything else – is merely an Irish version of the English myth of a lost generation of brilliant young officers cut down in their prime in the trenches of World War One. Both narratives have equally little basis in fact. It has been shown that although British losses in the officer corps were heavy, most who served came home – to become prime ministers, politicians and civic leaders. Similarly, most of the intellectuals and radicals of the Irish Renaissance also survived the experience of war and counter-revolution. In the case of England, Robert Wohl has argued that 'the myth of the missing generation provided an important self-image for the survivors' and 'a means of accounting for the disappointments of the present'.[61] (Thus – as Connolly had predicted, with bitter irony in this context – the worship of past heroes was really a deification of current mediocrity.) Moreover, the myth reflected the survivors' guilt at being alive at all while their comrades rotted in trenches, along with their conviction that 'they had been the victims of a dirty trick played by history incarnated in the evil form of the Older Generation'.[62] In Ireland, of course, these trends were reinforced by the loss of many more imaginative and energetic souls to emigration. The revivalists had won: the fathers with their heroes and ghosts from the past – the revolutionaries were snuffed out – and the sons with their hopes of self-creation in the image of an uncertain future.

REBELS OR REVOLUTIONARIES?

Yet the revenge of the fathers was barren in every respect. It represented a final surrender to colonialist modes of thought. The occupier who seemed to have gone left behind a ghost in every mind and machine. Ireland had taken two steps back only to find that after that retreat, instead of a liberating leap into the future, all movement ceased. By 1929 Daniel Corkery could describe the national consciousness as a quaking sod, neither English nor Irish nor any fruitful blend. And since then the sod has quaked and quaked.[63] A revival, which should have extended personal freedom, served only to confirm the pathology of dependency. Today the Irish Republic has the highest hospitalisation rate for mental illness in the world. On census day in 1971 two out of every hundred males in the west of Ireland were in mental hospitals; even today there are four times as many patients per thousand of population in Irish as in English psychiatric hospitals. When Nancy Scheper-Hughes visited the country, she found not the fighting Irish of ancient legend but men whose reserved behaviour indicated a terrible self-suppression. She found habits of verbal ambiguity that, however well they served a Swift or a Joyce, 'can provoke schizophrenia in vulnerable individuals'. The personality structure of the Irish male showed feelings of masculine inadequacy and high dependency – a dependency that afflicts even the nation's leaders, most of whom now celebrate the national holiday on platforms in Pittsburgh, New York or Birmingham. Scheper-Hughes found fathers to be marginalised in their own families, yet the sons also had no control, ceding much of the high ground to charismatic mothers.[64]

Such a depressing report might be taken as the jaundiced view of a clinical foreigner were it not for the massive corroboration by native analysts. By 1976 the chief psychiatrist of the Eastern Health Board, Ivor Browne, noted a growing belief among Irish adults, even in urban areas, that they would never take control of their own lives, government or economy. Commenting on the ridicule that greets persons of enterprise – a ridicule that by 1986 took the form of 60 per cent taxation on an income of a mere ten thousand pounds – he argued that apathy, selflessness and loss of autonomy characterised the post-colonial personality, along with civic indifference. Urging his fellow countrymen to cast off the security of oppression, he lamented that 'we are only concerned with aping our oppressors, with proving to ourselves that we are the same as they were and can use the same methods of oppression on each other'.[65]

The character structure sketched by Ivor Browne is what might be termed 'revivalist' – in which an individual depends on other peoples and past images to acquire the strength of self it lacks. Whether they know it or not, such persons betray symptoms of self-loathing and acquired incompetence. A Dublin psychotherapist, J. V. Kenny, finds in post-colonial Irish personalities evidence of a people who are in fact secret rebels, dragging like dead weights against authority. Because of their skills in verbal ambiguity, they can never, says Kenny, confront one another with feelings of anger or love, can never express inner needs nor appreciate them in others. Instead, each in the prison of a pseudo-self turns away from reality, ignores his or her appearance, and elaborates an inner world of fantasy.[66] These findings are a stunningly exact repetition of Shaw's allegation in *John Bull's Other Island* (1904) that 'An Irishman's imagination never lets him alone, never convinces him, never satisfies him; but it makes him that he can't face reality nor deal with it nor handle it nor conquer it: he can only sneer at them that do and . . . be "agreeable to strangers."'[67]

These problems are in large part a result of colonial oppression, but for the past sixty years the sole agents of that oppression have been the Irish themselves. Is there any hope for a change? To ask that question is to ask why Ireland has produced so many revivalist rebels and so few revolutionaries. If the country were to produce a generation of social visionaries the process would begin, as Fanon insisted, in the family. In Ireland today most psychologists still find that children with problems are mother-dominated, but they now concede that such problems can very often be attributed to the father's failure to assume full responsibility. This, indeed, is now the received international wisdom and the central argument of the best-selling book *Families and How to Survive Them*, by Robin Skynner and John Cleese. Their central theory casts much light on the Irish situation. Briefly, they argue that the father's role is central in the second year after a child's birth. The toddler needs space in which to achieve the beginnings of independence, but the mother feels a natural sadness at the prospect of a less intimate bond. The father at this point must try to compensate for this loss by reclaiming his place as a lover, as well as by fulfilling the duties of father. If he doesn't, so the theory goes, 'he's not helping the mother, or the baby, to cope with their next move of stepping back from each other'.[68]

Many emasculated fathers in colonial and post-colonial societies may lack the self-confidence, or hope for the future, that such a deed demands; by failing to act at the right moment they launch another generation into a further hopeless cycle. On the other hand, those fathers who *can* demonstrate that they are not under the mother's control help to cure the child of absolute dependency. By asserting his due authority over his children, the father allows them to explore their own anger until they can control it at will and learn to stand up for themselves. Even more important, the father thereby teaches the child that other people have needs too, and that we all function as members of wider and wider groups. When such fatherly authority is not asserted, the child may become a self-indulgent subversive with no respect for the configurations of the larger community – in other words, a rebel. Weak fathers lead to clutching mothers who raise rebel sons. If the father does assert himself, the child may begin the task of achieving a vision of society as a whole and the even more exhilarating challenge of framing an alternative. Irish rebels, feeding off the past, know what they are against; Irish revolutionaries, once they have learned to love the future, may yet learn what they are for.

NOTES

This essay is an extended version of a lecture given at the American Committee of Irish Studies, Tacoma, Washington, 1985. I wish to acknowledge helpful discussion of that lecture with Rob Garratt, Deirdre Bair, Vivian Mercier, Richard Murphy and John A. Murphy.

1 W. B. Yeats, *The Collected Plays* (New York: Macmillan, 1953), p. 112. Subsequent quotations are from this edition, cited parenthetically by page number in the text.
2 Peter Ure, *Yeats, the Playwright: A Commentary on Character and Design in the Major Plays* (London: Routledge & Kegan Paul, 1963), pp. 50–4.
3 Erich Fromm, *The Fear of Freedom* (London: Methuen, 1984), pp. 146, 148–9.
4 Simone Weil, *Waiting on God* (London: Collins Sons, 1983), p. 105.
5 Quoted in Rubem A. Alves, *Tomorrow's Child: Imagination, Creativity, and the Rebirth of Culture* (New York: Harper & Row, 1972), p. 110.
6 Fromm, *Fear of Freedom*, p. 142.
7 Norman O. Brown, *Life against Death: The Psychoanalytical Meaning of History* (Middletown, Conn.: Wesleyan University Press, 1959), pp. 92.
8 Frantz Fanon, *The Wretched of the Earth*, trans. Constance Farrington (Harmondsworth: Penguin, 1967), p. 135.
9 Karl Marx, 'The Eighteenth Brumaire of Louis Bonaparte', in *Surveys from Exile*, ed. David Fernback (Harmondsworth: Penguin, 1973).
10 Quoted in Bernard Ransom, *Connolly's Marxism* (London: Pluto Press, 1980), p. 46.
11 P. H. Pearse, *An Claidheamh Soluis*, 21 November 1908.
12 J. M. Synge, *The Complete Works of John M. Synge* (New York: Random House, 1936), p. 226. Subsequent quotations are from this edition, cited parenthetically by page number in the text.
13 See the chapters on *Ulysses* in Hugh Kenner, *Dublin's Joyce* (Bloomington: Indiana University Press, 1956), and in Frank Kermode, *The Sense of an Ending: Studies in the Theory of Fiction* (New York: Oxford University Press, 1967), pp. 113 ff.
14 For an extended version of this analysis see Declan Kiberd, 'Brian Friel's *Faith Healer*', in *Irish Writers and Society at Large*, ed. Masaru Sekine (Gerrards Cross: Colin Smythe, 1985), pp. 106–22.
15 Harold Bloom, *The Anxiety of Influence: A Theory of Poetry* (London and New York: Oxford University Press, 1975).

16 See Declan Kiberd, 'Inventing Irelands', *Crane Bag* 8 (1984): 11–26, for a fuller application of this idea.

17 Quoted in Thomas Mann, 'Psychoanalysis, the Lived Myth and Fiction', in *The Modern Tradition: Backgrounds of Modern Literature*, ed. Richard Ellmann and Charles Feidelon, Jr (New York: Oxford University Press, 1965), p. 677.

18 Heaney's fixation with Hamlet was taken by critics of the *Field Day/Crane Bag* enterprise as an example of how eternal students of phenomena may be immobilised by 'too much consciousness of the complexity of things'. In 'From Explanations to Intervention', Nina Witoszek and Pat Sheeran note Hamlet's ineffectiveness and ask if the ghost has anything to say (*Crane Bag* 9 (1985): 83–7). The present essay offers my alternative interpretation of the Hamlet tale, and a response to their critique.

19 W. B. Yeats, *Autobiographies* (London: Macmillan, 1955), p. 47.

20 Harold Rosenberg, *Act and the Actor: Making the Self* (University of Chicago Press, 1983), pp. 74–103.

21 Ibid., p. 102.

22 Marx, 'The Eighteenth Brumaire', p. 94.

23 Ibid.

24 John Berger, *About Looking* (London: Writers' and Readers' Publishing Co-op, 1980), p. 35.

25 Eric Hobsbawm, 'Inventing Traditions', in *The Invention of Tradition*, ed. Eric Hobsbawm and Terence Ranger (New York: Cambridge University Press, 1983), p. 22.

26 Seán de Fréine, *The Great Silence* (Dublin: Foilseacháin Náisiúnta Teoranta, 1965), p. 108.

27 J. M. Synge, 'Can We Go Back into Our Mother's Womb?' in *Prose*, ed. Alan Price (London: Oxford University Press, 1966), p. 400.

28 Quoted in Maurice Goldring, *Faith of Our Fathers: The Formation of Irish Nationalist Ideology 1890–1920* (Dublin: Repsol, 1982), pp. 80ff.

29 On this slot-rolling mechanism see Declan Kiberd, 'Anglo-Irish Attitudes', in *Ireland's Field Day* (London: Hutchinson Educational, 1985), pp. 92ff. Also see G. J. Watson, *Irish Identity and the Literary Revival* (London: Croom Helm, 1979), pp. 121ff.

30 Fromm, *Fear of Freedom*, pp. 160, 161.

31 Quoted in Desmond Fennell, *The State of the Nation: Ireland since the Sixties* (Dublin: Ward River Press, 1983), pp. 31–2.

32 W. B. Yeats, *Collected Poems* (London: Macmillan, 1951), p. 204.

33 Capt. Frederick Marryat, *Masterman Ready; Or, The Wreck of the Pacific* (London: Bell, 1978), p. 140.

34 Samuel Beckett, *Molloy; Malone Dies; The Unnamable* (London: Calder, 1959; reprint, 1976), p. 305.

35 Samuel Beckett, *Murphy* (London: Picador, 1973), p. 46.

36 James Joyce, *A Portrait of the Artist as a Young Man* (Harmondsworth: Penguin, 1969), p. 189.

37 Richard Poirier, *The Performing Self: Compositions and Decompositions in the Languages of Contemporary Life* (New York: Oxford University Press, 1971), pp. 8–14.

38 Irving Howe, *Literary Modernism* (Greenwich, Conn.: Fawcett Publications, 1967), p. 14.

39 Seamus Deane, 'Heroic Styles', in *Ireland's Field Day*, pp. 45–58. I wish to acknowledge a wider debt to Professor Deane, whose own critical writings have been a potent source of inspiration to me, and whose solidarity as a colleague has been an eloquent reminder that even in Ireland radical intellectuals have a right to a job.

40 James Joyce, *Ulysses* (Harmondsworth: Penguin, 1969), p. 31. Subsequent quotations are from this edition, cited parenthetically by page number in the text.

41 Fanon, *Wretched of the Earth*, p. 181.

42 Patrick Kavanagh, 'Memory of Brother Michael', in *Collected Poems* (London: Martin Brian and O'Keeffe, 1972), p. 84.

43 E. M. Forster, *A Passage to India* (Harmondsworth: Penguin, 1965), p. 58.

44 Quoted in V. S. Naipaul, *An Area of Darkness: An Experience of India* (London: André Deutsch, 1964), p. 209.

45 Ibid.

46 Goldring, *Faith of Our Fathers*, pp. 68 ff.

47 Quoted in Mike Milotte, *Communism in Modern Ireland: The Pursuit of the Workers' Republic since 1916* (Dublin: Gill & Macmillan, 1984), pp. 30–1.

48 David Fitzpatrick, *Politics and Irish Life 1913–1921: Provincial Experience of War and Revolution* (Dublin: Gill & Macmillan, 1977), p. 234.

49 José Ortega y Gasset, 'Pidiendo un Goethe desde dentro', in *Obras Completas* (Madrid: Revista de Occidente, 1966), vol. 4, 401.

50 Hannah Arendt, *Between Past and Future: Six Exercises in Political Thought* (London: Faber & Faber, 1961), p. 6.

51 Albert Memmi, *The Colonizer and the Colonized*, trans. Howard Greenfeld (Boston: Beacon Press, 1967), pp. 95–100.

52 Ibid., p. 101.

53 Kavanagh, 'The Great Hunger', in *Collected Poems*, p. 36.

54 Sean O'Casey, *Three Plays* (London: Macmillan, 1970), p. 71.

55 Frantz Fanon, *Dying Colonialism*, trans. Haakon Chevalier (Harmondsworth: Penguin, 1970), p. 81.

56 See Declan Kiberd, *Men and Feminism in Modern Literature* (London: Macmillan, 1985).

57 Fanon, *Dying Colonialism*, pp. 83, 85.

58 Ibid., p. 86.

59 Carl E. Schorske, *Fin-de-Siècle Vienna: Politics and Culture* (New York: Vintage Books, 1981), pp. 191–7.

60 Yeats, *Collected Poems*, p. 203.

61 Robert Wohl, *The Generation of 1914* (Cambridge, Mass.: Harvard University Press, 1979), p. 115.

62 Ibid.

63 Daniel Corkery, *Synge and Anglo-Irish Literature: A Study* (Cork University Press, 1931), chap. 1.

64 Nancy Scheper-Hughes, *Saints, Scholars, and Schizophrenics: Mental Illness in Rural Ireland* (Berkeley and Los Angeles: University of California Press, 1979), pp. 3, 65, 111ff.

65 Ivor Browne, 'Mental Health and Modern Living' (paper delivered 8 May 1976 at a seminar of the Eastern Health Board, reported in the *Irish Times*, 9 May 1976).

66 J. V. Kenny, 'The Post-Colonial Personality', *Crane Bag* 9 (1985): 70–9.

67 G. B. Shaw, *The Complete Plays of Bernard Shaw* (London: Odhams, 1937), p. 411.

68 Robin Skynner and John Cleese, *Families and How to Survive Them* (London: Methuen, 1983), pp. 189ff.

CHAPTER 12

The Elephant of Revolutionary Forgetfulness

(1991)

1991: WHO FEARS TO SPEAK OF EASTER WEEK?

On Easter Sunday 1991, the leaders of the Irish Republic gathered at the General Post Office in Dublin to remember the event that led to their state's foundation. The ceremony was spare. Five surviving veterans of the Rising attended (a sixth stayed away as a protest at what he saw as the current politicians' betrayal of the ideals of 1916). A revelation in the *Irish Press* during the previous week that no special travel arrangements had been made for the veterans, some of whom were infirm, had the desired effect. The former rebels were given seats near to state dignitaries.

Later, the Taoiseach, Charles J. Haughey, was featured in an interview on the six o'clock news. The reporter did not ask whether such a brief, sheepish ceremony was an appropriate way to mark the seventy-fifth anniversary, or whether it might be contrasted unfavourably with 4 July celebrations in the United States or Bastille Day in France. What transpired was far more interesting than that: the leader of a sovereign state was asked *why he was holding a ceremony at all*. If privately he considered the question insulting or stupid, he concealed his feelings with great skill and gave a civil answer. The reporter suggested that IRA terrorists might derive comfort and succour from the festivities. Mr Haughey quietly denied this.

In the weeks leading up to that moment, only one political group, the Workers' Party – with support levels in the community of about 5 per cent – had questioned the wisdom of commemoration. Its leader spoke, caustically and repeatedly, of the dangers of a 'triumphalist' celebration, such as had been conducted in 1966. RTÉ radio airwaves reflected this debate, giving equal airtime to both sides and conveying the impression of a community split down the middle on the issue.

On 27 March 1991, *Wednesday Report* was broadcast on RTÉ television as the station's documentary on the anniversary. In the event, it said little about the 1916 Rebellion, devoting itself instead to 1966. Photographs of a younger Charles Haughey, sitting alongside soldiers on state platforms in that year, were used to a background of an IRA ballad. Short sound-bites from nationalist intellectuals were juxtaposed with long monologues by critics of Irish nationalism. Conor Cruise O'Brien repeated his well-known analysis of the 'Brit-bashing' version of history taught (so he claimed) by the Irish Christian Brothers. Two of the Brothers' more illustrious graduates offered themselves as proof of the O'Brienite diagnosis. The writer Dermot Bolger contrasted the 'triumphalist' rhetoric of 1966 with the social realities faced by poor Dubliners in that year. Mr Bolger, who was born in 1959, would have been all of seven years old in 1966: at an age when most Dublin boys were falling off their first two-wheel bicycle, he apparently was amassing sociological evidence for O'Brienite historiography. On the same programme, the journalist Fintan O'Toole contended that RTÉ television's 1966 serial *Insurrection* had had a 'huge' influence on the revival of Sinn Féin in the North. A short clip was shown to illustrate the militarist ethos of *Insurrection*, but the programme as a whole could not be rebroadcast, said an RTÉ official, 'because repeat royalty payments to actors would be prohibitive'. Viewers were left to take Mr Bolger's expert word that Hugh Leonard's vivid script had helped the recruiting sergeants of Sinn Féin.

In fact, few Northern Irish homes were able to receive the RTÉ signal in 1966; and any nationalists who saw the serial would in all likelihood have wondered if they – living in a gerrymandered state based on religious apartheid – could decently share in the southern rejoicings. The possibility that these social injustices had contributed a great deal more to the current IRA campaign was not canvassed on *Wednesday Report*, nor was anyone allowed to recall that, as late as 1969, the acronym IRA on a Belfast wall was taken to mean 'I Ran Away.' Once again, southern 'radicals' were proving themselves addicted to the rather un-Marxist belief that cultural consciousness determines social being, rather than social being determining cultural consciousness.

At the end of *Wednesday Report*, a Leaving Certificate class at the Bishopstown Comprehensive School in Cork indicated that its members knew little and cared less about 1916. Most recalled, however, the 'triumphalism' of the 1966 anniversary and its serious contribution to violence in Northern Ireland. None of the speakers could have been born earlier than 1972.

And so the 'commemoration' continued. If, in fact, the Christian Brothers had brainwashed one generation with a set of nationalist myths, then their products-in-revolt could administer an equally simplified anti-dote. If, in the bad old days, rote learning of the approved post-colonial line secured you a scholarship and a place in college, now, in the bad new times, it could land you a spot on late-night television. The voices raised on *Wednesday Report* and day after day in the *Irish Times* were so determined that Ireland should complete the move from nationalist autocracy to workerist conformism that they left no space for any tedious interludes of liberalism. And so, fancying themselves the sponsors of a persecuted modernity, they smugly marginalised all other voices of dissent or challenge, whether feminist or environmentalist or gay or, indeed, nationalist. But not completely. There was, for one thing, the small but not utterly insignificant matter of actual public opinion. The workerist media operatives had been so busy 'shaping' opinion that they had never bothered to measure it. But the market-driven *Irish Independent* newspaper did. Its findings must have startled anyone foolish enough to rely on other outlets in the previous weeks. In a scientific survey, 65 per cent of respondents said that they looked on the Rising with pride, as opposed to a mere 14 per cent who said they regretted it. Fifty-eight per cent thought that the rebels were right to take up arms, as opposed to 24 per cent who would have preferred them to try political means. And 66 per cent thought that 'the men of 1916' [*sic*] would oppose today's IRA violence, as opposed to just 16 per cent who considered that they would endorse it.

Emboldened by these findings, perhaps, the *Irish Independent* (which in 1916 had called for the execution of the rebel leaders) printed on 30 March what was by far the most rigorous supplement of commemoration to appear in 1991, with the survey itself alongside major articles from different viewpoints by J. J. Lee, Conor Cruise O'Brien, T. P. O'Neill and Maurice Manning. On an RTÉ debate on 2 April, Professor John A. Murphy sought to distance himself from the views of Conor Cruise O'Brien, who had been arguing for two decades that the Easter rebels and the Provisional IRA were analogous. The fact that the Easter rebels obeyed the international rules of war and that they secured a retrospective mandate in 1918 clearly differentiated them from today's IRA, he contended. It was significant that the man who said these things was not only a professor of history but a politician active in the Irish Senate, who must have read the *Irish Independent* poll. It was becoming clear to everyone that the 2 per cent of votes given to Sinn Féin in the Republic's last general election was but a derisory fraction of the 65 per cent of citizens who took pride in 1916. For years, journalists in RTÉ and 'serious' newspapers had sought to enforce the O'Brienite equation, but it would no longer wash.

On a subsequent Saturday, a group of citizens, led by artist Robert Ballagh and frustrated at the government's failure to organise a more splendid celebration, held its own festival in central Dublin. Thousands of families took part, as did poets, musicians, face-painters and so on. RTÉ's six o'clock news reported the event for thirty-two seconds as its final item; and the camera focused not on the crowd of families, but on the presence of Sinn Féin president, Gerry Adams MP. Clearly, the *Irish Independent*'s poll had not yet got through to everyone in RTÉ.

While these bizarre events unfolded in Dublin, the peoples of Eastern Europe were asserting their national rights. Stalinism had all but crumbled there; but one might have been forgiven for thinking that it was still alive and well in Dublin 2 and 4. Such a situation was Orwellian, in the strict sense adumbrated by the author of *Nineteen Eighty-Four*: disciples of a single party were reaching into the past and saying of an event that it should be erased from memory. Nor was this the first bout of such amnesia in Irish public life: for decades, the 150,000 Irish who fought in World War One (for 'the rights of small nations', as most of them saw it) had been effectively extirpated from the official record. Now, it seemed that powerfully organised cadres within the Irish intelligentsia were keen to airbrush the 1916 rebels out of official history as well.

1966 AND ALL THAT

Amnesiacs, as Nietzsche joked, have good strategic reasons for their forgetfulness; and in an Ireland often accused of fixation on the past, such reasons would not be far to seek. For decades, conservative nationalist parties had encouraged the people to become drunk on remembrance: endless references by leaders to their part in the Rising conveniently distracted attention from their failure to implement the 1916 promise to cherish all the children of the nation equally. In such a context, it might have seemed reasonable to some that the fittest way to honour a man like James Connolly was a strategic forgetfulness of his life and sacrifice. After all, he himself had warned that, in Ireland, the worship of the past is often an excuse for an escape from the mediocrity of the present. So, an analysis was advanced to the effect that the best nations – like the most emancipated women – were those with 'no history'. History, after all, was a nightmare from which every Irish person was trying to awake: Joyce had echoed in that great line Karl Marx's reasoned lament that the past always seemed to weigh like a nightmare upon the brains of the living. When bombs began to explode again on Irish streets in graphic illustration of that image, it seemed sensible to many people to wind down the Easter military parade; otherwise, the people were 'in danger of commemorating themselves to death'.

During the fiftieth anniversary celebrations of the 1916 Rising, the sponsors of this radical analysis suffered something of a setback. Politicians and propagandists produced a sanitised, heroic image of Patrick Pearse, at least partly to downplay the socialism of Connolly, then attracting the allegiance of the liberal young. It took some years more before the genuine liberalism of Pearse's own views on education was established by scholars such as Séamas Ó Buachalla and Ruth Dudley Edwards (the latter, for all her sharp criticisms of the man, restored an essential humanity in her portrait). Much of the critique of Pearse in more recent times has been a necessary and overdue reaction against the plaster saint constructed in 1966 and by biographers like Louis Le Roux in the decades after Pearse's execution. It is the business of historians to revise knowledge, and there was a quiet kind of nobility about the attempts by a generation of historians, led by T. W. Moody and Robin Dudley Edwards, to interrogate the Irish past and, if necessary, the current public misunderstanding of it. Scholarly 'revisionism' of that kind is essential to any nation; and it had been proceeding since the 1940s as a disinterested pursuit of the facts by men and women anxious to question the journalistic simplifications of history, which are bound to arise in a recently independent state.

These simplifications reached their point of maximum publicity in the Republic in 1966, especially in *Insurrection*, which tellingly crossed the techniques of historical fiction with those of the Pathé newsreel. Many people can still recall their excitement as they watched Hugh Leonard's serial, and they are accordingly amused to find its author today featuring as a leading exponent of the *Sunday Independent* school of rebel-detection. Thus the whirligig of time brings in his revenges. It would be trite, however, to castigate Mr Leonard as a *laudator temporis acti* and scarcely more helpful to describe him as a conscience-stricken wordsmith worried that his play might have sent out men to shoot the English. The 1966 celebrations were a little more complex than that: they represented a last, over-the-top purgation of a debt to the past, which most of the celebrants secretly suspected would go unpaid. The Ireland of that year was embarked on a headlong rush to modernity, which so discomfited some returning emigrants from the United States that they found the homeland unrecognisable and vowed never to come again. Television – the agent of much of the change – was being put to a reassuring use on *Insurrection*, consoling the public with images of an Ireland it had all but abolished.

By far the most perceptive commentary on all this was written in 1966 by Conor Cruise O'Brien in a commemorative supplement to the *Irish Times*. In 'The Embers of Easter', he charged that there was 'no cause for self-congratulation', since the two major national objectives (reintegration of the national territory and restoration of the Irish language) had been quietly abandoned. Even more remarkable than this honesty was the essayist's insistence on placing the Rising in a European context. He took his epigraph from Lenin: 'A blow delivered against the British imperialist bourgeoisie in Ireland is a hundred times more significant than a blow of equal weight in Africa or Asia . . . The misfortune of the Irish is that they rose prematurely, when the European revolt of the proletariat had not yet matured' (O'Brien, 225). Cruise O'Brien speculated that had the rebels waited until 1918 when the country was united against conscription, then a Rising with mass support would have called forth a British reign of terror, with the inevitable consequence of mutinies by Irish troops on the western front. By then mass mutiny had taken Russia right out of the war, and the morale of both the British and French armies was very low indeed: so it would at least have been a possibility that the European ruling order might have collapsed. Cruise O'Brien cited Connolly's metaphor to the effect that 'a pin in the hands of a child can pierce the heart of a giant' (O'Brien, 227). This was all speculation, necessarily, but bracing nonetheless, when compared with the dreary platitudes being spouted by politicians at the time.

In the earlier 1960s, Conor Cruise O'Brien had played a leading part in African decolonisation and so he was better positioned than most Irish commentators to understand the significance of the Easter Rising in the history of anti-imperial movements. How, then, did he become by the early 1970s one of the Rising's foremost detractors? Doubtless his personal experiences in Irish politics had something to do with that change, but so also had the fluctuations of international affairs. Until the late 1960s, the 'Western' intelligentsia in general offered much support to anti-colonial struggles in Algeria, Palestine, Iran, Vietnam and so on. It was only in the following decade that a moment of exhaustion was reached when many writers repented and revised. Khomeini in Iran, Amin in Africa, Pol Pot in Cambodia – these were the new demons, as the image of the freedom-fighter was gradually replaced by that of the 'terrorist'. Back in 1937, sub-editors at the *Irish Press* had been instructed to replace the word 'bandit' with 'freedom-fighter' in processing stories from international news agencies; but, now, the traffic was more likely to flow in the other direction. Many of the regimes in post-colonial nations were barbaric; others were simply incompetent; but support for either kind was now often equated with obscurantism. The old, liberal–radical critique of colonialism, pioneered by Bertrand Russell and Jean-Paul Sartre, was usurped by the new, fashionable thesis of the 'self-inflicted wound', especially as propounded in the elegant travel books of V. S. Naipaul. His *India: A Wounded Civilization* contended that it was the native religions, rather than the colonial distortion, that accounted for the subcontinent's apparent helplessness: the undeveloped economy was a result of the underdevelopment of *ego* in Hindu religion (Naipaul, 43). A text such as this proved immensely popular among 'Western' liberals and conservatives, who were coming to a new-found consensus based on the conviction that, when the British left the colonies, things only got worse, and who needed to hear a convincing voice from within the Third World telling them that this was indeed so? By a subtle modulation, all remaining British guilt about the colonial adventure could be expunged, because one of the talented, witty natives had given permission, and in beautiful, eighteenth-century prose of which readers of the *Observer* or the *New York Times* could approve. More radical, liberationist writers like Salman Rushdie, on the other hand, have declared that the chaos of the post-colony cannot be simplified or homogenised into well-bred Enlightenment models: he would accuse a Naipaul or an O'Brien of a fatal willingness to pose Third World questions in the inappropriate language of the 'West' or to describe the culture of a colony in the discourse of the imperialist. This would certainly describe the shift in Cruise O'Brien's position on 1916.

Anti-nationalist revisionism is rightly seen as a journalistic phenomenon of the early 1970s, called into prominence after the dreadful provocation of the IRA's bombing campaign by such powerful polemics as Father Francis Shaw's 'challenge' to the nationalist canon in *Studies* and by Conor Cruise O'Brien's book *States of Ireland*. Both appeared in 1972, at a time when the collection of shattered civilian bodies into plastic bags was a commonplace televisual image and when the life-expectancy of a Derry IRA volunteer was about six months. Father Shaw's articles had been written for intended publication in 1966, as a bracing antidote to the largely uncritical commemorative mood; and Dr O'Brien's reservations about militant nationalism dated even further back, to his fruitless days in the Anti-Partition League of the mid-century. Both were refreshing and exacting interrogations of a prevailing stereotype, but they rapidly became the signal for a 'new consensus' in the media. When an Official IRA bombing in Aldershot left a number of working women dead, the movement called off its military campaign and instructed members to promote this new thinking. Through the years that followed, airwaves and news pages would be given over increasingly to exponents of the new philosophy, not all of them by any means members of the Workers' Party – the successor of Official Sinn Féin – but all in basic agreement with its new line on Northern Ireland. The salient point here is that many promoters of the new orthodoxy were the same people who had abetted the simplified media celebrations of 1966 – and so the rather complex analyses of an O'Brien or a Shaw became homogenised to the point of caricature for popular consumption. Most academic historians continued their work of disinterested scholarly research, but some who produced texts reflective of the new fashion were strenuously promoted in the media.

As time went on, it became harder for nationalists to get a fair hearing without leaving themselves open to a charge of being fellow-travellers of the Provisional IRA. The Section 31 ban on radio or television appearances by members of Provisional Sinn Féin was not only a suppression of democratic debate; it also put those nationalists who did appear in a double bind. On the one hand, they were at the microphone precisely because they were *not* Provisionals, and yet they were constantly asked by producers (who claimed to be 'concerned with balance') to guess at or articulate what Sinn Féin's thinking might be. By osmosis, many of these commentators became associated in the popular mind with the Provisionals, even though most had nothing to do with them. The object of the producers and editors was clear in method and intent: to try by every means to discredit left-wing intellectuals who adapted a nationalist but non-Provisional stance. Effectively, they were given a simple choice: either throw in their lot with the Provos, or go over to the ranks of anti-nationalist revisionism.

There was no room for liberal tolerance or intellectual subtlety in these matters, no middle ground to be occupied. If a person came out in defence of the 1916 Rebellion in the media, he or she was simply dubbed a 'Provoid' or 'Hush Puppy Provo'; and many careers were either aborted or retarded so that the 'new consensus' might flourish. Like all such movements, it attracted to its ranks not just committed ideologues but also self-serving hacks, who could construct lucrative media careers around the newly fashionable themes. Patrick Pearse was now 'accused' of homosexuality by persons who, quite properly, would not have considered it a crime in a Gide or a Wilde.

Nor did the profession of history remain entirely uncorrupted. Access to the Northern Ireland Public Records Office was denied to Michael Farrell, presumably because he wrote books of history from a nationalist viewpoint. There were few voices raised in protest among professional historians at this further denial of intellectual freedom. And so it came to pass that academics could write entire narratives of Irish history which contained no reference whatever to either 'colonialism' or 'imperialism'; and that the head of a sovereign state could find himself apologising to a weekend-roster reporter for his audacity in commemorating that state's foundation.

1916: FORGOTTEN, BUT NOT GONE?

These bouts of communal amnesia are characteristic of most post-colonial states. India provides a good example. In *Midnight's Children*, Salman Rushdie describes a 'nation of forgetters' and evokes a hero, Saleem, born at the moment of Indian independence but 'fated to plunge memoryless into an adulthood whose every aspect grew daily more grotesque'. All of Midnight's Children, born in 1947, suffer from the same terrible ailment:

Somewhere in the many moves of the peripatetic slum, they had mislaid their powers of retention, so that now they had become incapable of judgment, having forgotten everything to which they could compare anything that happened. Even the Emergency was rapidly being consigned to the oblivion of the past, and the magicians concentrated upon the present with the monomania of snails.
(Rushdie, 428)

Or take Latin America as another case in point. *One Hundred Years of Solitude* is the great novel chronicling its history, in the course of which Gabriel García Márquez portrays what happens when an entire community loses its memory. The pathology in the case of each individual is clear: 'when the sick person became used to his state of vigil, the recollection of his childhood began to be erased from his memory, then the name and notion of things, and finally the identity of people and even the awareness of his own being, until he sank into a kind of idiocy that had no past'. Everything in Márquez's mythical Macondo fails in consequence – industry: 'nothing could be sold in a town that was sinking irrevocably into a quicksand of forgetfulness'; labour agitation: a massacre of workers is erased with the phrase 'there weren't any dead; . . . nothing has happened and nothing will ever happen. This is a happy town' (Márquez, 283–7).

One Hundred Years of Solitude is, among other things, a caustic critique of 'revisionism' in the narrower, negative meaning of that word when used to indicate the process whereby the history of a colonised people is taken from them. Its protagonist, Aureliano, learns from the one honest man who remains in the town what the facts truly were, though, of course, 'one would have thought that he was telling a hallucinated version, because it was radically opposed to the false one that historians had created and consecrated in the schoolbooks' (Márquez, 322). In the end, the people of Macondo are made to believe that the Yankee perpetrators of a massacre, the banana company and its officials, never existed at all.

In Ireland, those who would erase or diminish the memory of 1916 are actuated by one simple conviction: glorification of the Easter rebels leads young people to join the IRA. The worries that keep *Insurrection* locked in RTÉ vaults are the same worries that troubled Yeats in old age:

> Did that play of mine send out
> Certain men the English shot?
> ('The Man and the Echo')

In his case the answer was: probably. The famous play *Cathleen ni Houlihan* (1902) did suggest that the old woman (played by Maud Gonne) would walk like a young queen only when men were willing to die for her. The rebels who walked into the Post Office some years later *were* writers and artists, consciously literary in their demeanour – in their choice of date (Easter, with connotations of renewal and redemption); in their clothing (kilts were worn and bagpipes played in the lulls between fighting); in their bearing (Pearse handed over a symbolic sword in surrendering formally to the enemy).

But that was then and this is now. All across Europe at that time, young men had been filled with the old, chivalric claptrap that it was a sweet and noble thing to die for your country. (The suicidal young assassin at Sarajevo epitomised the fashion.) They could believe this because, for decades, they had not experienced war at first hand. Pearse's view of bloodshed as 'a cleansing and sanctifying thing' for a youth grown supine from the long peace is horrible rhetoric by any of today's standards, but he was not exceptional in advancing it at the time. The liberal humanist Sigmund Freud wrote in 1915 that, unless it is placed constantly in jeopardy, life becomes 'as shallow as an American flirtation' and that only with the prospect of ten thousand deaths a day had it 'recovered its full content and become interesting again'. A majority of Europeans probably believed in these ideas. What is remarkable about Ireland is that only a tiny minority was willing to give them credence. The real lesson of 1916 for today is that acts of violence which have no popular mandate evoke little support in Irish people. Even *after* Pearse and the rebels had held out for a week of unexampled bravery against a mighty empire, they were jeered by Dubliners as they were led away. Only the official and prolonged violence of the British authorities could have rallied support to the rebel cause. As George Bernard Shaw pointed out, the rebels had fought a fair, gentlemanly fight and the executions seemed to Irish minds a bloodthirsty and illegal murder of prisoners of war. The subsequent victory of Sinn Féin in 1918 was based less on a glorification of Easter week than on a principled opposition among the electorate to conscription of young men into World War One. (This is the real mandate for the Irish tradition of neutrality.) In so far as Sinn Féin became implicated in violent deeds during the War of Independence, it suffered severe political reversals. This seems to indicate that, far from being the 'fighting Irish' of legend, the peoples of Ireland are remarkably pacific and that any movement seeking mass support for its policies, or any government seeking to commit the country to war, ignores this at great peril.

There is little in the ethos of Irish life or culture to glorify violence. The greatest work of modern Irish literature, *Ulysses*, is something of a pacifist tract whose central voice, Leopold Bloom, denounces all armies and insists that the only victories worth having are those won in the mind. Synge's exposure of the gap between a 'gallous story' and a 'dirty deed' has been updated in our own time by writers as diverse as Seamus Heaney and Brendan Behan. Even those who sing rebel ballads in public houses (the so-called armchair Provos) are in all likelihood purging an aggressive tendency which, otherwise, might take the lethal form of action.

The notion that a glorification of 1916 in poems or ballads leads to recruits for the IRA is insulting to the intelligence of the general public and of the IRA. What created the modern IRA was not any cultural force, but the bleak, sectarian realities of life in the corrupt statelet of Northern Ireland. During Operation Motorman in Derry in 1972, an *Observer* journalist interviewed a dying volunteer, who assured her that 'Mother Ireland' or 'Cathleen ni Houlihan' meant nothing to him; he was dying simply to defend the neighbours in the street on which he had grown up. The idea that IRA violence is rooted in the Christian Brothers' teaching of history is far too simple to account for today's complex and cruel world. It is endorsed by the only groups in Ireland today who really glamorise the IRA – those who confer on them the spurious aura of the outlaw by banning them from the airwaves, or by supporting such a ban. These are invariably the same people who have abandoned the attempt to get to grips with the underlying problem of a state built on ritual discrimination.

The most probing criticisms of 1916 have come not from latter-day castigators of Irish nationalism, but from the rebels and their immediate contemporaries. Michael Collins, who was in the GPO, found the theatricality too self-conscious for his pragmatic tastes: it had, he noted ambiguously, 'the air of a Greek tragedy'. The more ruthless methods he later adopted – such as killing government officials in front of their families – would certainly have shocked some of the men who vowed in the Proclamation to avoid all traces of 'inhumanity'.

Other paradoxes may be noted. The poet Yeats praised the theatricality of the rebels – the 'terrible beauty' is Aristotle's tragic compound of pity and terror – while the playwright O'Casey was wholly allergic to it. O'Casey had resigned from the Citizen Army when it decreed that its men should wear uniforms (he saw these as a foolish vanity which would simply mark out volunteers more clearly as targets for their military enemies). In *The Plough and the Stars* he mocked Uncle Peter's nationalist uniform, like something 'gone asthray out of a toyshop'. Doubtless O'Casey saw costumes as a bourgeois affectation, for in a real revolution the people would wear their own clothes.

There is a problem with that analysis, however. Every revolution nerves itself for the open future by pretending to be a reassuring restoration of some past glory. The French rebels of 1789 donned togas in the pretence that they were resurrected Romans restoring democracy; but, of course, the costumes were worn to conceal the disturbing radicalism of their new ideas. By analogy, Pearse summoned Cuchulain to his side in the GPO, but only to validate the ideal of a welfare state which cherished the children of the nation equally. Likewise, Connolly invoked the ancient Gaelic system, whereby a ruler held land in the name of all the people, as an instinctual, early version of his socialist ideal. The donning of historical garb or the adoption of ancient rhetoric may not be as conservative as O'Casey thought.

These radical ideas are all still relevant, but they are not often associated in the public mind with Pearse and Connolly. Those who organised the pageants of 1966 never mentioned child-centred education, Anglo-Irish literature or redistributive justice – all concepts promoted by rebel leaders long before they became fashionable. Instead, Pearse and Connolly passed into Irish history attired in that most inappropriate garb, the military uniform. How was this simplification possible? One answer is that the old-fashioned conservative nationalists removed all troubling complexities from these men's thought in the early decades of the infant state. This played right into the hands of the new-fangled 'revisionists', who were happy to demolish the cardboard caricature thus created . . . but they went on to replace it with an equally simple-minded caricature of their own. Although each school of thought likes to think of itself as the mortal enemy of the other, both are distorted interpretations that feed remorselessly off one another, and both are sponsored by rival sections of the bureaucratic middle class. As a result, the real complexity of the thought of 1916 has been all but lost from national debate. In 1966 people who seemed too interested by Connolly's socialism were dubbed 'reds' by conservative nationalists; but in 1991 those who still professed an interest in the Irish language or Gaelic cultural traditions were frequently called 'fascists' (and their castigators used the same word to describe Estonian or Lithuanian protesters against Soviet imperialism). Much of the political and cultural life of Ireland has been distorted accordingly. Organised cadres in the news media pilloried the Green TD Roger Garland for his effrontery in opposing extradition; not one of these cadres saw fit to report Garland's anti-violence picket on the headquarters of Sinn Féin. In the literary world, a major talent like Thomas Kinsella has been marginalised since his poem protesting about Bloody Sunday in 1972, while a minor figure such as Dermot Bolger has been programmatically proclaimed as 'the new James Joyce'. It is no coincidence that many of Bolger's celebrants or Kinsella's detractors played a leading part in the 1991 media 'commemoration' of 1916.

The alleged problem here is the 'nationalism' of a figure like Garland or Kinsella; but the real problem is that the designer-Stalinists who control so many Irish debates can deal with only one idea at a time: for them, it must always be a simple choice between tradition or modernity, nationalism or social progress, soccer or Gaelic football. Those who defend tradition, nationalism or the Gaelic Athletic Association are merely jeered; but those who try to combine both elements represent an insupportable 'ambivalence' and so are targeted for vicious attack. A case in point would be the early Field Day pamphlets of the 1980s, some of whose authors were called (in the *Times Literary Supplement*) the literary wing of the IRA. Yet the pamphleteers' arguments could hardly have been more balanced. In effect, they warned that one could not implement the dream of an absolute return to a mythic Gaelic past and that one should not submit to the shallow cosmopolitanism which sought to fill the ensuing vacuum. Instead, there should be a perpetual negotiation between both worlds.

This sane ideal is the real 'unfinished business' of 1916, and of the Irish nation–state. It rejects the dreary polarities of all binary thought, recognising that a vital part of the imperialist mission was to compel the colonial subject to see life only in these slot-rolling categories. Pearse himself wrote well in both Irish and English. Connolly fused international socialism with Irish nationalist traditions. Their direct contemporary, James Joyce, spent much of 1916 elaborating his portrait of Leopold Bloom, the new 'womanly man', who threw all such polarities into question. It was the British imperialists who had created the notion of a necessary antithesis between things English and Irish, but a sharp critique of such thinking was implicit in the writings of the generation of 1916. This critique was neglected by those who came later: for example, MacDonagh's fusion of Gaelic and Anglo-Irish traditions in his posthumously published *Literature in Ireland* has yet to be fully implemented in courses on Irish Studies in the nation's schoolrooms.

It was left to decolonising peoples elsewhere to complete the analysis, for Ireland after the executions was doomed to a cycle of imperialist violence and nationalist counter-violence. The militarist ethic thus cultivated, in Easter marches and in the regalia so proudly displayed in the National Museum, became a subtle form of collaboration with an imperial culture based on force, coercion and a devaluation of the female. Nationalism on its own, unredeemed by other enriching ideals, was always doomed to be a replica of its imperial enemy. For every British army funeral, there would be an IRA one; for soccer, there would be Gaelic football; for the parliament at Westminster, the Dáil. Such gestures could offer only what the Gaelic poets of previous centuries so feared, 'Sacsa Nua darb ainm Éire' (A New England called Ireland). Only in places like India and Algeria did thinkers like Ashis Nandy and Frantz Fanon break out of the inherited binary-thinking and opt for the 'third way' of liberation. Instead of, say, Irish against English nationalism, they would oppose either in favour of the ideal of international brotherhood; instead of male against female, they would set against either the notion of androgyny. A new set of criteria would thus emerge, according to which the martial ethos of the imperialist was found wanting.

There was, in fact, one participant in the events of 1916 who so perfectly achieved this transcendence of the old polarities that he was shot in the very space he opened between the traditional enemies: Francis

Sheehy-Skeffington. A pacifist and crusader for women's rights, he was also a socialist who was proud to name himself a friend of the republicans. In a magnificent letter to Thomas MacDonagh just before the Rising, he praised the future rebel's ideas, but denied that the war they proposed could be 'manly' or anything better than 'organized militarism'. The questions raised in his letter are still pertinent: why are arms so glorified?; will not those who rejoice in barbarous warfare inevitably come to control such an organisation?; why are women not more centrally involved? 'When you have found and clearly expressed the reason . . .', he added, 'you will be close to the reactionary element in the movement itself' (Skeffington, 151).

Skeffington was murdered by a British officer who arrested him and two other men. He had been trying to organise a citizens' watch to prevent the looting of shops, a looting that would, he felt, bring discredit on Dublin's working class (whom he loved) and on the nationalist cause (which he admired). His life is an eloquent reminder that it is possible to be non-violent and republican, that not all who sympathise with nationalism are autocratic reactionaries, and that people who are labelled 'subversive sympathisers' are often being punished for subtleties of which their assailants are incapable.

The 1916 Rebellion was a brave, clean fight against an empire. Its protagonists, who volunteered without pay and jeopardised their careers as well as their lives, deserve all honour. They were indeed the pin that pierced the heart of a giant, for they made certain that Ireland would be the first among many British territories to decolonise in the twentieth century. If critics today are free to use the publicly subsidised airwaves to sneer at their achievement, that freedom would never have been made possible without it, for there would have been no independent Irish institutions at all. The 1916 rebels, unlike the subsequent insurrectionists of both Official and Provisional variety, did all in their power to avoid civilian casualties, took enormous risks themselves, and quit the field with honour. They had no popular mandate, it is true, and this weakness has always been apparent. O'Casey, in *The Plough and the Stars*, has a retreating Citizen Army officer refer to the looters as 'slum lice'. Such a phrase (whether it was ever actually uttered or not) indicates the gulf of misunderstanding between the insurgents and many of the people in whose name they rose; ever since, that gulf has seriously damaged the prospects for a truly liberated Ireland.

O'Casey, however, was hardly the most objective witness. An urge to self-justification mars the artistic balance of *The Plough and the Stars*.

As a former Citizen Army member, he may have felt the usual survivor-guilt of one who took no part in a war. He recoiled, for honourable reasons, from the carnage, but the natural aggression that remained unpurged in his personality was finally vented on the rebels in his play. Operating a kind of Section 31 ahead of its time, he kept them on the edge of his stage and never allowed one of them to make a full statement of the nationalist case. Instead, he portrayed them as vain, strutting fellows, and the ordinary citizens who thrilled to their rhetoric as dupes – hardly the sort of portraiture expected in most countries of a people's playwright. By depicting his inner-city Dubliners as jabbering leprechauns, he appealed to the new middle-class elites which dominated the Free State and which cast the Dublin proletarian in the role once reserved by the Anglo-Irish establishment for the Stage Irish peasant. And, of course, O'Casey lied blatantly in claiming that the rebels used dum-dum bullets: even the British enquiry found no evidence of that. Like more recent ideologues disgusted by a violence they had once endorsed, O'Casey felt the need to distort the evidence, exaggerating not only the mendacity of some rebels but also the virtues of their British opponents. His play is tremendously popular these days, partly due to brilliant productions by Joe Dowling and Garry Hynes, but mainly because it is much touted by the designer-Stalinists who have so successfully impoverished the contemporary debate about the past. It should never be forgotten that those who first protested against the play in 1926 were *not* fanatical nationalists; they were radical socialists like Liam O'Flaherty and Hanna Sheehy-Skeffington, the widow of Frank.

The murderous IRA bombings of recent decades have made it hard to honour the 1916 generation, and the intellectual terrorist campaign of denigration against 'Provo fellow-travellers' has done great damage too. The authors of such activities will succeed, however, only if the great majority of Irish nationalists submit to the thesis that the Provisionals are the sole custodians of the 1916 flame. In 1991, despite a systematic campaign for over fifteen years on the national airwaves to promote this thesis, 65 per cent of the population still took a celebratory pride in the Rising. In the same year, the lessons from Eastern Europe and the Third World made it abundantly clear that nationalism was still a potent force. The challenge in Ireland, as elsewhere, was to learn how to sift the good in it from the bad in an unfettered nationwide public debate. There was pitifully little of that debate in evidence in the official media or in some 'quality' newspapers during the year: for, as in 1966, a critical exchange of ideas proved all but impossible. But begin that debate surely will, and when it does, the debaters could do worse than start with the writings of Francis Sheehy-Skeffington. He was in truth 'the finest of all the flowers that fell in Easter Week'.

Early in the nineteenth century, the Emperor Napoleon sought to commemorate his African campaign in an appropriate manner, so he decreed that a brass elephant be erected in central Paris. The siting of this animal in the Place de la Bastille was interpreted by some as a calculated snub to the French revolutionaries of the previous decade. However, things did not work out quite as Napoleon planned. His own campaign came unstuck and he fell from power. The government could raise money only for a gigantic *plaster* elephant, which soon began to disintegrate: first a tusk fell off, then a leg was infested with rats, and eventually the curator resigned in disgust. The beast was by then known to all amused Parisians as 'The Elephant of Revolutionary Forgetfulness'. There may be more than a few mordant citizens of Dublin who, after Charles Haughey's scaled-down ceremonial at the General Post Office on Easter Sunday 1991, are expecting a similar statue to appear in the spot vacated in 1966 by Admiral Lord Nelson.

FURTHER READING

Ciarán Brady, ed., *Interpreting Irish History: The Debate on Historical Revisionism*, Dublin, 1994.
Ruth Dudley Edwards, *Patrick Pearse: The Triumph of Failure*, London, 1977.
Brian Feeney, *Sinn Féin: A Hundred Turbulent Years*, Dublin, 2002.
Michael Laffan, *The Resurrection of Ireland*, Cambridge, 1999.
Richard Loftus, *Nationalism in Modern Anglo-Irish Poetry*, Madison, Wis., 1964.
Máirín Ní Dhonnchadha and Theo Dorgan, eds., *Revising the Rising*, Derry, 1991.
William Irwin Thompson, *The Imagination of an Insurrection: Dublin Easter 1916*, Oxford, 1967.
Francis Shaw SJ, 'The Canon of Irish History: a Challenge', *Studies*, Summer 1972, vol. lxi.
Robert Wohl, *The Generation of 1914*, Cambridge, Mass., 1979.

CHAPTER 13

Reinventing England

(1999)

'Virtues are individual; vices are national.' That witty Enlightenment formulation gained added authority through the twentieth century, as nationalists of one kind or another wrought havoc. By the 1980s the very notion of international solidarity had changed its meaning, having ceased to denote the pooling of national resources and become instead an alternative to nationalism, an international style. All talk was of 'world novels' and 'world music' in a global economy. Yet by 1998 cricket fans celebrated a famous victory in the test series with South Africa by waving English flags rather than Union Jacks. The Cross of St George flies ever higher on these occasions, while cultural nationalism enjoys a new vogue even among exponents of left–liberal Critical Theory. John Rutherford's *Forever England* concludes with a lament that 'England' remains as yet undefined.[1]

Only rare contemporary thinkers such as Tom Nairn have registered the fact that, far from being only a backward-looking philosophy, nationalism might also be the sign and shape of the future.[2] The collapse of communism in 1989 simply speeded up a process which had marked a growth from about fifty recognised nation–states in 1945 to something more like two hundred as the century ends. Critical Theory is now becoming open to the suggestion that many 'international' arrangements from Great Britain through the European Union to the Organisation of African States may be little more than mechanisms for reinforcing the hegemony of one strong power at the expense of all others. As yet, however, it has scarcely learned how to explain what happens to the people-nation which allegedly enjoys such hegemony. In *The Satanic Verses* a character remarks that so much of their history happened overseas that the British don't know quite what it all means.[3] The same might be said of many other peoples as well.

If social class has not become the basis of international solidarity which radicals once hoped it might be, perhaps a new kind of nationalism can, permitting peoples to pursue legitimate interests as a brake upon the global economy. Tom Nairn has complained that events since 1989 have prompted no new theories to explain the resurgence of nations.[4] Instead commentators have resurrected all the old left–liberal warnings against chauvinism and fascism, using the tools of yesterday to analyse the challenges of tomorrow. But perhaps some of the even older analyses, now forgotten in some quarters but still a part of the cultural record, could be of help to us now.

To explain this, I'll begin with the situation I know best. Post-colonial theory has talked itself into a profound depression on the subject of nationalism, which it routinely accuses of inscribing into its own actions and texts all the major tyrannies of the imperial system which it promised to extirpate. So, in Irish terms, the old colonial capital Dublin was allowed to continue swelling at the expense of the provinces; a compulsory version of Standard Irish was beaten into children as once a compulsory version of Standard English had been imposed on them; and British guns which had been used to suppress the 1916 rebellion were called back by Michael Collins to quell radical republicans.

But, if the post-colony carries the after-image of empire on its retina, might not the process be more complicated? Perhaps the colony before independence might be found to have borne a proleptic image of a liberated home country. The postboxes in Dublin whose *Victoria Regina* insignia were spray-painted green by nationalists too poor or exhausted to imagine an alternative are often cited as an instance of post-colonial torpor. But they may tell a deeper story, for Ireland in the 1830s and 1840s had a streamlined postal system well before England. The 'laboratory theory' of history reminds us that, for the rulers of Westminster, nineteenth-century Ireland was a sounding-board, a place in which intrepid experiments could be tried, a land that existed in a parabolic relation to England.[5] Some of the successful experiments were so radical that even a century later they have not been fully implemented in England, the delinking of an official connection between the Protestant church and state, the dismantling of a feudal aristocracy and so on. The colony was, in short, not only a site of nightmarish fears but also an anticipatory illumination of real potential, an image of a future England. Shaw liked to joke that all Englishmen should be sent for a spell in Ireland, so that they might learn flexibility of mind.[6]

Shaw was, of course, a reader of Marx, who had argued that Ireland was the key to revolution in Britain, since overthrow of the old paternalist aristocracy was more likely to occur in the land of the Fenians first. Far from being saved by British radicals, the Irish saw themselves as saving them, for the project of 'inventing Ireland' presupposed the task of 'reinventing England'. Hence the involvement of a Land League leader like Michael Davitt in the Labour interest during the general elections in Britain. That process was reciprocal, however, indicating that it was not only among left-wing activists that the dialectic was at work. Many traditional Englanders, sensing that a pristine version of their own cultural heritage was still to be encountered on the other island, came over to savour its ruralist ethos and Elizabethan locutions. Some, like Wilfrid Scawen Blunt, found themselves also supporting the Land League. Ireland just might be, as Shaw liked to suggest, the last spot on earth still producing the ideal Englishman of history, the freedom-loving defender of rural life.[7]

Blunt saw no contradiction between his support for the Land League which sought to expropriate landlords and his continuing prosperity as a landholding aristocrat in the south of England. He has been accused of misreading the political message of the Land League – but did he? After all, what followed the League's campaigns was not the communitarianism of Davitt's dream but a much more English kind of property-owning democracy. Anyway, whether Blunt's interpretation was right or wrong is scarcely important now. He is significant, rather, as an example of the emerging sort of intellectual who sought to undo the deforming effects of the British empire (with all its energy-sapping demands for service and self-extinction) on the English folk mind. Some of these intellectuals, from Blake to William Morris, were social radicals, while others were highly conservative Little Englanders. Today, after Powellism, Little Englanders often get a bad press, but their ideological range was broad enough to comprehend such figures as H. G. Wells, George Orwell and (in our own time) Tony Benn.

Wilde and Shaw were early exponents of this viewpoint. They considered that the strain of running an empire had left Britain a deeply distorted society. Whatever the material benefits (and they were questionable), the psychic costs were just too high. In order to harden themselves for the task of military coercion and colonial administration, the British had devalued in themselves all those qualities of poetry, sensitivity and imagination once celebrated by a Shakespeare or a Blake.[8] And the projection of despised or soft 'feminine' qualities onto Celts or Indians had led inexorably to a diminishment of womanhood at home. The colonial adventure had led not just to suffering overseas, but had corrupted domestic British society to the core. Worse than that, it had left the English with their own unresolved national question, for the motive of imperialism might not, after all, have been economic gain so much as an attempt to escape from some terrible emptiness within. In the very act of escaping, some hoped to find the 'England' which had eluded them at home. But, apart from the Noel Coward and Gilbert and Sullivan caricatures, few people had any clear idea as to what 'England' might mean.

Wilde and Shaw thus believed that England was the last, most completely subjugated of all the British colonies. Their espousal of androgynous heroes and heroines may be seen as a critique of the prevailing macho-imperial styles. 'I would give Manchester back to the shepherds and Leeds to the stock-farmers',[9] proclaimed the youthful Wilde, already as worried as any BBC2 presenter about the disappearing English countryside. 'Home Rule for England' became Shaw's favourite slogan, and whenever he was asked by bemused Londoners for the meaning of the terrible words 'Sinn Féin' he would reply 'It is the Irish for "John Bull".'[10]

That programme of English self-recovery had a set of cultural corollaries, best outlined by W. B. Yeats. His rereading of Shakespeare at the start of the century was based on the attempt to restore an 'English' in place of a 'British' Shakespeare – one who loved the doomed Celtic complexity of Richard the Second and scorned the usurper Bolingbroke's merely administrative guile. If Edward Dowden had praised Shakespeare for mastering 'the logic of facts' in pursuit of the imperial theme, Yeats saw him rather as one who would never deny his own or imagination for the sake of mere power. Bolingbroke, like all usurpers, was in flight from his own emptiness 'and saw all that could be seen from very emptiness'.[11] In his own plays Yeats sought to recover the earlier verbal energies of the English, the poetry of the carnivalesque. His resolve to tour London, Oxford and Cambridge with them was based less on a forelock-tugging desire for ratification in the great cultural centres of Britain than on a thoroughly admirable ambition to unfreeze the drama of post-Victorian Britain from its torpor, by restoring to it some of the authentic energies of English poetic drama. For he, too, was anxious, in inventing Ireland, to reinvent England.

Just how prophetic much of this was may be seen in any number of ways. I take, as a random sample, some of the London Sunday newspapers of April 1998. One contained a lengthy review of A. S. Byatt's attempt to define an English canon of shorter narrative prose in *The Oxford Book of English Short Stories*. The general verdict was that this was a difficult but fascinating task, one which might be taken further. In the 'Review' section of *The Sunday Times* of 26 April, the historian David Starkey followed a somewhat different line under the provocative heading, 'Hooray, England Doesn't Exist':

Once upon a time we were rather proud of this absence of national(ist) paraphernalia. H. G. Wells, that quintessentially English socialist, looked at plump, beer-swilling Bavarians squeezed into lederhosen and raw-boned Scots in kilts, and thanked God that the English had no national dress. But, as the world map has ceased to be coloured pink abroad and as the United Kingdom comes apart at the seams at home, we English have started to feel distinctly underdressed in the fashion parade of nations. And we are grasping at straws to cover our nakedness.

The reason for that crisis was the opportunist equation in the eighteenth and nineteenth centuries of Englishness with Britishness. Britain was really a flag-of-convenience for English interests but the price was that many specifically English traditions, such as the frock coat, were adopted as British and, therefore, imperial–international style. Even as it puffed Englanders up, the British scheme sucked from them what cultural identity they had achieved.

One of the insignia that the British imperial scheme did not rob England of was its cult of success. As W. B. Yeats wrote in an essay on Shakespeare, 'the popular poetry of England celebrates her victories; but the popular poetry of Ireland remembers only defeats and defeated persons'.[12] Now, despite the shapes currently being thrown in the name of Cool Britannia, even that has gone. David Starkey ended his *Sunday Times* article by posing a stark choice to the 'survivors', either to parade around with red roses and the Cross of St George or to decide that 'nationhood is a busted flush and become the first truly global multi-cultural society'. To some eyes that phrase 'truly global' might look suspiciously like some new post-modern version of the Pax Britannica.

On the editorial page of the same edition of the *Sunday Times* Ferdinand Mount wrote a thoughtful essay complaining that the Union was being 'kebabbed' (a telling coinage) by devolution in Scotland, Wales and Ireland. (On that very Sunday morning over in Dublin, the Irish Taoiseach Bertie Ahern was solemnly, if absurdly, insisting at a 1916 commemoration that the Belfast Agreement removed 'the British element' from the Irish equation.) Ferdinand Mount predicted that the Scottish National Party would engineer a bust-up with London, but that the loyalty of its diverse people to the United Kingdom idea would win though in the end. Asking just how far Prime Minister Tony Blair wanted to go in Balkanising Britain, he pointed very persuasively to the endless interactions of Welsh, Scots, Irish and English, 'as intermarriage and work further mongrelise us, it seems an odd time to split off into separate nations after three centuries together.'

But just how 'together' did these peoples ever manage to be? Linda Colley's *Britons: Forging the Nation 1707–1837* suggests an answer implicit in the *double entendre* of the word 'forge'. 'It was an invention forged above all by war'[13] she says downrightly at the outset – war against the Other that was Catholic Europe. But now both the empire and Protestant faith which gave that warmaking some meaning have all but disappeared, and so the question of separate nationalisms re-emerges, just as it is re-emerging among the nationalities of Eastern Europe which were held formerly as part of the Soviet scheme. Any Irish person who marvels at the immense 'militaria' sections in British bookshops (presumably bought by people who yet subscribe to the myth of 'the fighting Irish') can only endorse Colley's view that 'this is a culture that is used to fighting and has largely defined itself through fighting'.[14]

Those writers of English romanticism who objected to the imperial agenda, such as William Blake, insisted that it would be better to build a Jerusalem 'in England's green and pleasant land', and from the later 1780s the rebirth of England as England became a major theme of poets.[15] Many sensed that the strain of running a far-flung empire could bring down the home country. Edmund Burke suggested as much in his impeachment of Warren Hastings and Edward Gibbon openly toyed with the analogy in his *Decline and Fall of the Roman Empire*. But fighting a common external enemy helped to forge a unity at home, and to head off energies which might in peacetime have led to internal conflict. Perhaps Mr Blair is trying to find a peacetime way of saving the union by making it more fuzzy and less abrasive at the edges. However, once unleashed, the genie of devolution may, as Mount fears, take many people much further than they intended to go. That is certainly the interpretation which both Sinn Féin and the Irish government are banking on. There is a passing phrase in the Belfast Agreement of last April, which, though it went unremarked in the British press, gives the Irish hope. Strand 3, Article 2, says, *inter alia*, that membership of the British–Irish Council will comprise representatives of the British and Irish governments, devolved institutions in Northern Ireland, Scotland and Wales, when established, and, if appropriate, elsewhere in the United Kingdom, together with representatives of the Isle of Man and the Channel Islands. That can only mean some sort of parliament in England, so Bernard Shaw may have his wish after all.

Where might all of this lead? Where will the British Council stand in ten years' time? Perhaps its delegates and speakers will find themselves offering lectures on Milton, Blake and Shelley, safe in the knowledge that contemporary writing, post-colonial literature and cultural studies can all be left to the department of English in the local university. Certainly, the coming decade will witness many battles on the Bennite left as well as the Thatcherite right to reclaim and redefine an idea of Englishness. John Major's much-documented 'lift' of a passage from an essay of George Orwell on the theme was one kind of manifesto for a Protestant, cricket-playing, village culture. Tony Benn's invocation of the Levellers and Diggers is another. Even the developing republican undertone may ultimately be connected back to the monarchy, which was apparently so secure in the latter half of the 1700s that people felt free to engage in all kinds of subversive debate. One consequence was that Americans came to believe that, under the skin of monarchy, England was actually a republic in all but name.[16]

As these debates take on more focus, we may find that they have been already rehearsed in the dramatic art of England for the past two generations. I have sometimes wondered what might ensue if we were to carry forward the logic of Yeats's rereading of Shakespeare and subject some of the plays of 'modern Britain' to a post-colonial interpretation – to take them, no less than *Midnight's Children* or *Borstal Boy*, as post-colonial texts. One could, for example, analyse John Osborne's *Look Back in Anger* as a year-of-Suez drama and treat it in the light of some of the themes adumbrated in this essay. Jimmy Porter's late speech could then be read as climaxing in that long-postponed confrontation of the British male with his repressed *anima*:

There aren't any good, brave causes left. If the big bang does come, and we all get killed off, it won't be in aid of the old-fashioned grand design. It'll just be for the Brave New Nothing-very-much-thank-you. About as pointless and inglorious as stepping in front of a bus. No, there'll be nothing left for it, me boy, but to let yourself be butchered by the women.[17]

Porter's indictment is not that the upper-class is tyrannical, but rather that it has no remaining code of belief at all. Though seeming a rebel, he is really a superstraight. To himself, of course, he appears effeminate, a half-man. Brave enough to admit the *anima* as none of his military forefathers could do, he is nonetheless unnerved by that very freedom, and seeks to ratify his jeopardised sense of his own virility in talk and acts of downright misogyny.

The diagnosis offered by Osborne is astoundingly similar to that made by D. H. Lawrence after the previous world war. When the attempt at blood-brotherhood fails, one is left only with 'cocksure women and hensure men', leading to a moment when 'men lose their hold on the life-flow'.[18] Lawrence's remedy was to flee the country on the grounds that 'England's done for . . . in England you can't let go.'[19] Jimmy Porter cannot leave but, remaining, he becomes a study of what Lawrence might have become – a powerless witness of the decline of romantic England from a dynamic, open society to a packaged heritage industry. Porter's wife and her friends will stay in old cottages and visit ancient churches not because they retain any belief in the traditional codes, but simply as a style option, a matter of external form. Jimmy Porter is appalled, 'Reason and Progress . . . the old firm is selling out . . . all those stocks in the old free enquiry.'

For all his faults, Porter sees the English past as something to learn *from*. For his wife's friends, it is something to learn *about*, something now museumised but scarcely the basis for a national future. Porter's analysis of upper-class paternalism and pusillanimity is sound enough. The problem is that he has not worked the dialectic through and so his revolt in the end is less against the imperialism of the upper class than against the timidity with which its members gave the empire up. The rebel is a conservative at heart and there are moments in the play when he voices a very personal resentment against those seductive British forces which dispossessed his generation of the idea of England:

I think I can understand how her daddy must have felt when he came back from India, after all those years away. The old Edwardian brigade do make their brief little world look pretty tempting. All homemade cakes and croquet . . . Still, even I regret it somehow, phoney or not, If you've no world of your own, it's rather pleasant to regret the passing of someone else's.[20]

The clashes between Jimmy Porter and his wife might be taken as a version of the class war disfiguring British society, after the safety valve of empire has been removed, with the Welsh lodger Cliff cast in the role of a reluctant Celtic witness who is constantly tempted to opt out of the entire arrangement. Too young to have fought in World War Two, too old to forget, Osborne's generation could never subscribe to the warlike old Britannia described by Linda Colley. So it had no option but to look back in a kind of muffled anger on the rhetoric of a diminished empire.

One of the major themes of John Osborne's autobiography, *A Better Class of Person*, is, in fact, the sheer impossibility of recovering a personal or national past. England, allegedly underwritten by centuries of tradition, is depicted as a geriatric in the grip of a terminal amnesia. The famous challenge posed by E. M. Forster in an essay on racial purity is repeated, 'Can you give the names of your eight great-grandparents?' Forster had argued that the betting would be 8:1 against and, true enough, the young Osborne never could find out who his ancestors were or what they did. All he ever got were vague anecdotes from family members who never asked the boy about himself. The autobiography (a far finer work than the plays) becomes a long protest against the conditions of its own impossibility, and against a family which, having no sense of its own tradition or nation, substituted for them a tissue of platitudes about class and empire.[21]

It was only a matter of time before a play devoted to emptying the word 'Britain' of its residual content was staged. There was a certain inevitability about the fact that this finally came to pass at the National Theatre in London. Howard Brenton's 1980 drama *The Romans in Britain* implied an equation between the Roman rape of ancient Britain and the contemporary conduct of the British Army in Northern Ireland. At a time when the SPQR mentality, not to mention the study of Latin, had ceased to be a dominant element even in the public schools, Brenton might have seemed open to the allegation of taking a cheap and easy potshot. But his play was truly probing in suggesting a Celtic basis for British culture. Britain's current Irish enemies were their own secret doubles, just as King Arthur was 'one more fucking mick'.[22] Irish audiences knew that the converse was also true, in the sense that Sinn Féin leaders with names like Adams and Morrison had genealogies pointing back not to a Celtic past but, more likely, to Cromwell's invading soldiery. Yet Brenton chose not to make that point.

Some accused him of being overanxious to dismantle a British nationalism but unwilling to subject Irish nationalism to an equally stringent critique. In fact, Brenton portrayed the Irish (especially the women) as no less bloodthirsty than their enemies. Nevertheless, he did allow a sort of glamour to the Irish side. In the play they have a cultural code in which they believe, one that gives their lives coherence, whereas the members of the British Army do not. Brenton was setting his face less against national essences than against imperial ideas. It was the British scheme which he wished to drain of meaning, the better to make way for an English nation sufficiently at ease with itself not to want to run other people's affairs. The lesson was that already taught by Lévi-Strauss; our own system is the only one we can reform without destroying.

The current vogue for Irish plays in the London theatre (nineteen were playing at one time in March 1998) may indicate another theatrical revival among the Irish, but its location in the English capital also suggests that many of these plays – such as Frank McGuinness's *Mutabilitie* – allow audiences to approach their own national question from a safe remove. Once again, Irish culture exists in a kind of parabolic relation to England's; once again, the Irish in renovating their own consciousness, may also be helping, wittingly or unwittingly, to reanimate England's.

Englishness surely needs redefining. It is a mark of how sunken beneath the level of consciousness it now is that in large tracts of the world people entirely miss the element of parody in a comic-opera song like 'He is an Englishman' or in the drawing-room plays of Oscar Wilde. Those works which are known to be parodic, such as the lyrics of Noel Coward, have been esteemed among formerly colonised peoples for what are at best dubious reasons. They allow people to laugh gently at Englishness, while also reassuring them that as an act it is hilariously easy to mimic. But what is mimicked is not Englishness so much as an unconvincing, unconvinced imitation of those 'higher home types' who never really existed. The post-colonial diagnosis which Douglas Hyde reported from Ireland and Homi Bhabha from India may now be found to trouble the citizens of London and Manchester themselves, for they also are making the painful discovery that to be anglicised is not at all the same thing as to be English.[23]

The inner history of England will be found eventually elsewhere – not in a people given to play-acting (was it really *Englishmen* who went out in the mid-day sun?) but in a people who were, and remain, rather suspicious of play-actors. These are the people of whom E. P. Thompson and Christopher Hill, A. S. Byatt and E. M. Forster have written so well, the ones who (in Thompson's telling phrase) need saving from the enormous condescension of posterity. Whether they also need saving from the enormous condescension of those Irish who tried to help them to help themselves is another matter. But it should be said that the project sketched by Shaw and Wilde in no way militates against a multicultural society. Since all identity is dialogic, 'England' is more likely to achieve a satisfying definition in endless acts of negotiation with those of other identities, not just Irish and Welsh, but Indian and Trinidadian too. In that way, England might once again become truly interesting to the English.

NOTES

This is a shortened version of a keynote lecture delivered at a conference on 'Intercultural Relations' at Trinity College, Dublin, on 13 May 1998.

1 John Rutherford, *Forever England* (London, Lawrence & Wishart, 1997).
2 Tom Nairn, *Faces of Nationalism* (London, Verso, 1996).
3 Salman Rushdie, *The Satanic Verses* (London, Viking, 1988), p. 343.
4 Nairn, *Faces of Nationalism*, pp. 59ff.
5 For the exemplary application of the parabolic interpretation, see the writings of Gearóid O Tuathaigh, especially *Ireland Before the Famine 1798–1848* (Dublin, Gill & Macmillan, 1972).
6 Quoted by Michael Holroyd, 'GBS and Ireland', *The Sewanee Review* LXXXIV, 1 (Winter 1976), 41.
7 G. B. Shaw, 'Preface', *John Bull's Other Island* (Harmondsworth, Penguin, 1988), p. 18.
8 Ashis Nandy, *The Intimate Enemy, Loss and Recovery of Self under Colonialism* (Bombay, Oxford University Press, 1983), pp. 7ff.
9 Quoted by H. Kingsmill-Moore, *Reminiscences and Reflections* (London, Methuen, 1930), p. 45.
10 G. B. Shaw, *The Matter with Ireland*, ed. David H. Greene and Dan H. Laurence (London, Hart-Davis, 1962), p. 149.
11 W. B. Yeats, *Essays and Introductions* (London, Macmillan, 1955), p. 108.
12 W. B. Yeats, 'The Literary Movement in Ireland', in Lady Gregory (ed.), *Ideals in Ireland* (London, Batsford, 1900), p. 101.
13 Linda Colley, *Britons, Forging the Nation 1707–1837* (New Haven, Yale University Press, 1992), p. 5.
14 Ibid., p. 9.
15 John Lucas, *England and Englishness* (London, Jonathan Cape, 1991), pp. 75ff.
16 Gordon S. Wood, *The Radicalism of the American Revolution* (New York, Vintage, 1991).
17 John Osborne, *Look Back in Anger* (1957; London, Faber & Faber, 1966) p. 51.
18 D. H. Lawrence, *Selection from Phoenix*, ed. A. A. H. Inglis (Harmondsworth, Penguin, 1979), pp. 373–4.
19 D. H. Lawrence, *Women in Love* (Harmondsworth, Penguin, 1969), p. 341.
20 Osborne, *Look Back in Anger*, p. 49.
21 John Osborne, *A Better Class of Person* (London, Methuen, 1981).
22 Howard Brenton, *The Romans in Britain* (London, Methuen, 1980), p. 75.
23 See Douglas Hyde, 'The Necessity for De-anglicising Ireland', in Sir Charles Gavan Duffy (ed.), *The Revival of Irish Literature* (London, A. P. Watt, 1894), pp. 87ff.; and Homi K. Bhabha, *The Location of Culture* (London, Routledge, 1994).

CHAPTER 14

Museums and learning

(2003)

As far as modern writing goes, museums have got a bad press. If a novelist compares some institution to a museum, this is usually less than complimentary. In the second episode of James Joyce's *Ulysses*, for instance, Mr Garrett Deasy is headmaster of a school in Dalkey and a narrow-gauge Orange loyalist who believes that history is over, because the British empire is secure across the world. It soon emerges that Mr Deasy has a very limited view of his role; 'to learn, one must be humble', he tells Stephen Dedalus, 'but life is the great teacher'.[1] Yet the establishment he directs seems less devoted to the education of its boys – leading forth their essential natures – than to mere schooling. Everything is done by copying – the boys copy sums off the board but do not understand them; they recite a Roman History lesson by rote but miss its point – that Pyrrhus had won a battle but at a cost too great to be borne. Joyce uses the scene to capture the mimicry inherent in the colonial mission which turns natives into copycats and teachers into imitators of distant power-elites.

Mr Deasy is – or thinks he is – a Christian. He says that history is moving towards one great goal, the manifestation of God. Like the social theorist Karl Marx or the evolutionist Charles Darwin, he believes that it is going along a straight line towards a definite, discernible conclusion, and Joyce is quite mischievous in the way he links the teleology of Marxism and Darwinism to that of Christianity, as if they were but obverse sides of the same coin. The young poet Stephen does not agree; for him there can be no straight line. God is not the fulfilment of some long process but rather a 'shout in the street'; in other words, either God is with us now or he may not exist at all. Without God, history may just be a succession of civilisations without purpose or change. This is his greatest fear, confided with the scepticism of a modernist to Mr Deasy:

– History, Stephen said, is a nightmare from which I am trying to awake.
From the playground the boys raised a shout. A whirring whistle, goal. What if
that nightmare gave you a back kick?[2]

As he sits later, teaching his classroom of boys Roman History, Stephen
contemplates the futility of war by quoting Pyrrhus: 'another victory like
that and we are done for'. But his is also a mind which reflects Joyce's
experience of aerial bombardment of buildings near Locarno in 1917:
'I hear the ruin of all space, shattered glass and toppling masonry, and
time one livid final flame.'[3]

Most museums were built and based on the 'straight line' principle of
history: that the world was improving and that its progress could literally
be mapped by the straight lines along which a visitor to a gallery walked,
as he or she made the symbolic re-enactment of the passage from antiquity, through feudalism, into the Renaissance and beyond that into
the triumph of the modern individual. Those museums were rich in
material things – as were their sponsors, the triumphant bourgeoisie –
and not averse to displaying acquired trophies. Mr Deasy instinctively
understands this. His religion is a lot less spiritual that he'd care to
admit. He advises the young teacher Stephen to put money in his purse,
unaware of the fact that the source of the quotation is one of Shakespeare's villains, Iago. He fills his school with glass display cases containing Stuart coins and apostle spoons, symbols of a triumphant state and
church, those forces of Christ and Caesar which work hand-in-glove to
threaten Stephen. He claims to be a follower of Christ, yet epitomises the
truth of Nietzsche's aphorism that there was only ever one Christian – and
they crucified him. Ireland, Mr Deasy boasts with racist complacency,
has the honour of never having persecuted the Jews, because it had the
good sense never to let them in. 'They sinned against the light', he
explains to Stephen, but the young man responds, 'Who has not?'[4] It is
as if Stephen is unconsciously preparing for that later moment in the
book when he will meet Mr Leopold Bloom, at least one Jew who has
managed to get in.

So Mr Deasy's comfortable lies are exposed, and so is his view of
history as an opportunity to store up useless objects from the past – the
coins and apostle spoons, the symbols of a decayed polity and outworn
church. If Stephen appears in the scene as a reluctant prisoner of history,
the Orangeman is her willing slave. He has gathered the trophies of
the past, an 'old pilgrim's hoard', but (as Richard Ellmann noted) in
doing so he missed their spiritual point, and his inner emptiness is
epitomised by his third hobby, the collection of shells, 'dead treasure,

hollow shells'.[5] They actually remind Stephen of the hollow shells that pass for teeth in his own ruined mouth, further instances of history's nightmare and time's decay: but although Stephen's body may be rotting, at least he is living. Mr Deasy, by contrast, is a mere hoarder of things from the past, saving their outer shells but losing their deeper lessons. In the end he is shown to worship a false god, a version of the past which seems stabilised once and for all, no longer a dynamic process with an open future. His shells and coins and spoons are used by Joyce to make him seem more like the curator of a museum than the headteacher of a school. That may even be Joyce's central point: that museums are like schools, except that there are often more dead things in schools. Mr Deasy is a bleak illustration of Oscar Wilde's sad observation that 'in the modern world everyone who has forgotten how to learn has taken to teaching'.[6] He hoards dead facts as he saves dead shells but, in the very next episode of *Ulysses*, Stephen will crunch the shells of Sandymount Strand under his live feet, as if in deliberate repudiation of that notion of tradition.

When I read that telling scene now, I often think of Walter Benjamin's remark about 'the melancholy of the collector'.[7] Most museums have an aura of sadness and melancholy, which may first have attached itself to those colonial explorers and collaborators who made so many of the great museums possible. Benjamin, a great collector of books and photographs himself, never fully explained what he meant by that haunting phrase, but it seems to suggest a depressive streak in the collector, as if he were somehow trying to ratify and augment his own uncertain selfhood and identity by surrounding himself with beautiful objects – trophies which might testify to the final triumph of his fragile but purposeful spirit. The problem with nineteenth-century taxonomy was that it often seemed a prelude to taxidermy: you crossed the world, gathered specimens and examples, asserted your almost unlimited intellectual powers, and then discovered that you were descended from apes (who like to gather and store bright objects too). The more you asserted your own civil authority and refined knowledge, the more you were brought face to face with the implications of your own barbarism. When W. B. Yeats walked into London Zoo – itself a form of museum – late in the nineteenth century, he headed straight for the monkey-house and then wrote a letter asking a friend a leading question, 'Do you not think that monkeys might not be degenerate men? – hence their look of wizened age?'[8] In short, he offered a subversive reversal of the more 'optimistic' Darwinian model. In Yeats's museum, the visitor would first have confronted the present moment, and then gone back over time, to the period of primitive man, who had so much more to teach us. He would have had his visitors walk in straight lines but in the opposite direction to most, for this is what Yeats wrote in defence of his own theory of evolution or degeneration:

Science is a criticism of Myth. There would be no Darwin had there been no book of Genesis, no elections but for the Greek atomic myth, and yet when the criticism is finished, there is not even a drift of ashes on the pyre . . . There is no improvement, only a series of sudden fires, each, though fainter, as necessary as the one before it. The last kiss is given to the void.[9]

It is strange to think of that sort of lesson being drawn by Yeats from a visit to London Zoo. But then the case against traditional zoos may be rather like the arguments which can be advanced against museums: that they rip objects out of their natural settings, in which alone they have full integrity and meaning, setting them up as objects which exist solely for the education and pleasure of others. Not that there is an absolute equivalence: at least the objects in museums are dead before the thing is done.

However, even to state the case as starkly as that may not be to go far enough. Many of those objects collected in museums are works of art, or at least acquire that aura in the transition from the past to the present – think of old photographs – or in the transition from the fields of Bali to a European museum. In fact, as Margaret Mead found out when she first arrived in Bali and tried to discover whether the Balinese had any pictorial representations of their society, the most integrated and balanced communities would have no such thing. After some considerable time spent listening to Mead's descriptions of pictures, frames, representations of the body, etc., the Balinese laughingly said, 'We have no art, we simply do everything as well as we can.'[10] Yet objects from their artisan world acquired the status of art by virtue of being relocated in museums and galleries. So those who make the case against museums may have to face the fact that the argument against curatorial display may simply be one element of the much wider and deeper case against the very idea of art itself, of a separate art with a capital A.

Still, it's hard to deny the force of Walter Benjamin's thesis on the philosophy of history. Its most famous paragraph reads like – though not intended as such – a call to close down every museum in Europe:

Whoever has emerged victorious in battle participates to this day in the triumphal procession in which the present rulers step over those who are lying prostrate. According to traditional practice, the spoils are carried along in the procession. They are called cultural treasures, and a historical materialist views them with cautious detachment. For without exception the cultural treasures he surveys have an origin which he cannot contemplate without horror. They owe their existence not only to the efforts of the great minds and talents who have created them, but also to the anonymous toil of their contemporaries. There is no document of civilisation which is not at the same time a document of barbarism, and just as such a document is not free of barbarism, barbarism taints also the manner in which it was transmitted from one owner to another. A historical materialist therefore dissociates himself from it as far as possible. He regards it as his task to brush history against the grain.[11]

The questions raised by Benjamin are immense but they are rooted in one simple enough idea: that the victors always think history is over, having come to a culmination in them, and that knowledge has been stabilised once and for all. I remember having that feeling of great privilege, even as a nine-year-old child, when my parents first took me to the National Museum of Ireland in Dublin. We dutifully inspected everything: stone-age flints, bronze-age cups, brooches worn by Gaelic ladies, but the images which stayed in my imagination for years afterwards were the charred uniforms of the leaders of the Easter rebellion. This was as near as history got – it was a version of the sublime, evoking extreme danger, vicariously experienced by one not actually in peril himself, as I fondly imagined, because, with the permission of the glass case around the uniforms, it seemed possible to conclude that this whole aspect of our history was over.

In later years as a student at Trinity College, Dublin, I lived for four years within a three-minute walk of the National Museum, but never went in, because I had come to feel troubled by the implications surrounding the images. I was bothered not just by the idea that the history of the Irish struggle for self-determination was concluded (which it patently wasn't) but by the simplification of Patrick Pearse into a military hero, without a due weighting being given to his literary achievements as a poet, playwright, and storyteller, to his liberal child-centred philosophy of education, or to his insistence that tradition was living and vital and not a thing to be embalmed. As I considered Pearse's life and read his thoughts in Trinity's libraries, the museum version began to seem a misrepresentation of much that he stood for.

On another of my student courses at Trinity I was reading Shakespeare's *Hamlet*, whose fate struck me as strangely like that of Pearse. Here was another gifted, versatile man in his thirties, a courtier, soldier, scholar, about to come into his own when he met a ghost from the nightmare of history and henceforth could never become his true self. Although the role of military revenger was one to which he was thoroughly ill-suited, he was compelled to fill it and he became in consequence a character obsessed with role-playing, a frequenter of theatres, a coach of good and bad actors, a mimic who could in the end play many different parts except his own. In Act 5 of Shakespeare's play, Hamlet disappears and reappears as a sort of ghost come back from the dead, much as Pearse and James Connolly eternally return, their words and meanings simplified and insisting that those who follow them simplify themselves too. Having hovered for four acts between an assigned role and an emerging self, Hamlet finally surrenders to the revenger's plot. Anyone who has loved the Hamlet of the earlier acts can only feel betrayed by the gut-wrenching irony of that closing scene in which Fortinbras orders a *soldier's* burial for a man who was everything else but militarist – a poet, philosopher, scholar, lover, clown, but a soldier least of all. The true Hamlet wished to live his life as a thing particular to himself and had expressed huge reservations about a derring-do soldier such as Fortinbras, but he is doomed to have his meaning for posterity set by this man of action, 'Bear Hamlet like a soldier to the stage, for he was likely, had he been put on, to have proved most royally.'[12] In a similar tragedy of mistaken identity, Pearse and Connolly have passed into Irish iconography attired forever in that most inappropriate costume, the military uniform, whereas the real meaning of the revolution which they led was that there should be no more copying of approved costumes and that everyone would thereafter feel free to wear their own clothes.

In calling for a learning which brushes history against its own grain, Walter Benjamin implied an approach which would not just privilege the winners but also the losers of battles, and, beyond them, the vast majority who just got on with their lives and took little interest in such contests. The problem is obvious: how to document the subaltern, the marginal, the ones who leave few records of themselves and often none at official level? And who is to set and define the limits of such judgement? After all, if Joyce's Mr Deasy had lived long enough to see the Easter rebels' uniforms in the National Museum, he might well have regarded them as a wholly inappropriate presence, a subversion of so much that the earlier objects in the collection stood for. All we can say for sure is that every triumphant nationalism tends to use museums to mythologise itself, with the attendant simplification which seems too often to be the price of explanation at a popular level. Salman Rushdie's novel *Midnight's Children* provides a tell-tale example of how this very process of museumisation begins even before independence has been won.

In *Midnight's Children*, just before January 1948, a rising Indian businessman, Ahmed Sinai, buys a colonial estate from the departing Englishman, Mr Methwold, and he gets it at a bargain price but only on one condition: that the sale will be closed on Independence Day and that until then every ornament and item of furniture will be left exactly as it is. This is the greatest deceit perpetrated by post-colonial time – to make everything appear to stand still, and to freeze everything in just that state it was in at the moment of independence. One consequence in Rushdie's telling is that the emerging middle class which buys out the British doesn't inherit a dynamic, evolving society so much as a post-colonial museum, over which the new elites will merely preside as custodians. The task of curators, of course, is to resist this notion of a knowledge which has been stabilised once and for all, and to mount displays which recognise that history is an open process, never concluded, not even fully representable, and seldom agreed over by its chief interpreters. But the odds against such openness are huge, because it is a perfectly natural thing for peoples who have emerged victorious after a period of struggle to wish to memorialise that phase of their development, whether they be Jews emerging after the Holocaust or South African blacks recovering from apartheid.

The question curators face is how to give as full as possible an account without lapsing into nationalist apologetics. Some curators have to document nations without nationalism, and peoples who elude national categories altogether. By their nature, museums are as selective as literary anthologies, which in many respects they greatly resemble, precisely because they are often the result of a colonial encounter, and are based on the notion that a native culture need not be known whole and entire, but can be studied through representative examples or characteristic extracts. It is surprising how tenacious this tradition of anthologising has remained, even in an age of post-colonialism. While it might be easy to understand why British scholars produced anthologies of Indian or Gaelic literature in the nineteenth century in the task of attempting to know the mindset of their subjects, it is harder to understand why contemporary Indian and Irish scholars keep on producing such anthologies. It is a high irony that the most anti-colonial of all cultural movements in contemporary Ireland, the Field Day Company of Derry, is the one which produced a now five-volume anthology of the entire conspectus of Irish history and writing from earliest times to the present. Such an underlying idea – that you can study a whole civilisation from its rise to its demise – is deeply embedded in colonial ideology, for the colonialists felt that they alone could construe the natives who might never be expected to construe themselves. But in that last phrase lurks the makings of an explanation, for as Seamus Deane, the general editor, observed in justifying the Field Day anthology, if people are going to have to live in enclaves and ghettoes, they might at least be enclaves and ghettoes of their own making, as opposed to sites constructed by others.

This may serve better as a strategy for literary intellectuals, however, because words are less at the mercy of material conditions than objects, the lingua franca of museum-keepers. Slave narratives, oral traditions and folk tales all allow the literary scholar at least the possibility of reconstructing some of the counter-narratives which opposed the old world-systems, but the actual objects used in such acts of resistance are less likely to have survived intact. And because they deal in objects – palpable, solid, measurable – museums seem to give material form almost immediately to official versions of the past, reinforcing a type of 'public memory' which privileges the social over the personal and so narrows the definition of what the 'political' might in fact be.

Often the old structures of thought remain surprisingly unchallenged. For instance, the British imperial obsession with militaria was replicated in the Irish National Museum of my youth, despite the fact that Pearse saw soldiering as a mere means to the recovery of a cultural sovereignty which might have been more fully represented through exhibits. What I am suggesting is too obvious: if public memory has been powerfully shaped by a regime, it may need to be forcefully reshaped by its successor. This is all the more vital given the fact that children are among the most frequent museum users and will have their initial understandings of the past strongly influenced by the images on display and, even more crucially, by the uses to which such images are put.

For instance, in South Africa today, curators are quite rightly refusing to throw out many of the old exhibits first collected and mounted by the exponents of a racist regime, but they are recaptioning them in ways which ask pertinent questions of the past and its relation to the present. Questions such as: why is less than 1 per cent of the 4,000 national monuments of South Africa related to a pre-colonial African heritage? Large museums have semi-permanent exhibitions which militate against rapid change, but which can be destabilised by the use of counter-images, or by using captions which ask visitors to consider the relationship between knowledge and power. In whose interests was a particular collection first staged? Moreover, the South Africans, like the Irish before them, are converting famous buildings from past history into sites which investigate the ways in which the past may be reconstructed. If, in Dublin, Kilmainham Jail has gone from being an image of oppression to a centre for creative arts and thence to a dynamic, interrogative museum (which even shows how little poor prisoners got to eat compared with the comforts enjoyed by a VIP nationalist captive such as Parnell), in South Africa the Robben Island prison has been transformed, in the words of Patricia Davison, 'into a symbol of transcendence over oppression, an icon of hope'.[13] An exhibition there includes official documents of the apartheid regime but also letters from wives, children, friends outside, while interactive facilities (as in Kilmainham) encourage visitors to leave their own comments and analyses. Even in this process, alas, memory is selective, for Robben Island is not strictly being preserved so much as transformed to provide another use, and the sheer numbers of tourists now descending on it pose a new kind of threat to the archive of the African National Congress. One could imagine a similar fate for the Maze Prison in Northern Ireland in years to come. Just as there are now Robben Island T-Shirts, tea-cups and ball-point pens, there may some day be Maze wallets, Maze harps and Maze belts for sale in an interactive museum on site.

The best way of challenging the 'straight line', colonialist version of the museum is to subvert the seemingly timeless authority of all past exhibits by constantly reminding viewers of the present, and of the fact that every narrative construct is made at the mercy of the present moment, as is every subsequent act of interpretation. What is a past moment for us was once someone else's uncertain present. What is present now is no more privileged, no more secure or lasting, but liable to further subversion and disruption itself. If museums, in practising such subversion, can make viewers less sure of the ground on which they stand, they will have genuinely educated their users. They will do so most effectively of all if they cure them of that temporal provincialism of mind which used to make viewers believe that they were history's cutting-edge, the grand climax of civilisation rehearsed and approached in all those exhibition rooms. The ways in which museums once fed this illusion might well be one of the major topics for future study, and, after that perhaps, the ways in which more modern museums have thrown all understandings into question. Many of the older collections which purported to construe the lives of African tribesmen or Irish peasants were put together by confident aristocrats who never once stopped to think that some day a time would come when viewers of these exhibitions would begin to construe the texts that aimed to construe them. A telling question, now posed on captions in some museums, is whether the object on exhibition should be returned to its natural context.

If, in the post-colonial novels of Chinua Achebe, Alice Walker and Salman Rushdie, the empire writes back and, in the process, rewrites some of the classic narratives of Europe, the same thing is happening in many museums. Let me offer some working analogies. In 1966 the Sudanese writer Tayeb Salih wrote *Season of Migration to the North* (it was translated into English in 1969), the novel is about two Sudanese subjects, Meheimeed and Mustafa Sa'eed, and the privations they suffer in London before a return to the Sudan, but it was composed as a contrapuntal version of Joseph Conrad's *Heart of Darkness*. Whereas Conrad's Europeans had sailed up the Congo river into the bush, there to discover absolute barbarism and Africans who could be scarcely described in English, Salih preferred to perform his own reverse anthropology on the heart of darkness and the uncommunicative, unwelcoming natives of a European city. The Strokestown museum, curated by Luke Dodd in Roscommon, seems to work off a similarly contrapuntal method. It displays the impressive ornaments, paintings, stucco plasterwork, furniture, kitchen utensils and childhood toys of an Anglo-Irish residence, but not in their usual coffee-table-book style. That style, favoured by many exponents of the heritage industry, is to dehistoricise the Big House by separating it wholly from its past of domination over a local tenantry and to render it up solely as a timeless art-object filled with other *objets d'art*. What Dodd has done, however, is to create alongside the stately house a Famine Museum which examined local interactions between landlord and tenant in the Great Hunger, including the scheme of the local gentry to pay for the passage of 800 hungry tenants to the new world. Half died en route and one young man among the stay-at-homes, separated from his departed lover forever, took revenge by shooting the landlord, whose killing was celebrated by bonfires among the remaining tenantry. The Famine Museum uses local papers, court records and handwritten letters to measure the human cost of all the elegance in the Big House, but the contrapuntal method is subtle too, for it allows the record of the landed estate to show what great sacrifices were made by the landlord's own sons for the project of empire. These sacrifices finally included the house itself, whose refurbishment was made possible by the wealth and generosity of one of the 'risen people', a local garage owner.

This contrapuntal technique may be used most effectively of all in museums of Northern Ireland, where two utterly contested versions of the past exist side-by-side with no short-term likelihood of resolution.

A Dublin-born curator of the Orchard Gallery in Derry decided that, where a conflict seems insoluble, it is better to teach the conflict as such than to adopt Olympian positions. So the past century of sectarian conflict in the city is represented by a single street with two footpaths on either side – one nationalist, the other unionist. (At the official launch, the Reverend Ian Paisley was photographed by a mischievous cameraman under the signpost pointing to a United Ireland and John Hume under one pointing towards final, full integration within the United Kingdom.)

Northern Ireland in general has a wonderful variety of museums, many of them recreations of past communities, such as the American-Ireland Museum in Tyrone or the Folk Museum at Cultra. When I first visited Cultra with the critic John Wilson Foster, he pointed waggishly to the large sign outside which read 'Folk Museum' and said, 'There's only one thing wrong with that sign. It's in the wrong place. It should be at Aldergrove Airport at the entrance to Northern Ireland. The whole place is a folk museum.' This was not necessarily a serious criticism. After all, a people who have no art but do everything as well as they can are also likely to want to keep the tokens of the past within the integrated world of their own present, rather than sequestering them in the clinical conditions of a museum. The very existence of museums as sites of preservation suggests the predicament of a culture which lacks other, more natural, methods of preserving old things. Museums, in effect, are a sign of rampant modernity rather than of a fixation upon the past. They appeal to a society forever liquidating its own past more than they do to one which still has a practical use for it.

It is probably inevitable in such a context that museums will sometimes succumb to the temptation of giving idealised versions of past societies, especially when people begin to despair of achieving a transformed future, as was the case in Margaret Thatcher's Britain, which seemed filled with Victorian rediscoveries and re-enactments. However, Raphael Samuel has rightly questioned a tendency among socialists to engage in what he called memorably 'heritage baiting'. Many of the recently built heritage centres, for all their simplifications, have restored to ordinary people a sense of the material conditions in which their ancestors were asked to live their lives. Most who disapproved of such things were document-driven historians, fixated on archival research and on the textual. Samuel contends that if more demographic historians actually visited such heritage sites or actually dressed up as Victorian fathers and mothers, they might indeed write a more felt and convincing form of history. He asks whether some element of the critique of heritage centres might not be based on old-style snobbery in the face of a project which restores a mass-entertainment value to the analysis of lived history. And he ends his chapter on heritage baiting with a magnificent corrective:

The perceived opposition between 'education' and 'entertainment', and the unspoken, unargued-for assumption that pleasure is almost by definition mindless, ought not to go unchallenged. There is no reason to think that people are more passive when looking at old photographs or film-footage, handling a museum exhibit, following a local history trail, or even buying a historical souvenir, than when reading a book.[14]

All that said, the best way to connect ourselves and our children to past monuments is to take things out of glass cases and enclosing frames, in order to show that the past is never really past, never completely over. Rather it is a process, crying out for understanding. The task of the teacher or curator, like that of the historian, is literally to re-member the past, to put the different part of its body back together again, and to restore to it the fuller context which once it had.

There is a beautiful poem called 'Bog Queen' by Seamus Heaney which bears on this theme. Most of Heaney's bog poems are about bodies exhumed from the turf in Jutland, but this figure (feminine and Irish) speaks for herself:

> I lay waiting
> Between turf-face and demesne wall,
> Between heathery levels
> And glass-toothed stone.[15]

Caught between the native Irish boglands and the demesne walls of the ascendancy, she awaits (like rebels and rapparees) the 'moment when she may rise again'. The bog preserves not just her body but her consciousness. Like all who make Freud's desperate bargain to live with the discontents that alone make culture possible, she has been in fact preserved by the sheer weight of the earth which suffocated her. She is also proof that the dead, though often forgotten, are never truly gone, and, since they do not even know that they are dead, may just be wintering out:

> My skull hibernated
> in the wet nest of my hair.
>
> Which they robbed.
> I was barbered
> and stripped
> by a turfcutter's spade

who veiled me again
and packed coomb softly
between the stone jambs
at my head and my feet.[16]

The kindly turf-cutter who dug her up by accident in a quite literal sense 'remembered' her, reassembling her bones in proper order before the discreet 'veiling'. This was, of course, that very moment for which all along she had been waiting, that instant when she would re-enter human minds as a troubling challenge.

The facts, however, record that when she was dug out on Lord Moira's estate in 1781, her body was not accorded the dignity deserved by such patient, prayerful waiting. The cutter was paid off in cash and Lady Moira plundered the corpse, which the cutter might respectfully have restored to its resting place:

Till a peer's wife bribed him.
The plait of my hair,
a slimy birth-cord
of bog, had been cut

and I rose from the dark,
hacked bone, skull-ware,
frayed stitches, tufts,
small gleams on the bank.[17]

The grave decorum of the earlier stanzas is turbo-charged at the close and some readers have heard in its lines an echo of Sylvia Plath's 'Lady Lazarus', a witch back from the dead in vengeful mode, protesting the insult of a body reduced to mere exhibit. Deeper still is the anonymity of pain, as suffering erases all traces of the individual and past wars spill over into the present. Even the dead, as Benjamin said, can never be wholly safe from an enemy who wins. And this raises a deeper issue: are *we* that enemy who wins? Why is it all right to display the bones of a man who died in AD 52 but not of one who died in AD 1952?

Yet in 'Bog Queen', more in its rhythms than its statements, there is enacted a dignified hope. The greater the insult to the body, the surer the queen's eventual revival from it. Although she feels violated by the planter's wife, she also finds a sweet confirmation of her hope that she could rise again, to re-enter the human mind. Though made available for contemplation as an exhibit in an aristocrat's museum, she is rescued for human dignity by Heaney's imagination, which recreates a fuller context for her total story. His poem is actually an attack upon a certain kind of museumisation, that sort with which I began. It is a refusal to connive in the common curatorial desire to present anything old as an art work, an effect most often achieved by removing the object from its first enabling context. And the danger is that which attaches to so many old museums – that a discourse of connoisseurship (such as Lady Moira's) will take the place of the turf-cutter's honest workings. Better by far to return such objects to the bog which will preserve them more fully than any other museum. The problem with the colonial museum is the rather restricted role it accords the dead, for, unlike Heaney's poem, it gives them no chance to answer back.

A better model of the past would be more dialectical. It would recognise what Yeats once said: that the dead may not even know that they are dead but just keep on talking. Tradition can never be stabilised. The past can never be completely used up but will retain unfinished energies, still to be unleashed in a troubled present. This revolutionary use of tradition is quite at odds with that of the colonialist. It sees in a past moment a molecule which, as in a chemical experiment, collides into a molecule that is the present, releasing wholly new energies into the utopian museum that is the future. This is a knowledge incapable of fixity, but one that brings us face to face with our own strangeness as human agents in history.

Heaney's poetic project – so often linked to objects in the National Museum of Ireland – moves to a sort of climax in 'Bog Queen'. That project is to give the dead not just votes but voices, to recall them from the insolence of forgetfulness and what E. P. Thompson once called 'the enormous condescension of posterity'.[18] In the images of the museum Heaney found the real unfinished business of the modern Irish Republic, that sense of lost energies in need of reactivation, and a sense of his own as yet unexcavated depths as a person. And *that*, in the end, is the only really good reason to walk into a museum or gallery – in order to come, as if by accident, upon some unexpected, long-lost but immensely healing element of our own buried selves. If museums can reconnect us with our own strangeness, they can fulfil a useful and beautiful function.

The recent emergence of 'writers' museums' in Ireland offers a new set of challenges. The preponderance of such institutions in the former USSR suggested an official desire to control and curtail the subversive qualities of much good writing. Could the existence of a Joyce or Yeats or Dublin Writers' Museum imply a similar domestication of radical art? Perhaps the underlying desire is more subtle but less conscious: to make the present past, to consign art or artefact to the relative stability of 'tradition'. This is an impulse to be found within many art-works themselves:

the chorus in Yeats's *Deirdre* wishes to bring the tale to a conclusion, as does the narrator (Michael) in Friel's *Dancing at Lughnasa*, as does Winnie in Beckett's *Happy Days* when she speaks in the future perfect: 'This will have been a happy day.'

The literary museums have developed at much the same time as the 'interpretative centres' on the Burren or near the Blasket Islands. The critique of them repeats elements of the attack by such historians as Roy Foster and Tom Dunne on the 'lived history' aspect of some interpretative centres. What the academic historians have really been objecting to is the return at these centres of popular oral traditions (about 1798, the Great Famine, the 1916 rebellion, and so on), in place of the document-driven revisionist versions which their own bestselling volumes had done so much to advance. In retrospect, it is now clear that the revisionist moment has passed and that its flowering was a brief print phenomenon, before the repressed traditional and local memory of what happened was restored in community-organised centres.

Some of these centres have helped to expose serious gaps in the National Museum – for example, the lack of many religious artefacts. This lack might be a result of the desire of various churches to keep their artefacts to themselves, a desire which in turn may have suited a state authority which wished to maintain a sense of separation from all churchly things. (There is less shyness about displaying *ancient* religious objects, but far more about showing the sectarian Christian memorabilia of post-Reformation centuries.) Obviously, after the devotional revival of the nineteenth century, the Catholic Church did not see museums as replacing churches, preferring its churches to present old relics or saints' artefacts as part of a living ritual, much like the art of the Balinese which is taken to be a practical element of everyday life. A related irony may be found in the absence of many items of the struggle for national independence from the state's museum (which some might accuse in the past of simply tacking an Easter Rising room onto the old colonial structure). One telling reason for this may have been the reluctance of some republican families to recognise the state as embodying the historic nation for which their ancestors fought: the papers of Seán Mac Diarmada, for instance, remain in the United States because his descendants do not recognise the legitimacy of the Dublin government.

Clearly, the ideal museum would be one which could make its exclusions, both deliberate and regretted, part of its own explanatory narrative and which could disrupt previous narrative accounts, asking people to take sides as a new order displaces older ones. There is always a danger of these new structures replicating the old problems (by, for example, repeating the binary structures of life in Northern Ireland or South Africa, rather than mapping out more plural solutions). Maybe the best answer so far found is to 'federalise' the idea of a national museum so that all possible histories are included: and in Ireland that would embrace children's, labour and women's museums, as well as those of a nationalist or unionist disposition.

NOTES

1 James Joyce, *Ulysses* (Harmondsworth, Penguin, 1986), p. 29.
2 Ibid., p. 28.
3 Ibid., p. 20.
4 Ibid., p. 28.
5 Ibid., p. 25, and see Richard Ellman, *Ulysses on the Liffey* (London, Faber & Faber, 1972), p. 32.
6 Oscar Wilde, quoted in Richard Ellman, ed., *The Artist as Critic: Critical Writings of Oscar Wilde* (London, Allen, 1970), p. 291.
7 Walter Benjamin, *Illuminations*, trans. Harry Zohn (London, Collins-Fontana, 1974), p. 174.
8 W. B. Yeats, in Allan Wade, ed., *Letters of W. B. Yeats* (London, Hart-Davis, 1955), p. 108.
9 Yeats, quoted in Ursula Bridge, ed., *W. B. Yeats and Sturge Moore: Their Correspondence 1901–1937* (London, Routledge & Kegan Paul, 1953), p. 154.
10 Cited in Marshall McLuhan, *The Medium is the Message* (London, Random House, 1968), p. 41.
11 Benjamin, *Illuminations*, p. 246.
12 William Shakespeare, *Hamlet*, ed. Oscar Campbell, Alfred Rothschild and Stuart Vaughan (New York, Bantam, 1961), p. 175.
13 Sarah Nuttall and Carli Coetzee, eds., *Negotiating the Past: The Making of Memory in South Africa* (Cape Town, Oxford University Press, 1998), p. 154.
14 Raphael Samuel, *Theatres of Memory: Past and Present in Contemporary Culture*, vol. 1 (London, Verso, 1994), p. 271.
15 Seamus Heaney, *North* (London, Faber & Faber, 1975), p. 32.
16 Ibid., p. 33.
17 Ibid., p. 34.
18 E. P. Thompson, *The Making of the English Working Class* (Harmondsworth, Penguin, 1968), p. 13.

CHAPTER 15

Joyce's Ellmann, Ellmann's Joyce

(1999)

I am neither a full-time Joycean nor a strict theorist and at a conference filled with both types, my position somewhat resembles that of an atheist at an eucharistic congress. I want, nonetheless, to pay my own tribute to a very great forerunner. Ever since *Middlemarch* taught me that specialism can be but another word for self-love, I have gone in fear of academic experts. A colleague of mine at University College, Dublin, once pointed out how quickly scholars took on the character of those authors whom they made their sole study. The Yeatsians in his judgement were generally arrogant and autocratic; the Shavians all seemed to have overdosed on the life force; the Beckettians were all permanently depressed; the Gregorians flighty and feminist; the O'Caseyans pedantic and paranoid. But, he added by way of a modest qualification, 'the Joyceans are usually very nice'.

We think of Dick Ellmann, I suppose, as the essential Joycean: and he was in truth one of the nicest men you could hope to meet. Irish scholars in particular will tell one another of his many acts of kindness done by stealth and discovered long afterwards. As a young man, he bought a couple of paintings by Jack Yeats in order to show some gratitude to the family which had done so much to help him. They lay, neglected, in a corner of his office for years, before a visitor noticed them and told their owner of the fabulous cash value which they now represented. That was one case where his kindness was returned.

Ellmann features now in Irish literary lore not only as a Joycean but as a fully comprehensive figure in his own right. The writings of Yeats, Wilde and Beckett, as well as those of Joyce, seem quite inseparable from his explanations of them: and in helping the world to understand the Irish modernists, Ellmann inevitably helped the Irish to know themselves. It would hardly be an exaggeration to repeat of him what Yeats said of Standish O'Grady: that to him each Irish writer owes a portion of his or her soul.[1]

235

Not all the writers were immediately grateful for his contribution, of course: and in his earlier years Ellmann had to contend with the sort of ragging which many subsequent American scholars would experience at the hands of militant authors. He told me once of how, shortly after the poet Austin Clarke had written a rather savage review of one of his books on Yeats, he found himself facing the porcelain in the men's urinal by O'Connell Bridge, next to a man in a wide-brimmed black hat who looked eerily familiar. 'Are you who I think you are?' he asked, tentatively. 'I'll wait until we're both completely finished before I answer your interesting question', drawled the laconic Clarke, before adding the single word immortalised in a hundred cowboy films, 'pard'ner'. Clarke had been bemoaning the lack of a strong native Irish literary criticism[2] when Ellmann's books began to appear. Over time, he came to understand that Ellmann regretted it too and they became better friends.

It had been said that a literary revival occurred in Dublin because five or six people lived in the same city and hated one another cordially. Ellmann, entering this force-field just after World War Two, was bound to get caught in some of the crossfire. He remained convinced that he was the prime academic target of Patrick Kavanagh's poem 'Who Killed James Joyce?':

> Who killed James Joyce?
> I, said the commentator,
> I killed James Joyce
> For my graduation.
>
> What weapon was used
> To slay mighty Ulysses?
> The weapon that was used
> Was a Harvard thesis.
>
> Who killed Finnegan?
> I, said a Yale-man,
> I was the man who made
> The corpse for the wake man. . . .
>
> And did you get high marks,
> The Ph.D.?
> I got the B. Litt.
> And my master's degree.
>
> Did you get money
> For your Joycean knowledge?
> I got a scholarship
> To Trinity College.[3]

Yet within a few more decades a less querulous generation of artists was celebrating Ellmann in works of high literature dedicated to him. The phoney war between writers and critics was over. Both Seamus Heaney and Edna Longley would, after his death in 1987, deliver a series of lectures in his memory,[4] while the keynote talk each year at the Yeats International Summer School in Sligo bears his name. If the notion of Joyce as smutmonger is in danger of being replaced by a holy cult of Saint James Aloysius, memorialised in statues and busts across inner-city Dublin (at the last count there were more Joyces than Virgin Marys within four hundred yards of O'Connell Street), then there is a similar possibility that we may soon be confronted with a cult of Blessed Dick.

I first heard him lecture at the summer school in Sligo, 1971. Almost two years later, I was sent to Oxford by my teachers in Trinity in hopes that I might write a dissertation on Synge and the Irish language. The interviews seemed to go well enough but afterwards I was ruefully informed that there was no scholar of modern Irish literature in the English faculty. If I wanted to write about Synge, it would be wiser to look elsewhere for supervision. Resigned, I reverted to the role of tourist determined to enjoy a day or two in the city of dreaming spires and perspiring dreams, the home of lost causes. On the second evening of my visit, I spotted a bald, avuncular man walking along St Giles, a cross between Henry Kissinger and Sergeant Bilko. It was the same man who had lectured on Molly Bloom's menstruation in Sligo. I told him of my fruitless interview at the faculty and lamented its lack of an Irish Studies person in Oxford. 'Who told you that?' he gently enquired. It had been the Master of Linacre, Jack Bamborough, a Ben Jonson scholar and so, in his way, a Joycean. He was also the next-door-neighbour of the Ellmanns in St Giles: 'How could they have made such a mistake?' I asked in some bewilderment. 'Oh', Ellmann purred, 'They probably associate me with modernism.' And indeed they did. He was in Oxford because he embodied, more than any other critic of his time, the modern tradition. His career had by 1973 the look of inevitability about it and seemed all of a piece. In his books on Yeats and Joyce – as later in the study of Wilde – he had shrewdly fused the celebratory techniques of Victorian biography with the close analytic methods of the New Criticism, adopting an approach that was (to me) pleasantly inclusive but sharply innovative when first applied in the 1940s. Hence the double meaning of a phrase like 'The Identity of Yeats' – identity in the sense of personal hallmark of an author but also to indicate the internal consistency of a work.[5]

It is the destiny of original minds to appear less and less remarkable in direct proportion to their success in changing received ideas: a moment is eventually reached when few can recall what the world was like before they came upon the scene. Few of my contemporaries, least of all myself, could in 1973 have had a clear concept of the critical change wrought by Ellmann and his fellow-workers. When he began his university life, as he often told me, Robert Browning was cited generally as the representative instance of a modern poet. It took rare courage for a young graduate student to stake a career on the seemingly eccentric, convoluted writing of W. B. Yeats but 'the fascination of what's difficult'[6] was what held him to the task. He and his contemporaries launched themselves into a systematic explanation of the texts of high modernism with an audacity which must, at times, have unnerved not only their teachers but themselves. Like the monks of some unproven new religion they offered exegeses of apparently impenetrable works with no certainty that the wider world would concur that those texts were sacred.

The skills of the biographer were so immense that they risked obscuring the real power and originality of his critical thought. However, time settles all verdicts: and it's now clear that the chapters of criticism in the Joyce biography stand as definitive, essay-length treatments of their subjects ('The Dead' and 'The Backgrounds to *Ulysses*').[7] In a hundred pages of *Eminent Domain* Ellmann managed to say more about modernism than other outstanding critics might articulate over four hundred pages.[8] His lucid analyses of Yeats provided the basis for his recognition as a major genius rather than a brilliant Irish sillybilly. His discussions of *Ulysses* exploded the prevalent reading of Bloom as a debased satirical contrast with Odysseus rather than a modern hero in his own right. He outlined the mythic method of modernism in a beautiful sentence: 'we walk in darkness on familiar roads'.

In stressing the affirmative qualities of those writers, he may at times have carried his optimism a little too far, but that was a very American attitude. It was characteristic of him to suggest that the word known to all men in *Ulysses* was 'love' and that its final monologue was a lyrical assertion of the life force, summed up in the single word 'yes'. Irish readers, disposed more to tragedy than comedy, have found darker meanings in the plight of a Molly Bloom left with nobody to talk to but herself. They have made considerably more of her masturbation than her menstruation. Indeed, when the actress Fionnula Flanagan performed the monologue in this way in Minnesota, large numbers of her audience walked out in protest, as if the holy text had been profaned. This was a measure of how influential Ellmann's reading of the 'happy' ending had become. The fact that Molly's 'yes' might also be a Dublin 'no', or that this woman posted blank pages to herself in a form of epistolary masturbation, seemed of less consequence to Ellmann than it did to the Irish interpreters of yet another 'silent marriage'.[9] However, in terms of the wider explanations of modernism then current, Ellmann's reading performed a signal service: it destroyed the view of modern art as a surly refusal to celebrate the twentieth-century world. The Americans had always known that this would be their century but Ellmann also registered the latent optimism in any writer's conviction that the turbulence of the period could be committed to paper. 'Passivity in act; energy in thought; tenacity in conviction:'[10] these qualities which he observed as bonds between Leopold Bloom and Stephen Dedalus also described himself.

He was later to make an even more comprehensive effort to define the essential elements of modernism, when with Charles Feidelson he assembled and edited a vast compendium of texts which provide the intellectual backdrop to twentieth-century literature under the paradoxical title *The Modern Tradition*.[11] Even if the subjects of his major books remained steadfastly Irish, it was obvious from the elegant introductions and linking commentaries of this book that Ellmann was in command of all the major elements of European and North American thought. His French was excellent (a fact made clear in his edition of Henri Michaux) and he seemed to be one of those great comparative critics produced out of the migratory experiences of the first half of the twentieth century: a cosmopolitan polymath.

Yet for Irish people, as Clarke had so ungallantly noted, he was filling a vacuum left by the absence of a developed national criticism. Some aspects of his work troubled us. His over-optimistic reading of Molly Bloom's monologue was matched by an over-enthusiastic celebration of the interior monologue as such in *Ulysses*. It was as if he was so entranced by Joyce's technical triumph in rendering the human consciousness that he wanted the very contents of that consciousness to be similarly positive. My father once remarked to me after reading one of Leopold Bloom's monologues: 'Don't you sometimes think it might have been better not to have had quite so rich an inner life?' Ellmann was shrewd enough to notice the contrast, pervasive in Irish literature, between the richness of a person's private thoughts and the actual poverty of the social setting: and he knew the act of compensation for what it was, an attempt to find in the mind a spaciousness impossible in the world. But it never seems to have struck him that such a richness comes at an awesome cost. A person's inner life may become so splendid and challenging as to disable him or her for all contacts with the world, a bleak truth dramatised by Brian Friel in *Philadelphia, Here I Come*, where the musings and mockeries of Private Gar have the effect of leaving Public Gar hopelessly tongue-tied and ineffectual.[12] On Friel's stage, the inner monologist is more often a damned nuisance than a secret ratifier: and those who have pondered that play and return afterwards to the monologues of *Ulysses* may find in it a very different work.

These doubts – or doubts very like them – assailed Irish students of Ellmann and Joyce, but we usually suppressed them, having been taught to read literature in our departments as if we were young Londoners or Mancunians. When we wrote of D. H. Lawrence, we did so in the approved manner of a Leavis or a Kermode; when we constructed essays on Joyce, we practised the style of Ellmann, Hugh Kenner or Walton Litz. Only outside the classroom or the library did we permit ourselves to think that there was something very strange in Ellmann's attitude to Ireland. While he loved Irish people as individuals, the plain truth was that he did not particularly like Ireland. His natural gift for empathy with a valued informant like Stanislaus Joyce conditioned his portrait of James, but it also filled him with a certain bitterness about the land which Stannie despised.

There were plenty more Irish voices to endorse that judgement: for Ellmann arrived as a young man in the 1940s to discover that most of the modern classics which he revered had been banned by the Censorship Board. His early and deep friendships with Sean O'Faolain and Frank O'Connor, both arch-critics of the repression, could only have reinforced Stannie's assessment. O'Faolain in a memorable phrase described the Irish as a nation of apple-lickers, i.e. pathetic venial sinners who, if tempted in the Garden of Eden, would have licked rather than bitten the apple.[13] O'Connor said that he returned to Ireland from America whenever he could, simply to remind himself what a terrible place it was. 'It's a lovely country to visit', Ellmann remarked during our first conversation in 1973, 'but I don't know how you manage to live there.' By 1973, of course, the country had changed massively: the cultural censorship had largely disappeared and the special privileges accorded the Roman Catholic Church were being rapidly eroded. Nonetheless, Ellmann never seemed able to register the compelling force of John Montague's lines:

> Puritan Ireland's dead and gone,
> A myth of O'Connor and O'Faolain.[14]

In this he was, again, a rather representative example of an American scholar in his attitude to other ethnic goups. Edward Said has, for example, demonstrated just how many specialists in Arab Studies secretly despise those people, the professional study of whom has allowed them to make their very reputations.[15] Ellmann was never guilty of double-think on that grand hypocritical scale: he rarely spoke disparagingly of Irish individuals, even of those who might have deserved some criticism, but he never cared much for the prevailing ideas of 'Ireland'. For him vices were national, virtues individual.

A close reader of his major books on Yeats, Joyce and Wilde will find in them a linked set of narratives; each suggests that the act of becoming modern requires a transcendence of mere Irishness. The shortest road to modernity is via Holyhead. This is relatively easy to demonstrate in the case of Wilde, for his was a mind utterly translatable, apparently devoid of any sense of locality or nation. However, Ellmann was able to effect a similar reading of Yeats, the same Yeats who had made of Wilde's lack of locality a grand complaint. In 'Yeats Without Analogue' Ellmann pronounced himself willing to admit that Irish nationalism was probably an absurdity, but he added (which was very kind of him) that Yeats did not consider it so. Still, he went on, it was not very helpful to consider Yeats as one of a group of people who merely freshened up Celtic legends. 'When he wrote *A Vision*', proclaimed Ellmann, 'he forgot he was an Irishman. And while he calls the fairies by their Irish name of *Sidhe*, I suspect that they too are internationalists.'[16] So there it is: even the little people, transcending their Irishness, are secret subscribers to the Fourth International. In saying this Ellmann was, in fact, forgetting that Yeats had written *A Vision* with the idea that its spiritual teaching might underpin the constitution of the emerging Irish state, a fantastic hope, perhaps, but not a wholly ridiculous one.[17] And Ellmann was imputing the censoriousness of mid-century Ireland to the renaissance Ireland of fifty years earlier.

In some ways this refusal to make too much of the Irishness of his subjects was exemplary and in keeping with the best of the post-revival spirit among contemporary writers. 'Irishness is a form of anti-art', thundered Patrick Kavanagh against all literary Paddies, 'A way of posing as an artist without being one.'[18] Flann O' Brien argued that a single sentence of Joyce was worth the whole corpus of Synge. I had the feeling that Ellmann, though he was too tactful ever to say so, kept wondering why I was wasting so much precious youthful energy on Synge. Yet his denial of the value of Ireland as a possible explanatory category in the story of modernism was also disingenuous in the manner of much mid-century criticism.

Denis Donoghue could write an entire book on Swift (a very good one, let it be added) while keeping Ireland severely in the background rather than the foreground: yet, a couple of decades later, when he came to collect his essays for posterity, he found it easiest to group them in national categories: *We Irish, England, Their England* and so on. Likewise, Hugh Kenner wrote of different modernisms in *A Sinking Island* (English), *A Homemade World* (American) and *A Colder Eye* (Irish). When these critics were in their youth, the approved style was one of compulsory internationalism: yet when they came to summarise their work, they found the national categories rather helpful. As for Ellmann, he was unlike the other two men in that he virtually never strayed from a consideration of Irish writers and themes.

He would insist that his chosen subjects only happened to be Irish, and also only happened to be the major modernists still crying out for book-length study. Yet he kept coming back to the matter of Ireland. Why? Not out of specialist self-love, for Ellmann read and knew all the great European and American authors. There were certain qualities to be found in Irish writers which he was willing to admit he valued above all others. They, like he, had the gift not of simplification but of explanation. Yeats said that a poet should think like a wise man but express himself like one of the common people: and although Ellmann's words were always clear, his ideas were often deceptively sophisticated. From Joyce he had learned that literature is but recorded speech ('Nobody has read *Ulysses* until he has read it aloud'): and he recognised a similar impulse in the witticism of Wilde, characterised as a kind of aristocratic folklore.[19] Ellmann's own lectures had a somewhat writerly quality, even as his books have something of the urgency of the spoken word. The fascination with a vibrant oral tradition may help to account for his lifelong obsession.

Was he really filling large gaps left by Irish critics? The answer cannot be simple, for research has alerted us to the fact that much was going on beneath the surface. The Ulster poet John Hewitt agreed with Clarke and lamented the dearth of Irish scholar–critics – but while the absence of published criticism is one thing, the want of criticism per se is quite another. After all, in the American academy of the 1940s, there was little enough curricular study of the classic texts of the American Renaissance and much devotion to Austen, Tennyson and Arnold. Lectures there were daily exercises by scholarship boys (or, more rarely, girls) in upper-echelon English ventriloquy, daily demonstrations of their right to hold their exalted positions. Such persons suffered from a very vulgar dread of vulgarity: for them an author like Joyce or Melville posed a huge challenge, because of the mixture of obscenity and wit, of learning and vulgarity. Had Ellmann simply been in search of a viable subject, he need never have left his own country.

The paucity of published academic research in Ireland had many causes, among them a belief that oral tradition was paramount and that it was sufficient for any professor to instruct his or her own students in the received wisdom. Moreover, some of the best native critics were by no means sure that the island's writers really deserved sustained attention: perhaps familiarity had bred contempt. But the sheer weight of the teaching-load, the small numbers in most departments meaning that each person had to teach across a huge range, and the lack of sabbatical facilities – all these factors retarded the development of scolarly research. There was a further complication: Irish writing, like that of the American Renaissance, seemed to contain within itself its own auto-criticism, its own essential self-commentary. This was as true of *Ulysses* as of the poetry of Yeats, of *At Swim-Two-Birds* as of Kavanagh, and it left many scrupulous critics wondering just how much of value could be added. Yet these acts of auto-criticism were individual occasions and even when taken together would hardly amount to a national critical methodology. Hence the concern of Clarke and Hewitt, a fear which had once assailed the black American radical W. E. B. DuBois, when he suggested that a people is never fully mature until it has produced not only a corpus of creative texts but also a criticism of the national life which helps to interpret them.

Irish artists had often spurned critics and denied the value of their activity: now, when the post-war army of American scholars began to arrive with their boxes of file-index cards, they began calling for a native response. The Americans, it seemed, were the surveyors; the Irish were what they surveyed. This was demeaning. The Americans wrote criticism; the Irish were creative. That was uplifting. But the 'translations' effected within the whole situation were problematic. Two social anthropologists like Arensberg and Kimball might come from the United States to study the western peasantry and produce a functionalist analysis, in the course of which their description of a countrywoman in her kitchen would have much of the artistic beauty of a Dutch, interior painting. To understand the reality of life in that rural landscape, a reality marked by seasonal migration and family break-up, one would have had to read a novel by Liam O' Flaherty.[20] Something was clearly askew when the sociology written by outsiders was turning so fast into literature, and the literature produced by insiders was taking on the value of sociology. In a similar fashion, Ellmann, though ostensibly a critic, seemed intent on creating works of literature himself.

He had rightly opposed the common English view of Irish modernists as eccentric, weird, obscene. While Auden might mock magic as 'the southern Californian element' in Yeats, Ellmann was willing to take it with some seriousness. He treated Joyce as an uxorious family man, arguing that his concern for his family gave his work its human dignity: in saying such things, Ellmann might have been describing his own experience. His gift for empathy, with his subjects as well as his informants, was a decisive factor in winning the confidence of the writers' families as he went about his work.

He used each of the three great biographies to explore himself, managing in that process to convert even Wilde into a genial, witty, avuncular charmer (a portrait which, by today's standards, rather overlooked his unpleasant use of rent-boys). All of this amply confirmed Wilde's adage that every portrait reflects more of the artist than of the subject. For Ellmann was in the end an artist, a finished example of the critic as artist. Because of that, he may have trusted his chosen authors' own descriptions rather too often. Ulick O'Connor has, for instance, recently demonstrated errors in the treatment of Oliver St John Gogarty caused by an uncritical reliance on *Ulysses* as a factual source.[21] Similarly, in a doctoral dissertation 'Joyce in Trieste: Trieste in Joyce', John McCourt has not only corrected errors of detail in Ellmann's treatment, but also shown how seriously the biographer underestimated the impact of the Triestine years on Joyce's life and work.[22] These shortcomings were perhaps predictable given Ellmann's willingness to understand Joyce in much the same terms as he understood himself. In all of Ellmann's seminars, when a text came up for discussion, his first advice to students was: 'Let us take the writer's part.' Although he was honest enough to include much that was unflattering about Joyce's selfishness, his neglect of his children and his exploitation of his brother while writing *Ulysses*, he overrode those elements with a narrative of his own about the essential decency of a great artist. It was as if Ellmann were in agreement with Dr Johnson who believed that a good artist cannot really be a bad man.

Certain themes recur in much of Ellmann's writing. For example, the father–son relationship is treated in *The Man and the Masks* as crucial to an understanding of Yeats: and the issue is raised again in the studies of

Wilde and Joyce, in all three cases as part of an argument to the effect that each writer, faced with some inadequacy in his father, was left to invent or father himself. The involvement of the writers with what might be called popular culture – whether oral or printed – was well described, putting them at variance with most European modernists who shunned mass-culture in the pursuit of high art. Likewise, the androgyny espoused by representative characters in each man's work is fully celebrated as it all too rarely was in the world of *machismo* conjured up by other European modernists, whose cults of virility were often an aspect of an autocratic politics. And so on. It seems to me that Ellmann held many of the keys to the distinctive features which set Irish modernism apart from other modernisms but that, for his own reasons, he chose not to turn them.

Ellmann's reluctance to develop ideas of national identity may have had something to do with his background in a mid-western Jewish family. He was attracted as a youth by the high art of Europe and especially by a text such as *Ulysses* which celebrated a man like Leopold Bloom. Ellmann was a member of the American forces which helped liberate Europe at the close of World War Two and he must have been shocked beyond words at the revelation of what went on in the gas chambers and concentration camps. The knowledge that many Nazis who presided over these outrages were devoted students of modernism was also hard to take. Against that backdrop, Ellmann's project assumes a kind of nobility: to rescue the humanist content of European modernism after the Holocaust recruiting the Irish writers to the centre of the pantheon. The scholarship of Ellmann would, like the liberating American armies and navy, help to build a new European ideal. This entailed the rewriting of literary history. In this revised version Ireland would be described as a narrow, backward, rather intolerant place which drove a free spirit like Joyce into exile. By such means the Ireland of the 1950s was read back into the land of 1900, against the empirical evidence which showed that in fact the Irish at the start of the century were audacious in thought and that the reasons for Joyce's exile were more economic than cultural, since he could find no post commensurate with his qualifications or self-image at home.

Ellmann remained in some ways a rather naive observer of contemporary Ireland. The possibility that his own analysis of Joyce in 1959 accorded perfectly with the new philosophy of the Europeanising elite in Dublin probably never even crossed his mind: but it was so. A whole generation of civil servants, journalists, academics and writers had as its ultimate aim the entry to the European Economic Community, finally voted for in 1972. For these people, a writer who suggested that they might become modern by ceasing to be consciously Irish was saying something very interesting indeed. This, along with the wonderful clarity of his style, was another reason why Ellmann's books won huge audiences in Ireland well beyond the walls of the universities. Even today a random check at the bookshops in Dublin Airport will show that his biographies all remain steady sellers among the frequent flyers of the Celtic Tigerland.

The truth was, of course, somewhat different from what he or the new elite imagined it to have been. From the time of the Great Famine in the 1840s, Ireland was modern. Whether its people willed it or not, modernity was thrust upon them as a donné, not a choice.[23] To begin your life speaking one language in a windswept neolithic village and to end it speaking another in Hammersmith or Hell's Kitchen was to undergo the sort of wrenching contrast which would characterise modern life in the twentieth century for millions of migrants and exiles. But all this happened to Irish people in the middle of the nineteenth. Even those who stayed at home found themselves in a modern situation, living like Beckett's tramps without a key in an environment made all but incomprehensible by the rapid shift of languages. The Irish were now strangers in their own country, and strangers everywhere else too. Their artists, caring too little for the environment even to spurn it, had little choice but to go inside the human head and to seek new literary forms appropriate to that challenge.

For them the realist modes of European writing had never seemed real at all and the nineteenth-century idea of linear progress was reduced to risibility by the events of the Great Famine. Thereafter, for Irish writers history was not a straight line going somewhere definite but a circle of cyclical repetitions: it was impossible to view 'progress' as anything more than just another myth. Their search was for a set of forms sufficiently fragmented to accommodate all the splinters of national experience. Even the father–son conflict had a different meaning in Ireland. In other European countries, where fathers and sons had hands on the levers of power, the eventual triumph of sons over fathers could be translated into social progress: but in Ireland that conflict was turned back on itself, unbearably intensifying the stresses of family life. Elsewhere Oedipus was producing neurosis; in Ireland neurosis was producing Oedipus.[24] The revolt by sons was meaningless unless transformed into outright revolution: hence the 'himself his own father' theme in Joyce which Ellmann, with his unerring instinct, linked to the Oedipal dramas enacted also in the pages of George Moore, Wilde and Synge. However, though he might note those parallels, he could not see the obsession with the father–son theme as the certain sign of a society unsure of its general direction.

What strikes critics in the current generation is the sheer oddness of, say, *Ulysses* alongside other works of high modernism. Its plot moves, after all, towards a rapprochement between bohemian and bourgeois, Dedalus and Bloom. In an age when most modernists attacked the family unit, Joyce celebrated it: and at a time when others sought extreme situations, he savoured the quotidian, the middle range of experience. While others feared the forces latent in the masses, Joyce showed that art might engage with those masses, by minutely documenting the half-articulated thoughts and half-conscious feelings of very ordinary people. And so on.

Whereas in English, French or German literature the hero's arrival in the big city signalised liberation, in Joyce's books it is movement out of the city which heralds freedom. In most novels dialogue propels the plot, while in *Ulysses* it more often anaesthetises and retards it. At the very time when other European modernists declared cultural war on news-papers, Joyce was imagining *Ulysses* as a bookish version of a daily journal, with himself as scissors-and-paste man, editor-in-chief. The difficulties of reading his montage are in essence no different from those associated with rapid scanning of a metropolitan newspaper: and the experience calls more for quickness of response than for a training in the classics of European art.

All of which suggests that it is time for a discrimination of modernisms, a recognition that Irish modernism may be not at all the same thing as English modernism (which characteristically, as in Forster, attempts to pour the experience of modernity into the forms of a nineteenth-century novel). And French and American modernisms may be something else again. Ellmann often shrewdly noted the resistance of English readers and academics to Joyce: it was, he said, the expatriate intellectuals like Anthony Burgess who gave him a fair hearing. Had Joyce attempted his literary career in England rather than on the continent he might have appeared as just the sort of striving, educated, disadvantaged young man who is gently mocked in a work like *Howards End*. (In fact, he was so patronised by Bloomsbury in the deeply ignorant comments on his writings by Virginia Woolf.) Ellmann saw himself as on a mission in Oxford to bring the genius of Joyce to the recalcitrant English. In that he succeeded very well.

Ireland he left to another generation of critics. Over the past decade the publication of a Penguin Twentieth Century Classics series of Joyce's texts edited by a team of Irish scholars has led to predictable allegations that this is little better than a doomed attempt to assimilate Joyce to the ideas of a militant nationalism which he despised. In fact, its aim was to locate Joyce against the Irish background, demonstrating that one doesn't need to turn only to Europe to explain his modernism, for it was already inherent in the formal demands placed on artists by the Irish situation. The gap which Ellmann and his Oxford colleagues saw between 'Irishness' and 'modernity' has been closed in these editions.

What Hugh Kenner long ago demonstrated of America's home-made modernism, a new generation of Irish critics – notably Terence Brown, Emer Nolan and Seamus Deane – has shown of Joyce (with significant contributions by overseas scholars like Vincent Cheng, Joe Valente and Cheryl Herr). These have all restored to Joyce the integrity of his local moment. In a similar fashion, the Indian critic Homi Bhabha is currently writing a study of the elements of vernacular modernism as filtered through Bombay in the early decades of this century, just as Ann Douglas has monitored Mongrel Manhattan of the 1920s in a book of that name.

Each of these points on the global network of vernacular modernism will have many elements in common with other points, as well as many elements of difference. What is needed now is a restoration to the work of the early modernists of the intellectual openness which it once had. Accordingly, Terence Brown's edition of *Dubliners* allows us to read the stories as they were interpreted by their very first audience either in the pages of *The Irish Homestead* or in the first edition of the collection. I hope very much that this work will be taken for what it is: a recognition that, in historicising a great artist, critics must go back to a study of the field of force out of which he or she came. If the resulting readings suggest that Joyce has as much in common with the post-colonial or vernacular modernists as with the high modernists of Paris or Zurich, then so be it. If the artists chosen for intense study by Ellmann just happened to be Irish, then it may be time to concede that Joyce's own location in Zurich or Paris was a matter more of chance than of cultural piety. After all, he viewed the culture of those great cities with the detachment of an anthropologist who had come from another place entirely.

NOTES

1 W. B. Yeats, *Autobiographies*, London, 1955, p. 220.
2 Clarke's first statements to this effect appeared in the 'Letters to the Editor' columns of the *Irish Times*, during a controversy which lasted through January 1941. Ellmann's first book on Yeats appeared in 1949.
3 Patrick Kavanagh, *Collected Poems*, London, 1972, pp. 117–18.

4 These lectures have been delivered at Emory University, Atlanta, Georgia, where he had served as Visiting Professor; other recent lecturers have included Helen Vendler and A. S. Byatt.

5 Susan Dick, Dougald McMillan, Joseph Ronsley and Declan Kiberd, Introduction, *Omnium Gatherum: Essays for Richard Ellmann*, Gerrards Cross, 1989, pp. xiii–xviii. Many of my ideas on Ellmann owe much to our discussion in preparing the introduction. This point I owe specifically to Dougald McMillan.

6 W. B. Yeats, *Collected Poems*, London, 1950, p. 104.

7 Richard Ellmann, *James Joyce*, Oxford, 1959, pp. 252–63 and 367–90.

8 Richard Ellmann, *Eminent Domain*, Oxford, 1967.

9 For a fuller version of this reading see Declan Kiberd, *Ulysses: Annotated Student's Edition* (Penguin Twentieth Century Classics), London, 1992, pp. 1180–5.

10 Ellmann, *James Joyce*, p. 379.

11 Richard Ellmann and Charles Feidelson Jr eds., *The Modern Tradition*, New York, 1965.

12 Brian Friel, *Philadelphia, Here I Come*, London, 1965.

13 'Writer in Profile: Sean O' Faolain', RTÉ television, 5 April 1968.

14 John Montague, 'The Siege of Mullingar 1963', *Field Day Anthology of Irish Writing 3*, Derry, 1991, p. 1353.

15 See Edward Said, *Covering Islam*, London, 1981, pp. 3–64.

16 Richard Ellmann, 'Yeats Without Analogue', *Along the Riverrun*, New York, 1990, p. 25.

17 See for example Ellmann's own rather different treatment of *A Vision* in *Yeats: The Man and The Masks*, London, 1961, p. 249.

18 Declan Kiberd, 'Underdeveloped Comedy: Patrick Kavanagh', *The Southern Review*, Louisiana, July 1995, vol. 31, no. 3, 714–25.

19 Ellmann, *Eminent Domain*, p. 14.

20 See, for instance, Michael D. Higgins, 'The Gombeenman in Irish Fact and Fiction', *Etudes Irlandaises*, December 1985, no. 10, 31–52.

21 Ulick O'Connor, *Biographers and the Art of Biography*, Dublin, 1991, pp. 17–21.

22 John McCourt, 'Joyce in Trieste: Trieste in Joyce', Ph.D. dissertation 1996, University College, Dublin.

23 On this see Declan Kiberd, 'Romantic Ireland's Dead and Gone', *Times Literary Supplement*, 12 June 1998, 12–14.

24 For one similar case see Gilles Deleuze and Felix Guattari, *Kafka: Towards a Minor Literature*, Minnesota, 1986, p. 10.

CHAPTER 16

Multiculturalism and artistic freedom: the strange death of liberal Europe

(1993)

In 1991, a human corpse was used in a sculpture by an American artist; and another artist dipped a crucifix in a container filled with his own urine to make a model called *Piss Christ*. In 1990, the controversial photographs of the late Robert Mapplethorpe were exhibited, including depictions of one man stuffing his fist up another man's rectum. All of these cases provoked massive controversy, and they were part of a wider pattern of debate in the developed – some might say, overdeveloped – nations of the West. In February 1989, a British jury had ruled that the use of human foetuses as earrings in a work of art was an outrage to public decency. The ten-to-two majority, far from being seen as conclusive, provoked a new debate: should they have the right to dictate what can or cannot be enjoyed by the minority?

That question of a desirable balance between expressive freedom and the social order is as old as the law itself, but it has been posed with particular intensity in the past century, ever since art proclaimed itself the new religion and Matthew Arnold proclaimed that the place of the priests would now be taken by poets. The high modernists contended that life was justified as an aesthetic phenomenon, or else not at all. This led them to challenge bourgeois proprieties in a series of well-publicised contests, beginning when the Lord Chamberlain banned a performance of Wilde's *Salomé* in London in 1894, and culminating in the unbanning of *Lady Chatterley's Lover* after the famous trial of 1960. Within the realm of art, its exponents dedicated themselves with ever-increasing monastic zeal to a rigorous internal order, but this did not prevent them from asserting their absolute right to challenge public order and decency. This shift might seem of interest only to those concerned with the world of high art, but in fact it reflected a major modernisation in the wider society. Artists could now declare themselves above and beyond considerations of social decorum; and those who suffered for asserting those freedoms became the heroes and heroines of the modern movement from

Joyce to Genet, from Woolf to Plath. The autonomy – or, to put it another way, the honourable exemption – claimed by artists soon came to be demanded by many other citizens as well, with the result that the balance in practice, if not in actual law, began to tilt towards the individual. Henceforth, the effects upon an individual rather than its implications for society became the moral touchstone of an action. The decline in religious belief left men and women free to proclaim the individual godlike, autonomous; and the demonic or satanic forces, once strictly policed by the priests, were now released as a source of creativity and power. Freud could justly claim to have unleashed the lower depths, and the general development of modernism from Stephen Dedalus's 'non serviam' to Bulgakov's *The Master and Margarita* seemed to ratify this diabolical pact.

Central to this literature was the conviction that the whole world existed to be turned into a book, and that even the most remote parts of it might offer up valuable materials to the transforming hand of the artist – African statuary, Balinese murals, Latin American music, all were fair game. Though the solid middle-class administrators of various European empires liked to think of themselves as the polar opposites of feckless bohemian artists, both groups agreed on their right to expropriate any native artefact or tradition which could be turned to use. The mingling of disparate artistic modes which ensued was perhaps the first instance of multiculturalism, but it was predicated within the single text or art object, and justified by the artist on the basis that such resources assisted in the remaking of a self. What the peoples whose cultural artefacts were so appropriated actually thought of these developments is largely unrecorded, though we know that those who lived long enough or travelled far enough to sense what had been done were as angry as Martin Mac Donagh, the young Aran islander whose letters Synge reproduced without permission in a published essay and whose sentences Synge used in the closing lines of *Riders to the Sea*.

In recent years, as both travel and communications have still further improved, many Indian sculptors and potters have witnessed on television the use to which European artists like Stephen Cox have put their centuries-old traditions, after brief, often cursory visits; and they have voiced a resentment as bitter as that articulated by some South African musicians at the use made of their native melodies by the singer Paul Simon.

The licence claimed by modernist artists in Africa, Asia and Latin America did not unduly trouble the rulers of European and American societies, but when these freedoms were asserted in home countries, then it could be a different story. The jury which found against the foetal earrings might not have come up with a ten to two majority in favour of returning all the African woodcarvings in British museums to their original contexts. And the crusades of conservative politicians like Jessie Helms against gay art in the US are stern reminders that the rights of artists are under baleful scrutiny at all times. Indeed, the recent removal by George Bush of the head of the National Endowment for the Arts – a person who had defended grants to gay artists – might seem to indicate a new mood favouring curtailment of the expressive freedoms of the American artist.

If that is so, then it is only just to add that there is reason to believe that those freedoms may sometimes have been pressed too far. The case of sculptor Richard Serra is significant here. He is a hero of modernism, who builds in the gigantic manner. One of his structures killed a Minneapolis labourer in the 1970s during a removal. His *pièce de resistance*, however, was a four-yard high, forty-yard long steel wall, erected on the plaza of the Javits Federal Building in New York. This he called *Tilted Arc*. In October 1988, the *New York Times* reported that 'More than 1,000 government employees . . . signed a petition asking that the carved wall of three rusted steel plates be removed because it blocks access to the building, disrupts traffic patterns and destroys the plaza's vistas and amenities.' Insisting that his work was 'site-specific', Richard Serra said that any change in location would violate his Fifth Amendment right to free speech and to due process of the law protecting the moral rights of an artist. He sued the federal government and tried to halt what he saw as the malicious removal of his work. He lost and told reporters: 'I don't think this country has ever destroyed a work of art before.' Some endorsed his protest, while others castigated him for going to law at all, because thereby he seemed to submit art to the authority of the state. The case became famous largely because the artist *lost*.

Such recourse to law made sense, however, given that American and European law generally vindicates the rights of an artist. In Britain, for example, recent legislation has guaranteed that every time an author's book is borrowed from designated libraries a royalty will be paid. In a period when high-brow criticism has proclaimed the death of the author, both the government and judiciary have taken with an unprecedented seriousness the sacredness of the artist and of the art object.

This may signify that the law, as so often, is merely fifty years out of date and only catching up with the modernist view of art, now that modernism has been safely domesticated. It may even be that the freedom and immunity thus accorded the artist are not always indicative of a wider liberalisation of society but can on occasion supply the token exception that proves the bourgeois rule. The modern artist is often asked by the public to embody all that craziness, poetry, madness and even badness which a lifetime of cautious career-building has led the ordinary citizens to suppress in themselves. Art might even be seen as the safety-valve which ensures society's survival, and bohemia as the ghetto in which cluster those troublemakers who might otherwise disrupt the city streets. The decade of the 1980s, which expanded the freedom of artists, also saw a severe contraction in the freedoms of the individual citizen, even at the level of permitted thought.

There does indeed seem to be an inverse relationship between artistic licence and the individual citizen's expressive freedoms. Many who would consider protofascism unpardonable – even at the level of ideas – in some National Front extremist are nonetheless willing to forgive a Francis Stuart or an Ezra Pound their autocratic politics on one simple understanding: that these writers were, ultimately, artists. Being artists they can be afforded a fool's pardon, because artists are by very definition deviants, dissidents, liminal ones. But should artists acquiesce in what may be a trivialisation of the ideas-content of their work?

That debate has been brought into a sharp and sustained focus by the traumas following publication of *The Satanic Verses* in 1988. To most European intellectuals, the cruel *fatwa* of the Ayatollah Khomeini, which condemned a man to death for writing a satirical fiction, is a blatant denial of the freedom of artistic expression. To Islamic intellectuals, it is a more complex issue: in their view, *both* the *fatwa and* the book have together fed noxious Western stereotypes of a barbaric and vicious Islam. The portrayal of Rushdie in European papers as a secular saint of modern art has meant that Muslim rights to unfettered self-expression have been curtailed, to such a degree that most people do not understand why the book is as offensive to Muslims as *Piss Christ* was to Christian viewers. The liberal European sees a book burning and remembers the Nazis: could any analogy be more damning? The fact that Rushdie was offered only belated and seemingly reluctant protection by a government whose leader his book portrays as 'Mrs Torture' merely augmented the understandable zeal of Harold Pinter and other London intellectuals to protect a colleague and friend. And there was in truth something heroic about Rushdie's lonely exposure: disliked by the English authorities, but in danger of death from his own people, he seemed the very epitome of the post-colonial intellectual, the world author, the nomad as multicultural hero, the man with no place to hang his hat. Such a description would certainly fit the author of *Midnight's Children*, whose narrator suffers just that kind of loneliness. I want to ask, however, if *The Satanic Verses* gives us reason to question that description.

There is, after all, a liberal Islamic case against Rushdie (argued most eloquently in *Distorted Imagination* by Ziauddin Sardar and Meryl Wyn Davies), which calls not for his death but for his answer to certain charges, the major charge being that he is not a liberal at all but just as fundamentalist as the Ayatollah. This fundamentalism is accused of relying on its own rather narrow secularist ethic, a relatively recent development in world history but one which arrogates to its artists the right to freely expressed contempt for traditional beliefs and believers, in extremist language and images. How *multi*, in other words, is a *cultural-ism* which loads its language heavily in favour of the secular West, a West which supplies the Eurocentric framework through which all other cultures are subsequently judged?

That this is happening is incontrovertible: otherwise, most newspaper readers would know by now that the *fatwa* was opposed by the vast majority of Muslims. Freedom of expression exists in theory in Europe, but – as any anti-Maastricht campaigner will tell you – the power to exercise it is not equally distributed. The generality of Muslim opinion has yet to be represented. Hence the intellectual poverty of Rushdie's defenders who – with some exceptions like Tom Stoppard – have not thought the issues through to anything more developed than the old cliché of artistic licence. To some in Europe that argument has begun to seem suspect; to most in the East, it appears downright uncivilised. So far the Rushdie affair has demonstrated two things – that there is no truly free market in ideas, which is to say no true multiculturalism; and that freedom of expression is not unconditional, since every expression also involves a suppression.

This latter point is seldom appreciated, because those who have controlled the discourse in which the affair is debated do not care to note the limits which they have set to their own tolerance. Like all dominant forces, they assume where others have to prove, and one assumption is that their own secular rationalism is a fitting yardstick by which to judge all human behaviour and belief, even the behaviour and belief of peoples who remain defiantly anti-secular. The sceptic has thus become the surveyor, the believer the surveyed.

It would be hard to overstate just how lacking in analytic self-awareness such a secular rationalism actually is. But then, Europe has always prospered on such self-contradictions: it was Enlightenment Europe, after all, which gave the world the terrors of colonialism. The dehumanisation of native Asians, Africans and Americans found its programmatic justification in what is still called (with no sense of irony) humanism. Only the most radical European thinkers saw this disjunction for what it was. After the Algerian war of the 1950s, it became clear to Jean-Paul Sartre that 'the striptease of humanism' was 'not a pretty sight', nothing but 'a perfect justification for pillage'. Far from being a source of culture, Europe was itself a luxuried creation of the colonised world in its suffering, plunder and pain. Ever since that discovery, the humanist project has been discredited among thinkers like Foucault and Derrida (who, indeed, was Algerian). These writers exposed the injustices which it perpetrated and occluded in the name of humanism. Their analyses have now been co-opted by post-modernists, but seldom with any recognition that the critique of the subject was initiated on the periphery of Europe by analysts like Frantz Fanon and Aimé Cesaire. Fanon indeed wrote that 'The violence with which the supremacy of white values is affirmed . . . means that, in revenge, the native laughs in mockery when western values are mentioned in front of him.' The Oxford don Robert Young has drawn the logical inference for English Studies: 'every time a literary critic claims a universal, ethical, moral or emotional instance in a piece of English literature, he or she colludes in the violence of the colonial legacy in which the European value or truth is defined as the universal one'. The fact that the direct, visible violence of European colonialism is almost at an end, except in places such as Belfast and Derry, has made it all the harder for the perpetrators of epistemic violence to see it for what it is. Especially when they call themselves, or are called, liberals. For them Europe is still at the centre of the global map: it has not yet struck them that to the Japanese Europe now appears as a tiny, open-air boutique at the fag-end of Asia, or that the remoteness which Europe once shaped is now reshaping Europe.

Of all European nations, these observations are spectacularly true of Ireland, and true because of its ambivalence, at once post-imperial and post-colonial, as Europe's internal Other. The Irish were the first English-speaking people in this century to decolonise, and where they led, others followed; but, in more recent times, it is the Irish who have been learning from clergy, who have themselves returned from stints in the Third World, how to democratise parish councils and so forth. The official self-image of the Irish state is Eurocentric, but the cultural and social realities are more often post-colonial. This should have left Irish artists and intellectuals more responsive to the Islamic critique of Rushdie, but it didn't; they simply joined in the easy chorus of voices defending him against the *fatwa* and asserting his rights. A case in point would be Dermot Bolger, who posed as a persecuted fellow-artist in an amazingly self-regarding piece in the *Irish Times* ('Dear Salman. . .'): this came strangely from one who for years has enjoyed subsidy from and a seat on the Arts Council of the state, as well as being regularly fetishised as the next James Joyce by the literary bureaucrats of the *Irish Times*. In this, of course, Bolger does have something in common with Rushdie – a skill in using the rhetoric of an oppressed modernity when in fact he is securely empowered as a leading figure in the dominant code. No attempt was made, within that dominant code in Ireland, to ask how exactly Rushdie might have offended Muslims. Ireland, which enjoyed and enjoys much trade with the Arab peoples, failed itself and failed Europe in not bridging this gap of cultural understanding.

For the Irish know, better than most peoples, that the attempt by a post-colony to modernise, is a painful and uneven process. For a traditionally religious people, secular modernity is not something that flowers naturally out of a prior experience: rather it seeks to blot out much previous history and to insist that past memories will serve mainly to confuse and disqualify those who wish to become modern. Hence the massive amnesia induced in modern Ireland by historians who can chronicle four centuries of British domination of the island with no mention of the word 'colonialism'. Marquez observed a similar forgetfulness in Colombia and wrote of it in *One Hundred Years of Solitude*, and Rushdie recorded it in the India of *Midnight's Children*. Both regretted it and lampooned its perpetrators; and it is to their credit that they did.

Ireland, like India, has a republican-style constitution but, for all that, has yet to become in its practices a truly secular state. Modern European states arose – as Sardar and Davies contend – out of the secularising tendencies which followed hard upon the Protestant notion of self-election: for Protestant peoples they represented a natural development, but for many Irish and Indians they have seemed impositions, disrupting the bases of traditional culture without assuring the material comforts which make such emptiness tolerable. This consumerist modernism is provincial in temporal as well as in geographical terms, in as much as it cannot imagine any time or any place but its own: the past is an embarrassment, so whatever is embarrassingly different must, *ipso facto*, pertain to the past – whether it be Gaelic Ireland or Islamic protocol. The lore of Gaelic, like that of Islam, exists only to be mined by contemporary artists, who rip its elements out of their original contexts in the name of their expressive freedom. The works which result are most often seen by natives as just another in the long sequence of texts which have imposed a foreign domination, whether it calls itself Protestant Christianity, secularism or modernity. People who attack such books do not see themselves as Nazis, but as anti-colonialists.

'Those who clamour most loudly for liberty', wrote Dr Johnson, 'do not most readily grant it'; and of nobody is this more true than the modern liberal. Sardar and Davies have contended that one of the reasons why modern liberalism can be so illiberal is the fact that it is a creation of the Christian churches and, like them in their time, it seeks to permeate the state with its ethos: the Reign of Terror once unleashed on the streets of Paris to punish those who resisted secularisation has since gone global. In the eighteenth century, the secularists were still an embattled minority in Europe as a whole, but since then they have been empowered. This has not prevented them from continuing to use the rhetoric of the persecuted dissident, or from marshalling the language of glamorous marginality to lodge their claims. Rushdie has been super-effective in this regard, sounding at once like a darling of the Hampstead intelligentsia and an outlawed desperado. Like sections of the old Christian church, the secular pontificate has proven just as adept at extirpating the unortho-dox and, failing that, at devising the usual punishments of ridicule, imposed silence and marginalisation. Secularism reserves its greatest as-saults for those still committed to serious religious practice. Having long since, in its comedy shows, mocked Europe's vestigial Christians to scorn, it has in recent years had to turn east for whipping boys, and has found it fatally easy to portray Muslims as errata and deviants in the western master-narrative.

To the secular mind religion is intrinsically backward: the notion that it might have updated itself to the conditions of post-modernity seems almost unimaginable . . . as unimaginable as a liberal Islam. Yet it is the western liberal who often subscribes to medievalism, in unquestioningly accepting a Crusaders' view of Islam. The sleep of reason has brought forth many monsters. Sardar and Davies point out that witch-hunting happened under the Christian puritans because of their obsessive belief in the power of the rational intellect to expose witchcraft. They add that disciples of religion, precisely because their codes rely on faith rather than proof, tend to be more tolerant of differences nowadays. In marked contrast, the contemporary liberal accords to scientists an uncritical homage which not even the medieval laity offered to their priests. For all its rhetoric of scepticism, secularism now claims a totalising charter: the right to determine the ethos of a state.

So the conceptual frame brought to bear on Islamic realities is an impoverished thing indeed. The *fatwa* was the Ayatollah Khomeini's response to a crisis of his own authority within Iran, brought to a head at least partly because of a Western failure to understand his significance. His revolution could be understood neither in pro-communist nor pro-capitalist terms and, since it chose neither form of modernisation, it was derided as medieval: in Rushdie's own phrase 'a secession from history'. But history, in such a formulation, is simply European history . . . and well Rushdie knows that. He is far too sharp a thinker to have been unaware of the underlying issue here. Indeed, the problem faced with great wit and vivid imagination in *Midnight's Children* is the question confronted by Edward Said and all post-colonial intellectuals: how do you devise categories which reject the homogenising tendency of the West to proclaim itself the human norm and the East as a mere deviation from it? How, rather than level all differences, can you evolve a narrative devoted to the ideal of multiculturalism, and do this in such a way that you don't just redraw a fixed boundary at some other point?

Perhaps because he fears a spiritual repartition of that kind, Rushdie in *The Satanic Verses* shows himself averse to those Indians who, having arrived in England, become much more 'ethnic' in their loyalties than they ever were at home, and averse also to those who resort to the manic anglicisation of the adopted umbrella and bowler hat. But the scepticism which denies any one code the right to dictate the ethos of a whole society is suspended in *The Satanic Verses* for the benefit of scepticism itself: in that book, the narrative assumes a secular reader and uses sacred Islamic texts out of context to a brashly profane purpose. Those who burnt it felt less like the violators than the violated.

Their plight offered many interesting analogies with that of the protesters against J. M. Synge's *The Playboy of the Western World* who, in 1907, found blasphemous the playwright's use of sacred phrases to dignify a deed of parricide. 'With the help of God I killed him surely', says Christy Mahon, father-slayer, 'and may the holy immaculate mother intercede for his soul.' In each instance, the protesters felt that the steadfast faith of an oppressed people was being mocked by a patronising and secularised intellectual: and, in each case, the artist's defence was the same. Rushdie claimed that the offensive passages must be read as a dreamlike fantasy, while Synge told a newspaper reporter that his play was simply an 'extravaganza'. Rushdie's offence, being more extreme as well as more publicised, was much the greater, for coded into his book is the notion that Islam is based on the illusion of living in contact with eternity, of being 'a secession from history'. But of whose history does Rushdie speak? Europe's? Asia's? Or the wider world's?

To most Western intellectuals, Rushdie remains a hero because of his certainty that doubt is now the proper human condition, especially for an artist. His dialogic account of the novel as the form for conflicting voices, none of them privileged, seemed heroically at variance with religion, which is monologic in its devotion to a single text. The novel, he contended, in a clear paraphrase of Bakhtin, 'takes the privileged arena of conflicting discourses right inside our head'. The problem with such an analysis is that it fetishises an eternal scepticism, ignoring or discounting those strong minds which, having heard many voices and arguments, come to a conclusion of definite belief. Rushdie has no answer for them and so, in a sense, he fails his own test for a post-colonial intellectual, because he *does* privilege *one voice*, that of secular scepticism, and he does redraw the boundary between East and West as a border between belief and doubt. Since he writes for and lives in the West, he enjoys the immunity which it grants the artist from the usual intellectual sanctions placed on common humanity. This is why his defenders have so little analysed the logic of their position, and why his subtlest critics – liberal Islamic critics of the *fatwa* – have had virtually no hearing. Rushdie asked in his Herbert Read Lecture of 1990 'Is nothing sacred?' and came up with the easy reply, 'Art is.' But that is far too simple, as the fate of *Tilted Arc* has shown. It is not even an answer hospitable to multiculturalism, since it connives in a fundamentally Western reification of art as a separate category of human expression, divorced from other experience. In the East, however, many would concur with the Balinese who told the anthropologist Margaret Mead, 'We have no art: we do everything as well as we can.'

So, how to achieve a true multiculturalism, which is not just based on post-modern indifferentiation or smorgasbord consumerism? Too many have confused multiculturalism with token concessions to minorities. Rushdie himself, in his essay 'The New Empire Within Britain', has been eloquent in his criticisms of such catchword multiculturalism:

In our schools, this means little more than teaching the kids a few bongo rhythms, how to tie a sari, and so forth. In the police training programme, it means telling cadets that black people are so 'culturally different' that they can't help making trouble. Multiculturalism is the latest token gesture towards Britain's blacks, and it ought to be exposed, like 'integration' and 'racial harmony' for the sham it is.

But equally unsatisfactory is the view which holds that multiculturalism is akin to the ideal of academic freedom: that if you afford equal protection to every point of view, then the job is done. American universities have found, in practice, that while they can referee conflicts of ideas, and insert a text by Frantz Fanon or Alice Walker into a 'Great Books' course, they cannot go further and referee disputes among rival interest groups about inequities in society as a whole. Intellectuals formed in the 1960s thought that they could solve the question of cultural freedom, but by the 1980s they were driven to the reluctant conclusion that this was a question embedded in the deeper problematics of power – who had it, who had not. In society one group enhances its power only at the expense of another: rulers can't just add a new law, like teachers adding a few new, radical texts. When the debate ceases at the level of ideas, even campuses find the raw realities of power confronting them, since the Black Studies department can often gain a new lecturer only on condition that Renaissance Studies agrees to a corresponding cut.

This shows that power can never be evenly distributed and that, in consequence, freedom of expression is never unmediated, never absolute, because some people can exercise it more easily than others. For instance, the British blasphemy laws have not protected Christians from the subversive skills of the Monty Python team. All religions have become a lot more tender towards one another in the face of such Europe-wide secularism: hence the statements highly critical of Rushdie which have come from Pope John Paul II and from the Anglican hierarchy. The real problem of tolerance is raised by art, which insists on free and even ferocious exploration of all experience, including the religious, even at the risk of insult and blasphemy.

Such a freedom meant something in the days when the artist was a persecuted freethinker, but today its exercise merely aligns the artist with a triumphalist secularism. In ancient times believers could happily tolerate such deviationists precisely because the prevailing Christian codes of Europe remained so strong. Medieval Irish literature is filled with high-spirited blasphemies, like *Aisling Mhic Chonglinne*, often written by priests or clerical students safe in the knowledge that the Church could withstand their attacks. Similarly, even today, within the Sunni Muslim world, a vibrant anti-clericalism flourishes. Rushdie has pointed to that very tradition in his own defence, but it seems to me that the fact that he is writing in, from and largely for the West somewhat alters the argument. Though he may genuinely see his critique as an internal one, to Muslims it comes from a declared apostate who writes from a Western perspective which, over a thousand years, has invoked expressive freedom for itself while silencing, abusing or misrepresenting Eastern religion. That Western tradition has, in recent decades, entered a new secularist phase, with the consequence that Christian believers in the West are now also exposed to the same misrepresentation and ridicule.

The apparent collapse of the Enlightenment project among radical intellectuals has also led to a contempt for the liberal illusion – as it now seems – of freedom, and to a hermeneutics of suspicion which privileges doubt. (In his fine essay on Gunter Grass, Rushdie manages to spell the word with a capital D.) Those who in the 1960s sought cultural freedom now in the 1990s resign themselves to the eternal 'undecidability' of texts. The irony, of course, is that while thinkers in European and American universities were proclaiming the impossibility of meaningful language, the peoples of Eastern Europe, still convinced like Havel that language could yield miraculous meaning, recovered cultural freedom, including the freedom of religious belief.

That lesson will not have been lost on those who live even further east, or on the Muslim communities in Europe who will no longer settle for that invisibility which was the ultimate mark of the limits of European liberalism. The outbreaks of fundamentalism in the past decade are a result of the intolerance of many secularists, and of their inability to live alongside believers without belittling their pieties. Statues have moved and constitutional amendments have been organised in Ireland, as a direct consequence of secular triumphalism among the journalists and intellectuals. The cognoscenti have proclaimed that all gods and devils are dead, and then found that they cannot live at peace with themselves in the vacuum of doubt that ensues – and so they have promptly demonised all believers. One of the truly valuable ideas in *The Satanic Verses* is that every god had his corresponding devil, to a point where the two seemed interchangeable; and that such forces could not be denied or repressed without resurfacing elsewhere. The secularists have installed artists as the new gods, and believers as the new devils. Seeking further evidence that they are right, the secularists manufacture it on the spot, in the form of an ugly religious fundamentalism into which many believers have been driven by such intolerance. Though neither group would ever admit it, the secularists and fundamentalists feed happily off one another; and their interests march hand-in-hand.

In consequence, western commentators often make a false equation between 'Islam' and this or that extremist, beginning with the Ayatollah in Teheran. That this, of course, was exactly Khomeini's intention has never detained the secularists. It means that, to all intents and purposes, the Ayatollah Khomeini was a part of Orientalism, happily performing the role decreed for him by the secularists, by conforming to their worst fears of Islam. With Khomeini to the fore, the issue of a true pluralism, as opposed to a merely assimilationist secularism, had never to be broached in Western debate, because each side in the battle was openly playing to win.

Rushdie has often described himself as a nomad, a deracinated one, but he would surely be the first to admit that the real nomads are those who have been uprooted from their native cultures *by force rather than choice* and who (because of their strong beliefs) never feel fully welcomed or integrated into the culture of England. Like Irish immigrants in the nineteenth century, many Muslims take on the protective coloration of modernity, while continuing to practise their ancient *pietas* within their own tightly knit communities. The problem is how to build a real connection between these disparate existences, so that such peoples will not seek freedom from a secular society but rather freedom in a multicultural endeavour. The Irish in England never really solved that problem: they were simply assimilated, as is evident in the non-existence of the phrase Irish–English or Irish–British to put alongside Irish–American. It is also clear from the fact that when they were offered a Sunday morning programme by the BBC, as part of its service to ethnic minorities in the early 1980s, they refused point-blank. As the anti-Catholic ethos of British society waned, it was easy enough for the fair-skinned Irish to assimilate; but for Muslims it is a different story.

What I have sketched here is a secularism which fancies itself tolerant but is often in fact invasive and coercive. It imposes a narrow, and now questionable, European model of Enlightenment, ignoring the many Enlightenments enjoyed in the Third World, from Haiti to Harare. All religions and cultures have sought to modernise, to fuse tradition and innovation; and most would have happily persisted in the attempt did they not feel their traditions threatened and mocked by the dominant paradigm of secular modernity. If such Enlightenments were to be encouraged, nobody need feel a nomad except by choice; but the secularists have marginalised whatever fails to fit their model and have used their power to override embarrassing differences. A world which could savour those differences, without a levelling indifferentism, could valuably serve a multicultural ideal.

The question raised by the protesters in Bradford is the same issue raised by those Irish people who oppose the extradition of IRA suspects to stand trial under British law. How can there be a 'fair trial', a true understanding of the issues raised, when judge and jury have been prevented by the daily newspapers from seeing the accused as they see themselves? For this to happen, there would have to be a prior trial of judge and jury, not just as to their suitability to try this particular case, but as to their imaginative capacity to understand the codes which threw up those who stand before them. Otherwise the accused will be guilty until proven innocent. For them to be innocent until proven guilty would require a massive exercise in autocriticism by the British media as a whole. Such an eventuality is not likely as yet, which may be one reason why there has been no prosecution of Muslims for incitement to hatred, since if there were, this is an issue which the defence could be expected to raise. Lawyers for Irish suspects have found through bitter experience, however, that attempts to counter propaganda by explaining the crisis which produced the IRA are inadmissable in British courts, though almost always acceptable on the continent.

It is obvious from all this that any change in the blasphemy law – such as extending its coverage to all religions to secure their rights in an increasingly secular world – could occur only after a serious, self-critical public debate. The burning of Rushdie's book in Bradford was a breach of the peace, but a relatively minor one, given that the book was not and could not be suppressed in Britain. It was simply a signal from a long-neglected group that they could tolerate no more insults.

Intolerance is almost invariably the manifestation of a jeopardised identity, and it can be found as often among Muslims as among secularists, among Irish Catholics as among English liberals. No sane person would endorse a *fatwa* or ask others to live as he/she does; but the Ayatollah Khomeini did the first, and many secularists do the second. A multicultural society can never be decreed by law, but it will come about when people educate themselves not only in their own traditions, but in the sources of others too. Such an education might have led many to ask Rushdie why he chose to give unnecessary offence to a vulnerable minority, whose sufferings he knew better than most. Had that question been asked in repeated debates, there might have been no book-burning, no *fatwa*, no prolonged isolation for the author, no death for his translator, no murderous riots in Asia.

The issue raised by that controversy was anticipated with characteristic brilliance by Rushdie's friend and defender, Edward Said, at the climax of his book *Orientalism*: 'whether there can be a true representation of anything, or whether any and all representations, because they are representations, are embedded first in the language and then in the culture, institutions and political ambience of the representer'. Orientalism had relied on the silence of Islam, for there had never been any attempt by Western experts to deal methodically with Islam's own writings on Islam. For this to happen, for distance to be overcome, the West need not deny its own codes, but rather should admit them as *prejudices*, in the literal sense of that word as fore-meanings, pre-judgements.

'The important thing', says Hans Georg Gadamer in *Truth and Method*, 'is to be aware of one's own bias, so that the text may present itself in all its newness and thus be able to assert its own truth against one's shortcomings.' What is needed is some of that literal prejudice or pre-judgement, a prior acknowledgement of the blinkers worn when one approaches any code. This has always been difficult because prejudice, by its very nature, is hard to establish or prove; and my argument has been that secular fundamentalists have never brought their suspicion to bear on their own scepticism.

Conor Cruise O'Brien shrewdly foretold this development in *The Suspecting Glance*, when he remarked that the generation of 1968, though it suspected every authority, suspected itself not at all: 'They had not the slightest suspicion that in their own way of speaking to a policeman there might lurk the germ of some future Vietnam.' Germaine Greer has, more recently, offered the same diagnosis in *Sex and Destiny*, where she argued that in his attitude to sexual practices in the undeveloped world 'the modern liberal is a bigot and his bigotry may be heard in the corridors of all the international organisations', as he asks people, informed by very different traditions, to implement contraceptive and sterilisation programmes and to view sex as merely recreational rather than procreative. Accusing the overdeveloped West of having become a child-averse society, Greer pointed to the spiritual joy and sensuous pleasure brought by children to their traditional communities, to the indispensable work which they did. She argued that 'what we really fear from the exploding populations of the world is that they will challenge the superiority of our own sub-group, and compromise our survival as the biggest, richest, greediest and most numerous group on earth'. Whether she is right about the underlying psychology or not, one undeniable consequence of zero population growth in many European states has been a multicultural influx of peoples from the impover-ished periphery, from North Africa, Turkey, Greece, Spain and the ex-communist east. Their treatment by governments and by individuals leaves much to be desired.

This is why it is important that universities offer multicultural courses, not only to service members of minority communities, but also to enlighten those who will deal with them. Even if these courses do come to pass, it will never be enough merely to set great books of the east like *The Mahabarat* and *The Koran* alongside *The Odyssey* and the *Bible*. That, after all, was done in nineteenth-century imperial India, with the avowed aim of encouraging students to dismantle the myths which bound them to their own culture and, instead, in the words of one British administrator, 'to make them look to this country with that veneration which the youthful student feels for the classical soul of Greece'.

It might be objected that just such an ability to step outside an inherited culture is what I have been recommending for Western secularists here, so why complain of a similar training for nineteenth-century Indians? But that notion of a self-estranging canon is a relatively recent phenomenon, arising from Matthew Arnold's mission for a high culture which would free students from the philistinism of the middle classes. Arnold never dreamed of estranging students from their *national* culture: indeed, his central idea was that he was returning them to it. Two generations later, his American disciple Lionel Trilling did indeed ask students to use the classic texts of modernism in taking a famous step 'beyond culture', so that they might view Western man as if he were an anthropological witness of himself; but Trilling went on shrewdly to note the speed and gratefulness with which they stepped back inside the charmed circle. It might be that if they had stayed outside just a little longer, their understanding of other cultures could have been enriched: in effect, my call is simply for that liberal imagination, summoned up by Trilling, to be implemented in all its rigour.

The Indian students of English in the nineteenth century, like the Irish, the West Indian and other colonised peoples, were invited to step outside their culture on the strict understanding that they could never step back in. Rushdie is one of the many victims of that process, like the V. S. Naipaul in whose writing he finds the self-hatred of a colonial mimic-man caught in a 'life without love'. Rushdie's case is complicated by the fact that he has kept three toes within the original circle and has used Islamic and Indian traditions more extensively in his work than Naipaul would ever care to do. Because Naipaul is perceived as having gone over to the West, he is a target for contempt rather than for angry revenge. Better things, however, were expected of Rushdie, who had castigated Richard Attenborough for decontextualising Indian traditions in the film *Gandhi*. Yet, even after these discriminations have been made, it would be foolish to define such writers on the basis of who is for European civilisation and who is not: *all are victims of it*. The issue is not whether to know that civilisation, but rather how to know it. And a tentative answer would be the time-honoured liberal one: with passion and vigilance and an abiding sense, in submitting to any one experience, of other experiences which, in a slightly different setting, one might as easily have had.

Rushdie, it seems to me, has scarcely more right to an unqualified freedom of expression than a person who shouts 'Death to Rushdie' on the streets of Bradford. The case in his defence, on the grounds that he has apologised for his slur on the prophet and has suffered more than proportionately to his offence, is incontrovertible; but it should not ground itself on any European principle of free artistic expression. As Tom Stoppard wrote in a recent analysis, the *fatwa* raises questions of multicultural tolerance *for Iranians too*. 'We should not be busy standing up for the rights we have accorded ourselves', said Stoppard; 'we should instead be busy questioning the rights assumed by Iran, beginning with the assumption that Islamic law prevails over all other law in all other countries.'

It is obvious that the wrongs committed in a society cannot be put right by the nation's teachers or texts, and that a culture is more likely to be mummified than revitalised in a classroom. Current calls by feminists, Third Worlders and others for books which answer to their experience with idealised role-models are an understandable response to centuries of repression, but there is a danger that they may lead to a tedious rectitude in texts, such as offended Irish students in the post-independence decades. Similarly, the relentless insistence on books which contain characters with whom students might identify is a denial of an elementary function of literature: its delight in encountering other voices and other worlds than our own. To seek to identify fully with a character or text is to fall victim to the same quality of thinking which caused so many of these problems in the first place. Equally, to conduct monotonous head-counts of the number of blacks, women, regions or whatever represented in certain anthologies is to debase debate to levels of quantity rather than quality, and to forget that the books of dead white European males need not so much to be discarded as reread by way of prelude to setting them in vibration with Fanon, Walker, Walcott and so on. Those who wrote the classic texts of Europe did so in the blithe assurance that their control of global discourse would last forever. In constructing that narrative, they offered 'natives' everywhere a priceless, if ambiguous, gift: the story of how they had been banished from their own land. Those peoples have since learned how to read and reread the texts which ignored or misrepresented them, texts which assumed that they could never intervene. It is vital to retain these, not just for their intrinsic value, but for the sharpness and confidence with which they render a monocultural world. Otherwise, we shall all be in such a hurry to revise that we shall forget what it was that was in such need of revising.

What I am arguing for is a muscular form of that liberalism which only seems dead because it has never been properly tried. I am suggesting that any religion, any code, any culture should – if worthy of the name – be able to remain open to the essential criticisms which might be made of it. Though European humanism has been under a cloud ever since Sartre mounted his critique, it should be recalled that in its earliest phase the Enlightenment had a message that went far beyond Europe. It was indeed a code which contained an autocritique, and so it gave to those peoples who studied it the means to expose the master-narrative in its glaring moments of self-contradiction. The results were, among other things, the 'Black Jacobins' in Haiti.

Even Fanon, that fiercest of decolonising theorists, paid Europe the subtlest of tributes, when he invoked Hegel and Sartre to repudiate French colonialism in Algeria. In *The Wretched of the Earth* he argued that Europe had only known a false Enlightenment, one destined for Europeans alone but one which never managed to construe itself: that is why the radicals of the Frankfurt School, like so many university historians, could never bring themselves to write the dreaded word 'colonialism'. But, alongside that impostor lay the true Enlightenment of which many had dreamed, a real multiculturalism which would arise in the peripheries and eventually find its way back to that Europe which, in its horrific rape of the Other, had planted that very seed. I hope that Fanon was right.

FURTHER READING

Frantz Fanon, *The Wretched of the Earth*, London, 1967.
Hans Georg Gadamer, *Truth and Method*, Princeton, 1987.
Germaine Greer, *Sex and Destiny*, London, 1984.
Conor Cruise O'Brien, *The Suspecting Glance*, London, 1972.
Salman Rushdie, *Midnight's Children*, London, 1981.
    The Satanic Verses, London, 1988.
    Imaginary Homelands, London 1992.
Edward W. Said, *Orientalism*, New York, 1978.
    The Question of Palestine, New York, 1980.
    Covering Islam, London, 1981.
Ziauddin Sardar and Meryl Wyn Davies, *Distorted Imagination: Lessons from the Rushdie Affair*, London, 1990.
Robert Young, *White Mythologies: Writing History and the West*, London, 1990.

CHAPTER 17

The Celtic Tiger – a cultural history

(2003)

Charles Stewart Parnell, the great man whom we commemorate here, was a believer in an inclusive, agreed nation: 'we cannot afford to lose a single Irishman' was a favourite rallying cry. Another was his call, repeated on occasions when things seemed to be going wrong, that 'we must resign ourselves to the cursed versatility of the Celt'.[1] Perhaps this was just a colourful version of the better-known English political mantra to account for the inevitable frustration of plans – 'events, dear boy, events' – but I like to think that Parnell in those cryptic sentences was proclaiming the link between the ideal of a pluralist nation on the one hand and the expressive potential of the individual on the other. In the very year of Parnell's death, after all, Oscar Wilde straight-facedly told his disciples that the only way to intensify personality was to multiply it.[2]

That, for me, is the true significance of Parnell's career – that he opened up a debate about cultural sovereignty. Although the yearnings which he articulated seemed solely political in their language, they were also implicitly cultural: he wished for a form of sovereignty in the cultural domain so that Irish people might once again become interesting and metropolitan to themselves. The poet W. B. Yeats had the shrewdness to sense this point: in his writings Parnell is presented as an image of great conflicting passions marvellously controlled, whether the picture is of Parnell holding Kitty O'Shea over the turbulent sea-waters of Brighton or facing down his enemies at Westminster, the lesson is one of self-conquest, self-command, self-reliance.[3]

It is customary to treat the period from the fall of Parnell in 1891 to the founding of the Gaelic League in 1893 as the crisis in which the leaders of opinion turned away from politics in disillusionment and instead sought to express their aspirations by means of culture. In particular, the failure of the government at Westminster to deliver a promised version of Home Rule in 1893 seemed like a signal that all the political excitements of the previous decade – Parnell's decade – had come to nothing. Into that vacuum, so the received version goes, came the Gaelic League, the Agricultural Co-operative Movement, the National Theatre Society and a great modernist literary renaissance.

The historian R. F. Foster has warned against such simplified Yeatsian analyses, pointing out that after 1893 politics continued much as before, even showing new forms of vitality in the later 1890s with immense improvements in local government.[4] However, like F. S. L. Lyons and Conor Cruise O'Brien,[5] Professor Foster does find in the clashes between the clerks and schoolmasters of the Gaelic League and the more upper-crust artists of the Abbey Theatre, or in the many rows between local nationalists and Horace Plunkett's Co-operative Creameries, the sources of deep cultural divisions, endured to this very day.

But, I wonder. What all of these movements have in common is their basis on the idea of self-help, self-reliance, self-conquest. This is the theme of a brilliant book called *Revival* by P. J. Mathews, to be published later this year.[6] After 1893 Irish leaders began to realise that freedom wasn't something you sought from others but an attitude of mind, something you assumed for yourself. This had been already implicit not just in Parnell's utterances, but in the man's very bearing, his address and his style, his final indifference to his adversaries. What strikes me as false in the new 'revisionist' orthodoxy is its confident separation of politics (equated with the Parnellite movement) from culture (equated with the Gaelic League), as if culture might not be politics by other means. Also false is its obsessive search for tell-tale divisions within the cultural renaissance. Research has shown that it was, as so often in Ireland, basically the same group of intellectual leaders who got caught up in the work of the Gaelic League, Co-operation, and the Abbey Theatre. For instance, the split between the Gaelic League and Abbey Theatre following the 1907 riots against Synge's *The Playboy of the Western World* was a row internal to both the League and the National theatre, for the simple reason that many in the Abbey's cast of actors and back-stage crew, as well as in the audience, had been recruited directly from branches of the Gaelic League.[7]

One of the most impressive aspects of the Abbey Theatre was that it was a truly free and open space, a fully national institution in an occupied territory, but also a class-free zone in which the sort of ambitious clerk or artisan who might in London have been the subject of a patronising encouragement by E. M. Forster's Schlegel sisters could mix on a basis of equality with an aristocrat like Augusta Gregory. The same was true of the Gaelic League, at whose summer schools could be found an amazing blend of socialists and socialites of a sort which might have joined the English Fabians at one of their weekend seminars in the countryside. If there were deep controversies within the Abbey Theatre or the League, they broke out because people from such different backgrounds existed in close enough proximity to conduct them. Culture, far from being a source of terminal division in the period, was a healing presence in many, many lives.

What happened in the Ireland of the 1890s was, as P. J. Mathews has demonstrated, repeated in the 1990s. When Mary Robinson began that period with her own campaign for a reforming presidency, she chose Allihies, a village in county Cork: and in her launch speech she blended a sense of local pride with the idea of self-help. A few years later in Dublin's north inner city in 1994, the James Larkin Centre for the Unemployed announced that its members had voted to become something more than a drop-in community. Now people with specific skills, such as tailoring, were using the centre as a place from which to set up businesses and put other members back to work. The tremendous success of a new Irish-language television station TG4 after 1998 seemed to embody this new spirit. Its newsroom in Port na hAbhann is the only non-metropolitan TV news centre in western Europe, but it also embodies the Parnellite thesis of a necessary link between social creativity and cultural self-confidence. In keeping with this new spirit, a young emerging generation of scholars began to revise the 'revisionists'. It was noted that the Gaelic League after 1893 had originated not only Irish-language classes but also the first industrial parades to promote Irish industries on St Patrick's Day, or that the Abbey Theatre, for all its other-worldly interest in fairies, had also been run as a going business without subsidy for the first two decades of its existence.

In strictly linguistic terms, the Celtic Tiger was born in 1994, when David McWilliams, a young Irish dealer at the Banque Nationale de Paris, used the phrase in a report on the Irish economy. He correctly predicted that the availability of cash at low rates of interest in the following years of the decade would unleash the creativity and initiative of a people who had made shrewd use of European Union subsidies and had in their labour relations achieved a remarkable degree of social consensus.[8] But the roots of that creativity and initiative lie, as Professor Rory O'Donnell has contended, back in the revival movements of the 1890s.[9]

The real question is not why there is now such prosperity but rather why its coming took so long. In the decades of Parnell's own childhood and youth, the Irish gained such mastery of English as the lingua franca of the modern world – a mastery of huge commercial value now in a global market – that they went on to produce one of the great experimental literatures in that tongue. Three decades after the passing of Parnell, the process of global decolonisation was headed by men like Michael Collins and Eamon de Valera, who managed to dislodge the greatest empire the world until then had known. The British left a good system of education, an honest Civil Service and a people with a growing belief in their own powers. Why then did the leadership fail to develop a relatively small economy to levels of some prosperity in keeping with the Sinn Féin ideal? (The words 'Sinn Féin' mean 'ourselves' and betoken self-reliance, a fact about which George Bernard Shaw liked to joke. 'Whenever Londoners ask me the meaning of the words Sinn Féin', he laughed, 'I always tell them it is the Irish for John Bull.')[10] But why did it take a further seventy years for economic progress to catch up with attainments in culture and politics?

The sheer energy expended in removing British forces may be one answer. The Civil War is another. Both left people very little energy with which to reimagine a society. Instead, exhausted revolutionaries lapsed back upon the inherited British forms. There was no decentralisation and no educational innovation along the liberal child-centred lines recommended by Patrick Pearse. The Civil War induced a profound caution, leaving many distrustful of innovation. Fancy theories about a republic had, after all, cost thousands of Irish lives.

Many of those republicans who lost the Civil War in 1923 could not bear to live on in a land which was a sore disappointment. A large number emigrated to a real republic, the United States, where some made fortunes in business – and some even in bootlegging.[11] (This may explain the motto now current on some American tea-towels: 'Hire the Irish – before they hire you.') Even today, if you walk the streets of New York, you see vans plying up and down Broadway with names like 'F. X. Brennan, Established 1926' inscribed on their doors. The republican idea has always been linked to entrepreneurship. After all, the French revolutionaries of 1789 were the first politically organised business people of the modern world, keen to replace a parasitic upper class living on unearned income with a society of careers open to talents. The loss of so much entrepreneurial flair to the Ireland of the mid-1920s was something which the fragile young state could ill afford; and those who remained at home often cast envious glances at their successful cousins who had gone. The Irish were successful in the US in ways in which they never seemed to be at home. One reason was that Irish–Americans could get money and put it to use. Another was that, now ratified by Emersonian ideas of self-reliance, they continued to support their national culture long after many of their sophisticated stay-at-home cousins appeared to have given up on it. It is surely significant that the recent revivals of Irish dancing and fiddle-playing have been led by Irish–Americans such as Michael Flatley and Eileen Ivers, both of whom have also known how to market their artistry to a global audience.

In doing as much, Flatley and Ivers were returning to the values of the Irish Revival which, unlike other forms of European modernism, did not proclaim the need for eternal antagonism between bohemian and bourgeois. James Joyce, for instance, shocked bohemian admirers by his incessant mockery of 'arty' types. When one young admirer asked whether he might kiss the hand that wrote *Ulysses*, he laughed and said, 'You can indeed, but before you do remember that that hand has done many other things as well.'[12] Joyce had in fact opened the first cinema-house in Dublin in 1909 (acting for an overseas investor). It failed only because Joyce was, as always, so far ahead of his own time.[13] He also began a side-business trying to sell Aran sweaters in continental Europe – another project which really began to blossom on a global scale in the 1990s when Comharchumann Inis Meáin sold its wares in fashion-houses in Tokyo, Milan and New York. Yeats not only ran a theatre but also a couple of publishing ventures. Shaw wrote mainly for money and earned lots, as did Wilde. Flann O'Brien liked to joke that Hitler started a war in 1939 with the main aim of preventing him from becoming a millionaire on the basis of the sales of *At Swim-Two-Birds*.[14]

All of these writers shunned the artist-in-a-garret cliché, seeing it as a snobbish inflection of the old notion of the aristocrat as one above common toil. A feature of their writings is a conviction that people emigrated from Ireland not just to seek employment but because the life available there had gown dull and mediocre. Attitudes to work in the new state were frankly disgraceful: it was something poor people did in order not to starve, for only the rich could afford to be idle. In the revolutionary year of 1922, a blacksmith expressed a hope for change. When asked who now would take the place of the toppled Anglo-Irish aristocracy, he said: 'We will in our arse have our own gentry.'[15] It might have been expected that the new rulers would develop instead a vibrant, productive middle class, but no such thing happened. Professional men often worked a short day or a partial week to demonstrate their gentility; and the Civil Service, even more brilliant than it had been in the British days, attracted those creative minds which might otherwise have sought greater challenges in business. The Irish bourgeoisie which did emerge was not extensive. It was consumerist rather than productive. The early novels of Edna O'Brien unerringly evoke its world in which children most often entered shops merely to beg or borrow cardboard boxes for their play, a world of consumerism without goods.[16] As Frantz Fanon would observe of other post-colonies later in the twentieth century, its middle class seemed to have arrived too late, missing out on the heroic phase of the bourgeoisie in the mid-nineteenth century, when factories were built and trading companies established. The post-colonial middle class was less an imitation of the European bourgeoisie than its caricature.[17]

The 'crash' of 1929 came at a particularly bad time for the new state, as did the Economic War of the 1930s, which deprived Irish suppliers of access to the British market. World War Two further curtailed possibilities and by the 1950s it was obvious that Eamon de Valera's policy of frugal self-sufficiency could never work in a now global economy. The continuing talent for experiment in literature was not being matched by a similar audacity in economics; and the Catholic Church was second only to the Civil Service in attracting many of the most gifted men and women into its ranks.

Those of us who attended secondary school in the 1960s lived through the consequences. Bright children were put to the study of Latin in the same period after lunch which saw less intellectual pupils set to study a strange subject called 'Commerce'. Then we were herded with absolutely no sense of irony into inter-school debates at which speakers agonised over the reasons for Ireland's poor economic development. (It seems to have struck nobody that the answer was staring us in the face – our own syllabus.) Later still, as arts students of the universities in the early 1970s, we learned to despise those who did something called 'Business Studies', and to mock those class traitors among us who put on sober suits for the annual round of interviews with Lever Brothers, Arthur Andersen and other companies. The socialism of the 1960s had blended with the professional snobbism of the 1920s, creating a real allergy to technology and to business. This was summed up in a dismissive description of the new University College campus at Belfield as a 'Polytechnic'. What was a term of pride in Germany or France was a word of abuse in swinging Dublin. It was as if we were all characters in a novel by Jane Austen, an upper-crust grouping which taught its children to speak with lofty condescension of those involved in trade.

None of this was accidental. The cultural self-image of the stage was ruralist. It is well captured in the novels of Dermot Bolger, where civil servants, solicitors, teachers and nurses speak, after forty years of adult life in Dublin, of a farm in Derry or Mayo as 'home'. Even the Donnycarney boy, Charles Haughey, signalised his strange rise to immense wealth by the act of riding to hounds and buying a rural seat. We did 'in our arse have our own gentry'; and its name was Haughey. In some advanced boys' schools after World War Two, science was grudgingly taught, but with a strong hint that too many scientists were atheists. Science was presented to children in much the same way as literature was in some other countries – it had its uses but shouldn't be taken overseriously. The result was that for years senior policy-makers lacked much scientific or economic knowledge, unlike their counterparts in Germany or the United States. In all of this, we were merely imitating one of the less admirable features of British life, as any reader of Martin Wiener's *English Culture and the Decline of the Industrial Spirit 1880–1980* will readily recognise.[18]

Today, all has changed. University dons no longer scoff at polytechnics, but shower honorary degrees upon Irish–American business leaders, from whom they anxiously seek endowments for chairs and from whom they anxiously conceal the handiwork of their resident 'revisionist' historians. Free secondary education for all, introduced in 1967, proved not only a progressive, democratic thing in itself, but the presence of so many less wealthy children in classrooms led very rapidly to a more pragmatic type of education. In 1955 67 per cent of all students sitting the Leaving certificate (equivalent of A levels) took Latin. By 1979 that figure had shrunk to 5 per cent – but subjects like Business, Engineering, Building Construction and Accountancy had made it onto the syllabus.[19] (While I am sad to see such a sharp decline in the study of Latin, it is sadder still to realise that people felt that this was an either/or decision.) It may be no accident that the Celtic Tiger came to life just over twenty years after Donough O'Malley's Free Education scheme of 1967. In a very similar sequence of cause and effect, the Civil Rights movement emerged on the streets of Northern Ireland about two decades after the passing of R. A. Butler's Education Acts of the 1940s in the United Kingdom.

Over the past decade the numbers at work in the Republic have risen by hundreds of thousands and could reach 1.8 million. In the early 1980s for every 100 people working there were 250 dependants, giving a dependency ratio of 2.5 – nowadays that figure is 1.1. In the year 2000 the growth rate was over 10 per cent. This year it is down to about 4 per cent – and though this seems a relatively poor performance, it is one which leaves our German neighbours still envious.[20] This generation in Ireland has inherited wealth but also a willingness to spend as well as save. It is almost as if the promise latent in those words 'Sinn Féin' has at last begun to be made good. As if to symbolise all this, one of the major exports of the last five years has been plane-loads of Viagra, from the land of Eternal Youth.

It would be hard to imagine a James Joyce or a Sean O'Casey passing up the rich pickings for an artist in such a profound social change, yet that, most incredibly, is what the current generation of writers, with only rare exceptions, has so far done. There is no major celebration or corrosive criticism of these developments in good novels, plays or poetry. There is no Trollopian *The Way We Live Now*, much less a Tom Wolfe-style *Bonfire of the Vanities* even among our younger writers. The pace of change may be just too fast for most, for it is never easy to take a clear photograph of a moving object, especially when you are up close to it. Nothing, after all, is more difficult to realise than the present – we are always at its mercy more than we are its masters. There is also a fatalism among the intelligentsia, who seem unable to believe in the recent affluence, preferring to see it as a blip on the radar screen rather than the natural state of things. One might semi-jocularly blame some of this on the late Samuel Beckett who made elegant desperation fashionable among our writers, for if you praise the day's sunshine to an Irish writer, you will in all likelihood hear the same thing: 'It'll never last.' For roughly similar reasons, many writers find it hard to believe sufficiently in the shiny surfaces of Celtic Tiger Dublin to go to the considerable trouble of rendering them. In fact, many disbelieve in those surfaces as only a profound post-colonial sceptic can, turning from them to the deeper philosophical question: 'But how do we know what we know?'

The almost inevitable answer to this question is a sort of autobiographical writing, set in a period at some remove from the present, forty or fifty or even sixty years ago. This, like an expansive rear-view mirror attached to a fast car, has the merit of giving the reader some implication of just how much things have changed since Brian Friel's 1930s, Frank McCourt's 1940s or John McGahern's 1950s. These writers, in rendering so clearly the landscape left behind, may give some sense of where the country is now. To contemporary Irish people, nothing seems more remote than the recent past. So for them, as for overseas audiences, Ireland must be forever staged as the Other (rural, storytelling, heroic),[21] but not of the present – only a measure of how far we've travelled getting here.

It is in a context such as this that one must assess the success of a book like *Angela's Ashes*. It appealed through the late 1990s to two very different constituencies – *internationally* to those WASP readers who wished, in spite of the Celtic Tiger, to read a book which showed them an Ireland as colourfully desperate as ever; and *nationally* to a confident, even brash people keen for some measure of how fully they had transcended the old world of failed fathers, smug priests, harrassed mothers and so on. It may be that, in a much subtler way, the artistic work of John McGahern or Brian Friel also cast an angular, refracted light across the past and onto the present.

McGahern's *Amongst Women* was published within a year of Mary Robinson's accession to the presidency. In both its opening and closing passages, it refers to the trumping by modern Irish women, back in the late 1950s, of their father's old heroic world of ambushes and flying columns – as if the advent of Mrs Robinson were over three decades in the gestation. *Dancing at Lughnasa* by Friel also appeared within weeks of the president's inauguration and by a brilliant technical feat found a form in which to dramatise that phenomenon known as uneven development,[22] a characteristic of many post-colonial societies. The narrating Michael, from the retrospect of the swinging 1960s, wishes to rush the story he tells onto fast-forward, while the five aunts whose farm life of 1936 he describes, struggle to prolong their moment, to slow down the reel, to make their sweet but doomed world last just a little bit longer.

The confidence with which McGahern and Friel could formulate past experiences suggested some hope for the present, even if that present could not yet be directly depicted as such in a major art-work. For them, the present was to be excavated, never frontally rendered. Those younger writers who have written a play or a novel about 1990s Ireland have had nothing like the same success, although in 1999 Éilis Ní Dhuibhne's *The Dancers Dancing*, by overlaying a plot set in 1972 with a knowing late-90s consciousness (one chapter-heading said 'The Peace Process is over, but don't worry; it's only 1972') managed greater things, by making the underlying problem a central element of her narrative. In January 2003 *The Parts* by Keith Ridgway offered a series of glimpses of the derangement which characterised some lives in contemporary Dublin,[23] but the very word chosen for title indicated the author's conviction that nothing like a whole portrait of the city could be attempted. There has been no really major art-work about the Tony O'Reilly dynasty or about a conflicted, interesting figure such as Dermot Desmond, because most writers are still caught in that old 1960s time-warp which decrees that business people are irretrievably boring compared with the staples of Irish fiction – brutal fathers, sad mothers, crazy aunts. McGahern has shown in his novel how the family-unit, far from being the bedrock of Irish society as proclaimed in the 1937 Constitution, was promoted in the mid-twentieth century as an alternative to the very idea of the social as such. Having been the largest social unit to which a colonised people could subscribe in acts of effective resistance to the old imperial power, it then became fetishised after independence and thus turned into a barrier to the development of a truly republican notion of community.

Most Irish writers seem unable to move beyond the family as the central unit of investigation into a more panoramic social novel of the kind written by a Martin Amis or a Jay McInerney. The reluctance of artists to celebrate or castigate those business leaders who provide daily fodder for excited journalists at the many public tribunals is all the more baffling when one recognises that both artists and entrepreneurs have one thing in common: each is a broker in risk, a devotee of an instinctual insight which can only be confirmed or negated by subsequent years of exhausting hackwork. It was on the basis of such self-identification that the writers of revolutionary France celebrated the genius of the revolutionary energisers of 1789, of those who favoured a career open to talents, but contemporary Irish writers have chosen not to reinvigorate that Enlightenment tradition. Instead, they pursue a tradition of intellectual dissidence, belatedly picked up from European modernism, but never practised by the real Irish modernists of the revival period.

In recent years, civil servants and socialist groups, like the Larkin Centre, have wakened up to the fact that the setting up of businesses, far from being immoral, is the very essence of a republican democracy. Yet most journalists, trapped in the modes of inherited dissent, dismiss such activities as a sort of Hibernian Thatcherism. They fail to recognise what a good thing it is that the characters of Roddy Doyle's Barrytown are now strictly historical, or how a station like TG4 can act as a useful cultural brake upon the forces of globalisation. The new fashion for self-help is neither asocial nor Thatcherite: rather is it a return to the civic republicanism preached by the inventors of modern Ireland over a century ago.

Its current leaders are radical on economics, liberal on matters of politics and personal freedom, and (if anything) somewhat conservative on culture – but only because of the dynamic, creative nature of the 1890s mindset which has enabled and underwritten the very nature of the latest flowering. And that is why it is worthwhile to commemorate the gifted men and women who created the Irish Renaissance in the years after the fall of Parnell.

There are some who would deride such commemorations as the folly of a people fixated upon the past. It is now almost three decades since Conor Cruise O'Brien, objecting to the holding of military parades on Easter Sunday, delivered the mordant complaint that 'we are in danger of commemorating ourselves to death'.[24]

Superficially, the evidence might seem to support his view. One promise held out by revivalists at the start of the last century was that Cuchulain might again walk through the streets of Dublin. But a central tendency of that revival was its critique of those who wished only to go back in time. The socialist James Connolly warned, for instance, against a Celtic Studies which might be 'glorious and heroic indeed, but still only a tradition'.[25] *Only* a tradition. He went on to suggest that too often in life the apparent worship of the past was merely an attempt to escape from the mediocrity of the present. For him the logic of revival was not found in the urge to repeat some past moment of glory but in the desire to experience once again the revolutionary nature of tradition: the power of the past moment to tear open, disrupt and re-energise the present.

As in the collision of molecules in a chemical experiment, a past moment might form a constellation with a present one, releasing a wholly new energy into the future. So Connolly contended that socialism would also be an act of Gaelic revival, a return to the system whereby the chieftain had held the land in the name of all the people, the crucial difference being that now the place of the chieftain would be taken by the state. Connolly turned history into science fiction, discovering the lineaments of his desired future in the remote Gaelic past. So did Patrick Pearse when he summoned the image of Cuchulain to his side to validate his dream of a welfare state which would (in the words of the Proclamation of the Irish Republic in 1916) 'cherish all the children of the nation equally'.[26] So did James Joyce, when he had the most experimental prose narrative of the twentieth century gift-wrapped in the structure of one of Europe's oldest tales, the *Odyssey* of Homer. They all knew that in a land filled with nostalgia, you must present the very new as a return of the very old. Hence also Mary Robinson's use of ideas from Douglas Hyde and the Gaelic League of the 1890s in her campaigns of the 1990s.

This is, of course, a revolutionary use of tradition, but it is founded on the intuition that mere change is not growth. Growth is a synthesis of change and continuity. For such thinkers, the past still holds untapped energies and unused potentials, which may be released in the present moment. Its wisdom was summed up by an old Connemara woman who told an anthropologist in the 1950s that it is our duty to use those energies. She asserted that old people get wrinkles on their faces not as a punishment for all the nights of drink and debauchery wasted in youth, but rather because of those wasted moments of their lost youth when the passions knocked and we were not in to answer them.

Far from being fixated upon the past, the Irish are obsessed instead with their power over it, including the power to change its meaning whenever that seems necessary. Theirs is a genius for adaptation to new circumstances, with the consequence that they can be both modern and counter-modern at the same time. The Connemara woman just cited was a functional illiterate, but she knew dozens of oral tales, some of which lasted well over an hour. Her visitor (who brought an early tape recorder) couldn't help noticing that she herself was surrounded by many modern conveniences, a telephone, fridge, electric meat-mincer, and so he asked: 'Do you really believe in the fairies?' She thought for a moment and then replied with sophisticated derision: 'I do not, sir, but they're there anyway.' He then probed further, asking why there were more stories in her village than in any other in Galway. 'I think, sir', she said meekly, 'it owes something to the post-war influx of North American anthropologists.'

The country has gone through in the past century and a half the sort and scale of changes which took four or five hundred years in other parts of Europe. No wonder that people have looked in the rear-view mirror and felt a kind of motion-sickness, or have sought to conceal the underlying modernity of their lives by giving them the surface appearance of the ancient. They have followed the advice of those who say: 'Mask, and it shall be given to you.'[27]

In most ways, this masking process has worked too well, convincing the outside world that we were more addicted to the past than was really the case. And *some* of our writers, journalists and revisionist historians have bought into the resulting illusion. For instance, many official historians now routinely tell children that the Easter Rising was a hopeless, hyper-romantic attempt to restore a lost medieval Gaelic world. These accounts fail to mention that about seventy women fought in the rebel forces or that, if those forces had succeeded, Hanna Sheehy-Skeffington would have been the first female government minister anywhere in the world (a whole year before Alexandra Kollontai). The sheer modernity of that moment escapes most current historians, who notice only the back-references to Cuchulain and so on. It did not escape Lenin, who wrote that the misfortune of the Irish was that they rose too soon – surely the only occasion in history on which the Irish have been castigated for early rising – 'before the revolt of the European proletariat had matured'. According to Lenin, this transpired one year later in 1917.[28]

Wherever you look in the story of Ireland over the past hundred and fifty years, you find evidence of this masked modernity. Precisely because the island was a colonial laboratory, new projects were tested there first, from state-run schools in the 1830s to streamlined postal systems in the 1840s (both tried in Ireland before their success ensured their replication in England). In a similar spirit, the disestablishment of the Anglican church as the official religion of the state was achieved in 1869 (something that has yet to happen in the United Kingdom). The famines of the 1840s, unutterably traumatic, were also modernising in some of their effects. To give up speaking your own language and learn that of another people, or to move from a rural parish into a major city or town, was to find yourself living without interpretative keys in a baffling new environment. The result was that even those who stayed in Ireland felt, in the words of Friedrich Engels, 'like strangers in their own country'[29] – and they themselves were like the estranged inhabitants of some new bohemia, finding themselves suddenly alienated from the available environment, decontextualised as any Beckett clown, living without any existential key in a coded but now-indecipherable setting. No wonder that these people learned the virtue of adaptation, of wearing masks.

All of this helps to explain the paradox of an experimental, high-modernist art, futuristic in tone, emerging around the year 1900 from a culture believed by many (including most of its own sponsors) to be deeply conservative. It accounts for the obsession with masking in the literature – conservatives like W. B. Yeats used radical new forms of art in order to protect what little of the past remained, while socialists such as Sean O'Casey employed the old-fashioned devices of music hall and melodrama to disguise the radicalism of their ideas. It explains above all the strange blend of backwardness and forwardness in that Connemara woman's kitchen – or more generally in Irish life. Even in the decades of economic stasis after independence, many modern schemes were tried: Ireland was the first country to run a live broadcast of a sports event on radio in the 1920s and the first to create semi-state companies (somewhat along the lines of those public–private partnerships which came into favour many years later).

A people hurtled into modernity at such speed are bound to seek reassurance in images and edicts of stability: but in my opinion such conservatism is largely formulaic and only skin-deep, a matter of law and public propriety rather than anything else. Actual Irish behaviour has more usually been innovative. Daniel O'Connell, for example, was the first mass-democratic politician of the modern world, his 'monster meetings' anticipating by a century and a half the rock concerts for Live-Aid and Farm-Aid of the 1980s. In the mid-1980s I once asked a good student at University College, Dublin, how he spent the weekends. 'On Saturday night I go out with my girlfriend and we sow our wild oats', he told me with grave decorum, 'and on Sunday we slink into Mass and pray for crop failure.' Pious conservatives would doubtless have called him a hyprocrite, but I know that Joyce would have considered him an Irish modernist. Within the rather conservative official scheme of the 1980s, that student and his generation created a virtual world of freedom, just as their grandparents had done in setting up Dáil Éireann and Dáil courts within the prevailing British order of 1919,[30] or as their parents had done within the censorious Ireland of the 1950s, of which the novelist John McGahern observed that on the night of a summer dance, 'there was not a hayrick safe within five miles of the dance hall, but the whole parish going off like alarm-clocks'. It was no accident that by the end of the 1980s my student's generation helped to elect a president who only slightly masked her left-wing social philosophy (on world economics, women's rights, ecology, Third World debt and so on) by speaking in the style of the headmistress of a high-toned girls' finishing school, a cross between Julie Andrews and Pegeen Mike.

There are indeed many conservative elements in Irish society, much maligned in the Dublin 'liberal' media and much reported overseas (and invariably reported as if they were the only elements of the equation): but these are largely understandable reactions against the extreme modernity of the underlying situation. There is, however, an immense difference between this surface *conservatism* of bruised, baffled minorities and an underlying social process which is openly and dynamically *traditional*.

Back in the 1970s, in any course given on literature and identity, I would tell students that there were three keys with which they could unlock the secret sources of the Irish mindset – language, religion and nationalism (I based these inevitably on the three forces which troubled Joyce's Stephen Daedalus, those 'nets' he hoped to fly past – and dutifully noted that Daniel Corkery's three bases of Irish culture were much the same). I don't do this any more. Instead, I urge students to consider the fate of each of these forces. My conversion experience came during a debate with Father Peter Connolly, a liberal priest–professor of English at Maynooth, who had bravely opposed literary censorship in the 1950s but subsequently became apprehensive about the undiscriminating, hedonistic Ireland which seemed to be taking its place.

Our debate in the autumn of 1980 led him to make a shocking prediction: 'Religion will go in Ireland in the next generation: and when it goes it will go so fast that nobody will even know what is happening.' At that moment his comment seemed ridiculous, for the Holy Father, Pope John Paul II had on a visit in the previous year been acclaimed by hundreds of thousands all across the island: but after the debate over a cup of coffee, I asked Peter Connolly what he meant. 'Exactly what I said', he smiled: 'after all, look at the speed with which our people got rid of their own language when it no longer seemed of practical use to them.' It was then that I realised that the papal visit of 1979, far from signalling the Church Triumphant, was a symptom of and panic reaction to the gathering crisis. For no Pope had ever felt the need to secure the green island with a personal appearance in the past.

Peter Connolly was right. The Irish are among the least sentimental people on earth and have little compunction about dumping a once-sacred core-value or identity-marker. The fate of the Irish language in the nineteenth century is indeed indicative. In the classrooms of the independent state, children were given three reasons for the collapse of Irish in most areas (there were three causes for everything in those days, as there were three markers of identity): the devastating effects of the famines especially in Gaeltacht areas; the official insistence on the use and promotion of English in National Schools; and the exemplary use of it by that arch-moderniser, Daniel O'Connell. This conveniently took away most of the responsibility from the people themselves: but it *was* the Irish who coolly decided, after centuries of speaking their own language despite official disapproval from the colonial authorities, that they would no longer do so.[31] It was indeed the people themselves, and not their imperial masters, who invented the *bata scóir*, that tally-stick on which notches were etched for every time a child spoke English, with a calibrated system of corporal punishment to be administered in keeping with the number of notches at the end of the school day.

The people did all this because they were modernisers who wished for mastery of a world language and they rightly sensed that English would be the language of international travel and commercial transactions. They were in fact the only European people who taught themselves English in their own country, even before their exiles reached England or the New World. The choice which they made was not a completely free one, but was forced on them by their own economic vulnerability and by the growing importance of a state apparatus in which English alone was used: for as Karl Marx wrote, 'men make the world but not in conditions of their own choosing'. Those who so chose were traumatised by what they did, by this desperate bargain which they felt compelled to make with modernity. Like most traumas, this one couldn't even be registered as such at the time: the cataclysm appeared to have destroyed all those instruments which might have measured it. Even after the independent state was over half a century old, there was still no scientific survey of popular attitudes to Irish, for both its supporters and detractors were terrified of what might emerge. One sociologist tersely complained in the 1960s that the movements of cows and pigs were more studied than the movements of Irish speakers.[32] Only in 1975 did an official government survey finally reveal that 91 per cent thought Irish essential to identity but only 23 per cent considered that it would survive as a community language.[33]

Following a series of sexual scandals through the 1990s, many involving serious abuse of children, some institutions of Irish Catholicism appear to be in free fall. But they were already in crisis by the time that Peter Connolly made his prediction. After 1967 the number of religious vocations each year dropped sharply.[34] Between 1971 and 1991 the average family size dropped from four to two children. Throughout that period church attendance continued to slump badly, but so also did the obedience of that flock which remained. At the present moment, more than one in five children are born out of wedlock.

Most intriguing of all, perhaps, is the speed with which in 1998 the people in a referendum abandoned the third core-value, that political nationalism which (along with religion) had filled for so many the vacuum left by the loss of the Irish language as a marker of identity. 94 per cent of the citizens of the Irish Republic voted in May 1998 to rescind a constitutional claim to the six northern counties, a claim which they had been taught since childhood was a force of nature and a recognition that God had made our island a singular space, destined for unification. For the sake of peace and good neighbourliness, they voted for a Belfast Agreement which included the contention that a county such as Antrim could be British or Irish or both. In effect, they abandoned nineteenth-century concepts of sovereignty for a recognition that identity is never fixed, perpetually up for renegotiation and certainly not based on territory. Are we the inhabitants of the first nation–state in Europe to vote to reduce its territorial claims? Such a gesture seems to come out of the coming century rather than the nineteenth.

A conservative might well weep at this point and ask what of our past identity will survive in this pragmatic, post-modern land. Will we be just another aircraft-carrier for the Americans? Or a place, as Shaw said, to which every rule-bound Englishman should be sent for a spell in order to learn flexibility of mind? What would Parnell, who said that no man had the right to set the boundary to the march of a nation,[35] think of what we have done? Perhaps he would be cross, but on the whole I think not. When he praised the cursed versatility of the Celt, he did so in the knowledge that the alternative was to fossilise. There is nothing at all abject about a genius for adjustment. And it is in fact that strange, ambiguous gift for masking which may protect and save us in the end: for it has meant that our traditions *seem* to die, only to be reborn in newer, modified forms. The ruined Gaelic bards or *filí*, after the defeat of their chieftains at the Battle of Kinsale in 1601, announced the death of Gaelic culture – but in a poetry of such renewed and awesome power as to rebut that very claim. In such a land death is never final, merely another career move: 'I can't go on, I'll go on.'[36]

The Irish language didn't finally die, but is still, like so many of our national corpses, alive and shouting (about four hundred books are published in it every year, which compares very well with the five books in print at the foundation of the Gaelic League in 1893). But in those areas where Irish did die it was reborn in the brilliant Hiberno-English used by a people who continued to think in Irish while employing English words. Unlike standard English, which relies on tonal underlining for emphasis ('Are you going to *town* tomorrow?'), Hiberno-English brings the key word forward in the sentence, just as Irish would ('Is it to town that you are going tomorrow?'). The people found that if they translated their Irish almost word-for-word into English, then the results could be strangely poetic. In other words, much was gained as well as lost in the translation. The magnificent achievements of Augusta Gregory, J. M. Synge, Joyce and O'Casey in that English provided one way of coping with the trauma of a lost ancestral tongue, a compensation-mechanism, certainly, but also a great intellectual feat.

Will people be as traumatised by their apparent rejection of institutional religion? It is probable that they already are, but also that many among them are finding forms in which the residual yearning for ritual and meaning is reborn. The sales of the Glenstal prayerbooks, which were number one on the bestselling booklists between June and December 2001 (except for the few weeks when they were out of print) might be one indication. The three million souls who turned out to worship the relics of St Thérèse of Lisieux could be taken as another.[37] These suggest that it is simply the power of an institution which is collapsing rather than the authority of religion as such. If the language analogy of Peter Connolly is anything to go by, there may soon be founded new institutions to embody and carry forward the religious hopes of a people, just as the Abbey Theatre and Gaelic League arose out of the apparent ashes of Irish-language tradition.

It is in that same context that political nationalism seemed to accept its own demise in the Belfast Agreement, but only so that it could be reborn as cultural pluralism – a civic nationalism which would devise structures calibrated to the needs of all cultural traditions, unionist as well as nationalist, Protestant as well as Catholic – in truth, a return to Parnell.

All that said, some cultural contradictions remain. Although Irish business schools produce American-style graduates, committed to naked market forces and a strong work ethic, the arts and economics faculties create public servants to a more European mould, imbued with social-democratic values and a belief in welfare systems. These contradictions are more deeply rooted than the 'Boston-or-Berlin' debate of the past two years might suggest. For a very similar sort of contradiction one has only to consider the career of Flann O'Brien (Brian O'Nolan), who worked as a senior civil servant by day and as a savage satirist by night, when he penned his 'Cruiskeen Lawn' columns for the *Irish Times*. If the Anglo-American world viewed the intelligentsia as a loyal and logical extension of the establishment, the European world has generally preferred to follow Jean-Paul Sartre and Simone de Beauvoir, casting intellectuals in the role of a perpetual and vigilant opposition. Irish writers have yet to work out where they stand on such questions. Their relative silence over the past decade on a whole range of issues from political corruption through the Celtic Tiger to the Belfast Agreement may indicate an underlying bafflement in the face of contradictory demands and of rapid social change.

Parnell believed that every country needs a distinctive philosophy. Right now Ireland lacks one, caught between legal adherence to European Union codes and an economic identification with the values of the United States. It would be good if business leaders were to help shape that debate. One way would be for some to write autobiographies, as do their counterparts in both the US and France, where such works are often bestsellers. Then the creative artists might respond to that challenge, outlining their own views. At present the country is in the strange situation of having both gifted artists and major entrepreneurs, yet neither group contributes (or is asked to contribute) significantly to public debate. Confronted with a hostile media, business people keep their heads well down: and soured by memories of the bad old days of censorship, artists tend to do in like manner. The ensuing stand-off does the country no good at all.

The great renaissances of national culture in the past have flowered right across the globe against a background of economic confidence – ancient Greece and Rome, Shakespeare's London, the United States in the age of Whitman and Emily Dickinson and the United States again now. The Irish Renaissance of a hundred years ago was, by contrast, aberrational – its leaders had little cash or funds. The current affluence, far from threatening art, imperilling identity or killing the Celtic soul, is a great opportunity for a second national flowering, this time in film perhaps as well as in literature, in religious life as well as economics. (It may indeed emerge that it is wrong to look for sustained renditions of the Celtic Tiger in literature when the major centre of interest for the rising generation is to be found in other forms.) If we could only bring the revivalist tradition of self-help once again into alignment with cultural pursuits, then the unfinished project of national renewal could come to fruition, and economics and art might harmonise. Then the bohemian and bourgeois might be as one, as they were briefly at the close of Joyce's *Ulysses* when an ad-man named Leopold Bloom took an artist named Stephen Dedalus back to his house, in order to explain the workings of the real world to him.

NOTES

This is a transcript of the Parnell Fellowship Lecture delivered at Magdalene College, Cambridge, on 27 January 2003.

1 F. S. L. Lyons, *Charles Stewart Parnell*, London, 1977, p. 362.
2 Quoted by Richard Ellmann, ed., *Oscar Wilde: The Artist as Critic*, London, 1970, p. 234.
3 Lyons, *Charles Stewart Parnell*, p. 590.
4 R. F. Foster, *Paddy and Mr Punch*, London, 1993, pp. 22–35.
5 F. S. L. Lyons, *Culture and Anarchy in Ireland 1890–1939*, Oxford, 1979; and Conor Cruise O'Brien, *States of Ireland*, London, 1972.
6 P. J. Mathews, *Revival*, Cork, 2003.
7 Declan Kiberd, *Synge and the Irish Language*, London, 1979, pp. 236–60.

8　See David McWilliams's weekly columns, *Sunday Business Post*, Dublin, 2001–2.

9　Rory O'Donnell, 'Reinventing Ireland: from Sovereignty to Partnership', Jean Monnet Inaugural Lecture, 27 April 1999; and for a critique of this analysis see Peadar Kirby, Luke Gibbons, Michael Cronin, eds., *Reinventing Ireland: Culture, Society and the Global Economy*, London, 2002.

10　George Bernard Shaw, *The Matter with Ireland*, ed. David H. Greene, London, 1962, p. 104.

11　Tom Garvin, *The Evolution of Irish Nationalist Politics*, Dublin, 1981, pp. 160–73.

12　Richard Ellmann, *James Joyce*, Oxford, 1959, p. 167.

13　Ibid., p. 432.

14　Conversation with Evelyn O'Nolan, 8 April 1978.

15　Breandán Ó hEithir, *The Begrudger's Guide to Irish Politics*, Dublin, 1986, p. 2.

16　Edna O'Brien, *The Country Girls*, London, 1963, pp. 7–21.

17　Frantz Fanon, *The Wretched of the Earth*, translated by Constance Farrington, London, 1967, p. 157.

18　Martin Wiener, *English Culture and the Decline of the Industrial Spirit*, London, 1985.

19　Louise Fuller, *Irish Catholicism Since 1950: The Unmaking of a Culture*, Dublin, 2002, p. 172.

20　I am grateful to Damien Kiberd for these figures.

21　For more on this, see Nicholas Grene, *The Politics of Irish Drama*, Cambridge University Press, 2001.

22　For more, see Declan Kiberd, 'Dancing at Lughnasa', *Irish Review*, no. 27, Summer 2001, 18–39.

23　Keith Ridgway, *The Parts*, London, 2003.

24　Conor Cruise O'Brien, RTÉ television, 3 April 1973.

25　Quoted by Bernard Ransome, *Connolly's Marxism*, London, 1980, p. 18.

26　Proclamation of the Irish Republic, Easter 1916.

27　*Oscar Wilde, The Artist as Critic*, p. 27.

28　See Declan Kiberd, *Inventing Ireland*, London, 1995, p. 196–217.

29　Quoted by Nicholas Mansergh, *The Irish Question 1840–1921*, London, 1965, p. 88.

30　See Mary Kotsonouris, *Retreat from Revolution: The Dail Courts 1920–24*, Dublin, 1994.

31　Maureen Wall, 'The Decline of the Irish Language', in *A View of the Irish Language*, ed. Brian Ó Cuív, Dublin, 1969, pp. 81–90.

32　J. J. Lee, *Ireland 1912–1985: Politics and Society*, Cambridge, 1989, pp. 658–74.

33　*Report of Commission on Public Attitudes to Irish*, Dublin, 1975.

34　Fuller, *Irish Catholicism Since 1950*, p. 167.

35　Quoted by Lyons, *Charles Stewart Parnell*, p. 317.

36　Samuel Beckett, *Molloy, Malone Dies: The Unnamable*, London, 1962, p. 510.

37　Fuller, *Irish Catholicism Since 1950*, 251.

CHAPTER 18

The city in Irish culture

(2002)

In its heroic phase, the city was a site of pluralism, an example of the uses of diversity. It was in such a period that Dr Johnson could observe that when a man is tired of London, he is tired of life. The celebration of urbanity was not confined to cities – even the greatest of all Lake Poets could join in:

> Earth has not anything to show more fair:
> Dull would he be of soul who could pass by
> A sight so touching in its majesty:
> This City now doth like a garment wear
> The beauty of the morning; silent, bare,
> Ships, towers, domes, theatres, and temples lie
> Open unto the fields, and to the sky;
> All bright and glittering in the smokeless air.
> Never did sun more beautifully steep
> In his first splendour valley, rock, or hill;
> Ne'er saw I, never felt, a calm so deep!
> The river glideth at his own sweet will:
> Dear God! the very houses seem asleep;
> And all that mighty heart is lying still!
> 'Sonnet: Composed upon Westminster Bridge'

Wordsworth (1807) here explicitly says that no valley, rock or hill can bring out natural beauty as well as does Westminster Bridge. The city still in sleep becomes an illustration of that romantic definition of poetry which sees it as might half-slumbering on its own right arm. The sonnet is a useful reminder that there can be an urban as well as a rural pastoral – that the city may even for the most romantic of poets be a site of enlightenment as well as of corruption, of beauty as well as of squalor. Yet Wordsworth's London is, for all that, an *imperial* city. The rest of the world has nothing to compare with its majesty or its mighty heart.

There could be no similar poem devoted to Dublin in the eighteenth or nineteenth century. For a writer such as Jonathan Swift, the city was always an imitation of the real thing:

> If you have London still by heart,
> We'll make a small one here by Art.
> The difference is not much between
> St James's Gate and Stephen's Green . . .

But, the difference was marked off all the same by his friend Thomas Sheridan:

> Instead of Bolingbroke and Anna
> Shane Tunnelly and Brian Granna

What struck Swift most about the streets of Dublin was the amount of excrement on view, both animal and human, in cobblestone walks and in the gutter of the thoroughfares. It could never be the site of a pastoral; insofar as it recreated the effects of rural living they were all the less desirable features. The city even then struck its leading writer as a zone of failure and death, a centre of paralysis.

Only in the fantastic imaginings of Gaelic storytellers and poets could Dublin have ranked as a brilliant, heroic capital. When Standish O'Grady came to write down in translated form the *History of Ireland: Heroic Period* in the 1870s, he caused Cuchulain to visit Dublin in the hope that this might touch off a sense of aristocratic pride and self-possession in its masters. There was only one problem with this: Dublin was not founded for hundreds and hundreds of years after the death of Cuchulain. In the national saga, it was a virtual city, an imperial capital perhaps, but a capital of the pure imagination.

The real city was rather different. In Swift's time, one-third of its population was Irish-speaking, and over twenty men of learning were listed as Gaelic scholars in its environs, perhaps the most famous being Seán Ó Neachtain, who produced a famous parody of old romances. Areas with names like Irishtown indicate the existence of vibrant Irish-speaking communities, even while names like Ballybough (Baile Bocht) show that their inhabitants lived on the less fashionable fringes of the city, as among the poorest of the poor, in what were in all likelihood the barrios of Georgian Ireland. In time, all the great imperial cities would come to have such settlements. After Swift's death, Dublin enjoyed a brief period of glory as a metropolis with its own parliament and cultural autonomy and this was the time when the great squares and thoroughfares of the city were laid out. But it was not to last for long. The Act of Union not only deposed Grattan's Parliament but it also put an end to the idea of a stately city on Irish soil. Ever since, songsters and writers have lamented the loss of a utopian city of their early childhood. Here is Charles Maturin in 1818:

Its beauty continues, but it is the frightful lifeless beauty of a corpse, and the magnificent architecture of its public buildings seem like a skeleton of some gigantic frame, which the departing spirit has deserted (p. 295).

Or here is George Moore over 60 years later in *A Drama in Muslin* (1886, p. 159), for whom Dublin's plaster is falling like scabs from a diseased body, as its chief administrators 'strive to strut and lisp like those they saw last year at Hyde Park'.

Long before Jane Jacobs wrote her classic study of *The Death and Life of Great American Cities*, these writers were lamenting the death of the capital – being 'a part of what was Dublin in the rare aul [*sic*] times' is nothing especially new. But we need to be more precise. What was dying was Dublin as an imitation Georgian city, as a simulacrum of the old imperial capital, and nobody knew this better than George Moore, who recounts a clap of thunder over Dublin Castle 'so terrible that it seemed as if the heavens were speaking for the freedom-desiring action, now goaded and gagged with Coercion Bills' (Moore, 1886, p. 172).

It has long been fashionable in Irish nationalist discourse to denounce the city as an essentially English phenomenon, a place of fuming chimneys, dirty factories and (in the jocular words of John B. Keane) 'perverts from a built-up area'. Some even go so far as to critique the city as a place of modernity and, as such, of corruption and immorality. Those readings have, however, been over-emphasised. The rural–urban split seems far more rooted in British than in Irish culture. Most of Restoration comedy, for instance, feeds off a dichotomy between the sky-high sparks of the city and the tedious rectitude of country folk. Insofar as these forms were adopted and adapted by Irish writers, they were used in ways which subverted the foolish notion that all innocence is rural and all decadence urban. In *The Importance of Being Earnest*, Oscar Wilde shows how the city slickers, Algy and Jack, are truly open to life in the root meaning of the word innocence (in-nocentes, Lat., open to injury), while characters such as Canon Chasuble and Miss Prism, though living in the country, can be seen to conduct conversations filled with cynical innuendo and a corrupt knowingness. One of the female leads, Cecily Cardew, has her most interesting (i.e. evil) inspirations in the garden, rather in the manner of her biblical predecessor, Eve. Wilde dismissed all English stereotypes of rural rectitude with his joke about a Bible story which begins in a garden but ends in Revelations.

I have shown how Wilde dismantles the binary thinking off which late Victorian thinking fed – he challenged not just the notion of a necessary, inevitable split between urban and rural, but also between male and female, evil and goodness, Irishness and Englishness – showing that each of these forces was interpenetrated by its opposite. One reason for this may have been the fact that, coming from Ireland, Wilde may have found it difficult to make a clear distinction between rural and urban at all. Mid-nineteenth-century Ireland was predominantly an agrarian society and nobody had yet begun to think of such alternatives as real. 'Rural Ireland' as an idea would be largely an invention of the revivalist generation at the turn of the century, a concept made possible only when a sufficiently large number of Irish people began to live in cities and major towns. In 1901 that figure was 28 per cent, still fairly low, but it would rise steeply thereafter, and with that rise emerged the image of a beautiful rural life, whose beauty is in direct proportion to its jeopardy. Like all such images of pastoral, the very naming of rural Ireland as a concept was a sure sign that the culture it reflected was already doomed to disappear.

It would in fact be possible to rewrite the story of Irish independence not so much as a narrative of national self-determination but rather as an account of the transfer of responsibility for the management of the crisis in a rural civilisation. The long decline of rural Ireland began well before the famines of the 1840s and is still not quite over: but the flight from the land into towns and cities, whether in Ireland or further afield, has been a constant theme. The decline of Dublin after the Union was matched, in short, by a slow-motion collapse of rural societies. In that charged context, it might make more sense to see the assault on urban values in revivalist and nationalist literature less as an attack on the city as such than on the idea of a colonial or imperial capital, less as an assault on the city as a non-Irish phenomenon than an attempt to imagine an Irish alternative, less a critique of one of the forms of modernity than an attempt to imagine an alternative method of modernising human experience.

Of all the revivalist authors who made rural Ireland a theme, J. M. Synge is arguably the most famous – yet his notebooks in Trinity College, Dublin, are filled with musings on ways of solving the simultaneous crisis affecting Dublin and the countryside. His answer was to use modern technology to secure for citizens the full benefits of rural living – a complex system of railway lines, radiating across the land, would permit workers to live in country cottages and to commute by that network to industrial centres and factories. In England the answer to that same question was the sprawl of suburbia, which was really a victory of the urban over the rural by a sort of stealth. Synge's response has the merit of working to a wholly alternative frame of reference, in what may rank as the earliest anticipation of the idea of the electronic cottage, a world in which all urban/rural splits cease to have much meaning.

Synge's solution, with its attempt to map an urban modernity onto a rural existence, was something he had already done in his great travel masterpiece, *The Aran Islands*, where he purports to rediscover the values of the Paris Commune of 1871 among the farmers and fisher-folk of the islands. In other words, he rediscovers the attempt by the capital of the nineteenth century to blast open a revolutionary future in one of Europe's oldest and most traditional societies, the ultimate in rurality. In doing as much, Synge may simply have been engaging in a cultural tradition not all that different from that engaged in by those people who moved into Dublin and other Irish cities in the later decades of the nineteenth century.

Unlike Paris, with its radial system of boulevards, centrally planned by Baron Hausmann in the nineteenth century, Dublin as a city is scarcely planned at all. No single mind or imagination lies behind it. It has never been destroyed and rebuilt in such a pattern – and apart from those Georgian squares at its very centre, it is more an agglomeration of villages like Ranelagh, Rathmines, Rathgar, Clontarf, Killester, Marino, all of which eventually got 'joined up'. When James Joyce called it 'the last of the intimate cities', he was in all likelihood recalling fondly this very villagey feel. His own masterpiece, *Ulysses*, mimics the structure of Dublin, being a collection of micro-stories and anecdotes, bolted together into the shape of an experimental narrative. The same is also true of two other modernist masterpieces written by Dubliners: *At Swim-Two-Birds* by Flann O'Brien and the trilogy of Samuel Beckett.

Rather than thinking of Dublin as a backward, deposed ex-capital of empire, it may be possible to imagine it even more profoundly as an instance of emergent modernity. Joyce deliberately treats his city as a site of the modern: he once said, 'if I can get to the heart of Dublin I can get to the heart of the world'. Much has been made of the 'Wandering Rocks' chapter of *Ulysses* which projects the city as a maze, an image of that labyrinth beloved of post-colonial writers from Octavo Paz to García Márquez. The text itself in its structuring is like a maze, enterable and leaveable by many different routes. The psychoanalyst Jung even suggested that it was best started in the final chapter. And the streets rendered therein were not anonymous zones of danger to be traversed as quickly as possible by persons moving from one private experience to another, but places of sociability and excitement. American readers are often annoyed by the sheer amount of walking done and lovingly described: one student once suggested to me that Bloom must be ill, because he seemed to be walking something off. Frank Delaney long ago noted that Bloom's movements, if traced on a map, form a shape something like a question mark – but the real point is that in the Dublin of those years, everyone was a *flâneur*, a stroller in a city still felt to be cheerfully negotiable. One of the reasons for the awesome popularity of *Ulysses* in Ireland today, if not in its own time, may lie in the fact that it seems to suggest that the city is viable, friendly, and yet for all that, mysterious. People in Dublin in the early decades of the twentieth century felt that they owned the streets in a way that few enough of them would ever hope to own their own houses, and they spilled out on to the streets at every opportunity. My uncles and aunts thought nothing of spending over an hour and a half walking to a game of cards which itself might last no more than an hour – and walking all the way home afterwards, often stopping to chat with friends and acquaintances. Being open and public, the streets allowed for a sort of intimate exchange less likely in enclosed and more monitored settings – a paradox Joyce exploited brilliantly through use of the interior monologue. What he also captured was the expressive dignity of ordinary men and women in working conditions – in 'Wandering Rocks' the camera pans back and away from Leopold Bloom and Stephen Dedalus, with the implication that any one of the thousands of other citizens passing might be enjoying interior monologues of similar poetry and complication. At a time when European modernists voiced fear and loathing of the many-headed mob, Joyce celebrated mass men and mass women in the word-city, demonstrating how lovable such people were.

What was produced in the Dublin of the early twentieth century was a form of vernacular modernism, quite different from that of London, Berlin or Paris (even if *Ulysses* was written to a finish in the French capital), but somewhat similar to that to be found at the same time in places like Bombay or Buenos Aires. Because Ireland was a colony, it was also a laboratory in which new social experiments could be tried out – a postal system, universal education – and because the crises at the centre of the empire often first manifested themselves on the periphery, it also witnessed developments like the separation of church and state or the expropriation of the aristocracy long before such things happened in the colonial home country. Hence that odd mixture of backwardness and forwardness which characterised Irish modernism – the sense that the ancient and modern, far from being opposed, might in fact be complementary. Those country people who crowded into the city, as in other parts of the decolonised world, brought with them a set of ruralist values which they were all the keener to maintain in the new setting. This is why a left/right ideological politics of the kind to be found in major British cities could never fully emerge in Dublin – its political activists cut their teeth in country villages, where a brokerist, clientelist politics led most political activists to avoid clashes and search for consensus around the ideological centre. In a somewhat similar way, the rural character of Irish life was maintained even in a capital of 300,000 souls by the daily sight of cattle being herded past Rathmines clock, down to the city centre, and across Carlisle Bridge, for export from the docklands. Small wonder, then, that *Ulysses* should in its second episode focus so intensely on the cause and cure of foot and mouth disease in cattle. Dublin was a classic Third World capital, a centre dominated by the cultural values of the peasant periphery – its policemen, civil servants, teachers, even its city planners and architects, for most of the twentieth century, were people who came in from farms and villages in the countryside. Their formative years had been spent in rural backdrops; and since their arrival in the capital indicated a degree of social success, and the self-confidence which that success engendered, they had far more effect on it than the rhythms of urban life could ever have on them.

Even eight decades after the day on which *Ulysses* is set, a contemporary novelist like John McGahern, in a story called 'Parachutes', could describe a school-teacher strolling up Grafton Street and all too sharply aware that behind the gilded façades of Brown Thomas and Switzers lay small fields of brambles and nettles among which grew those dandelions, which sent forth the clocks blowing over the roof tops: 'backyards and dumps and yards and gardens'. The teacher has just one response: that the place will never be a city. Or never a European city maybe – but perhaps a post-colonial one (1985, p. 23).

Of all the writers who came to Dublin and mapped a set of rural co-ordinates on to the capital, Patrick Kavanagh is surely the most greatly loved – and loved most of all by those new Dubliners who were undergoing the same transition. He treated Baggot Street as a glorified rural village and daily performed the 'Baggot Street Gallop' (this involved a morning going from pub to pub on the left side of the street, and an afternoon doing in like manner on the right side). The Grand Canal, with its trees, grassy knolls and running waters he dubbed 'my Pembrokeshire', in a faint reprise of Swift's idea – but it was an idea he also sought to develop, since he found the values of his lost farmland community of County Monaghan around the canal, in a classic *rus in urbe* setting.

Kavanagh, O'Brien and Brendan Behan are often coupled as mid-century absurdists, and a favourite story has the triumvirate locked in conversation at the end of Grafton Street, all of them solemnly lamenting the decline of the Dublin eccentric. This too was another translated tradition. Like Gaelic Ireland, Dublin was always dying, always in a state of near-terminal collapse. Brendan Behan won fame in both modes because his generation permitted such bifurcation. In Irish poetry he wrote 'Jackeen ag caomeadh na mBlascaod', bemoaning the last Golden Eagle of the Blasket Islands and the loss of its island community to the mainland – but in English prose he bemoaned the break-up of that inner-city Dublin which had so sustained Joyce and the relocation of its citizens out on the wilder shores of Kimmage and Crumlin, out among those very rural idiots and wild men of whom he had written with such tenderness in his other mode. And this lament for a lost inner city of 'aul wans', doting grannies and throaty street-dealers has become ever since a leitmotif among nationalists and republicans, an astonishing number of whom have written laments for a lost locality. Eamonn MacThomáis was once sent for a spell in jail as editor of *An Phoblacht*, the Sinn Féin weekly newspaper, but is far better known as a guide to the inner city's historical sites and as author of *Me Jewel and Darlin' Dublin* and *Me Darlin' Dublin's Dead and Gone*. Similarly, the current leader of Sinn Féin, Gerry Adams, has had bestsellers with such books as *Falls Memories* and the collection of short stories called *The Street*, most of them sentimental exercises in nostalgia for a 1960s world of prelapsarian innocence, non-sectarian delivery men and lovable old rogues conspiring to breed champion greyhounds.

It is indeed truly remarkable that the major voice of Sinn Féin, the one political party with an all-Ireland vision and profile, should in his creative writing be so rooted in his immediate locality and parish. It recalls the young IRA man who was wounded during Operation Motorman in Derry during the Summer of 1972 and told a journalist for the *Observer* that he wasn't really dying for a United Ireland, rather to protect the neighbours in his own street. It recalls also the question put to Gerry Adams at the start of the Peace Process in 1994: whether his followers were defenders of a locality or genuine United Irelanders? Much of the recent fiction about Northern Ireland stresses the way in which young people there have felt penned into a little world of their own – but the fiction of the republicans like Adams and Morrison, who are a generation older than those young novelists who grew up within the Troubles, suggests that they are also localists. Only in very recent work does the younger generation repeat the move of Wolfe Tone and attempt to see Belfast whole. Geoffrey Beattie, in *The Corner Boys*, has written about loyalist youth:

I sat there with Keeper and Trucker that afternoon looking down at the Belfast beneath us and thinking, is that all there is? We worked our way across town, up streets that we knew and down streets that we didn't know. Streets me and him would never walk. You could see how streets joined together from up there . . . Just round the hill a bit I could see tight little rows of streets like ours that meant nothing to me, streets that led nowhere. Fenian streets where we would never dare go. (p. 113)

The loyalist gangs, like the Republican writers, only feel secure among their own immediate community – but in *Eureka Street*, Robert McLiam Wilson celebrates Belfast as a city where narratives might meet and a true dialogical novel become possible, although at present that is more an aspiration:

It is only late at night, if you stand up high, that you can see the city as one thing, as a single phenomenon. While all sleep, the daytime jumble is unified and, geographically at least, the city seems a simple thing. (p. 213)

We are back perhaps to Wordsworth and Westminster Bridge.

Edmund Burke once remarked that everyone cleaves to the little platoon from which they came: and so it is in Ireland. Even after living forty or fifty years of their adult lives in Dublin, many incomers feel ill at ease, and this despite the fact that they have made over so much of the city in their own image. What this suggests more than anything is the persistence of the *ancien régime*, Burke's image of an organic and ordered society. Fintan O'Toole has shown how even the forms of drama pioneered by Yeats, Synge and Lady Gregory, while well fitted to capture a rural community, were quite inadequate to deal with the layers of urban life. Every time the characters of Sean O'Casey attempt to seize the streets and make them their own, they are repulsed either by the armies of nationalism or imperialism, and driven back to tenements which, with multiple families in one building, work like a rural village community. O'Casey had to describe the urban in ruralist forms, because the city was intent on so conceiving of itself.

Yet out on the edges of the new Dublin, among those transplanted souls in Kimmage, Crumlin, Raheny and Coolock, was to be found a new form of urban living, combining urban and rural modes, more like that imagined by Synge. The inhabitants of Roddy Doyle's Barrytown could hardly be classed as 'suburban' in conventional British or American meanings of that word – yet in the Irish literature of the 1980s they played much the same role as had once been discharged by the peasants of Synge. They were as poor and as disempowered in the 1980s as the Western peasants had been in the 1890s – the subject of anxious government reports. Yet along with their poverty went a tremendous energy of language and fertility of comic playfulness – the qualities which allowed both Synge and Doyle to build a sort of utopian community out of such unpromising material. These people were largely unknown to the literate middle classes who would marvel at them in plays or read about them in books – and so the urban writers of the 1980s were able to recycle the 'Hidden Ireland' rhetoric of the national revival as a way of adding conspiratorial and counter-cultural glamour to their new discourse. The echoes of such a discourse may be heard even in the flyer circulated for the 'Writing the City' conference held in Dublin in 2001 :

Ireland has long had a problematic relationship with the urban life. The city, passed over routinely by anthropologists, painters and poets in their search for the 'real Ireland', has often been seen as an alien intrusion. It has, however, also been the inspiration for some of the last century's most important artistic achievements: the source of another, alternative construction of identity.

Change the word *city* to *countryside* in the paragraph and you have a perfect Gaelic League poster, *circa* 1901.

When the Australian poet Vincent Buckley lived in Dublin for a sabbatical year in the early 1980s, he was appalled by the housing developments on the city's rim. He remarked on the high-minded aimlessness with which boys performed amazing tricks on bicycles with one wheel airborne, or on the fact the builders tended to leave the estates looking at once 'unfinished' and 'used up' – that is, of course, what *Ulysses* itself once was, what happens when you follow Walter Benjamin's advice and build a ruin as a way of overcoming the ravages of time. Yet Buckley was also haunted by such sights – he called his book *Memory Ireland*, in recognition of an advance factory that collapsed and of a seeming amnesia among the inhabitants of such featureless places about the memory of the dead. Yet he needn't have worried. The decade that followed was to be filled with books which revealed the hidden contours of this lost Ireland to readers. In *The Journey Home*, Dermot Bolger (1991) did for Finglas what Doyle would do for Barrytown – beneath the nihilism and aimlessness, he sought to return to official history the lives of the new Dubliners and to return to them some sense of their historical setting. While Peter Sheridan was invoking a Joycean tradition to the effect that the inner city was the authentic urban experience, Bolger and Doyle lodged a counter-claim, rather like that made by Corkery for the Munster peasant poets of the eighteenth century in *The Hidden Ireland*. And yet in Bolger's work at any rate there is a dire contradiction: the squalor of city life is such that the depiction becomes a form of propaganda for the superior vitality of rural life. Beneath the high-minded aimlessness of Finglas lurks an – you've guessed it – ancient village culture, implicit in the beautiful placename Fionn-ghlas, a point of origin, but almost lost to urban sprawl as here and there older bushes give way to patios and crazy paving:

'Remember the stories from school? . . . The secret tunnel from here out to Dunsoughly Castle, the grave robber who died of fright . . . I doubt if the kids tell them to each other in school any more. We caught it, Hano, the very tail-end of one place and the start of another. And it's fucked me up till now . . . I just want to lie here in my own home place which no longer exists except in my head.' (p. 207)

In the words of Astrid Gerber, both Bolger and his characters time and again feel homesick for a place in which they never felt fully at home – Finglas.

With the characters of Roddy Doyle, adjustment seems to come more easily. Yet, nevertheless, their world has much in common with that of the revivalists, being so well known that, like the Emain Macha of Cuchulain, it scarcely needs to be described. It is a local world, whole and entire unto itself – as in ancient epic, subject only to intermittent invasion by alien forces which are usually repulsed. The trees and woodlands and hills exist all around it, in direct proximity to the cement mixers and domestic railings which betoken a new form of civilisation – but the Paddy Clarke who grows up against that strange backdrop feels no sense of conflict, merely the happy amenities of green fields and TV soccer, side by side. Where Bolger's characters seem traumatised by cultural loss, Doyle's are imbued by a sense of gain, in the best of both possible worlds. Yet what both have in common, with Gerry Adams as much as with one another, is an intense devotion to capturing the experience of a given locality. And in no case is the locality a synecdoche for the wider city as such – rather a sort of alternative to its blandness. Not for nothing has Gerry Adams been called the Alice Taylor of West Belfast – but something similar could be said of Bolger and Finglas.

Nor are these isolated instances. While Bolger was excavating a lost Finglas beneath the crazy-paved gardens and the local laundromat, Martin Amis in *London Fields* was attempting to probe beneath the cynical surfaces of 1980s Thatcherite London to the town once inhabited and recorded by the radical poet William Blake. And well beyond the zones of fiction, writers have devoted themselves to studying the history, topography, dialect words and character of individual areas, boroughs and parishes. Every Christmas three or four books appear in the bestseller lists, many of them penned by retired civil servants, teachers, priests or librarians who, after a lifetime of study, commit the story of Terenure or Chaplelizod or Inchicore to print. Even high-toned places like Rathgar or Dundrum are now honoured by such volumes, which seem to be avidly read.

What is behind this localism? Cities have now grown so large as to seem undesirable – far from being aberrational, Belfast is a telling contemporary example of a place which nobody seems able to describe as a whole, other than from a great distance. No longer is a 'Wandering Rocks' chapter or book possible. People prefer, if they can, to have a job, and a shopping centre, in their own immediate area. The cult of the local may indeed be a panic reaction to the forces of globalisation. For a century nationalism seemed to offer some kind of resistance to the forces of global capital, but this seems less and less viable, as the leaders of nation–states pool their powers.

The reaction, however, may be as much to the growing homogenisation of cities, all of which now seem as alike as one airport or one university campus is to another. The problem posed for many by rural life a hundred years ago – sameness, boredom, anomie – is now more likely to be identified with life in a great city. The heartless monitoring mechanisms once discharged by the clergy or the local gossips are now performed by CCTV; and, paradoxically, a private life seems less and less possible, as the state and the junk mail companies intrude on everything. Many of those students who graduated in the early 1990s and left Dublin report themselves dispossessed of the city which they left, but whose image they carried everywhere in their minds, when eventually they return. The nostalgia once felt for Belmullet in Dublin has been replaced by a feeling for a lost version of the city itself. That the bestselling books of the past twenty years are the ones I mentioned suggests that we are already also mourning a lost sense of locality. Yet the forces that took that sense away in the 1980s, the decade of compulsory internationalism, of world music, world novels and the United Colours of Benetton, are already in retreat – because the power of technology now permits the cheaper printing of books by local authors, the use of local radio and television, the supporting of local publishers and local theatre companies. It could be argued that all this began in the Gaeltacht, that crucible of post-modernity, in the 1970s, and slowly fanned out across the country-side, from west to east, hitting Dublin last because, as in Swift's day, too many of its minds were still turning east, to London and beyond.

If vernacular modernism helped to produce Joyce, then a localist post-modernism has already created in Ireland and elsewhere a wholly new kind of art which doesn't look to any distant centres of authority for its sanctions. It remains only for architects, road-planners and local adminis-trators to create more fully an environment which fits those impulses. If they succeed, one thing is sure – the words 'country' and 'city' will have to be taken out of circulation. They only had meaning when their under-lying concepts were dying but now that they are very dead, it's time to move on.

The recent arrival of immigrants from Eastern Europe, Africa, China and so forth will further enrich and complicate the pattern of localisms that is contemporary Dublin. For example, the area from the Parnell Monument to Summerhill is now known as Little Africa. Out of the experiences of such people will emerge new hybrid strains of music, painting, poetry and (in due time) novels and film. Their struggle to maintain strong elements of their inherited culture within their own enclaves, while yet being recognised as participatory citizens of an Irish democracy, will make for interesting reading.

FURTHER READING

Beattie, G. (1999) *The Corner Boys*. Belfast and London: Orion Mass Market Paperback.

Beckett, S. (1959) *Trilogy: Molloy/Malone Dies/The Unnamable*. London: Calder Publications.

Bolger, D. (1991) *The Journey Home*. London and New York: Penguin Books.

Gerber, A. (2001) *Tradition and Ephemerality: Suburban Voices in Dermot Bolger and Roddy Doyle,* Ph.D. dissertation, Trinity College Dublin, 63–80.

Jacobs, J. (1997) *The Death and Life of Great American Cities.* New York: Random House.

Joyce, J. (1960) *Ulysses.* London: Bodley Head.

Maturin, C. (1818) *Women, or Pour et Contre*, vol. 3. London.

McGahern, J. (1985) *High Ground.* London: Faber and Faber.

(1993) *The Collected Stories*. London and New York: Faber & Faber.

Moore, G. (1886 (1993)) *A Drama in Muslin*, with an introduction by James Plunkett. London: Appletree Press.

O'Brien, F. (2000) *At Swim-Two-Birds*. London and New York: Penguin Books.

O'Grady, S. (1878) *History of Ireland: Heroic Period*. London.

Synge, J. M. (1992) *The Aran Islands*. London and New York: Penguin Books.

Wilde, O. (1996) *The Importance of Being Earnest*. London and New York: Penguin Books.

Wilson, R. M. (1997) *Eureka Street*. London: Minerva.

CHAPTER 19

Strangers in their own country: multiculturalism in Ireland

(2001)

The seductive charm of Irish culture no longer seems to work in quite the old way. A *céad míle fáilte* is not extended to all new arrivals any more. Yet the historical capacity of the Irish to assimilate waves of incomers should never be underestimated. Eight centuries ago, after all, the Normans became 'more Irish than the Irish themselves'. Who is to say that the latest group of arriving Nigerians might not know the same destiny? If there is no zeal like the zeal of the convert, there may be no Irishness quite like that of the recent recruit.

The fear of being assimilated too readily to Irish culture haunted those colonisers who came in the armies of the English queen, Elizabeth I. Their official artists painted portraits of men who had gone native and been barbarised by contact with Gaelic culture. In them, hybridity, far from being a desirable state of cultural fusion, was seen as a negation of humanity itself, as two discrepant codes cancelled one another out, leaving the victim a prey to evil instinct and uncontrolled lasciviousness. On the other side, Gaelic poets lambasted those overlords who were keen to anglicise themselves, dubbing them half-breeds ('a dhream gaoidhealta gallda'). Nobody wanted to be a hybrid in those far-off, pre-post-modern days: yet somehow quite a lot of writers (and, one assumes, ordinary persons) managed the trick.

By the eighteenth century, macaronic songs and ballads were all the rage in a patently bicultural community, yet the fear on both sides of being wholly absorbed by the other never went away. It surfaced again at the start of the twentieth century in the claim by D. P. Moran that the Gael must be the element which absorbed – a claim which simply underlined the fact that by then it was the Gael who was being co-opted massively by the forces of the English language. When the new Irish state of the 1920s and 1930s appeared intent on defining itself in mainly Catholic and Gaelic terms, Moran's counterthesis might appear to have staged a late rally: and even today his statement has the power to terrify some critics, who are so fixated on it that they ignore the more progressive elements in his thinking. Routinely, they cite it as further proof of a covert assimilationist tendency in Irish nationalism, whose siren-call to unionists must be resisted. Yet that same siren-call is all but inaudible to Africans and Eastern Europeans. Suddenly, the fear of assimilation seems to have struck the assimilators.

Yet the stubborn facts of history remain. Those English who have 'opted' for Ireland have been effortlessly assumed into the national narrative: from the fictional John Broadbent to the factual Jack Charlton, Ireland has gone on bearing out Bernard Shaw's claim that it is one of the last spots on earth still producing the ideal Englishman of history. In recent years, the number of converts has, if anything, increased. When Daniel Day-Lewis pronounced his win at the Oscars a triumph for Ireland, he effectively dismantled the English-when-they-win, Irish-when-they-lose equation. But he *chose* Irishness, just as much as the Anglo-Normans did before him: in neither case was it forced upon a hapless victim.

There has never been any problem in embracing such figures, despite the fact that in some senses they were products of the traditional 'enemy'. So why the reported reluctance to embrace Nigerians or Romanians? Many people have been shocked by racist attacks on foreigners (not all of them confined to black visitors) and some have wondered whether this is a new phenomenon. Back in the 1980s, when the late Phil Lynott sang 'Whiskey in the Jar', there was little evidence of such intolerance: or even in the 1980s when soccer fans sang the praises of Paul McGrath (although the famous 'ooh-aah' chant had something slightly iffy about it). Perhaps such figures were sufficiently rare as not to seem threatening: what Joyce's Mr Deasy said of the Jews might have been indicated of the blacks – that Ireland had the distinction of never having persecuted them, because it had the sense never to let any numbers of them in. Yet even in those decades, change was afoot. I had a young friend who went to England and when I warned him about the danger of racist attack on the streets of London, he laughed and said: 'Nobody there minds my skin-colour: it's only when they hear my Dublin accent that the trouble starts.'

It would be too simple to explain the recent racist outbreaks as a legacy of the colonial system (in which so many Irish served) or even as a copycat version of contemporary yob culture in England. After all, Irish soccer fans have not bothered to emulate the hooliganism of their English counterparts. Nor can it be mainly an after-effect of the encounter between triumphalist Catholic missionaries and African or Asian communities.

Many of those Nigerians who have come to Ireland did so in the hope that the people would be as kindly and civilised as those missionaries who taught them at school and cared for them in medical centres: and they have reported themselves as shocked by the blatant difference in behaviour.

Liberal intellectuals, who had long viewed Irish racism as a largely North American phenomenon, have also been amazed. While Phil Lynott was being acclaimed in Dublin as the inventor of Celtic Rock, over in Boston the lace-curtain Irish who voted for the Kennedys were also quite capable of refusing to share buses and schools with black neighbours. Nor were these problems of recent vintage. Tensions between the two communities went back to the 1840s, when emancipated black Americans lodged formal complaints that the arrival of the Irish was reducing the value of real estate in their neighbourhoods. A century and a half later, a more inflected version of this complaint surfaced with the claim that those scholars who placed Irish Studies in a post-colonial category were really guilty of gazumping black and Hispanic academics in the search for university posts under affirmative action programmes.

Back home in Ireland (and nearby in Britain), relations between Irish and Africans seemed far less tense. Bob Geldof invoked a communal memory of famine in helping to make his own people the largest *per capita* contributors to Third World relief in Live-Aid. In the arts an emerging talent like Roddy Doyle could build an entire comic novel around the contention that the Irish were the blacks of Europe: and *The Commitments* became a film which enjoyed popular success. By 1990 Brian Friel had created in *Dancing at Lughnasa* a play which explored analogies between the Ryangan culture of Africa and the harvest festivals of Donegal. Its central character is a returned priest who himself 'went native' in Uganda, losing the capacity to distinguish between the codes of the two cultures. Again, though a play by a complex artist might seem to appeal only within the traditional constituency of liberal intellectuals, Friel's masterwork won huge audiences, not just at home but overseas, and most of all among the American Irish.

The backdrop to those debates was, of course, the return of many priests, nuns and 'development' workers from missionary activity. Many brought with them radical new ideas about democratising parish life or applying the principles of liberation theology, learned out in Africa or Latin America. Ireland, which had once given a lead to other decolonising peoples, now seemed to be following their example. Nor was this wholly surprising. Missionaries are in the business of transforming conciousness, unlike military governors or colonial administrators, who simply need to know how to give orders and impose rules. Once you make an appeal at the level of the spirit, you are open to a counter-appeal: and that is what happened to many missionaries, like Friel's Father Jack or to the returned theologians of liberation.

Anyone who studies Irish art over the past two decades couldn't but be impressed by the amount of inspiration derived from other cultures, mostly in the Third World. What is even more remarkable is that in every case the foreign input, though major, has somehow assisted some element of traditional Irish culture to present itself more stunningly to a modern world audience. At one level, there is the marvellous fusion of Latino elements with native forms in Riverdance (which has obvious parallels with Latino influence in theology); at another, there is the Caribbean collaboration of Seamus Heaney with his fellow-Nobellist Derek Walcott (with analogies in the fusions of style achieved in various musical bands); and, even at the level of high theory, the inspiration derived by David Lloyd and other critics from the Subaltern Studies Group in India seems to replicate the uses to which W. B. Yeats put Indian culture early in the twentieth century.

In the time of Yeats and Joyce, the Irish had little difficulty in identifying with people of colour. Popular magazines like *Pat* in the 1880s and 1890s were filled with cartoons on the theme, of which Joyce would make much in the 'Cyclops' section of *Ulysses*. There the drinkers in Barney Kiernan's pub make common cause with those African slaves recently defended by Roger Casement. The entire tradition of comparative analysis reached a climax in Richard Ned Lebow's book *White England and Black Ireland* (1976), which suggested that the Paddy and Sambo stereotypes had worked in distressingly similar ways, creating a perceptual prison for the English which left them quite unable to recognise what was actually happening on the ground.

Against that rich background, one might reasonably ask where the roots of Irish racism are to be found. There are some commentators who believe that much of what is being expressed is not racism in the strict sense so much as distress-signals emitted by local communities, who find the ecology of their street or village massively disturbed by a bureaucratic central government, which suddenly 'plants' refugees in their midst. The 'Corofin effect' has been replicated in more than one rural town: and the government's failure to brief or persuade communities on the positive potentials of its policy has been at times lamentable. Journalists have managed to convince themselves that all forms of protest against such policies must be racist in tinge: yet most of the trouble-spots featured in media reports of 1999 have since settled down, once local people began to come to terms with their new neighbours. If there was some racist element in the initial outcry – and there surely was – it was often broken down once first-hand relationships began. That complex was long ago observed in attitudes to the English, whom the Irish were supposed to dislike 'in theory' but often came to love as individuals. The accusatory tone of some media reports hindered rather than helped progress, for the old journalistic obsession with trouble and strife may sell papers but often at the cost of increasing the sense of crisis.

In a similar way, it is sometimes hard to fathom whether the jibes and punches thrown at Nigerians in Parnell Street are manifestations of race-hatred or of a beleaguered community seeking to defend itself as such. 'We fought the culchies when we had to', said one veteran of a night's brawl, 'and then we fought the cops. And now we have to fight the darkies.' The elision there suggests an advanced paranoia about outside groupings, but whether it is classical racism is a moot point.

Yet racism of the most ugly kind undeniably exists in Irish society: and the presence of ever-growing numbers of refugees and migrants from overseas has brought it to the surface, making all foreigners (not just people of colour) arguably more vulnerable than once they were. It is probable that in other countries of Western Europe anything from 10 per cent to 15 per cent of the the community harbours such prejudices against guest-workers: and the same is probably true in Ireland. In order to account for the scale of this phenomenon, it may be useful to return to the fear of hybridity with which I began.

Humans sometimes display a dreadful need to make other people more like them. Irish people may feel this desire more than most. Even our 'liberal' press finds it hard to understand or speak respectfully of those who don't endorse all elements of the liberal agenda. The French are a bit like this too. Wherever they went as colonisers, they felt ratified rather than mocked when natives perfectly imitated them, to the extent of awarding special prizes to Africans who wrote like Frenchmen and French women.

Official Irish policy towards asylum-seekers, as spelled out in the 1999 Illegal Immigrants Trafficking Bill, works in a somewhat similar way. Anyone who fails to gain asylum has just fourteen days in which to appeal, despite the fact that ordinary citizens of the Irish republic have up to six months in which to seek reviews of verdicts. This was one of the clauses which President Mary McAleese found questionable enough to refer to the Supreme Court, which went on to vindicate it. That clause has interesting psychological implications. For instance, the extreme speed with which the appeal is to be processed suggests a problem in the official mind with the 'in-between' state of the applicant. Either the applicant 'becomes Irish' straight away or not at all: and there can be no sustained and troubling period of ambiguity. Either he or she is a wonderful addition to our society or a damned nuisance – but nothing in between.

A further aspect of the judgement is its ready acceptance that the political rights of nationals and non-nationals are not necessarily the same. The ruling of Judge Ronan Keane states:

The non-national or alien constitutes a discrete category of persons whose entry, presence and expulsion from the State may be the subject of legislative and administrative measures which would not, and in many of its aspects could not, be applied to its citizens. The rights, including fundamental rights, to which non-nationals may be entitled under the Constitution do not always coincide with the rights protected as regards citizens of the State, the right not to be deported being an obvious and relevant example.

In reporting this judgement, Carol Coulter of the *Irish Times* remarked that this went against the spirit of some previous adjudications, which tended to give non-citizens the same rights as citizens, once they were before the courts of the state, on the principle that the rights of man are universal. The new distinction seemed to reflect a harmonisation of immigrant law across the European union. Such harmonisation might not be a bad thing in itself, if only to prevent states from deporting immigrants to hard-line regimes for summary despatch: but the effect in this case was to make Ireland as hard-line as everywhere else. Patricia McKenna MEP observed that 'there is something seriously wrong with our Constitution if it cannot afford all people equal rights of access to the courts and surely it is our Constitution that should be amended to reflect modern-day reality'.

The issue broached here is central. Although the sovereignty of nation–states has been eroded in recent decades, they are likely to remain with us for many years to come. In the absence of a universal political system, people will have to ask themselves what happens in such a context to stateless persons. It seems that one can as little survive without a nation as without a gender. The need is, therefore, to develop a legal code which offers real protection to foreigners. The problem has been summed up in a savagely satirical question put by Julia Kristeva: 'is he fully a man if he is not a citizen?' If a foreigner is defined as one who is not a citizen of the country in which she/he resides, then where does that leave her/his political rights (such as the right to vote)? Most foreigners are useful contributors to the national economy and payers of taxes, yet their exclusion from the voting process ultimately denies them influence over decisions which affect their lives. It should be obvious that a process of law-making which excludes them may easily lead to a disinclination to respect state laws, or to respect the entire culture which is bound up with those laws.

The Gardaí have done their best to negotiate the new challenges: and a special unit has been set up to educate members of the force in the specificities of Muslim and other cultures. That wise example should be followed more generally in state schools, which should anyway have long ago offered basic classes in world religions and cultures. What militated against such study in the past was the exceptionalist philosophy of Ireland as a unique island, comparable to nowhere else. The Roman Catholic dogma taught in most schools evoked other -isms only to discount them. Those Irish people who eventually found themselves living next door to Muslims or Rastas had to learn about their codes in less theoretical ways: but now that the home society is becoming so variegated, there is an unanswerable case for such study. Once these classes begin, students may find that island status provides a good point of contact with that, say, of Caribbean peoples, even as the general Catholic background could be a useful aid in understand-Hispanic groups. What were once impediments to the development of an Irish multiculturalism may soon help to enable it.

Let us develop the latter point just a little. Central to the Christian faith is the conviction that this world is not our true home and that we are all nomads passing through it. Early Christianity emphasised the vital importance of offering lodging to those in exile, for they might be a chosen people. The history of the Irish, themselves dispossessed yet ever more sure of their communal identity, seemed to bear out the idea of a nation open to endless joiners: for as the Book of Leviticus taught, 'love him as yourself – for you were once strangers in Egypt' (19:33–4). What is romantic in Christianity is its openness to the notion of the Other: Jesus taught each man to love his neighbour as himself. Julia Kristeva has commented that 'the idea of a chosen people at once defines a rational entity and implies its eternal openness – as aliens'. Of course, even that liberal Christianity too often had its own set limits: the Other was put in the place of the loved self only if he or she was a Christian.

Nonetheless, the basic implication was priceless: if you are cruel to another, it must be because you are taking revenge on some hated aspect of yourself. The fear of hybridisation is really a terror in the face of potent but repressed forces within one's own culture. James Baldwin remarked many years ago of his fellow-Americans that at the root of the white man's inability to live at peace with the negro was his prior inability to live at peace with himself. It's a point worth applying more generally to human-kind. The attacks by English soccer hooligans on foreign fans may well have roots in a sense of jeopardised identity, consequent upon the fact that for two centuries Englishness has been drained of much of its content to make way for Britishness. Whenever English fans were up against other groups who knew who they were, they seemed to react badly. Equally, when some German racists have burned out Turkish guest-workers, that may have been a murderous distress-signal emitted by people who have turned their backs on their own traditional culture (a turning-away which was in some senses understandable, given what some elements of that culture had led to).

In the United States today multiculturalism has posed a problem. It is presented as an ideal to various recently arrived peoples (Hispanics, Africans, Eastern Europeans) who have no sense of a common American culture, and who thus become obsessed with the identity politics of their own ethnic group, leading to that 'fraying of America' about which Arthur Schlesinger Jr has written. The old secular republican ideal, as evolved in the American revolution, should provide the tissue uniting all, but seems no longer to do so. One manifestation of that failure is the evolving multicultural syllabus, which may in some ways serve as a warning of how *not* to do multiculturalism in modern Ireland. This is one which presents students with entirely separate versions of Hispanic, African or Indian cultures, each of them honourably rendered in some of its richness, but none of them shown in interaction. Like the admissions policy of modern states, the admissions policy to the syllabus is also passing strange: texts are admitted single file, so to speak. Texts by black or native American authors which offer interesting accounts of their culture from within are welcomed, but there is less engagement with texts (like the poetry of Langston Hughes) which show how effectively black culture has challenged and been challenged by other traditions. The activity of the migrant worker, who challenges one sexual, religious or ethnic code with another, has been replicated in great literary works like *The Color Purple*, which mingle traditional genres (slave narrative, epistolary novel etc.) to create brilliant new forms. This is the benefit of a necessarily messy, disputatious, promiscuous multiculturalism, or what Stuart Hall has pithily called 'a multiculturalism without guarantees'.

Irish teachers are likely to support a multicultural syllabus. They may then find themselves confronted with the same challenge which faced their American counterparts – the further reduction of subventions from government to colleges on the grounds that they are harbourers of 'tenured radicals'. Similarly, as more and more children of recent immigrants enter our public education system, we're likely to hear calls from right-wing politicians for a cutback in spending on it. Private colleges are bound to reblossom at secondary and even university level, and public utilities such as hospitals will be left to run down even further.

One of the mysteries of modern Irish politics has been the fact that politicians, ordinarily compassionate on most questions, seem determined to underfund such traditional public institutions as hospitals or universities, despite the massive overflow of expected cash in the state's coffers. Many politicians seem to fear 'floods', 'invasions', 'swamps' of immigrants (the language always suggests a loss of control) and invoke 'clearance centres' as an antidote. Yet one also gets the sense that there are real divisions of opinion. The editorials of the *Sunday Business Post* (hardly a left-wing paper) repeatedly call on government to provide efficient, humane facilities for immigrants and asylum-seekers, on the grounds that our economy needs all hands to the pumps. One may assume that within Fianna Fáil there is a liberal wing, epitomised by David Andrews or Tom Kitt, which is somewhat embarrassed by all their colleagues' talk of 'flotels' and so on. It is past time for such politicians to take a more active role in debate, pointing out just how much every newly arrived person can contribute to making Ireland a better place for everyone. The old theory that the unemployed secretly gloried in their own idleness has been exploded by the willingness with which people went back to work when work materialised: and the same will be true of immigrants, who will want to augment rather than drain the public purse as soon as they can. Such people will bring with them all kinds of unseen benefits – new kinds of medical therapy and holistic practices which will greatly enrich the local medical lore.

The more liberal politicians in the two main parties have remained rather quiet for their own reasons. All around them they see signs of a materialist individualism which seems to mimic that of British yob culture. The Christian churches, which might have provided a powerful moral crusade against selfishness and racism, have lost much of their teaching power and authority: and the politicians know that theirs is now in danger of a similar decline. If the belief of over 50 per cent of the public in the integrity of our system were to collapse, the country (small though it is) could disintegrate into various discrete groups, each proclaiming its moral superiority and clinging to victim-status. Already, there are signs that such a polity is emerging, thanks to the editorial policies of the major media networks, few of whom appear to invest much importance in the ideal of the republic as a guarantor of civic rights. Racism is often born of a search for scapegoats and is more likely to emerge in a climate of scapegoating, such as that promoted in the media today. Politicians, now on the defensive, are wary of espousing what may be an unpopular cause.

Yet they should proceed bravely on the basis that the great majority of Irish persons are not incipient or overt racists. They should support the editors of the *Irish Times* and the *Sunday Business Post* in seeking to explain why the accession of even more people may lead to even more business success. The unspoken but popular fear is that the current affluence, like sunny weather, 'will never last' and that, when it goes, the hungry immigrants will remain. Ordinary people who, at a time of affluence, see long waiting-lists for basic medical care are worried that more Nigerians and Romanians will merely lengthen the queues. It is up to leaders to lead and show why the prosperity is deep-rooted – and one way of stilling those fears is to provide proper medical services.

The fear of failure is far stronger among the old than the young. The latter don't fear losing jobs to outsiders, or losing their identity to people who might 'take Ireland away from them'. They have grown up seeing more and more black persons not just on TV but in the streets: and most of today's primary schoolchildren seem quite unaware of skin colour. When they grow a little older, most of them enjoy the diversity of ethnic art and ethnic restaurants. And most, if asked, would vote to increase the miserly amount of overseas aid voted annually by the government, not just because it's morally right for a stronger economy to help a weaker one, but because they are shrewd enough to know that such policies will make Africa and Asia happier places in which to live and so less likely to produce the sort of desperation that creates political refugees and economic migrants.

What these young people grasp most clearly of all is that Ireland itself was always multicultural, in the sense of eclectic, open, assimilative. The best definition of a nation was that given by Joyce's Leopold Bloom: the same people living in the same place but not necessarily all one thing. As an outcast Jew, condemned to wandering, Bloom may in fact have had more in common with the members of the historic Irish nation than most of the characters in *Ulysses*: and would certainly endorse the view that monoculture works as badly in the body politic as in agriculture, rapidly wearing out the earth's potentials.

Joyce wrote almost all his major texts in European exile, yet every one of them describes his native Dublin, which proved, to his satisfaction at any rate, that there is more than one way in which to live a national life. The recognition during the Robinson presidency that the overseas Irish were also part of the national family suggested a corollary: that many immigrant peoples living on the island of Ireland might also have their own global communities over and above the immediate society to which they belong. In such a context, the word 'foreigner' may begin to seem a little preposterous: and that was in all probability the understanding which led Ted Turner to ban its use on CNN Global News.

When *Ulysses* headed the lists on both sides of the Atlantic as 'book of the century', Irish people everywhere felt a surge of pride, as they do when Sonia O'Sullivan wins an athletics medal. In the same spirit, following the revelations of corruption at various political tribunals, they have experienced an onset of shame. To belong to a national community is to feel personally implicated in its performance: and that is one of the moral values of such belonging. Yet there never really was a pure essence of, say, Frenchness, a fact which we all register in recognising that nations claim historic sanction and are at the same time cases of recent invention, if not instant archaeology. Nations are invariably conflations of various constituents – for instance, the Basques, Catalans, Burgundians, Provencaux and Franco-Germans all contributed to the making of modern France. Nations are in fact a response to the hybrid nature of living conditions, yet for all their claim to essential unity, they create even further hybridities. Joyce, as an early guest-worker on the continent, knew that an unprecedented knowledge is possible on the borders between cultural traditions: if *Ulysses* conflates elements of the novel, drama, lyric poem, play, opera, inventory and so on, that is to produce a wholly new genre, for which even at the time of Joyce's own death, there was as yet no name. The central figure of that narrative, Leopold Bloom, is valued to precisely the extent that he can recognise the stranger in himself. He is, in fact, more Christlike than any of his anti-semitic fellow-citizens and constantly able to put himself in the other fellow's position. His wife chooses him by a similar line of reasoning: 'as well him as another'.

Joyce was one of the first artists, therefore, to imagine 'a world without foreigners', a world possible once men and women begin to accept the foreigner in the self and the necessarily fictive nature of all nationalisms, which are open to endless renegotiation. He was also highly astute in locating the racist impulse in those who have an impoverished sense of history. That may seem paradoxical but isn't really: those who lack a sophisticated sense of their own origins are more likely to seek a simplified version of the past, in whose name to lash out at the 'foreign'. The other side of this dreadful coin is, of course, the sort of loathing for history disseminated by revisionists, as Julia Kristeva has explained:

As an expression of hatred the glorification of origins finds its matching opposite in the hatred of origins. Those who repress their roots, who don't want to know where they come from, who detest their own, fuel the same hatred of self, but they think that they can settle matters by fleeing.

Kristeva goes on to assert the need for 'a nation of strangers' – one which would in turn produce a world of 'nations without nationalism'. She wishes in short to launch a critique of the idea of the nation, but without a sell-off of all its assets. If the right-wing obliterates the symbolic capital and cultural value of immigrants, she says, the left is often equally at fault in tending to question or erase the value of the national community. But without the idea of the nation, a host-people can make no claim on the respect of immigrants. Those immigrants, she avers, must also honour the 'strangeness' of the culture whose sponsors welcome them in. It is worth stressing that point, because many who preach a policy of tolerance towards the cultural needs of immigrants are often the very ones who have done most to junk the claims of traditional Irish culture. Yet the national ideal has survived, for all the mockery by the media's designer Stalinists, in rather better shape than the crude forms of Marxism in which once they believed. Millions have, rightly or wrongly, died for the nation in the past century, but nothing like those numbers have died to defend or vindicate their own social class. A national entity is, as W. B. Yeats found, a glove placed over the hand with which we reach out to hold a world: and (another happy paradox) one can never fully know one's own country or culture until one has been outside for a time and found something with which to compare them. A rich national tradition will offer its children the tools with which to critique it, just as Europe as a whole created not just colonialism but also the opposition to it, out of Hegelian dialectics.

The nation is less a legacy of the past than the site of the future, a zone of pluralisms which will prove its durability precisely by the success with which it embraces refugees, exiles and newcomers. Ireland, far from adopting a defensive policy or meekly following prescriptions from the European Union, should lead in the development of new policies. If the North–South interface will be, as the Brandt Commission hinted, the key relationship in the coming century, there is a sense in which that relation has already been enacted symbolically within an Irish culture which is at once post-imperial (recognising the many Irish who helped to build the British empire) and post-colonial (aware of the great role played by those who began its dismantling).

How would this new, positive treatment of immigrants emerge? By studying the errors committed in other republics which, years before our own, tried as best their leaders could to solve these problems. Both the United States and France attempted to restrict the number of immigrants and to submit those who arrived to an Enlightenment definition of republican virtue. The result is there for all to see. In the United States, immigrants sometimes show scant respect for laws which they had no hand in framing. In France, Muslim schoolgirls are humiliatingly compelled to give up either the veil or the prospect of a state education. In both lands, the common public culture was republican, and matters of religion, cultural piety or ethnic identity were left to a purely private enactment. Congratulating itself on being neutral, the nation–state was anything but, enforcing a code of Enlightenment values on incomers. The failure of this form of 'liberal' democracy may be read in the current fraying of America and of France.

At the core of all societies, even bad societies, is a set of cultural codes: and nationalism has always been no more than a political and economic means by which to protect and deliver certain cultural values. There is nothing inherently wrong with any set of values being inscribed at the core of a nation–state's self-designation: but this should be done in a way which encourages respect for cultural traditions. There will always be a bedrock element of civic culture to which all tax-paying citizens (and all tax-paying workers should be voting citizens) subscribe. For this to work properly in a multicultural society, it will be necessary to abolish the old distinction between the public sphere as the zone of reason and the private area as a place of emotion. The public sphere should now be able to project the diversity of cultures within it, rather than suppress them. In Ireland, this would involve not just showing respect for Muslims, Hindus, Jews and Buddhists, but also Catholics and Protestants – and *that* would entail a reversal of many recent trends, which have worked to make even Catholicism a matter more of private than public symbolism.

Everybody has a right to practise their own cultural or even national traditions: and in the emerging world this should be possible even for minority cultural and national traditions within larger structures. It should, for instance, be possible for schools to ensure that Hindus or Jews or Catholics have their own special periods for internal doctrinal instruction set aside, within a teaching system which also ensures a minimal academic study of the main global traditions. In her book *Liberal Nationalism*, Yael Tamir has shown how the growth of large federal structures like the European Union should help to relax the pressure on minority groups within states, ensuring recognition for all in more relaxed configurations. Far from encouraging peoples to transcend localism (as was once thought), it may sufficiently loosen structures to allow for their more ardent pursuit. Tamir contends that not all nations can realistically have self-rule of a political kind but that all should have the right to cultural self-expression, a view which seems to coincide with that taken of nationalism within Northern Ireland under the Belfast Agreement.

Tamir argues that everyone has the right to choose a national culture and that this may be more and more a choice rather than a fixed birthright. A child of Algerian parents in a French school or a child of Catholic nationalists in Northern Ireland can decide to join a national culture: and that choice is a right because

Outside such communities they cannot develop a language and a culture, or set themselves aims. Their lives become meaningless, there is no substance to their reflection . . . A right to culture thus entails a right to a public sphere in which individuals can share a language, memorise their past, cherish their heroes, and live a fulfilling national life.

The removal of Catholicism from the public sphere, rather than the existence of the northern state as such, was therefore the primary sin of a triumphalist unionism. This right to practise one's own culture in public should go very deep, but it can never be absolute in cases where it may override the rights of others. However, the wearing of a veil by a schoolgirl, or indeed of a turban by a motorcyclist, can hardly be said to infringe others' rights. A country whose political system works on a principle of proportional representation is in a good position to recognise and amplify all the traditions within it. And a people who have already endorsed the notions of hybridity coded into the Belfast Agreement should have no difficulty in recognising identity as both multiple and chosen in the modern world. Such a people should, as Tamir suggests, distinguish between the rights of refugees (who have an absolute entitlement to sanctuary) and immigrants (who must recognise a state's right to exercise some controls): but they would also, as a voluntary association, grant citizenship formally to those, born within its physical confines, who finally seek it. Identity would be tied much less to ideas of land and sovereignty and more to acts of negotiation between cultures.

Ninety-four per cent of those who voted in the republic's referendum of May 1998 decided to endorse such a working assumption: and that is an excellent start. As Julia Kristeva says: 'by recognising the other within ourselves, we are spared detesting him in himself'. If everyone recognises her or his own strangeness, the very notion of the *foreign* dissolves, to be replaced by the *strange*. (This may be why the Irish language speakers tended to call the English 'stráinséirí' rather than 'eachtrannaigh'.) That recognition needn't be as difficult as it might seem, for the whole object of British colonialism in Ireland through the nineteenth century was, in the words of Friedrich Engels, 'to make the Irish feel like strangers in their own country'. That ordeal is something which even the stay-at-home Irish have in common with refugees and asylum-seekers: and in a re-configured educational system, the story of that struggle should be narrated to the incomers. Extracts from Tim Pat Coogan's recent *Wherever Green is Worn: The Story of the Irish Diaspora* would be a good start. In such discussion, of course, it might also be recognised that if the Irish have often found it difficult to feel at home in Ireland, they are entitled to express some surprise at others who seem better able to feel at home, even as they feel some solidarity with those who do not.

The experience of exiles has much in common with the cultural strategies of the Irish over the past two centuries – the use of psychological masks for self-protection; the idea of the lost homeland as vanished paradise; the certain knowledge that one was an 'Other' to a host people; the need in such circumstances to self-invent and to ignore parental connections (as both Wilde and Shaw did in London); the inventive use of a new language by those who have no superstitious investment in its received protocols. If the migrant is a sign of the modern, then the Irish were modern earlier than most peoples, enduring the fate of uprooting, of learning a new language, of leaving a neolithic civilisation and settling in modern conurbations. Even those people who have moved from country to city in the past two generations have an experience which gives them something in common with that of immigrants.

The fear of the outsider is often a version of the fear of the future – for instance, those middle-Americans who interned Asians during World War Two may have subliminally anticipated that their children would become the major beneficiaries of the new technological dispensations in west-coast colleges fifty years later. In the fast-changing world of the future, a world filled with travel and resettlement, we are all likely to feel like foreigners not just at home but overseas too. Like Swift's Gulliver, we shall all find ourselves using other places as a way of analysing and improving our own, based on the understanding that our own society is the one we can reform without destroying.

Artists have traditionally asked people to recognise their own 'Otherness', to understand whatever is repressed in the subconscious. Beckett took this more literally than most, producing many of his masterpieces in a second language. The French have as little difficulty as the Irish in claiming Beckett as one of their own: and his achievement is to have recognised that hatred of the Other is often rooted in some prior wrong done to the Other, who is punished a second time for simply reminding the unjust of their own guilt. This may well explain some of the maltreatment of immigrants from former colonies in countries like France or England, but it should cause fewer problems in Ireland. However, the fear of the foreign as a fear of what people have been schooled to repress in themselves may cause some difficulty. At the most rudimentary level, the presence of black Africans in the streets of Dublin is a reminder of a colonial past of shame and shared humiliation which some might prefer to ignore. Yet, even in that painful challenge, the new immigrants are providing a priceless service, reconnecting people with their own buried feelings.

Bernard Shaw once described himself as a sojourner on the earth. That state in which everyone is open to his or her own strangeness seems a good basis on which to build a cultural democracy, which calls for respect for its own products even as it offers a similar tenderness to newcomers. Once one recognises the 'Other' within the self, one has begun to engage with the thinking of the Belfast Agreement, for as Kristeva has written:

We must live with different people while relying on our personal moral codes, without the assistance of a set that would include our particularities while transcending them. A paradoxical community is emerging, made up of foreigners who are reconciled with themselves to the extent that they regard themselves as foreigners.

The problem is one that faces every country, not just Ireland: how to create a true multiculturalism without levelling everything or redrawing borders between what is permissible and impermissible at some other point. The need is to create a civic nationalism. Like Irish immigrants in nineteenth-century England or the United States, many Muslims today take on the protective coloration of modernity, while continuing to practise their religious rituals in their own communities. The challenge is to build a real connection between these disparate existences, so that groups will not seek freedom *from* a secular society so much as freedom *in* a multicultural endeavour. The Irish in England, to be honest about it, never really solved that problem, but were simply assimilated.

Given the low levels of population growth in most European countries, it is inevitable that a shortage of labour will create a demand for immigration over coming decades. It is important that universities offer multicultural study-courses, not alone to service members of these communities, but also to enlighten those who will deal with them. Faced with such wide choices, students are more likely to admire and endorse those codes which allow for a self-critique, rather than those which begin with the assumption that their law should prevail over all others.

At present only 500 applicants have received asylum status in Ireland. Thousands still wait to hear of their fate. In that period of uncertainty, they are prevented from taking jobs and are instead subject to 'Direct Provision', supplied with accommodation, food and £15 spending money per week. The identification of asylum-seekers with possible criminality feeds the assumption that many are bogus. Given the need of the economy for workers, that is a pity. The Minister for Justice, John O'Donoghue, has said that racism threatens to become a major illness of our society. While only a minority of people are abusive to non-nationals, they are having a disproportionate influence on the social climate. If politicians gave a lead in outlining the benefits brought by immigrants, ugly incidents could be much reduced in number: and if members of society were generally more willing to intervene in cases of assault and attack, the number of violent acts would drop further still. The evil of racism is a subset of an even wider problem: the collapse of respect for *res publica*, the loss of faith in society as such. Such a faith can only be restored if leaders outline a national philosophy and not just programmes of economic self-interest. For the ultimate paradox is this: that only a people secure in their national philosophy are capable of dealing confidently with those who come among them with deep commitments to alternative codes.

FURTHER READING

June Caldwell, 'Are we Becoming a Nation of Racists?', *Woman's Way*, vol. 38, no. 37, 22 September 2000, 10–11.

Carol Coulter, 'Courts to Face More Challenges on Asylum Question', *Irish Times*, 29 August 2000, 7.

Oscar Handlin, *Old Boston*, New York, 1989.

Robert Hughes, *The Culture of Complaint*, New York, 1993.

Declan Kiberd, 'Reinventing England', *Keywords: A Journal of Cultural Materialism*, 2, 1999, 47–57.

Julia Kristeva, *Strangers to Ourselves*, translated by Leon S. Roudiez, New York 1991.

    Nations Without Nationalism, translated by Leon S. Roudiez, New York, 1993.

Tom Nairn, *Faces of Nationalism*, London, 1997.

Cary Nelson, *Memoirs of a Tenured Radical*, New York, 1997.

Robert Schmuhl, *Indecent Liberties*, Indiana, 2000.

Yael Tamir, *Liberal Nationalism*, Princeton, N. J., 1993.

Index

AAP-1933